Hunger: Theory, Perspectives and Reality

Analysis Through Participatory Methods

COMMUNITY PERSPECTIVES IN ENVIRONMENT & DEVELOPMENT

No. 1. Alternative Perspectives on Livelihoods, Agriculture and Air Pollution: Agriculture in urban and peri–urban areas in a developing country
—Neela Mukherjee

No. 2 Perspectives of the Silent Majority: Air Pollution, Livelihoods, and Food Security–Indepth studies through PRA methods on community perspectives in urban and peri–urban areas of Varanasi and Faridabad, India
—Amitava Mukherjee

No. 3 Hunger: Theory, Perspectives and Reality
—Amitava Mukherjee

To
My Mother

Prof. Amitava Mukherjee Ph. D. is an expert on food security, hunger and poverty. He is currently the Executive Director of Development Tracks, Research Training and Consultancy plc, a knowledge company, in New Delhi and is consultant to several UN agencies and international organisations in and outside India. He has lectured extensively on these issues almost worldwide, including at the UN and has 25 books and numerous papers to his credit. His contributions to micro-level planning, participatory development, food security and hunger are internationally recognised.

Community Perspectives in Environment & Development-3

Hunger: Theory, Perspectives and Reality

Analysis Through Participatory Methods

AMITAVA MUKHERJEE
Executive Director, Development Tracks, RTC, New Delhi and Professor, Insititute for Human Development, New Delhi

CONCEPT PUBLISHING COMPANY, NEW DELHI -110059

Originally published by
Ashgate Publishing Limited,
Grower House, Croft Road,
Aldershot,
Hampshire GU11 3HR
England

Ashgate Publishing Company
131 Main Street
Burlington, VT 05401 - 5600 USA

Ashgate website ://http:www.ashgate.com

This South Asian edition is for sale in the Indian Sub-Continent only.

ISBN 81-7022-985-5 (Series)
ISBN 81-7022-988-X (Vol. 3)

South Asian Edition 2002

South Asian Edition
Published and Printed in India by
Ashok Kumar Mittal
Concept Publishing Company
A/15-16, Commercial Block, Mohan Garden,
NEW DELHI-110059

Phones : 5351460, 5351794
Fax : 091-11-5357103
Email : publishing@conceptpub.com

Contents

List of Charts, Boxes and Figures

Charts

Boxes

Figures

List of Tables

Glossary of Indian Terms

Terms	Meaning
Aganwadi	A government child welfare day-care centre where children upto the age of 5 receive free food and health check up.
Baithak	Living Room
Bajra	A Coarse Cereal
Banga	Disease afflicting Buffaloes. It affects the feet which get swollen.
Baroo	A type of weed which looks similar to Jowar and is found mostly in Jowar fields.
Barsam	Fodder sown in winter
Basti	Ward or colony in a village organised mainly on the basis of caste/religion.
Bathua	A weed
Bigha	Measure of Land: 5 Bigha = 1 acre
Biswa	Measure of Land: 5 Biswa = 1 acre
Burela	Another name for Dhola

Chepa	Tiny white insects suck juice out of leaves in Cabbage, Bajra, Mustard, Sugarcane leaves. It gives a sticky texture.
Chhedak	Any caterpillar that bores hole. It is also called Dhola/Burela.
Chitli	A worm that eats vegetable roots
Chula	Oven or stove made out of mud which uses wood, animal dung, etc. as fuel.
Congress Grass	A weed having small white flowers. Also called Parthenium.
Dhencha	Medium sized fodder plants sown in summer
Dhola	Caterpillars that bore holes
Fatinga	Any pest which is a grass hopper
Galaghotu	A disease found in buffaloes. It chokes buffaloes to death
Gander	A general term for caterpillars
Gram Samiti	A village Co-operative Society
Gram Sewak	An appointee of the Block Development Office for supervising development work in the village. He/She looks after 3 villages
Gurchawa	A disease which results in wilting and crippling of leaves
Hara Kira	Small green caterpillar

Harwawa	A disease which turns leaves yellow
Jhansi	A cluster of small caterpillars (pest)
Jhulsa	A disease resulting in wilting and blackening of leaves.
Jowar	A inferior cereal used also as fodder now
Kanduwa	A disease which affects the ear-rings of wheat turning them black.
Kasba	A village which is the centre of rural growth having a population of 7000 or more.
Kateli	A medium sized tree-weed having thorns.
Katui	A pest which cuts down paddy ear-rings.
Kirona	Any pest which is a caterpillar.
Koria	Crippling of leaves and plants like a leper. The fruits of the affected plants look deformed.
Lalrii	Red coloured small sized pests which can fly. It eats leaves of leafy vegetables.
Machchi/Makhi	House-Fly
Mandi	Wholesale market
Morya or Gurchawa	A disease which wilts and cripples leaves especially of Chilies and Tomatoes.
Muhalla	Ward/Colony
Najla	Ailment: running nose, headache and nose burning

Nakshatra	A Constellation
Nilagai	Blue Bull
Pankhi	Any pest that can fly.
Pradhan/Sarpanch	Village Head, usually elected to the village level unit of governance.
Rani Jai (Ghan Jai)	A weed similar in looks to wheat and whose seeds are identical to wheat grains, though slightly black in colour.
Safed Moondi	A weed having small seeds (coriander type), mainly found in wheat fields.
Sambar	A kind of deer
Sati	Small sized weeds which mainly grow in Bajra fields.
Soondi	Small sized caterpillar found in paddy leaves. It sucks the sap.
Telchatta	Small sized pest which can fly. It sucks juice out of mustard pods and cauliflower.
Tidda	A current variant of locust which is small in size.
Tiddi	Large sized locust (the earlier variant)
Tikuli	A beetle that sucks juice from leaves of vegetables mostly found in summers.
Titri	A small white moth which sucks milk from paddy ear-rings.

Months of the Year in the Indian Calendar

Vernacular Month	Corresponding Period in Roman Calendar
Baisakh	Mid-April to Mid-May
Jeth	Mid-May to Mid-June
Asard	Mid-June to Mid-July
Sawan	Mid-July to Mid-August
Bhado	Mid-August to Mid-September
Kuar*	Mid-September to Mid-October
Kartick	Mid-October to Mid-November
Aghan	Mid-November to Mid-December
Poos	Mid-December to Mid-January
Magh	Mid-January to Mid-February
Fagun	Mid-February to Mid-March
Chait**	Mid-March to Mid-April

Notes: *In some villages called Aswin. ** Also spelt as Cheth .

Introduction

Jerome K. Jerome in a delightful essay on "Idle Thoughts of an Idle Fellow", once said that kitchen is the temple of God and cook the high priest. Food as a metaphor of foremost divine concern is present in almost all major religions. Lord Krishna's first commandment at the closure of the Royal Battle of Kurukshetra to Yudhistir, the eldest of the victorious Pandavas, was "*Dadaswa Annam, Dadaswa Annam, Dadaswa Annam*". "O' King, *provide food, provide food, provide food*".

The importance of food in modern times has been widely accepted. A resolution on Right to Food was adopted by the U. N. General Assembly in terms of the Universal Declaration of Human Rights, vide resolution No.217A (III) on 10th December 1948. The Universal Declaration rightly elaborates both civil and political rights, as also economic, cultural and social rights. These rights are inextricably interwoven into one fabric. One set of rights cannot be guaranteed without the other sets being enjoined. Just as civil and political rights are indispensable to communities struggling to secure food security, enjoyment of other rights is seriously jeopardised if people spend all their energies to keep their body and soul together. These Rights have been repeatedly reaffirmed in one form or the other, in numerous bilateral and multilateral declarations and international instruments. Notable amongst these are the declarations and plans of action emanating from the World Food Conference, Rome, 1974; World Summit for Children, 1990; the International Conference on Nutrition of the WHO/FAO, 1992; Conference on Hunger and Poverty of IFAD, Brussels; World Summit for Social Development, Copenhagen, 1995 and finally World Food Summit, Rome, 1996. Indeed the World Food Summit, called upon the United Nations High Commissioner for Human Rights, "to better define the rights related to food...and to propose ways to implement and realise these rights as a means of achieving the commitments and objectives of the World Food Summit, taking into account the possibility of formulating voluntary guidelines for food security for all" (FAO, 1996).

Yet every seventh person worldwide and every fifth person in the developing parts of the world are hungry today. Nearly one third of Indians suffer from food insecurity and hunger in one form or the other. They lack access to adequate food. The "inherent dignity and........the equal and inalienable rights of all members of the human family" are violated with impunity. Due to limitation of resources an estimated 84 million people in the world are undernourished, 1.2 billion do not have access to safe water (a vital ingredient for food security), 1.6 billion are illiterate and 2 billion do not have electricity (Sinha, 2000). These have led several international civil society organisations to start a movement for adoption of a code of conduct on the right to food, which will set out standards of behaviour for Governments, international NGOs, international organisations and private enterprises (BFWI, 1999). There is also the move to have a closure on the International Food Security Treaty directed towards binding the Governments to enact enforceable international laws guaranteeing the right to be free from hunger and implement, wherever existing, national laws to the effect.

India is a signatory to all the declarations and instruments mentioned in last but one paragraph. The Directive Principles of State Policy, enshrined in the Constitution of India, have enjoined that it shall be the duty of the State to provide for such policies that will secure food and nutrition to all its citizens. Yet we have no flattering record on food security and hunger, to write home about. The World Bank in its Report Number 197471 have concluded that the number of people below the poverty line in India is 33 per cent. That is, more than 326 million people in India today live below the poverty line, an increase of 46 million in the last decade (Guruswamy, 2000). While we can debate till the cows come home, whether all those who are poor are hungry or not, and whether all those who are hungry are poor or not, our field experiences have shown that while many non-poor may be hungry, due to good reasons, like disparity in intra-familial distribution of power, but those who are poor are generally hungry. Human beings, like all living beings, do not opt to be hungry, unless they are forced to be so. Hunger and starvation, though not necessarily famine, hit us every year.

And yet, if we look at the nature of economic and social debates we have had throughout most of the nineties, and in even political polemics, the key words often heard are privatisation, globalisation, liberalisation, investments (or more accurately foreign direct investments) and disinvestments. Movements in the stock markets, rates of interest, e-commerce, information technology and the wealthiest men (and on some rare occasion women) have attracted an unduly large portion of the limelight. There are at times (read budget times!), some breast beating about mounting fiscal deficit, low agricultural growth and industrial growth. When the Parliament is in session, the antics and activities of our Hon'able Members of the Parliament occupy television news bulletins and hit newspaper headlines. If there are elections and Ministry-making, the role of the Governor, otherwise not heard except for ribbon cutting and innocuous Convocation Addresses, come under sharp scrutiny. If there is space still left, all you hear is how the government machinery is pre-occupied with utter non-issues like the lifting of the ban on RSS by a State Government, conversion (a right guaranteed by the Constitution of India), putting out "Fire", stopping the shooting of "Water" or screening of "Hey Ram".

This faux pass is a sad commentary on the national consensus that we have on subjects that require urgent attention. It is even sadder that broader issues that confront the majority of the people are forgotten. That 33 per cent of our people are living below the poverty line, as we mentioned above, and that 40 per cent of our people are illiterate do not bother us. I am told that there has been no debate in the 11th, 12th and 13th Lok Sabhas, on the question of poverty except perhaps incidentally while discussing Plan allocations. Food insecurity and problem of hunger, as matters of immediate concern never seem to hit the headlines, except when a major calamity visits some part of the country like the super-cyclone that hit Orissa in October 1999, only to be forgotten once the chips are down.

There is a kind of a mistaken complacency in official circles about hunger simply because we produce around 200 million tons of food, give or take a few per cent. We often hear that we have no problem of food insecurity because we produce so much of food and because we have the State Trading Corporation which has godowns full of food grains (upto 30 million tons against the warranted 15 million tons of buffer stock). If nothing, the bureaucracy believes, we can import food and take care of any residual problem of food shortage that may arise. Some scientists even tell us that the advances in bio-technology and genetically modified food should solve our food problem, if there be any. It is believed that there may be some sporadic cases of hunger, which are transitory in character and temporary in nature, but then, it is felt, these are problems only at the margin and are no causes for sleepless nights. In short, food security and hunger has fallen off the national agenda.

But we have not conquered the problem of hunger. We have not been able to guarantee a right to food for all our people. We need to stir out of our slumber. We need to act. We need to realise that agricultural growth which averaged 4.04 per cent per annum during 1981-91, has come down to 2.3 per cent per annum in 1991-99, despite an uninterrupted series of good monsoons (Indian agriculture is till prone to the vagaries of monsoon). Additionally, it is a serious matter that the area under foodgrains and oilseeds has remained unchanged or nearly so at around 150 million hectares. But the number of people dependent on land has increased by 42 million between 1990-91 and 1999-2000, as against an increase in food grain production by about 22 million tons during the same period. The implication is that a major slowdown in the growth of real incomes and wages in the rural sector has taken place. Such slowing down in agricultural growth rate and a freeze in the area under foodgrain and oilseeds, against a growing population, only indicate lower availability of food in the system for the people to access.

Whether slower agricultural production had any impact on food prices or not, need not detain us for long, but the rise in food prices is telling. The average annual price rise during the last decade has been 5.6 per cent for rice, 5.7 per cent for wheat and 11.2 per cent for pulses. During the current decade the price rise has been much steeper: 10.2 per cent for rice, 9.5 per cent for wheat and 11.4 per cent for pulses.

And how has the wage rates behaved? The annual average growth rate of wages of unskilled agricultural male workers in the eighties was about 4.6 per cent as opposed to a paltry 2.5 per cent in the nineties. When we pitch this against the increase of the Whole Sale Price Index, the picture becomes murkier. In the period 1991-2000, the WPI rose by about 8.8 per cent annually as against 6.9 per during the corresponding period in the last decade. Employment generation in the organsised sector was growing at 1.6 per cent in the eighties. It is now 0.8 per cent in the nineties exactly half the rate of the eighties. Both these have a strong bearing on the economic access that people have to food.

A redeeming feature of the nineties is that the GDP has increased at the rate of 5.8 per cent as opposed to a slightly lower figure of 5.46 per cent in the eighties. But given the stubbornness of the percentage of people below the poverty line, there seems to have been nothing of the much trumpeted "trickle down" effect.

These realities make a strong case that at the begining of a new century, it is high time we reflect on and assess what we have done in the last one and then act to move on to the future. Charting the future is always more fruitful when done with a sense of history. However, too much history may have its debilitating impact. It is best to see what we have done in the most recent past, because in a rapidly changing world, rate of obsolescence of variables affecting our lives is very high. Much of what we have done in recent past is all that are likely to have the maximum impact at the present time and in the foreseeable future. They can show us the blind alleys to avoid that blot the pages of our economic history. They tell us the leeway to make for.

In the light of the foregoing, we believe that food security and elimination of hunger are much more than food production and food availability. It is much more than running a better targeted Public Distribution System for food. It is an issue that requires a concerted national attention and must be brought back to the national agenda. It is our intention to make a contribution in this book towards bringing back the problem of hunger and food insecurity on the national agenda.

This is not just a book investigating the existence or otherwise of hunger and the suggested remedies. In this book we first examine the perspectives of "outsiders" (the experts, economists, political scientists and sociologists) on hunger and its causes, and see from first principles if what our leaders, bureaucrats and managers of the economy say are all correct. We then go on to examine the perceptions of the "insiders", those who suffer the pangs of hunger (*such as the poor communities, farmers, women, poor people, landless-labourers and the tenants-at-will*), on hunger and attempt to learn what they have to say about the state of food security, and the forces that cause or mitigate the pains of hunger. We finally look at the contrasts between the perspectives of the hungry or near-hungry with the perspectives of "outsiders". We then make an attempt to see the congruence between what the theories of hunger have to tell us and the reality of hunger that stares on the face of millions.

The views of the community are critical both in understanding the problem of food insecurity and hunger, and in working out the policies and strategies most appropriate to solve the problem. It is widely known that even in a vast country like India, decisions affecting the lives of teeming millions, diverse and deeply stratified are often taken at a central location without consulting them. There is indeed no institutional mechanism to consult the people on vital matters and bring to bear on the issues at hand their view. And whatever mechanism has been put in place, viz., the Panchayati Raj Institutions, it has been kept in a state of suspended animation by not providing them with resources and by not investing them with any function or authority to be effective instruments of the state.

In this book, therefore, we have attempted to present the perspectives of the community on livelihood, hunger and food security together with the perspectives of economists, gender specialists, political scientists and sociologists on hunger and food insecurity. Thus we have attempted to examine how far policies framed in accordance with the received theories, postulates and conceptions, of hunger and explanations of it, are in conformity with the perspectives of the community.

Box 1
Key Hunger Terms

Key Terms	Definitions
Hunger	A state in which people do not have **enough food** to provide them the required nutrients such as carbohydrates, fats, proteins, vitamins, mineral and water, to an active and healthy life.
Malnourishment	A state in which people can suffer impairment of physical and mental health due to **excessive consumption**, and be the cause or consequence of infectious diseases.
Under-nourishment	A state in which people have **inadequate consumption of calories**, protein and nutrients to meet the basic physical requirements for an active and healthy life.
Food Insecurity	A state in which people consume **inadequate amount** of food because they do not have **access** to sufficient nutritious food to sustain an active and healthy life.
Food Security	A state in which, at all times, there is **enough** food in the system. People have both **physical and economic** access to food. Food that is available is **culturally acceptable,** has the **required nutrition**, and there is **no institutional sanction** against accessing the available food.

There are a large number of terms like food insecurity, hunger, undernutrition, etc. used interchangeably in the context of food and related matters. We need to distinguish these terms, which are critical for putting the discussion in perspective. Hunger, mal-nourishment, under-nourishment, food insecurity and its obverse, food security, are different things. They have different meanings. We are concerned here with food insecurity and hunger. These are the principal focus of this work.

Of all the writers on hunger and food insecurity, Amartya Sen's work has been by far the most influential. Not that no one before him had said much of what he had to say but that he approached at the problem of hunger from a refreshingly and fundamentally new perspective. That was his path breaking contribution, which brought the problem of hunger on to the global agenda with new dimensions. In Chapter 1, we deal with the philosopher's perspective in terms of Sen's thesis, which we call the entitlement and deprivation thesis (ED) and attempt at its extension in terms of institutional sanctions, choice and secondary food system as elements in explanation for hunger. We also examine, briefly though, some other attempts made to extend the ED thesis. In terms of the ED thesis, hunger visits a person or an household because of a failure on the part of the individual or the household to access food, whatever the reason.

In Chapter 2, we look at the perspectives of economists and non-governmental organisations on hunger, its consequences and what needs to be done for ensuring that people do not suffer food insecurity and hunger, where we begin by looking at the reasons for which people fail to access food. There are several reasons and it is not necessary that individuals or households fail to access food because they can be classified as being afflicted by all the conditions that cause failure to access food. Any one or some combination of these conditions prevents individuals from accessing food and it is possible that all conditions may afflict an individual or a household at the same time, but that is not necessarily the case always. It is also possible that some of these causes may flow from other causes and they are generally self-reinforcing.

Of all the causes that prevent an individual or a household from accessing food, poverty seems more fundamental at least from one perspective. It has inter-generational implications, like gender bias in accessing food, on which we will focus in Chapter 2. In order to explore this dimension of hunger we move on to the "nutrition-poverty trap", because it brings out the inter-generational implications remarkably well. To complete the picture we discuss the ways and means, which have been presented both from theoretical and empirical perspectives, to overcome hunger.

Ways and means to overcome hunger so far discussed are from the economists' or the philosophers' perspectives. Hunger has also to be viewed as social and political problem. We need to have the political scientists' and sociologists' perspectives. For an understanding of hunger in all its horrific dimensions we need to know the social and political processes which prevent people from accessing food. In Chapter 3, we analyse the social and political approaches to understanding hunger. These lead us to an examination of some of the reductionist approaches to solving hunger and then arrive at the conclusion that a solution to the hunger problem, "a prirori", must have a multifaceted approach and must be, what we call for want of a better word, holistic in content. This necessitates a detailed analysis of the different layers of causes of hunger and helps delineating different policies to address the problem of hunger at different levels.

Having discussed the understanding of hunger as emerging from the views of the experts, we move on to understand how communities view hunger and how they cope with its pangs. This has important lessons for us both from the point of view of extending the frontiers of knowledge about the hungry person's perspective on hunger and in evaluating public policies directed towards solving this problem. This marks the beginning of the second segment of the book, viz., of listening to the voices of the silent majority. In Chapters 4 and 5, we discuss community perspectives on hunger from a backward state. We discuss what villagers have to say from two peri-urban villages, viz., Chandpur and Tikri, in the district of Varanasi, Uttar Pradesh. We take these views as representing what poor people have to say from peri-urban villages of a backward State and its under-developed region, viz., eastern Uttar Pradesh. These views emerged in course of the study on the impact of air pollution on crop yields conducted under the aegis of the T. H. Huxley School of the Imperial College of Science Technology and Medicine of the University of London, and the International Institute for Environment and Development, London.

To contrast the perspectives of the villagers from two peri-urban villages of a backward State we also look at the perspectives of areas from the heartland of the "Green Revolution" belt, viz., Uncha Gaon, in Faridabad district, Haryana.

Chapter 6 gives us the glimpse of what villagers from Uncha Gaon have to say and this provides the perspective of an area which is primarily a cash crop growing area, viz., vegetable growing. These have significant implications. The views from the Haryana village also emerged in course of the study mentioned in the foregoing paragraph.

In Chapter 7, we shift the scene to a tribal village in West Bengal, and learn about what the women of the village have to say. The village is Krishna Rakshit Chak in Midnapore. This Chapter gives us both the perspectives of tribal women and of villagers from a State ruled for decades now by a left front Government and at once helps us to compare and contrast the state of hunger in other situations. It is in this Chapter that we have the rôle of Common Property Resources coming out in sharp proportions. It also brings into the picture questions of seasonality, gender and role of women, in tackling hunger and the consequences on education.

In Chapter 8, we carry out a Field Force Analysis of the hunger situation of the four villages discussed in Chapters 4 and 5. Field Force Analysis was first used by Kurt Lewin who developed the Field Force Analysis (FFA) as a way of looking at and analysing forces that have a bearing on any problem or situation. We prefer the word problem, because in the villages studied, hunger and food insecurity are problems for the communities, only the degrees vary. We apply the FFA method to the situation depicted by Sagarpur, Uncha Gaon, Chandpur and Tikri, though not in the same order. This helps to work out a point of view of public policies and do suggest, even if tentatively, a course of action to bring about positive changes to the hunger scenario.

Chapter 9 is a *brief note* on what Food Calendars reveal of seasonality of the intensity of hunger from a perpetual hunger belt, viz., from villages in Bolangir district in Orissa. The role of forests and cultural traits in causing and mitigating hunger is revealing. They have important implications for policy formulations and forest laws.

Finally in Chapter 10, we summarise the findings and do a reality check of the perspectives of "outsiders", discussed in Chapters 1 to 3, with what the "insiders" have to say. While this enabled us to examine and compare some aspects of the received wisdom, with the perspectives of the communities, a complete debate on the gap between theory and reality, between what communities perceive and experts enjoin, has to be reserved for a future volume.

Acknowledgements

In the preparation of this book, I have received help and assistance from a large number of institutions and individuals. To all of them, I am thankful. I am particularly indebted to the following people for their help, comments and suggestions:

Professor G.S. Bhalla, Professor Ravi Srivastav of Jawaharlal Nehru University, New Delhi, Dr. S.S. Suryanarayana of the Indira Gandhi Institute of Development Research, Mumbai, Professor S. Mahendra Dev, Centre for Economic and Social Studies, Hyderabad, Professor Y.K. Alagh, M.P. (Rajya Sabha), New Delhi, Professor Neela Mukherjee, New Delhi, Dr. Meera Jayaswal, Ranchi University, Ranchi, Dr. (Ms.) B. Jena, Patna and Ms. Sudipta Ray, New Delhi.

I thank the librarians of F.A.O. Library, New Delhi; British Council Library, New Delhi, American Centre Library, New Delhi; NIRD Library, Hyderabad and Library of the Centre for Economic and Social Studies, Hyderabad.

Finally, my gratitude to the villagers where the primary work was done.

1 Institutional Sanctions, Choice and Secondary Food System as Elements in Explanation of Hunger

I. Introduction

The prevalent literature on the subject of food security, drawing from the "Entitlement and Deprivation (ED) Thesis" *(Sen,* 1981 and *Dreze* and *Sen,* 1989), defines individual to be food secure when there is enough food in the system that he/she can buy (food availability), when he/she has the capacity to buy that food (ability to buy food), and when the food that the individual buys provides her/him with the requisite nutritional value *(The World Bank,* 1986). Where any of these conditions is not satisfied, the person's food security is endangered and consequently the person becomes food insecure.

We are of the view that individuals can be food insecure even when these conditions are satisfied and to that extent there are gaps in the ED thesis. There are three more conditions, namely, the existence of institutional sanction to access available food, the exercise of choice to access the food that is available and the presence of a secondary food system which must be satisfied before individuals could be guaranteed to be food secure. The principal concern of this chapter is to establish the conditions that must be met before individuals could be treated as food secure. These additional arguments have been comparatively neglected in the food security debate.

This chapter is divided into four sections. Following the introduction in section two, we will examine the different concepts of entitlement and deprivation, and how they relate to food (in) security, based on Sen's thesis. In section three we will examine the gaps in the ED thesis, and establish the conditions that need to be **additionally** satisfied together with certain evidences to establish the criticality of the same. Finally, in section four brief conclusions will be drawn.

II. Conceptual Specifications

According to Food Availability Decline (FAD) arguments, an individual is food insecure because there is not enough to eat. The protagonists of the Green Revolution believed in this theory and they therefore argued that all that matters is producing more food for people to be relieved of hunger. The miracle seeds of the "Green Revolution" increases grain yields and therefore are key to ending hunger. Now bio-technology—actually manipulating the genes of plants—we are told, offers an even more dramatic production revolution just down the road (*Financial Express*, November 1999). The second Green Revolution based on these advances in bio-technology will have greater impact on our food security situation than the first Green Revolution. More food means less hunger. The then Chairman of the Consultative Group on International Agricultural Research (CGIR), overseeing Green Revolution research, S. Sahid Husain, went so far as to suggest that the poor are the beneficiaries of the new seeds output and proceeded to claim that "added emphasis on poverty alleviation is not necessary" because increasing production itself has a major impact on the poor (Quoted in *The Bank's World*, 1985, p. 1). Whether one agrees with CGIR Chief or not, the subsequent turn of events clearly establishes that advances made in production of food were for real. For instance, food production in excess of 204 million tons in India currently estimated is laudable.

There were skeptics, however, who held that focussing on increasing food production cannot alleviate hunger because it fails to alter the tightly concentrated distribution of economic power, especially access to land and purchasing power. If individuals do not have land on which to grow food or the money to buy food, they would go hungry, no matter how dramatically food production and hence food availability is pushed up. It was even argued that a narrow focus on production ultimately defeated itself as it destroyed the very resource base on which agriculture depended *(Lappe and Collins*, 1988).

The World Bank itself found the curious paradox that with increasing food production, the world was possessed of even more hungry people. The number of hungry people increased throughout the world during the 1970s, reaching 730 million by the end of the decade *(World Bank,* 1986, p. 49). And where were these hungry people? It was in South Asia, precisely where Green Revolution seeds had contributed to the greatest production success *(Lewis,* 1985), that lived roughly two thirds of the undernourished in the entire world. And in India, an estimated 300-400 million people are today hungry, despite the massive strides in food production.

It was in this scenario and in the high noon of the "Green Revolution", Sen came with the Entitlement and Deprivation Thesis (E&D Thesis) challenging the received theory that people are hungry because there is scarcity of food. We would now turn to examine the thesis, as it is the principal strand of thinking in currency as the explanation of hunger in contemporary world.

Box 1.1
Paradox of Hunger

It is paradoxical but hardly surprising that the right to food has been endorsed more often and with greater unanimity and urgency than most other human rights, while at the same time being violated more comprehensively and systematically than probably any other.

Richard Cohen, in Causes of Hunger, 1994

According to the E&D Thesis *(Sen,* 1981) food insecurity has to be seen as the characteristic of the person not having enough to eat. This is not tantamount to saying that "there isn't enough to eat". The latter could be the cause of the former, but it is not the only cause. It is argued that whether and how food insecurity is related to food availability argument deals with things about food considered on its own, whereas food insecurity statements are about the relationship of the person to food. Except in cases where an individual deliberately starves, so argues the E&D thesis, to understand food insecurity, one has to go into the structure of ownership of food.

Ownership relations, according to Sen, are one kind of entitlement relationship, which as accepted in a private ownership market economy, typically include the following amongst others:

a) **Trade-based Entitlement,** where an individual is entitled to own goods and services, which the individual obtains by trading something, owned by her/him with a willing party or parties.
b) **Production-based Entitlement**, where an individual is entitled to own goods and services, he/she obtains by arranging production using resources owned by her/him, or by hiring resources from willing parties meeting the agreed conditions of trade. Production–based entitlement may also be construed as exchange with nature when considered in the context of food security.
c) **Own Labour Entitlement,** where an individual is entitled to one's own labour power and thus to the trade–based and production–based entitlements related to the individual's labour power.
d) **Inheritance and Transfer Entitlement,** where an individual is entitled to own commodities that are willingly given to the individual by another who legitimately owns them, which could be either during the life time of the latter if commodities are transferred in the nature of a gift, or after the latter's death, in case they are transferred by way of a Will, inheritance or bequest.

What an individual owns is called the endowment entitlement or **direct entitlement**, but in a market economy individuals can also exchange the commodities they own for another, or another collection of commodities, either through trading (trade-based entitlement) or through production (production-based entitlement) or through some combination of the two. The set of all alternative bundles of commodities that an individual can acquire through such means, has been collectively called **exchange entitlement** of what the individual owns. We shall discuss this in greater detail in the next section.

Apart from non-entitlement transfers like inheritance, there could be, according to Sen, other kinds of entitlements as well, such that an individual may be entitled to enjoy the fruits of some property without being able to trade it for anything else. For instance individuals can use the river water for personal use, but cannot sell or buy a river. The case with the tribal's entitlement (in India) to minor forest produce is very similar. One could also inherit the property of a deceased person who leaves behind no deed of conveyance such as a **"Will"** for anyone to inherit, through some kind of kinship-based inheritance, accepted in the statutes as by law established. It is not hard to imagine that individuals may also have some entitlements related to unclaimed objects on the basis of "discovery".

Exchange Entitlements

The exchange entitlement **mapping** is the relation that specifies the set of exchange entitlements for each ownership, which defines the possibilities that would be open to individuals corresponding to each ownership situation. An individual, accordingly, would be food insecure if the **exchange entitlement** set does not contain any feasible bundle, which includes enough food. It is, thus, possible to identify those ownership bundles that must lead to food insecurity in the absence of non-entitlement transfers (such as charity). Sen identified five factors, which determine an individual's exchange entitlement, namely, the following:

a) The individual's ability to find employment, its tenure and the wage rate at which the individual will be able to secure the employment.
b) The individual's ability to earn by selling the relative individual's non-labour assets, and the costs to be incurred by the individual to buy whatever he/she can buy and manage.
c) The commodities that the individual can produce with his or her own labour power and resources he/she can buy and manage.
d) The cost, to the individual, of purchasing resources or resource services and the value of the produce which he/she can sell.

e) The social security benefits to which the respective individual is entitled to and the taxes, levies, fees and charges, to which he/she may be subjected, as enjoined by law.

Food insecurity of individuals and their ability to avoid it depend upon both individuals' ownership of commodities and on the exchange entitlement mapping. A general decline in food supply may indeed cause an individual to be exposed to food insecurity through a rise in prices with an unfavorable impact upon the individual's exchange entitlement. Even where food insecurity of the person is thus caused by food shortage, the immediate reason for the individual's food insecurity will be decline in that individual's exchange entitlement.

Significantly enough, according to Sen, an individual's exchange entitlement may worsen for reasons other than a general decline in food supply. For example, imagine that there are two Groups, A and B. An individual belonging to Group–A would be adversely affected, if the income of Group–B increases and starts buying more food (induced by higher income), causing food prices to rise, without any adverse variation in systemic availability of food. The reason is that this would lead to worsening the exchange entitlement of the individual belonging to Group-A. It is also possible that some economic changes, which as an IMF–World Bank enjoined structural adjustment programme may adversely affect the employment opportunities of the individual whose exchange entitlement may worsen because her or his wages lag behind price increases as it happened in India during 1991-92, when prices rose by upto 17 per cent on a month to month basis but wages remained nearly stagnant, during the same period, on a month to month basis, particularly so in the rural areas *(Government of India,* 1992). Thus, according to the ED Thesis, differential incomes of various sections of people, policy changes leading to changes in employment opportunities, wages and prices of commodities for production and consumption may lead to a worsening of the individual's exchange entitlement. These diverse influences on exchange entitlements, according to the ED Thesis, are as relevant as the overall volume of food supply vis-a-vis population of one's country.

Food Supply and Food Insecurity

The discussion, therefore, on food insecurity emanating from food supply falling behind population growth according to the E&D Thesis, is only part of the picture. According to the thesis, it is not merely falling food availability but food entitlement failure, which is responsible for causing food insecurity.

Ensuring food insecurity then would revolve around influencing different factors, which determine distribution of food between different sections of the community. The Senian entitlement approach directs one to questions dealing with ownership patterns and, less obviously, to the various influences that affect entitlement mapping. The influence of food supply itself on the prevalence of food insecurity, works through the entitlement relations. If one person in eight is food insecure regularly in the world (according to the Secretary General of the Food and Agricultural Organisation, Rome and Commitments and Plan of Action worked out at the World Food Summit, held in Rome in November, 1996, there are 800 million people who go to bed hungry every night in the world today) *(Diouf,* 1996) this is seen more as the inability of those who are food insecure to establish entitlement to enough food, where the question of the actual availability of food is not directly involved.

Endowment and Exchange

Clearly enough, entitlement approach to food insecurity of an individual concentrates on the ability of the individual to command food through the legal means available to the individual, including the use of production possibilities, trade opportunities, entitlements vis-a-vis the state, and other methods of acquiring food. Individuals are food insecure either because the individuals do not have the ability to command enough food, or **because the ability to avoid food insecurity is not used**. The entitlement approach concentrates on the former, to the exclusion of the other possibility, and it concentrates on those means of commanding food that are legitimate under the legal system for the time being in force. As Sen puts it :

> "While it is an approach of some generality, it does not make any attempt at including all possible influences that can cause food insecurity, for example illegal transfers (e.g. looting) and choice failure (e.g. owing to inflexible food habits)."

The entitlement approach focuses on the entitlement of each individual to commodity bundles which include food. It views food insecurity as resulting from a failure of the individual to be entitled to be bundle of commodities with enough food in it

Normally, there is a menu before an individual to choose from. It is argued by Sen that, suppose E-1 is the entitlement set of an individual in a given society, in a given situation, where E-1 consists of a set of alternative commodity bundles, any one of which the individual can decide to have. In an open economy, with private ownership typical of capitalist system, E-1 can be characterized as depending on two parameters, viz., the **endowment** of the person (the ownership bundle) and the exchange **entitlement mapping** (the function that specifies the set of alternative commodity bundles that the person can command respectively for each endowment bundle).

Take the case of a farmer, having a piece of land, labour power and a few other resources such as a pair of bullocks and a plough, which taken one with the others make up the farmers' endowment. With that endowment the farmer can produce a basket of goods, say rice and pulses, which will be farmer's own, or she could sell her labour and buy some basket of commodities which may include food. The farmer can alternatively produce on her piece of land some cash crops, say sugarcane, that she can sell to buy food and other goods and services that she may wish to buy. There are farmers who produce rice, consume rice to meet their own food consumption requirement. But to meet some of their other needs, say of clothing, they may sell a part of the rice grown by them. They would sell rice at as favourable an exchange rate as possible, to buy clothes.

A person can face food insecurity if some economic change takes place in the system, which makes it impossible for her to acquire any commodity bundle, which has enough food to survive. Such entitlement failure can be caused either by a fall in the person's endowment (like alienation of land for the landowner, or loss of labour power of a mason due to accidental loss of limb caused by a fall while at work), or by an unfavourable shift in exchange entitlement (like loss of employment, fall in wages, rise in food prices, drop in the prices of goods or services the individual sells, decline in self-employment, in production and so on).

It is added, however, by the E&D Thesis, that an individual who is engaged in growing food, and succeeds in growing more than enough food for survival, may still be food insecure despite the food produced by him/her. This is because he/she may not have the legal right to use the food so produced. History is replete with instances of food insecurity during famines, where the majority of the hungry lot are indeed agricultural labourers. These labourers are in the main engaged primarily in the production of food but are not entitled to consume the food so produced due to the legal nature of their contract, with the owner of the land or the farmer for whom they worked. The nature of the contract gives the agricultural labourers a right to receive only a wage in exchange for the labour sold, which may not meet the food demands of the household and may face exchange entitlement failure in the event of scarcity of food in the market. The contract typically excludes right to the food grown by the person's own labour, that is, the contract enjoins no entitlement to the food produced by the individual's own labour. Thousands perished in the Great Bengal Famine of the 1940s, in front of granaries (owned by landlords) full of grains, which they themselves produced.

Where a labourer is employed whether in food production or otherwise, and receives wages in cash, he/she has to convert the cash into food through exchange in the market, to move towards food security. The amount of food which the labourer could have command over, however, would depend upon the ruling food price at the time of exchange. Were food prices to rise rapidly, without nominal wages rising correspondingly (wages always lag behind prices), the labourer would be food insecure. The food grown by the employer (typically the owner of the land) and the wage payment, are in the end the right of the owner and the labourer (primary producer) respectively. The right of the labourer (the primary food producer) is limited to the wages earned, irrespective of whether the wage so received does or does not yield enough food for the labourer for his / her food security.

Similarly, an individual who acquires food by producing some other commodity and selling it in the market to acquire food, has to depend on his/ her actual ability to sell the produce as also on the relative price of that product vis-à-vis food prices. If either the sale of the commodity produced by the individual fails to materialise, or given the food prices, the individual succeeds in having command over food, which is insufficient for his or her survival; the person would be food insecure.

It is also important to note that uncertainty and vulnerability can be features of subsistence production involving both 'exchange with nature' and 'market exchange', whose precariousness is particularly visible in economies, where a substantial proportion of the victims are frequently small and marginal farmers, hit, *inter alia,* by a collapse of their 'direct entitlement' to the food they normally grow. It would be misleading, according to E&D Thesis, to hold self-provisioning as being synonymous with being food secure. The peasant farmer, like the landless labourer, has no guaranteed entitlement to the necessities of life including enough food.

Extended Entitlements

While the concept of entitlement so far focused on a person's legal rights of ownership, the E&D Thesis accepts that there are some social relations that take the broader form of accepted legitimacy rather than legal rights that are justifiable. For instance, by a well established convention, the "male-head" of a household in several parts of traditional societies, such as in India, receives more favourable treatment in the division of the family's total consumption. For instance, they have the first call on, say, the meat or fish in the family's diet, or receiving better and greater medical attention in case of illness. This is more often the case in households where the male head of the household is the breadwinner *(Greenough,* 1982; *Arnold,* 1985, p.89). It has even been found that when food is short (or when disease strikes) the male children get more medical attention and food resources. Such a claim to preferential treatment, which is accepted as legitimate and is thus effective, is neither enjoined by Law nor justifiable in a court of Law or enforced by the State.

This is more often the case in households where the male head of the household is the breadwinner. For instance, *Greenough* (1982) held that "the patriarchal values of Bengali Hindu society required priority to be given to the feeding of the male members of the household so as to ensure the continuance of the make line". Continuing this investigation further, it has been found that in many parts of South Asia "even in normal times men are fed first in peasant households. Women eat after the men, receiving a smaller and poorer share of food" *(Arnold,* 1985, p.89). Women eat last and the least. It has been even found that when food is in short supply, or when disease strikes, the male children get more medical attention and food resources.

The foregoing are legally weaker forms of entitlements, nevertheless such socially sanctioned rights may be extremely important and will play a part in the analysis of food security. For Sen, "extend entitlement is the concept of entitlements extended to include the results of more informal types of rights sanctioned by accepted notion of legitimacy", concepts that are particularly relevant while examining intra-familial division of available food, though it has other uses in social analysis to which we will presently turn.

In effect, according to the E&D Thesis, individuals acquire control over food in a number of different ways which in the last analysis are a function of dominant mode of production in their societies and where the individuals are positioned within that production scheme of their societies. Consequently, obstacles to have control over food varies from context to context. The E&D Thesis has attempted at organising the discussion about the variety of ways in which individuals acquire food, by linking them to the concept of "food entitlement", where acquisition or control over food is the realisation of one's food entitlement. Thus, in terms of arguments for "right to food", the E&D Thesis is extremely useful in taking account of the obstacles and remedies in relation to right to food. However, to be fully operational in defense of food rights, we need to look a little beyond, building up on what has been discussed above. To this we will presently turn.

III. Extensions

Sen's Thesis has been the subject matter of intense research and debate. One strand led to some notable extensions.

Some scholars have argued that Sen's approach could be extended to cover two special types of entitlements which neither fall within the purview of ownership nor are specifically exchange entitlements. These are entitlements stemming from individual's traditional rights to communal resources and from external social support systems that individuals enjoy, such as those provided by patronage, kinship, friendship, embodying relationships between social groups or persons in which considerations other than the mere economic take precedence. That is, they fall under the rubric of *moral economy*. Entitlements emanating from traditional rights and from external social support systems, are typically non-market exchanges, though not fully beyond market exchanges, such as those between a grocer and his/her favoured customers, who get privileged treatment in accessing goods, services, goods on credit, etc. Taking these analytical starting points noted commentators *(Agarwal,* 1999) have proposed that:

(a) An individual's "fall back position" as also her/his bargaining position within the household vis-à-vis, say food, would be a function of her/his ownership endowments, exchange entitlements and external (social and communal) support systems like patronage, kinship, friendship and right to communal resources. In other words, factors which impinge on an individual's command over food in general, would also impinge on intra-familial co-operative conflict over food. Any inequality among members of household in their ownership endowments, exchange entitlements and access to external support systems will place some members of the household in a weaker bargaining position in relation to all others in the household. Gender, vulnerability and age are obviously the basis of such inequality.

(b) Crisis of seasonality and calamity negatively affect ownership endowments and exchange entitlements as well as the strength of external support systems for both men and women. However, in so far as men and women are affected unequally, seasonality and calamity would alter their relative intra-familial bargaining strength as well. Suppose a calamity hits a community, which causes a total collapse or even a major deterioration in the women's fall back position (a likely event in case a famine strikes community in which the household is situated) while the "fall back position" of the men sustains (relatively speaking). This could weaken women's bargaining position even upto the point where non-cooperation becomes more beneficial to the men than cooperation, creating a tendency towards the disintegration of families and the desertion of spouses. Similar could be the consequences for the children and the aged and the disabled.

IV. The Additional Conditions

We saw above that the issue of food insecurity analysed above in terms of Sen's E&D Thesis is concerned with two basic conditions: one, availability of food and two, individual's ability to access food either through endowment or direct entitlements or exchange entitlements. In effect, if it is ensured that enough food is available and people can access the food so available, then right to food can be guaranteed. There would be no one going hungry. However, satisfaction of these two conditions may not always guarantee food security and even where these conditions are satisfied, individuals may not be able to exercise the right to food. There are three more conditions, namely, *existence of institutional sanctions, choice of food* and *the existence of the secondary food system,* that need to be met before individuals can be said to have the right to food. We now turn to examine each of the three additional conditions.

V. The Existence of Institutional Sanctions

First, the existence of *institutional sanctions.* Whatever be a person's basic endowment and whatever be that person's exchange entitlement, they have to be either objective goods like land, bovine wealth, stock of poultry and the like, or subjective goods like skill, knowledge, traits, technology, aptitude, capacity to work hard and so on. Sen's thesis laid considerable stress on possession based ability, where ability is shaped by institutional sanctions, availability and system of markets and prices. We will presently deal with all these briefly.

It has been rightly held that if individuals cannot access food, there would be widespread food insecurity of different degree: hunger, starvation (of different intensities) and in the limiting case, of even death caused by starvation. As it was pointed out by Sen, famines occurred when there were no systemic food shortages. In support of this position evidence from the Bengal Famine of 1943 and the Famine in Bangladesh of 1974 were summoned. In both cases inability of the people to access food caused greater havoc than food shortage *per se*. Therefore, distribution of food is a critical variable in causing or preventing famines. This is quite true, but this is only a part of the story. There are other parts to the story, of which institutional sanction is an important one.

An individual's exchange entitlement is seriously circumscribed by a fairly wide spectrum of legal, political, economic, religious, social and cultural elements, according to Sen's own theory. Exchange entitlement is not institution–neutral. Even where the availability of food is not the real problem and individuals have the ability to access food, right to food may not be enjoyed. Possession of food, direct endowment in Sen's terminology, or other commodities, which admit of conversion into food, exchange entitlements are important in exercising right to food, but not without constraints. What an individual possesses as a basic endowment can be converted into exchange entitlement, subject to constraints imposed, *inter alia,* by institutional sanctions. Thus the extent to which an individual can command food through exchange entitlement is determined also by institutional elements like cultural traits, customs, usage, traditions, religion, practice, beliefs and value system. That is why, we are arguing that exchange entitlement is not institution-neutral.

It is best to start with an illustration to establish this point. Consider a village in India which has both Hindu and Muslim population, say like Palanpur in Uttar Pradesh (*Bliss and Stern,* 1982; *Kynch and Maguire,* 1994). Both the communities have members who are engaged in agriculture and allied activities, such as dairying, whereby owning cattle. Some of the inhabitants of the village grow crops, including food crops, which are consumed at the household level, then sell their labour to buy alternative commodity bundles which includes food, to wipe out whatever food deficit they may have. The village is reasonably well endowed in terms of functions such as grocers, butchers and a bazaar at a nearby place.

In the event of a drought and a pest attack which, taken one with the other, wipes out completely whatever crops were grown in the fields, some food would still be available from the fields and some food would be available from the butchers who sell beef. This could have two-fold effect; **first** the direct entitlements of the cultivators are all gone and **second,** all those who used to rely on exchange entitlement (by sale of labour and non food crop as well) would find that their exchange entitlement has sharply come down because they have no non-food crop to sell, and also because their employment opportunities have shrunk owning to the destruction of the crop (*Mukherjee,* 1993). Further, if in keeping with the tradition of State action, a wage employment programme, such as the Employment Assurance Programme of the Government of India or the Employment Guarantee Scheme of the Government of Maharastra, is launched and people earn wages in lieu of labour, this wage can then be used by the wage earners to access alternative commodity bundles which include food.

Now the Hindus and the Muslims both have the ability to access food in terms of the wages earned from the wage employment programme. But food is available only in the form of beef in the village under discussion. While the Muslims will also suffer hunger in the absence of food crops, or on account of destruction of food crops, they will still be able to access some commodity bundle, which will contain food to consume from the available supply of beef. But the Hindus will suffer food insecurity (starvation), because they cannot or will not access commodity bundles containing beef, as they do not have institutional sanction to consume beef. Here religion is taken as an institution, and it is a matter of history that the Hindus by their prevalent religious practice are forbidden to consume beef. Therefore, even where food is available, people may still not be able to enjoy the right to food and be hungry despite having the ability to access food and despite food being available.

It is possible that some of the Hindus driven by hunger, or because they do not believe in the religious practices, or for whatever reason, may opt to acquire commodity bundles containing food in terms of the beef, being sold by the butchers in the village under reference. That is, the institutional sanction is obtained (in the breach) by one party to the exchange, viz., the buyers. But still the Hindus may not be able to acquire commodity bundles containing the food (beef) because the Muslims (vendors) will not sell them for fear of a reprisal. Typically in a rural situation in India, such a sale of beef by Muslims to Hindus, can trigger widespread disturbance, since it could be interpreted as a veiled attempt on the part of the Muslims to "defile" the Hindus or as an attempt to convert them to Islam (1). The history of partition on both sides of the border is bloodied with senseless killings associated with butchered animals being thrown at religious places by the "other community" *(Sahni,* 1998).

A situation similar to the above can arise when the parties to the exchange are high and low caste people. Some years ago Kusum Nair investigating the socio-economic scenario in Bihar graphically illustrated this landscape. Hark these words :

> "Thus, not very long ago, in the village of Mucharin, one Gopal Prasad went to work on a bundh (2) on the river Lilahana. According to him : "It became late and decided to spend the night at the bundh and not to return to the village. I am a Koeri (3) by caste. Some other people also were camping here for the night but they were all Bhoomiyar Brahmins .... Since I had not taken anything with me, they told me to cook and eat in an old earthen pot, which was lying in the sand. I was told that pot has been used by a Koeri before, so I could use it. But it looked very dirty and old, and I thought to myself, how am I sure who used it. Since the Bhoomiyars were cooking their meal, I decided to eat the food cooked by them, and did so. They gave me some. Next day there was an uproar in the village. They called me insane and threatened to ex-communicate me; they wanted to beat me up. My family also turned against me. Not a soul would take my side. Even if a Harijan was working the latha (4) on the well I could not bath there. All this because I had eaten food cooked by a Bhoomiyar. I was young then, and it made me angry. So I ran away to Gaya (5). There I stayed with a tailor and learned to trade. For more than a year I lived in exile. The purohit advised me to have Shuddhi done, but I was obstinate. I decided to fight it out, even if it meant that I could never return to the village. Since I had become independent economically I did not really care.
>
> Then fortunately for me, my grandmother died, and the priest advised me to utilise the opportunity to undergo the rites of purification as well. I agreed and went to Vishnupad Temple in Gaya and had my head shaved. I had to do that in

> any case for my grandmother, and then the purohit did shuddhi also. Only then was I accepted back into my caste and family" *(Nair,* 1979).

In anthropological studies the issues revolving around ceremonial purity of food in the rural areas of India, have been studied at length and the issue of ceremonial purity of food operates both ways. Just as the case illustrated indicates that a lower caste person would not eat cooked food handed down by a higher caste person, a higher caste person does not have institutional sanction to eat food prepared or served by certain lower caste people. "........ eating is actually a ritual and, like other Hindu rituals, has become associated with caste and status regulations *(Coon,* 1948, p. 471). The ramifications being too complex to be explored in detail were avoided by Coon and he concentrated on indicating briefly the 'rules of the game' followed by the Thakurs (an upper landed–caste) in so far as consuming cooked food is concerned. Thakurs are free to consume fruits, raw vegetables and milk products obtained from the hands of anyone. However,

> "The Thakur must closely observe the caste of anyone who prepares cooked food (kacha) for him or touches it before it is eaten. He may take food fried in butter (Pakka) from the hands of all but eight low caste Hindu groups and four Muslim groups from the village. (Muslims, because they eat beef, are always capable of rendering the food and water of Hindus impure). But he can accept baked or boiled food only from one higher in caste than himself, namely, a Brahmin, or from another Thakur. Actually, the Thakur hesitates to take food from a Brahmin household, for in theory the Brahmin is the one to receives service and alms, and it is considered in bad taste to accept his hospitality. Therefore, the Thakur, like other Hindus, actually freely inter-dine only with members of his own caste. He must be circumspect, also, about the identity of those from whose hand he takes water. In general, the rule is that he may take water served by those from whom he may receive fried food; thus the Thakur of Senapur may not take water from the Muslims of the village or from those Hindus of Senapur who belong to the eight low castes" *(Coon,* 1948, p. 270-271).

Even Mushars, who eat rats, about whose food habits we will have occasion to reflect later in this chapter, "have their standards and insistences. They decline to take cooked food at the homes of Chamars,

Khatiks and Dhobis" *(Coon,* 1948, p.488) as they are in popular conception looked upon as belonging to lower castes than the Mushars.

This holds true even where people are on the verge of starvation. If food is provided or served by people to hungry individuals, the latter can not accept the food provided by the former, if institutional sanctions permitting such acceptance are not operative. Evidence available from the famine in Chotanagpur in 1866 is a pointer in this regard. The Santhals of the area had a long history of struggle against the Brahmins and the Santhal Chiefs had issued fiats prohibiting any interface with the Brahmins. During the famine in 1866 the Government had decided to undertake relief operation by way of distribution of cooked food amongst the starving Santhals. Distribution of cooked food was organised. But the Santhals refused to eat the food so provided by the government because the Brahmins cooked them.

> "During the 1866 famine in Chotanagpur, British officials found to their astonishment that starving Santhals refused to eat the food distributed by the relief committees because it had been cooked by the hated Brahmins" *(Guha,* 1985, p.120).

The starving Santhals did not access the food available, despite the fact that they had the ability to access the food provided through "non-entitlement transfer" as the food was being distributed free by the Government. This was because there was no institutional sanction to access the food, as it was cooked by the Brahmins and there was injunction issued by the Santhal Chiefs against the Brahmins.

Institutional sanction can also take the nature of food being actually withheld from people, through arbitrary criteria. In some societies, women may not have access to food even though it may be available, in which event the possibility of food insecurity looms large, even though there may be no paucity of food in the system and individuals have the capacity to access food. This is truer still during hunger periods. For instance, in the Bengal Famine of 1943-44, in the rural areas in particular, food was withheld from women based on gender discrimination. Greenough argued that "some kind of persons in Bengal are regarded as inherently more valuable than others and they will be favoured and protected from extinction during crisis" *(Greenough,* 1982.p.214). He goes on to argue that as the economic situation deteriorated during the Bengal Famine of 1943-44, the head of the household (called Korta) "favoured more valued members at the expense of the less valued members. Since adults and males in Bengal are valued more than children and females... the master tended to deny the latter in favour of the former" *(Greenough,* 1982, p.217). Granted the foregoing it seems "that during the Bengal famine food was deliberately *withheld from women* and given to men", *(Arnold,* 1988 p.89. Emphasis added) though arguably there could be alternative interpretations of the facts stated by Greenough. Thus, food was seemingly available, but there was no institutional sanction for a section of society, namely, women, to access the food so available. Indeed gender discrimination in matters of accessing food, health and education in developing countries like India, reflected in greater women malnutrition. Higher female illiteracy rate, and poorer health among women are matters of our economic history *(World Bank,* 1989; *NCAER,* 1999). These are all, at least in part, on account of absence of an institutional sanction available to women, to access these functions, without demur or recourse, at par with men.

The essential point that emerges out of these recitals is that in a stratified society, defined, for instance, in the vocabulary of castes, it is not possible to access food even where food is available and the people have the ability to access food, in the absence of institutional sanctions. Thus enjoying the right to food will remain a rhetoric.

Sen was apparently aware of such eventualities when he said that what an individual can command in a society is constrained by a bundle of relationships covering legal, political and economic phenomena as well as social and cultural ones *(Sen,* 1981, p.47). There is, therefore, an implicit admission of the fact that institutional sanctions are required. But its role and significance has been seen underrated. In the entitlement and deprivation approach to ensuring right to food, institutional sanctions at best indirectly influence an individual's ability to access food through either exchange entitlement or transfer entitlement. An individual's ability to exercise right to food can be constrained by absence of institutional sanctions without the institutional arrangements being mediated in any way by possession of food or the means to access food.

The Issue of Choice

Even where food is available, where people have ability to acccss food and where institutional sanction to access food exists, there could still be difficulty in exercising right to food and people go hungry if people do not choose to access food available. That is, the element of choice has to be fitted into the food rights picture to ensure that people exercise the food to food and prevent hunger. The genius of Sen did not miss this problem but for some reason, not entirely clear why, elected to relegate it to the background with a one-sentence disclaimer :

> While it (entitlement approach) is an approach of some generality, it makes no attempt to include all possible influences that can in principle cause starvation, for example illegal transfers (e.g. owing to inflexible food habits)" *(Sen,* 1981 p.45).

Apparently Sen was emphasizing that starvation would almost always be caused by the inability of the individuals to access food. He argued that "there is indeed no evidence whatsoever of people starving because of *unwillingness* to change food habits" (Emphasis ours. *Sen,* ibid., p.165). He summons the evidence of the great famine of Ethiopia in 1888-92, for example, and suggests that people would eat almost anything under the grip of starvation *(Pankhurst,* 1968).

While this may be true only in some cases of sustained failure to exercise the right to food, Sen's thesis missed out in making a distinction between choices people make in the matter of exercising the right to food before and after they are starving. Sen seemingly looked at the limiting case of extreme hunger and his arguments, therefore, may apply in cases of extreme food insecurity. And if one were looking at the causative factors for non–exercise of the right to food then one of the more relevant issues, particularly so from a policy framing perspective, relates to choices made about exerting right to food prior to setting in of conditions resulting in death due to starvation. We do have the evidence from the Bengal Famine of 1943 when people in Bengal would not change their food habits even in the face of famines. That is, of people chosing to ignore the available food despite the fact that they were confronted with famine, even when food was available, they had the power to access food and there was institutional sanction for accessing the available food. Note these words :

> "During the famine large supplies of wheat and millet were sent to Bengal and helped to relieve food shortage. They were supplied to rice eaters through the free kitchens but efforts to persuade people to eat them in their homes in place of rice met with little success" *(Government of India,* 1945).

Thus failure to exercise right to food may persist despite food being available in the system, people having the ability to access food, and there being non-entitlement transfer, where the starving individuals do not choose to consume the food. This is so because the individuals may deem the food that is available (Wheat and Millet in the example of the Bengal Famine of 1943) as something which is not what they would normally regard as acceptable food.

Even at the cost of suffering the stricture of being repetitive, it is worth pointing out a real life situation to reinforce the argument relating to choice. We have mentioned that rats are eaten by a class of people called Mushars in Bihar *(Grierson,* 1926) as food. The situation remains almost unchanged to date. Thus it was reported :

> "The scorching summer sun beats down on the ground relentlessly. But the bunch of emaciated half clad children don't care....for the children of Mushar in a village near Bodhgaya in Bihar, the search for food is almost like trailing God. Some 5 kms away in Sarvodayapuri village ... another group of starving children too forages around the countryside for food. A half-crazed look comes into their eyes as they spot some holes in the fields. Bending over the mouth of the holes, they burn cow dung cakes while anxiously watching the black smoke billowing out of the other end of the tunnel-like space. The reason for this peculiar behaviour soon becomes clear as an army of rats scampers out. The villagers triumphantly bludgeon them with sticks, roast them and eat them as part of their mid-day meal" *(Ahmed,* 1992)

Rats are, therefore, accepted as food, by at least a section of the people, in some parts of Bihar in India even today as they used to be nearly half a century back. Similarly, rats are eaten by Mushars in U.P. as well, as we mentioned earlier *(Coon,* 1948, p. 488). If food in the form of rats is provided to the people like Mushars they would probably be accepted as food and consumed, as rats find a place in their menu of edibles. Similar choice may not be made, say in West Bengal, even during acute food insecurity (starvation) as people would rather starve than choose to eat rats, because rats are not normally seen as food. The element of choice in the exercise of right to food or starvation cannot thus be ignored, without leaving the canvas incomplete, except in very limiting cases.

In traditional societies of developing countries like India, where practices, traditions, usage, customs and beliefs about food and work are powerful, failure to adhere to these practices, traditions, usage, customs and beliefs are fraught with dire consequences, either by society or by nature embodied in deities and gods. The influence of such practices, traditions, customs and beliefs and adherence to them may be calculated and principled so that the actions of the poor people (who are most vulnerable in matters of food) are so chosen that they are consistent with the deep rooted cultural practices and traditions, religious beliefs and customary law, and therefore, they are in one sense incapacitated in acting differently. A concept of food security and right to food ought to be more general to take account of this eventuality as well. If it is maintained that food insecurity (famines or starvation) is caused by the failure (inability) of the people to access food, then it is very important to explore, in all its dull details, the causes on account of which people fail to access food and hence are unable to exercise the right to food. It would not be infrequent when the causes on account of which people would fail to enjoy the tight to food, could be traced to the impact of practices, traditions, customs and beliefs.

Existence of Secondary Food Security

In a developing country situation, it would be little unfair to define food security, as has to be done both by the protagonists of Food Availability Decline Arguments (FAD) and Sen, in terms of food produced by the application of technology in the economic sense alone. We will call this here "primary food". Food security has also to be informed by the existence of what we call **secondary food system**. In addition to primary food available, there is also a whole range of food from forests (*FAO,* 1982, 1983, 1984 1986, 1989), from common property resources (*Jodha,* 1989 and 1990) and from micro-environments *(Chambers,* 1991). And people have access to this food, which is produced without the application of technology in the strict economic sense. Fruits, nuts, tubers, leaves, gums and mushrooms gathered and harvested from forests; animals, birds and insects hunted from the jungles and CPR; fish, crabs, snails, etc. caught from rivers, collected from common property resources are the core constituents of the secondary food system.

Food derived from the secondary food system, "for most rural people... provide essential vitamins, proteins and calories" *(Falconer,* 1989). In several cases, as in the semi-arid regions of India, in absolute and in percentage terms, the quantities of food culled out from forests, common property resources and micro-environments may be as much as upto 30 per cent of the total food consumption of the rural households *(Jodha,* 1990) and more importantly, the essential nutrients, otherwise missing in the primary food consumed by the poor, provided by the secondary food system are vital not only in themselves but in terms of when they are available *(Falconer* and *Arnold,* 1988). Such food provide cover during periods of extreme stress, and at times of temporary scarcity of primary food during certain parts of the year, which have been rechristened "hungry seasons": when stored food supplies are dwindling and the next harvest is as yet unavailable particularly in the rainfed areas, peak agricultural periods when labour is in short supply and disposable time available to the women for cooking falls dramatically.

The secondary food system also provide a lifeline to the poor people during what is called "famine periods", times of natural and man-made calamities such as floods, earthquakes, famines, droughts (when additional energy rich foods such as nuts, roots and tubers and rhizomes are indispensable to provide an important buffer), riots *(Arnold,* 1991) and even wars such as in Somalia over the last few years, which is why these foods have also been given the appellation of "famine foods".

Our own findings in Midnapore district, West Bengal, showed that during the two "hunger periods" that people face every year, food from the secondary food system plays a critical role in helping them to tide over the difficulty *(Mukherjee* and *Mukherjee* 1994 and elsewhere in this volume). And this occurs year after year, on a fairly regular basis. And this is not a new phenomenon in the Indian context. As far back as in 1908-1915, it was found that the people of Hazaribagh, Bihar, depended on such food as forest food to meet their food requirements (*Final Report* of the Survey and Settlement Operation of the District of Hazaribag, 1908-1915). Although no quantitative data pertaining to such food are available, there is little doubt that they occupied a substantial portion of the common people's diet.

It is true that "famine foods" from forests, common property resources and micro-environments are different from food derived from these sources during normal times. It is also true that in times of famines such foods are more complicated to gather and process. Nevertheless, famine foods are characteristically energy rich and not infrequently, remain the only food available to the poor during famine periods. Additionally, gathering and processing foods from forests, common property resources and micro-environments provide valuable income during these difficult times which helps the rural poor in augmenting their (primary) food intake by accessing them in the market. And fortunately a secondary food system exists, in some form or the other, in almost all economies, though there may be variations, often at the margin, in the magnitude of contributions made by the secondary food system in the overall food security scenario.

Acquisition of food from the secondary food system can, however, be also explained in terms of the ED Thesis. In case of food gathered and hunted from CPR, microenvironment, forests, etc., there is an acquisition of food within the meaning of "other entitltments". There is in one sense an exchange with nature. Here individuals can be seen as expending labour for food gathered, collected or hunted from these sources but they do not give anything back in return to these sources. The individuals are exchanging their labour for food, but the sources, which provide such food do not get anything in return.

Thus even if all the three conditions of Sen's thesis and the additional two described above are not fulfilled, there would still be no absolute food insecurity (starvation), if there exists a secondary food system. Or even though there may be systemic hunger yet it would be relatively far less acute than what could have been in the absence of the secondary food system. From a reading of either Sen's works or the FAD arguments, it seems that this dimension of what we have called "secondary food system" (or food provided by forests, common property resources and micro-environments) was not taken cognizance of.

VI. Conclusions

Thus the elements of a regime of right to food ought to be written in terms of five crucial variables if the right to food is to be made a reality. These are

a) (primary) food availability,
b) ability of the people to access (primary food),
c) institutional sanction to access that food,
d) individual's freedom to choose food which is culturally acceptable, and
e) existence of secondary food system.

Just as the E&D Thesis argues that defining food security in terms of food availability alone, will be erroneous, so would defining a regime of right to food in terms of entitlements, regardless of **institutional sanctions** to access food, exercise of **choice** in favour of the available food, and the impact of a **secondary food system,** be incomplete. Unless all the five variables are incorporated in any analysis of hunger or starvation and in the structure of right to food, the theoretical constructs would be unable to explain a good deal of hunger. Consequently, policy making and corrective action, built on the foundation of such theoretical constructions, could only provide a partial solution to the problem. This is particularly true of societies which are strongly influenced by religious edits and where the sharp relief of social stratification can be easily discerned.

For the purposes of public action it is, therefore, necessary that, in the face of increasing hunger or in the event of a famine or in the event of trying to prevent an increase in hunger or starvation, in addition to the conditions laid down in the E&D Thesis, the public authorities ensure that additional supplies of food to be brought in to the food deficit areas be such that they would be chosen by the hungry; access to forests, common property resources and micro-environment is kept open and unhindered; and institutional sanctions exist to access food that is available.

Granted these, it follows from above that property rights in respect of common property resources, forests and micro-environments, need to be redefined and laid down clearly and unequivocally. In the absence of such clearly defined and unequivocal property rights, the people who are dependent upon common property resources, forests, etc., for their secondary food intake, will be in a disadvantageous position in exercising their right to food in avoiding and / or reducing hunger. Such property rights must have an explicit recognition that those dependent on the secondary food system to prevent or reduce hunger, have an inalienable right to the fruits of CPR, forests and micro–environments. It also stands to reason that whatever remains of CPR, forests and micro-environment can be put to sustainable use only when the people dependent upon them are guaranteed access to their fruits/products. Such guarantee, *inter alia*, will prevent people from abusing these sources of food. The success of the Joint Forestry Management in Midanpore, West Bengal and of Sukhamajri experiment in Haryana, are examples in point.

In the context of choice, the role of both the procurement and distribution of food in India assumes significance. If one looks at the procurement scenario, it would be apparent that the procurement basket and procurement prices relate principally to rice and wheat. And for good reasons into which we are not probing for the present. It automatically follows that the food to be distributed through the PDS would be, in the main, confined to wheat and rice. The "choice" of foodgrains by the people in India is thus influenced and/or reinforced by the kind of food distributed through the PDS. This is indicative of the fact that there is a possibility of changing food habits over the long-run and hence, alter the choice/ preference of the public by supplying successively higher quantity of a particular food grain through the PDS. For instance, in Bengal, the system of consuming wheat was non-existent, till the era of controls and statutory rationing emerged when wheat came to be supplied through the PDS together with rice. Although no statistics is available, people in Bengal who previously consumed only rice, have partially substituted wheat for rice, whatever the extent. Thus, it is possible to influence "choice" to a limited extent. This is why, it is important for food policy planners to have a long term perspective in sight. The policy planners must decide whether they seek to change people's preference in "choice" of food, by varying the kind of food that is supplied through the PDS, so that during crises, famines and acute hunger periods, supplying food, which is easily available and acceptable as food to the people, through different channels becomes a relatively easy proposition.

Endnotes

1. There is no expressed prohibition against consumption of beef in Hindu scriptures.
2. A bundh is a small dam on a river or a rivulet (Author's own footnote).
3. A sub-caste of Sudras (Author's own footnote).
4. An irrigation device.
5. A District Headquarter Town.
6. Thanks are due to Upendranadh, CARE India for very useful suggestions on an earlier version of this Chapter.

2 The Theory of Hunger: The Economists' Perspectives

I. Introduction

We saw in the last Chapter that the elements of a regime of right to food to eliminate hunger ought to be written in terms of at least five crucial variables if the right to food is to be made a reality. Availability of food (from the primary food system), the ability of people to access (primary food), existence of institutional sanction to access that food, existence of individual's freedom to choose food which is culturally acceptable, and the existence of secondary food system have to be the components of a right to food regime. Where all the five variables are incorporated in any analysis of hunger and in the structure of right to food, the theoretical constructs would be on sound footing. And policy making and corrective action to eliminate hunger, built on such foundation, would enable people to exercise their right to food.

Box 2.1
The Serenity Prayer

Thousands, if not millions, of people pray the serenity prayer each day:

God grant me the serenity to accept
the things I cannot change,
the courage to change things I can,
and the wisdom to know the difference.

II. Why Do People Fail to Access food?

Thus people (and their number runs into billions) go hungry because there is not enough food to meet everybody's needs, or there is a decline (read failure) in entitlement. Hunger can be caused by absence of institutional sanctions to access the available food and available food being culturally unacceptable. In many cases people may be more hungry than they otherwise would have been if there is no CPR, micro-environment, forests, etc. which provide food, from, what we have called, the secondary food system. Entitlement failure or decline in entitlement or absence of institutional sanction to access food etc. are the proximate causes of hunger. For instance, if an elderly person faces hunger due to entitlement failure, what are the reasons behind the entitlement failure: is it lack of income, absence of physical access to food or absence of physical access or what? The basic causes of hunger lie somewhere else, which need to be examined.[1].

There are at least seven basic reasons why people are unable to exercise their right to food and go hungry. Powerlessness and politics, violence and militarism, poverty, rapid population growth exerting strain on environment and over-consumption, racism and ethnocentrism, gender discrimination and vulnerability and age, are the seven of the more important causes of entitlement failure *(BFWI,* 1995). Let us see very briefly how each of these threatens the right to food and causes hunger.

Powerlessness and Political Will at the National and International Levels

Hunger is often caused and perpetuated by issues of politics, powerlessness of hungry people and hungry nations, and power-status-structure in domestic and global society. Whatever the form of governance, lack of political influence of those in the grip of food insecurity contributes to persistence of hunger. This explains why infusing aid and food aid cannot ensure right to food and they cannot solve the problem of hunger and food insecurity.

Assistance in terms of food aid and aid *per se* may help reduce hunger as a very-short run to short run measure. But they do not challenge the power-status-structure in the economy that controls the allocation of and access to productive resources, vital for eliminating hunger in the medium to longer term to guarantee right to food. Food aid creates a dependency syndrome, kills the spirit of community effort at solving communal problems and destroys the ethos of self-help that has sustained communities for ages. In many cases, leakages from food-aid breed corrupt practices and corrupt even those who receive food aid, in that they are lured to sell the food they receive as aid. Thus, food aid is not a solution to hunger problem though it can be a measure for temporary relief under conditions of food scarcity, for whatever reason: either famine, war, earthquake, floods or civil strife. This is best illustrated by what is happening in the aftermath of the super-cyclone that hit Orissa in October 1999.

The cyclone ravaged coastal districts of the State of Orissa, India such as Jagatsinghpur, Kendrapara and Paradip, amongst others, are receiving considerable amount of food aid. But it is feared that the relief measures in terms of food aid and aid, undertaken by some aid agencies might lead to another human disaster in these areas. The ad hoc approach adopted by the aid agencies has negated initiatives to make villagers self-reliant. "The villagers turn up at the relief supermarkets when they need something and are promptly given a bag of goodies. The villagers don't realise how difficult it will become for them once these agencies leave and the handouts stop" (*Shivshanker,* 2000). Recognising the seriousness of the situation, the government and some important development agencies like Eficor, Care India and Rama Krishna Mission have started "food for work programme" to resurrect the sense of community participation and stimulate the ethos of self-help.

Thus because food aid and aid are not the answers to end hunger, one of the answers to ensuring food security and eliminate hunger lies in ensuring that appropriate public policies are in place. These policies could include providing special access to food for the vulnerable and specially disadvantaged sections of society, access to basic education, and availability of primary health care services. Policies promoting sustainable agricultural practices, arranging for sanitation and safe drinking water, expansion of employment opportunities (including diversification of industry and general economic growth) and providing to the poor access to, and control over productive resources, are other elements of a basket of policies that need to be in place.

Box 2.2

The Problem Now is Aid Addiction, Jagatsinghpur

The Pradhan of Kunjakothi village in Jagatsinghpur district—one of the three most affected by cyclone—says that though there are agencies in the region that have begun programmes aimed at making the villagers more self-reliant, their efforts might go in vain as the villagers have got used to "living off dole". "The villagers are not interested in working in the fields any longer. They feel if someone is constructing their homes, clothing them and giving them food, they do not need to work".

A. K. Samantray, working with the Orissa Disaster Mitigation Programme, set up by the German Red Cross, says that a large number of villagers had taken to selling food supplied to them in the black market.

M. M. Rajendran, says, "To encourage self-relienace the state government had stopped distributing relief supplies after the first month. It now plans to supply seeds for the cultivation of cash crops, provide fertilisers, low interest loans, housing and even fishing boats".

Rahul Shivshankar, *The Sunday Times of India,* New Delhi, April 23, 2000.

It is necessary to have a strong public constituency to garner political will to make policies for guaranteeing right to food a top priority for the State.

The people who go to bed hungry every night (estimated at 800 million now) require the support of resources and organisations, which can be their own, in order to be empowered. They lack resources: they generally do not **own** land to grow food, though they may grow food on other's land, and their incomes are so low that they fail to provide their families with adequate diet regularly. They do not have organisations to articulate their interests, which is why Governments do not very often have a set of truly anti-hunger programmes in substance, though they may exist in form. This is abundantly exemplified by Government of India's Budget for 2000-2001. Subsidy on food sold through the Public Distribution System has been cut, for making a paltry saving of Rs 1000 crore. But many redundant Ministries involving expenditures aggregating several times more than this saving on food subsidy, have been left untouched, which prompted a leading newspaper to scream on the front page on the morning after the budget: "*Short on big ideas, Sinha lets Govt get away*" (*Indian Express*, 1st March, 2000, New Delhi). And despite the fact that it is now well accepted that policies to eradicate hunger have extremely high pay-off, yet not much is done very often. Less of malnourished and undernourished people means more productive workforce, healthier women and, therefore, healthier children, who can reach the full potential of human beings.

Hunger and politics are also related in another fashion. Not only does lack of political will cause and perpetuate hunger, hunger can contribute to lack of political, social and economic clout to seek elimination of hunger. People who are in perpetual struggle to somehow eke out a living, find it difficult to be effective participants in decision making at the socio-political levels and influence policy making, affecting their lives. Chambers in one of his most influential works had forcefully drawn attention to the powerlessness of the poor, to which so much attention is now being given (*Chambers*, 1972) in improving their own lot. Forces that render the poor powerless take a variety of forms.

Box 2.3

A Scientists' Resolution

"A hundred times a day, I remind myself that my inner and outer life depends on the labours of other humans, living and dead. And that I must exert myself in order to give in the same measure as I have received and still receiving".

Albert Einstein

Politics at the international level also militates against eradication of hunger. Developed countries maintain their economic power through a variety of means. For instance, they maintain higher tariffs on processed imports from developed countries than on raw materials. These reduce sales of more profitable goods whose production could have created jobs and help cut down hunger or at least its severity for large sections of needy people in developing countries. For instance, many of the developing countries manufacture clothing and textile for exports, but the countries to which these exports are directed restrict such imports into their countries.

The Multi-Fibre Agreement that regulated international trade in these items through quotas clearly bear this out. Such barriers cost the developing countries, according to one estimate, at least $ 80 billion per year. This is far more than the $ 55 billion that the developing countries globally receive in aid from all sources, including U.N. Agencies, per year. True, the MFA has been replaced by the Agreement on Textiles at the WTO, which will dismantle the quotas, but it is as much true that not much progress has been done in this regard till date. Where developed countries import goods at reduced tariffs from developing countries, it involves shipping parts to the developing countries for assembling and then re-importing, which results only a small portion of the profit going to the developing countries.

The imbalance of international power has now been codified in various other agreements entered into under the aegis of the World Trade Organisation (WTO). Like the Multi-Fibre Arrangements (which is to be phased out gradually), the agricultural subsidy rules enjoined in the Agreement on Agriculture, both at the insistence of the developed countries, in particular, are clearly inimical to hunger-reducing potential of the developing countries. The reduction of Quantitative Restrictions on Trade and bound Tariff Rates are other provisions that will create further problems for the developing countries in terms of employment and income. No less a person than Verghese Kurien himself, the father of the White Revolution in India, has beautifully put it which bears repetition here:

> "We produce milk at a very competitive cost. There're indeed subsidies in the West. If domestic prices for milk powder in the US are $700 or $800 per tonne more than the price at which they sell milk powder abroad—and if the same is true for the EU—then clearly there're subsidies. The Uruguay Round agreements on agriculture did not do away with those subsidies. It is more a matter of modest reductions of tonnage and subsidy amounts that'll still end up being very substantial. Indian milk is safe unless these subsidies are further raised.... Producing milk isn't a hobby for our farmers, it's their source of income. If a competitor has access to his government's exchequer and drives down our farmers' milk prices, in time we'll have farmers reducing investments in producing milk. If it continues, farmers will sell their milch cows and exit dairying. Our milk prices will rise and foreign milk will start coming in at a much higher cost to our foreign exchange and to our consumer" *(Anandan, 2000)*.

And on why the developed countries are trying to ram down agreements which lower restrictions on trade, he remarked: "As to the WTO's effect on milk producer, one should look at its effect on the world. If our dairy industry grows, India will be a threat to advanced dairying nations" (Ibid).

The soundness of what Kurien argued is best seen in the context of what M. S. Swaminathan, the father of India's Green Revolution, said:

> "Food imports are of two kinds—raw and processed. Imports of raw food grains, pulses, fish and milk will badly hit farmers, fishermen....Processed food imports will ruin micro-enterprises.
>
> The western concept of trade is "survival of the fittest". If there were a level playing field, there would be no problem in this. In agriculture, it is heavily loaded in favour of the west. The level of subsidies for the farm sector there is very high. Investment in post harvest technologies and methods, including cold storage chains and automation, is higher than the GDPs of many developing nations. The order of subsidised investment in farm infrastructure is that for every one dollar invested by a country like India, the investment in the developed world is about $ 100,000" *(Panneerselvan,* 2000).

The operation of the Agreement on Trade Related Intellectual Property Rights will further weaken the position of the developing countries even further *(Correa,* 1999a and 1999b). There is every chance that the developing countries would lose out to corporate raids on their indigenous knowledge, technology and bio-wealth. The two best known cases to illustrate the point are the patent granted in US on Basmati Rice and Turmeric to a US company and to two US scientists respectively. Fortunately, these could be challenged and the patents granted were cancelled on the ground that these were not inventions in that these were "prior-art" and recorded in written documents *(Chengappa,* 1997). There is a lot of hard work that the developing countries have to do before they can turn the TRIPS agreement to their advantage. But whatever the case, corporates will use the Agreement to have control over seeds and food, which is detrimental to the prospect of food security in the developing countries. Indeed, the manner in which the global economy is ought to be driven by the agenda of free trade, mirrors an impression that there has never been any commitment to fight hunger whether at the national or at the international level.

The trade negotiators were fully alive of the fact that as consequence of the Uruguay Round Negotiations developing countries would face hardships on account of these trade agreements. They were clear that higher food prices and market instability would cause increased hunger in some developing countries. Thus in Marrakesh in 1994, during the final adoption of the Uruguay Round Agreements, a separate agreement was reached to provide for compensation to developing countries who would face hardships. But as usual the terms of the agreement have been left vague and couched in normative terms, as opposed to *binding* terms used for the obligations of the developing countries, so that the developed countries could interpret the way that suits them the best. And as a consequence, there has been little follow up on these to make any meaningful difference to the developing countries, following the implementation of the different agreements.

Box 2.4

Major Commitments to End Hunger

Year	Event	Major Commitment Made
1974	**World Food Conference, Rome**	Gave a call to accept the goal that in 10 years time, no child will go to bed hungry, no family would fear for its next day's bread and human being's future and capacities would not be stunted by malnutrition
1979	**World Conference on Agrarian Reforms and Rural Development, FAO, Rome**	Encouraged Governments to pursue agrarian reforms and rural development interventions in partnership with non-governmental organisations and farmers' organisations to improve agricultural food production
1989	**Bellagio Declaration: Overcoming Hunger in the 1990s, Bellagio, Italy**	Called for ending world's hunger before 2000, by: • Eliminating deaths from famine; • Ending hunger in half of the poorest households; • Cutting malnutrition in half for mothers
1990	**World Summit for Children**	Reduce Child malnutrition by 50 per cent

1992	**World Declaration on Nutrition from the International Conference on Nutrition of WHO and FAO, Rome**	There is enough food for all people in the world, yet hunger and malnutrition persist because of inequitable access. Call given for reducing severe and moderate malnutrition of Children under 5 years of age to half of 1990 levels.
1994	**The Salaya Statement on Ending Hunger, Salaya, Thailand.**	• Reaffirmed that ending hunger is a credible and achievable objective. • Called upon nations at redirecting increased funds towards meeting the needs of the poor people, especially rural and urban households at the risk of food insecurity. • Recognised that continued progress can be achieved by better communication, community organisation and collaboration with local governments. Specific actions include empowering poor communities, better education for women and providing safety nets for vulnerable populations.
1995	**World Summit for Social Development, Copenhagen, Denmark**	Recognised right to food as a basic right of human beings and committed to reduce the proportion of people living in extreme poverty in developing countries by at least 50 per cent, towards achieving the basic rights of people, including the right to food.
1995	**Conference on Hunger and Poverty, IFAD, Rome**	• Recognised the importance of the role of civil society organisations in addressing the international causes of hunger. • Established a popular coalition for, *inter alia,* increasing public awareness about effective policies for ending hunger, and advance agrarian reforms.
1996	**World Food Summit, FAO, Rome**	• Committed to reduce the number of under-nourished people by half the present number by 2015. • Gave priority to poverty eradication and promoting food security of future generations.

It is indeed a curious paradox that though the developing countries and the developed countries have the same voting rights in trade negotiations, and the system driving the governance of WTO is democratic, yet the developing countries always loose out. Key to understanding the paradox lies in going into the process, rather than the form, of governance followed at the WTO. Major proposals for passage at the WTO are never put on the table as is taken for granted in any democratic system, because the wealthier members can be outvoted in the process. Decisions are, as a rule, therefore, made on the basis of "consensus building", with volleys of proposals coming from different informal and formal meetings of negotiators, at times even embodied in what is called a "non-paper". This consensus building process, *prima facie* appears efficient, but it reduces transparency and accountability because core bargains are made in informal and unrecorded meetings, where such "meetings" are neither open, nor accessible to countries, which are not part of these meetings. Consequently, those countries, which are not a party to such "consensus building", get no chance to put forth their case when formal negotiations begin and are, more often than not, quite unaware of the bargains struck. Fortunately enough, during the 1999 Seattle Ministerial Meeting of the WTO, this method of "consensus building" was strongly resented by the developing countries, notably the African countries which ultimately led to the collapse of the meet *(Economist,* 1999).

In this context of "consensus building", the size of the delegations, as much as their quality, which negotiate at the WTO level, hold the key to a *successful* negotiation. Developing countries can hardly afford large delegations comprising specialists to negotiate numerous and technical issues involved in trade negotiations. Many African countries cannot send delegations to the negotiating table. Thus they cannot get the best bargain out of this unequal process. And, therefore, the "truth is that the number of countries deeply involved in the negotiations on most issues does not exceed two dozens" *(Tironi,* 1995). Trade delegations from rich countries overwhelm developing country negotiators, both in terms of numbers and technical expertise, and levels of authority.

Violence and Militarism

Violence and Militarism is the second element that causes hunger and militates against exercise of right to food.

Violence are of two broad forms: **one**, harmful actions of institutions or individuals against persons or property, which are easily visible; **two**, destructive actions which do not necessarily involve a direct relationship between the victim and the institution or person responsible for the harm, which are largely invisible. "In every society, violence perpetrated by social institutions denies human dignity and human rights to many, notwithstanding legal safeguards and religious edicts enjoining that all men, women and children are born equal" *(BFWI,* 1995). Discriminations based on social norms, race, gender, sex, age, class, caste and colour and language and religion, are forms of institutional violence. "Violence at this level very often results from oppressive social policies, which have necessitated the emergence of prophets and apostles of peace to redeem the masses" *(Ibid).* Lord Mahavira, Gautam Buddha, Emperor Ashoka and Mahatma Gandhi were not mere accidents in the evolution of Indian history but were the natural and logical consequences of a long chain of antecedent events in the evolution of our civilisation.

Militarism is one of the most extreme forms of institutional expression of violence. History is replete, since the stone-age, with instances of conflicts and war based on desires of communities and nations to gain control over land and sea in order to produce or trade food. The cold war in the post–World War II period, between the two blocks led by the erstwhile Soviet Union and the United States, for decades drained resources towards war-preparedness and building numerous weapons of mass destruction to kill people in even greater numbers. Small wonder, military expenditure increased throughout the cold war period not only in the super powers but also in the newly independent nations as well. Even today, even after the collapse of the Soviet Union and the end of the cold war, all over the world and within each country, war preparedness continues. Because resources are not unlimited, resources so expended on war preparedness are obviously diverted from alternative uses in producing food, providing basic education and primary health care, and providing for R&D and extension services to farmers to improve food production, better food distribution and increase people's access to food. The Indian Budget for 2000-2001 provides for Rs. 13000 odd crore for social sectors (basic education, primary health, housing, drinking water and roads). It at once increases the allocation for defense spending by Rs. 12,865 crore *(Devidayal,* 2000), taking total defense spending to a staggering Rs. 45,694 crore during the fiscal 2000-2001. It is nobody's case that security needs for India can be compromised, but the fact remains that had it been *all quiet on the western* and *northern fronts*, the Finance Minister would have been more than happy to swap the numbers between social sector spending and defense expenditure. This will become even clearer if we have a fleeting glimpse of the costs involved in a modern war. The military cost of first day's attack on Serbia, borne by NATO, was estimated at GBP 44 million. The Cruise Missiles fired cost BGP 8,30,000 each and the US Bombers dropped bombs costing GBP 40,000 each. In the first day's raid 15 human lives were lost and in one week of the war, the bill for aviation fuel was GBP 150 million *(Ninan,* 2000).

Diversion of resources to war and war-preparedness and civil strife has serious consequences for food security and hunger *(Koomson,* 1999). Koomson notes four consequences of war and civil strife. First, countries at war invariably hack down social sector spending, which includes both human and economic resources. Such curtailment has adverse impact in the long run on economic access of the people to food. Second, civil strife affects the timing of increasing the intensity of war and therefore, food production. The intensity of war increases in the periods before the rainy season, which disrupts agricultural activities that must essentially be completed before the onset of rains and therefore, dislocates food production. Third, war and civil strife takes a heavy toll of infrastructure. Roads, hospitals, schools, water sources, drinking water supply, food storage facilities and sewer systems are damaged or destroyed. These are contributory factors in worsening the food security situation of a country.

Let us again turn to the war in Yugoslavia in 1999. After the first week the Allies turned to targeting Serbia's infrastructure. "We took out key bridges", said a NATO Spokesperson. NATO bombed bridges across river Danube, which carried 100 million tonnes of freight per year and acted as the main link to Hungary. The Danube Commission says the river's closure is now costing GBP 600 million per year and there is no money to clear the river of the debris, that blocks it to traffic. It cost GBP 6 million to destroy each bridge, rebuilding one would cost GBP 10 million. Rebuilding them all would cost GBP 80 million. The NATO destroyed the car plant of YUGO, which was the largest source of employment in the country, built at a cost of GBP 6 million. It would need GBP 40 million to rebuild it. The total military cost of the war has been put at GBP 2.5 billion, ten times that of the Gulf War.

Not only do wars and civil wars, divert resources away from sectors which contribute to food security of nations and communities, but they also destroy investments, real and potential, which could help fight hunger. They also create conditions to perpetuate hunger in future as well. While wars generate large number of refugees in other countries, civil wars produce large number of internally displaced persons and refugees in their homeland. The internal refugees are hard to identify and very often go hungry, because they have neither land to grow food on nor do they have money to finance farming operations. They do not additionally have either wages or employment to buy food, if they can't grow food.

The hunger effects of wars and civil wars are a function of the intensity of the fighting that goes on. Severe fighting has almost immediate consequences. If people flee their homes for their lives, hunger is almost complete and immediate. In the absence of food, fuel, and safe water for drinking, symptoms of hunger emerge within as little as a week or so. The effect of Bangladesh War in 1971 is an example in point.

There is, however, a much more fearsome dimension of the relationship between food and war, and that is, using food as a weapon in war. In places like Bosnia, Sudan and Cambodia withholding food to smother the enemy, was a deliberate strategy of warfare. This is the deadliest manifestation of hunger in War. Even where in war, deliberate withholding of food, is not a strategy, fighting even on a scale less severe than what we saw in Rwanda, Bosnia and Burundi, attacks food security ruthlessly. Fighting leads to breakdown of markets and transportation networks, disruption of fuel and food supplies, rise in food prices, fall in investments, rising unemployment and decline in both nominal and real incomes. On a long term basis, if warfare continues, food production per capita starts to fall. Frances Stewart demonstrated that in almost all the countries she studied, food production dropped by more than 15 per cent *(Stewart,* 1993) on account of war.

Box 2.5
What Causes Hunger in War and War Preparedness?

Destruction of Hunger Reducing Elements	Effects on Hunger through
Economic Overheads	Breakdown of transport and communication networks. Destruction of irrigation systems. Decimation of power plants and transmission grids.
Social Overheads	Destruction of schools. Breakdown of healthcare facilities.
Human Capital	Poor health. Under and Malnutrition. Loss on information and knowledge.
Institutions	Crumbling of extension services. Disfunctional credit delivery system. Disuse of marketing linkages. Deterioration of educational and health care institutions.
Social and Cultural Capital	Loss of mutual trust and faith. Decline in work ethic. Loss in social cohesion.

Source: Adopted from BFWI, 1995.

Violence and militarism, thus, almost inevitably lead to hunger, and where hunger exists, exacerbate it beyond recognition.

Poverty and Globalisation

Poverty and globalisation in its present incarnation, cause hunger and deprivation.

It is almost axiomatic to say that poverty is a cause of hunger. Very poor people are almost always chronically hungry. State policies, social and economic processes, structures and institutions are among the basic causes of poverty. Poverty, defined as lack of access to and control over productive resources *(Mukherjee,* 1999), leads to insufficient resources at the disposal of individuals or households, to access (either by outright purchase or by exchange) food, clothing, shelter, basic education and primary health care. Judged at from this perspective, poverty may not be an exact indicator of hunger. Nevertheless, poverty's correlation with hunger and undernutrition is high.

On a global scale, in this present day world more than 1.4 billion people have an income of one U. S. dollar or less per day, or its equivalent, and a vast majority of them (more than 899 million) are chronically hungry. The remaining 600 million live at the brink of hunger so much so that even a small emergency such as illness of the bread-winner, industrial strife, lay-off, fall in seasonal employment, drought, floods, price volatility, civil strife, communal disturbances, etc pulls them down into the hunger domain.

The people who are so poor that they are disproportionately affected by hunger are located in Africa. The largest number is in Asia and South Asia *(U.N.* 1999). A significant number are in Latin America and Carribean Islands. But the United States, European Countries and Australia also have large blocks of people who are hungry, which is one reason why some people talk of a "Global South". In most of the developing countries, the incidence of hunger is higher in the rural areas than in the urban areas, and nearly everywhere the women and girl children and elderly people suffer more from hunger than men or male children.

In India poverty is still a big problem. Though India has seen a sharp decline in poverty with the percentage of people living below the poverty line coming down to a little over 36 per cent in 1993-94, from 56.44 per cent in 1973-74, but after that percentage of people below the poverty line has remained unchanged *(Guruswamy,* 2000). This means that the number of poor people has increased and according to one estimate, during the period 1993-1999, about 46 million people have joined the ranks of the poor.

More distressingly, within India, incidence of poverty has been increasing in the poverty heartland of central and eastern states, notably Assam, Bihar, Orissa and Uttar Pradesh, even during the period when overall percentage of people below the poverty line for the country as a whole, was declining. For instance, percentage of people living below the poverty line in Bihar grew from 53.6 per cent to 58.2 per cent between 1987-88 and 1993-94 and the percentage of people living below the poverty line in Assam grew from 39.35 per cent to 45.01 per cent during the same period. The states of Bihar, Madhya Pradesh, Rajasthan and Uttar Pradesh, account for 51 per cent of the country's poor. Chotanagpur and Santhal Parganas of Bihar; Koraput and Phulbani in Orissa; Jhansi region in Uttar Pradesh and its adjoining region in Madhya Pradesh, including Betul, Khandwa and Hosangabad have very high poverty ratio *(Press Trust of India,* 2000). And these are the states where hunger is reported as a matter of routine every year and from where most migration in thousands, if not in lakhs, take place every year in search of work and food and hope.

The fact that the number of poor people is on the increase is accepted, but there is far lesser agreement on the inter-relationship between hunger and poverty in India. It is accepted that poverty is a hydra-headed monster and hunger is one, undoubtedly the most critical of its elements. It has been suggested that incidence of hunger as suggested by the people could be considered as an alternative approach to assess the extent of poverty in India. The 38th round household consumption expenditure survey of the National Sample Survey Organisation (NSSO) of the Government of India in 1983 included a question addressed to the head of the household on whether all members of the household get two square meals a day throughout the year or not. The responses to this question varied, and they were classified as follows:

(a) Number of persons who got two square meals a day throughout the year.
(b) Number of persons who did not get two square meals a day during some months of the year.
(c) Number of people who did not get two square meals a day even for some months of the year.

People falling under category (a) are taken as not hungry. People falling under category (b) are considered "Seasonally Hungry". People falling in category (c) are considered "Chronically Hungry". The ratio of chronically hungry to total population is termed as the "hunger ratio". It was also found that hunger is more concentrated in some regions than poverty. For example, the proportion of those chronically hungry varied from 39.6 per cent in rural West Bengal, 37.2 per cent in rural Bihar and 36.8 per cent in rural Orissa, to 0.85 per cent in Haryana and 1.6 per cent in rural Punjab.

Based on this question "it was found that the incidence of hunger was less than the incidence of poverty" *(Planning Commission,* 1993). But we have reservations about this conclusion and the reasons are not far to seek. No consideration was given as to what was the meaning of the term, *Square Meal.* The possibilities of subjectivity of the respondents and of the enumerators in interpreting the term were not taken cognizance of. The pitfalls of using a questionnaire method of survey, too well known to be laboured here (See *Mukherjee,* 1997) apparently did not weigh with the powers that be. One single question cannot be precise and objective enough to capture views, on hunger from those who are hungry, by outsiders who are reasonably well fed. The cultural dimension of the issue, namely, that people who are hungry are not always willing to say that they are indeed hungry, needs to be factored into this debate. For the head of the household to say that member(s) of her household go to bed hungry, even on some days of the year, hits at the very root of the dignity of the people. "Questions about how much people ate and shortfalls of food when asked to people who are regularly hungry, are not easy to broach. Some people are willing to make it clear about what they thought about such questions. They often use interrogative form when replying, showing a *mock contempt* of the person making the inquiry, a common practice in India. In addition, estimates ..... of food consumption should be taken as such. As one man put it: 'we don't measure how much food goes into our stomach'" *(Beck,* 1994).

Thus on the whole, taking an overall view of the matter, based on broad probabilities, we are unable to agree with the Planning Commission that the incidence of hunger was less than the incidence of poverty. Our own work at the grassroots level and village level has demonstrated that those who are poor are the ones who are hungry *(Mukherjee* and *Mukherjee,* 1994 and 2000). Indeed this was found to be so across the globe by the team, which was consulting the poor for the World Development Report 2000 of the World Bank. "Lack of food, shelter and clothing was mentioned everywhere as critical" *(Narayan, Chambers, Shah* and *Petesch,* 1999).

Even if we take the official poverty line of Rs. 11000 per household in the rural areas per annum, that the poor go hungry is a forgone conclusion. For a family of five, the per capita expenditure per day works out to be no more than Rs. 6.30. According to Government's view, any one who can spend this amount (which is expected to cover food needs, lighting requirements, clothing, schooling and health care facilities on himself/herself) is not poor. For anyone who lives in India of today, it will be hard to believe that there is any way that a household, which has an income as high as this or below this, can survive without hunger.

Let us now turn to globalisation.

Globalisation, in its current incarnation, was projected as the answer to the seemingly intractable problems of poverty and hunger, beginning with the Structural Adjustment Programme, which came to India in its final form in 1991. Globalisation has done many wonders but how far it has helped India is still debatable. There are three things notable in this regard.

First, the current phase of globalisation is through knitting the economies of the world via factor movements defined as capital, trade and technology flows. There has been an evolution of a single worldwide system of producing and exchanging money, goods and services. Instantaneous electronic transfer of information and capital funds, controlled by multi-national corporations and international agencies, allows for "on time delivery" of components for assembly wherever labour costs are the lowest or markets nearby. The shift of manufacturing, assembly and some service tasks to low wage areas offers the possibility of more jobs and higher wages in those countries which has abundance of labour. This is, however, under attack at the WTO by the United States, in the garb of imposing labour standards and social clauses on the developing countries *(The Economist,* December, 1999).

Second, there has been a shift from a resource-based economy to a knowledge-based economy. In the new economic world, wealth and employment result less from the processing of raw materials and more from the ability to process information or "manipulate symbols". The richest men are neither the Rockerfellers nor the Fords nor the Dhirubhai Ambanis, but Bill Gates of Microsoft, Milken of corporate-merger fame, Azim Premji of Wipro and Narayan Murthy of Infosys. The richer companies are Wipro,

Monsanto, Calgene and Boston Chicken and not Standard Oil or Krupp or Reliance Industries.

As assembly jobs move to computerised (read "robotised") assembly lines, semi-skilled workers find themselves out of the job market, unless they learn and re-learn new skills every few years. This is easier said than done. In the best case scenario they may find some work but have to face increasingly lower-wage jobs in competition with poorly educated or poorly trained workers.

The shift to knowledge-based economies can lead to enormous gains in productivity, achieving more with fewer resources but in an inequitous world with imbalance of power status structure, the new knowledge systems could prove to be socially destructive as monopolies and trusts were in an earlier industrial era. Indeed the US Anti-Trust Laws have been applied to Microsoft recently and the legal proceedings are in progress. The benefits of this gain will not flow to those who are hungry and needy but to those who can muster the power of knowledge.

Third, the acceptance of the market based economies as the best way forward for economic prosperity of nations, by most political leaders throughout the world, is somewhat disturbing. "There is no alternative to free market system", seems to be the only refrain. Even Marxism's senior citizens like Hobsbawm have come to the conclusion that capitalism is securely in saddle *(Habsbawm,* 2000) and that game is up for socialism *(The Economist,* 2000). Countries in the developing world have opted for market-led economies, because the well-developed market economies are the wealthiest and have least of hunger. Because centrally planned economies have collapsed and are plagued with widespread poverty and hunger. Because they see rapid growth and dramatic reduction in poverty in South East Asia, notwithstanding setbacks in 1997/98. Markets may do many things which help the poor, such as ration goods like clothing better than centrally planned economies and at times are fairer to poorer people than the Governments and the bureaucrats, often manipulated by groups of elite and vested interests. Large and sophisticated corporations carry out tasks not otherwise possible and which the State has failed to do: quickly putting together mechanism of movement of grains for emergency needs, or maintaining inventories of spare parts for repairing 20 year old tractors.

Nevertheless, it is widely accepted that markets by themselves will never eliminate hunger of poor and poorer people. It will eliminate the poor, because the market is an excluding mechanism, where the rule is "survival of the fittest" and by definition, the poor are not the fittest. That explains, at least in part, why poor people are acutely skeptical of grand claims made on behalf of the "magic of the market place". The existence of hungry people in the developing and developed countries alike, with differences in kinds and intensities, even in rich countries like the United Kingdom (often evidenced by beggars on the streets of London selling the "Big Issues"), punctures the infallibility of the market in eliminating hunger. Indeed, hunger remains a pervasive reality for millions of people even in the United States. An U. S. Department of Agriculture study reports that in the 12 month period immediately preceding April 1995, as many as 11.2 million people belong to hungry households that cannot afford enough food for all its members. And 34 million people live in food insecure households, or in households at risk of hunger *(Brown,* 1997).

Markets are also not benevolent. They admit of abuse by wealthy landlords, private and corporate businesses and multinational corporations, who fail to meet out a fair treatment to their employees, suppliers and customers, and the public at large. Large landlords and corporations sometimes may achieve their aims in collusion with each other or with Governments in their own countries as also elsewhere, which are inimical to eliminating poverty and hunger. They even have been found to rely on military support for protection. The East Asian crisis in 1997-98, as also the crisis in Latin American economies, have raised the issue of volatility of capital flows and the impact of international shocks on growth and poverty. The fastest growing economies of East Asia were not the ones, which have reduced poverty significantly *(World Development Report,* 2000). In India the nexus of the "Dada, Neta, Lala and Babu" have played havoc with the lives of the hungry. The market cannot deal with these elements. The markets could neither do anything to prevent unprecedented drought, famine and water shortage in large parts of the country like Gujarat, Rajasthan, Orissa and Andhra Pradesh, nor responded to mitigate the sufferings of humans and animals once famine and scarcity of food and water had hit an estimated 50 million of them in India in their face in 1999-2000. The market could not prevent people dying of starvation in Orissa and Rajasthan, when godowns of the Food Corporation of India is overflowing with 60 million tons of food grain in July 2001.

If we want to see the record of what the market has done to India in the last one decade, we need to look at the fundamentals of the Indian economy during the nineties, the "decade of the markets". We need to realise that agricultural growth which averaged 4.04 per cent per annum during the decade 1981-91, has come down to 2.3 per cent per annum in 1991-99, despite an uninterrupted series of good monsoons (Indian agriculture is still prone to the vagaries of monsoon) for ten years in a row. Additionally, it is a serious matter that the area which gives food, viz., under foodgrains and oilseeds, has remained unchanged or nearly so at around 150 million hectares in the decade.

The number of people dependent on land has increased by 42 million between 1990-91 and 1999-2000, as against an increase in food grain production by about 22 million tons during the same period. The implication is that a major slowdown in the growth of real incomes and wages in the rural sector has taken place. Such slowing down in agricultural growth rate and a freeze in the area under foodgrain and oilseeds, against a growing population, only indicate lower availability of food in the system for the people to access, to leave their food security unimpaired.

Whether slower agricultural production had any impact on food prices or not, need not detain us for long, but the rise in food prices is telling. The average annual price rise during the decade of the eighties has been 5.6 per cent for rice, 5.7 per cent for wheat and 11.2 per cent for pulses. During the decade of the nineties, the price rise has been much steeper: 10.2 per cent for rice, 9.5 per cent for wheat and 11.4 per cent for pulses. Rise in prices of foodgrains *ipso facto* indicates that economic access to food has been reduced, at least for the millions who survive at the margin, for the simple reason that wages are always sticky and wage increases always lag behind price rise and almost never fully neutralise price increases.

And how has the wage rates behaved? The annual average growth rate of wages of unskilled agricultural male workers in the eighties was about 4.6 per cent as opposed to a paltry 2.5 per cent in the nineties. When we pitch this against the increase of the Wholesale Price Index, the picture becomes murkier. In the period 1991-2000, the WPI rose by about 8.8 per cent annually as against 6.9 per during the corresponding period in the previous decade. Employment generation in the organised sector was growing at 1.6 per cent in the eighties. It is now 0.8 per cent in the nineties. It is half the rate of the eighties. Both these have a strong bearing on the economic access that people have to food.

"Thus no macro-policy based on market-led growth will be successful in dealing with either poverty or employment in India. Very often development under market–led growth benefits those who are qualified enough and socially well placed to take advantage of the opportunities of capital-intensive and labour displacing global technologies" *(Gupta,* 1999). Because of the reality of an unequal skill base, it is imperative that the government have target–oriented programmes and pursue public policies that help the 'left-out' groups like marginal farmers, unskilled labourers and people in the backward areas, to maintain a reasonably good standard of living and leave their food security, however fragile, intact.

A redeeming feature of the nineties is that the GDP has increased at the rate of 5.8 per cent as opposed to a slightly lower figure of 5.46 per cent in the eighties. But have the poor people benefited? The World Bank in its Report Number 197471 has concluded that the number of people below the poverty line remains at what it was in 1991, viz., 33 per cent. That is, more than 326 million people in India today live below the poverty line, an increase of 46 million poor people in the last decade *(Guruswamy,* 2000). But given the stubbornness of the percentage of people below the poverty line, there seems to have been nothing of the much trumpeted "trickle down" effect.

Population, Unsustainable Consumption and Environmental Degradation

The link between population growth, unsustainable consumption and environmental degradation on the one hand and hunger on the other has been a hobby horse of economists for a long time.

Staggering strides in science, technology and medicine have improved living standards dramatically, resulting in the phenomenal growth in population. Many countries seem to be in the early stages of declining fertility rates. But the number of people in the world continues to grow at an alarming rate and most of this growth is in the poorer areas and poorer households, who are already food insecure. We entered the 20th century with a population of less than two billion but left it when earth's population was six billion. And if the population wheel runs at the same pace, we will reach seven billion mark by 2015 and it is expected to reach 8.9. billion by 2030, levelling-off at 11.5 billion around 2050 *(Sinha,* 2000). Of this increase, in excess of 8 billion people will be in developing countries, according to at least one estimate. And it is increasing at the rate of over 90 million per year, most of which is in the poorer parts of the world, notably South Asia and Sub-Saharan Africa.

It is believed that Sub-Saharan Africa, troubled perennially by famines at regular intervals, chronic malnutrition and civil strife, which has attracted the appellation of the "hopeless continent" for Africa as a whole *(The Economist,* 2000), will in all probability double its population by the year 2020 *(Christian Science Monitor,* 1994). Thus, it is estimated that though the world currently produces enough food for everyone to consume 2500 calories per day, if it was distributed equitably, such increases in population may change the situation quite dramatically. Add to this, the problem that over three quarters of a billion people are chronically undernourished because they suffer various degrees of hunger, not because food is unavailable, but because they cannot grow food (have no direct entitlement) and /or cannot buy food (have no exchange entitlement).

Without going into the polemics of whether poverty leads to population explosion or population growth leads to poverty, it is safe to say that explosive population growth contributes toward increasing hunger and poverty. Indeed, in many parts of the world, high birth rates lead to lower standard of living for many people, because, *inter alia*, too few jobs and too little land for growing food, are being chased by too many people. The need for more living space, more food and drinking water and the need to tackle stupendous waste generated by the rapidly increasing urban population, are all emerging as intractable problems. Rapid population growth in several low income communities is exerting pressure on the delicately poised capacity of the poor countries to absorb the increases in the number of people given the biological, ecological and environmental parameters within which they operate. In these countries such population growth exerts enormous pressure on their fragile ecosystems. This is particularly important to note because the poor are usually located in the environmentally and ecologically fragile areas, so much so that more than 500 million people live on marginal lands.

Food systems and the soil, water and air on which poor people depend already show signs of deterioration and stress *(World Resources Institute,* 1994). The consumption of natural resources by modern economies remain very high between 45 and 85 tonnes per capita annually *(Sinha,* 2000). To meet the demands of a growing population, there will be greater turnover in agricultural, mining, fishing and industrial activities, at a huge environmental cost. Indeed, an estimated one billion people in 40 developing countries are at the risk of losing access to fish stocks, their primary source of protein, due to over-fishing to meet export demands, mostly for animal feed and oils. Deforestation is concentrated in the developing countries, so much so that the loss in tropical forests has been 7 million hectares in Latin America and the Caribbean Islands, and 8 million hectares in Asia and Africa. Many observers doubt whether food production and distribution can match population growth and in the areas where they will grow, on a sustainable basis, especially so when the poor people raise their standard of living. As Sen has noted elsewhere, though none seriously believe that the Malthusian doomsday will ever dawn, yet there is no denying that slowing down of population is highly correlated to improved well-being, implying at least some increases and improvements in levels of food consumption among poor people.

While it is true that population growth in poorer households and in poorer countries have strained the environmental, ecological and biological resources, it is as much true that over-consumption of non-renewable resources among the relatively well-off people and countries, puts a huge strain on the global environment. Some experts even maintain that the latter exerts greater strain on the global environment than rapid population growth in the developing countries. Worldwide, only 20 per cent of the world's population in the highest income countries accounts for over 86 per cent of total private consumption expenditure and uses over 80 per cent of its resources. "More specifically the richest fifth consume 45 per cent of all meat and fish, the poorest fifth 5 per cent; consume 58 per cent of total energy, the poorest fifth 4 per cent; have 74 per cent of all telephone lines, the poorest fifth 1.5 per cent; own 67 per cent of the world's vehicle fleet, the poorest fifth less than 1 per cent" *(UNDP,* 1998). These are only some indicators of the consumption explosion to which the global system has been exposed to, running as it were almost parallel to the population explosion in the developing countries.

This runaway consumption has exerted a strain on the environment, never seen before, from two perspectives. One directly, by straining the resources used to sustain this consumption or over consumption. "The burning of fossil fuels has almost quintupled since 1950. The consumption of fresh water has almost doubled since 1960. The marine catch has increased fourfold. Wood consumption both for industry and for household fuel, is now 40 per cent higher than it was 25 years ago" *(UNDP,* 1998). Second, by wasting resources needed to treat the ailments resulting from this unsustainable over-consumption, that shows up as obesity. "The number of overweight people world wide has for the first time caught up with the number who are underfed..." *(Rogers* and *Nduta,* 2000). In case of India it is even worse. Heart diseases caused by over consumption by the rich (read stinking rich) minority, rather than hunger or tuberculosis are India's biggest killer of people under 70. The burden of treatment of such a huge number who get sick due to over-eating will be severe for a country that does not have proper basic health services in many areas.

It is often heard that rapid population growth has not been met with the eventuality of inadequate food supply in the aggregate sense. There is, therefore, no real cause for alarm. But it is not realised that this has been possible because of food production has been ruthlessly augmented through two channels: one, through expanded use of nature's four major biological systems, and two, through increasing intensity of cultivation. As a consequence of these dual processes that have characterised our food production oceans have been fished beyond their regenerating capacity; rangeland has been overgrazed as never before; forest are disappearing at an alarming rate and cropland has expanded vastly at the expense, in most cases, of forests and rangeland. This has also resulted, amongst other things, in loss in bio-diversity and wildlife. Such expansion and over use of nature's biological systems have reached their limits and in many cases must be rolled back as soon as possible. By 2010 per capita availability of rangeland will drop by 22 per cent and fish catch by 10 per cent. The per capita area of irrigated land, which now yields about a third of global food harvests, will drop by 12 per cent. Cropland area and forest cover per person will come down by 21 and 31 per cent respectively. The global economy is expected to increase five times of the current level of $ 16 trillion, by the middle of this century, which will cause a gigantic depletion of world natural resources. Thus, those who are comforted by the thought that rapid population growth has not been met with the eventuality of inadequate food supply in the aggregate sense, need to take cognizance of the counterfactuals now staring at our faces as never before. They have to realign their sights very substantially, if not wholly.

Box 2.6
Revolt Against Consumer Materialism in Religion

Restraint in consumption has been recognised as a virtue throughout the ages by many religions, as reflected in their texts and teachings.

In Hinduism:
"When you have the golden gift of contentment, you have verything".

In Islam:
In Islam: "It is difficult far a man laden with riches to climb the steep path that leads to bliss".
"Riches are not from an abundance of worldly goods, but from a contended mind".

In Taoism:
"He who knows he has enough is rich".

"To take all one wants is never as good as to stop when one should."

In Christianity:
"Watch out! Be on your guard against all kinds of greed: a man's life does not consist in the abundance of his possession".

In Buddhism:
"By the thirst for riches, the foolish man destroys himself as if he were his own enemy".
"Whoever in this world overcomes his selfish cravings, his sorrow falls away from him, like drops of water from a lotus flower".

Source: UNDP, 1999

The increase in the intensity of cultivation that has contributed to increase in food production can no longer be sustained. The increase in the intensity of cultivation have been brought about by more intensive use of "external resources", that is, by shifting agriculture from "Low External Input Agriculture" (LEIA) to "High External Input Agriculture (HEIA), or what is often called the introduction of "new technology" or the "Green Revolution". Irrigated acreage on a global scale increased at the rate of 20 per cent per decade in the 1960s and the 1970s. Use of chemical fertilisers grew by as much as 900 per cent between 1950 and 1984. New and improved varieties of seeds brought about dramatic increases in rice and wheat yields during the two decades of the "Green Revolution".

Arguably the increasing use of fertilisers, pesticides and irrigation have resulted in environmental damage, a part of which is due to carelessness and a part of it was wholly avoidable, manifesting, ***inter alia***, in a fall in productivity, such as in the Punjab and Haryana. Extending crop production into marginal lands has also resulted in damage to environment, also due partly to carelessness. But even in the best case scenario, the world will need to double its food production on a global scale by 2050, if it is to maintain the same level of food availability per capita in the aggregate sense as is obtaining today. In India, demand for food is estimated to increase to 271 million tons by 2020, if the current level of availability of food per capita is to be maintained *(Bhalla,* 2000). Given that it will be difficult to maintain the increases in food productivity as the world and India has seen over the last 40 years or so, this looks like a daunting task staring the world in its face.

Not just population and unsustainable consumption, but also unjust land distribution and unfair social arrangements have added to the problems of hunger and environmental degradation in developing countries in South Asia and Latin America. Pangs of hunger and poverty have also forced farmers to take recourse to unsustainable agricultural practices. In many societies like the Jhum Cultivators in North Eastern States and Orissa in India, and in Sahel region in West and Central Africa, people traditionally left land fallow for long periods to allow time for land to regain its nutrition. With forests and common property resources providing fuel wood, animal dung was used as manure. But with population pressure and pressure of growing number of livestock to feed, particularly after the second World War, the "fallow period' got successively reduced. This deprived land a fair chance to recuperate and people cleared forests for cultivation to feed growing numbers, cutting off (at least severely reducing) sources of fuel wood, leading to use of animal dung as fuel, depriving soil of a vital source of nutrition.

Box 2.7

Agenda 21 from the U.N. Conference on the Environment and Development 1992 at Rio de Generio

"Land degradation is the most important environmental problem affecting extensive areas of land in both developed and developing countries".

Racism and Ethnocentrism

Racism and ethnocentrism contribute significantly to hunger and poverty of millions of people in the world today. Ethnocentrism describes the belief that one's own patterns of behaviour are preferable to those of the all other cultures. Because people are taught the values of the culture in which they grow up, they tend to view their own patterns of behaviour as being right, normal and best. Other cultures, as a corollary, are viewed as wrong, or irrational and misguided.

Ethnocentrism and racism are the foundation of many famines, wars, ethnic conflicts, communal violences, tribalism and colonialism. Racism and ethnocentricity are associated with power, and both are apparent and easily detectable when one group enslaves another. They are, however, less apparent in other forms of domination. Governments in several countries may intentionally deny racism and ethnocentrism in order to marginalise any group within their borders. However, often the results in these countries confirm the intention: marked disparities in income, opportunity and rights for the groups who are subjugated.

Some of the most serious consequences of racism and ethnocentrism are primarily economic, and economic problems have considerable influence on ethnic relations: struggle for scarce resources, regional imbalances, infrastructure investments that dislocates indigenous economic systems, conflicts in the labour market and distributional conflicts. Under the guise of development, many ethnic groups are impoverished and suffer hunger.

Competition for scarce resources is inherent in modern development, which can lead to the extinction of ethnic groups, the exodus of marginalised people (such as indigenous peoples, tribals or nomads) or the destruction of local eco-systems upon which these groups depend. A dominant group may "develop" the area for its purposes, making it uninhabitable for the local population, which are often the marginalised groups. Access to the State is the way for a group to achieve economic development. In an ethnically divided society, government often intervenes in ethnic struggle by the way it distributes services.

Box 2.8

Shrinking Land and Meals of Seeds.....

By Poornima Joshi in Phulbani

"...of Badgaon's 585 inhabitants, 265 belong to the Scheduled Tribes (mainly Kandha) and 123 to the Scheduled Castes. The rest are upper caste and have built concrete houses in the nearby upcoming town of Baliguda...

There is something static about Badgaon: in the broken plough propped against the cattle-sheds, in the algae-covered pond, in the women carrying pitchers on their heads, and in the resigned, almost numb expressions of villager elder Sarveshwar Malik and his companion sitting in the afternoon sun.

Most tribals have "sold" off their land to the money lenders that can buy them provisions for a year at most. An official ban on the sale of tribal land has done little to stop this. This shrinking of cultivated land has further reduced their yield and finding two meals a day is a problem for almost half the year.

Their meals comprise water boiled with rice and, when even that is not available, they boil mango seeds with water and drink the syrup residue. "We have a tradition of eating five meals a day. We never get that much food, so eat twice a day. When that also is difficult we make do with water", says Sarveshwar.

The Hindusthan Times, New Delhi, Sunday February 6, 2000

Different countries in Africa, notably Rwanda, Sudan and South Africa, and in Asia, such as Iraq, Sri Lanka and East Timor, who suffer from societal stratification in terms of racism and ethnocentrism, are also the countries which face considerable hunger and poverty, emanating from different forms of racism and ethnocentrism. In India, States which suffer from stratification of society in terms of ethnic groups and ethnocentrism of different forms also face massive problems of hunger: Bihar, Rajasthan, Uttar Pradesh and Orissa are examples in point. Even in a rich society like the United States, hunger occurs disproportionately among the African Americans, Hispanics, Native Americans and other racial and ethnic minorities *(Tidewell,* 1994 and *Harrington,* 1962).

On the other hand, societies which, while divided along ethnic groups, live in harmony achieve considerable development and succeed in having food security. Zimbabwe and Jamaica are examples in point. However, the spate of attacks in April 2000, on white farmers in Zimbabwe who control most of the farms by the war veterans, who are mostly blacks, has led to destruction of productive resources. It will be a while before the impact of this ethnic violence on food security will be seen.

Gender Discrimination

One of the root causes of hunger is gender discrimination. "Discrimination against women and girls is an important basic cause of malnutrition" *(Manuliak,* 1999). Because of their gender, females in almost every society do not have the same opportunities for development and growth as their male counterparts have. Cultural, social, religious and Governmental practices and policies often prevent female children from reaching their full potential and their mothers from gaining access to the jobs and education that could alleviate the cycles of hunger and poverty.

A UN estimate puts 400 million women of childbearing age as weighing less than 100 pounds, who are in all probability undernourished and vulnerable to obstetric complications. Almost 50 per cent of the world women suffer from iron deficiency anemia. In India, almost 80 per cent of pregnant women are anemic. This increases the risk of illness, pregnancy complications, maternal mortality and a fall in their productivity.

Not long ago the general perception was that hunger and poverty afflict all sections of society uniformly. Hunger was seen as an undifferentiated problem. As a consequence, hunger and poverty data were gathered on the presumption that all people in a family or community were affected equally, without taking cognizance of the fact that women have different nutritional needs. Women work longer hours than men do in many cases and hence their energy needs are much more than their men counterparts. As a matter of fact pregnant women and lactating mothers experience greater stress and demands on their bodies, than those who are not and they must, therefore, satisfy increased nutritional requirements. Micro-nutrient deficiencies, such as lack of vitamin A and Iron, can have serious consequences for women and their babies. Death at childbirth, a leading killer of women in reproductive age in most developing countries, frequently results from malnutrition. Recent studies have, therefore, made a strong plea for disaggregated data on critical areas of measurements. There has been on account of these studies, and even more because of women's movement, a greater realisation of the need for disaggregated data on all aspects of our social and economic life. Development thinking and practice have, of late, become more gender sensitive than in the eighties, but lot more needs to be done.

Hunger and malnutrition of women have inter-generational consequences. Women are either mothers or would be mothers tomorrow. Malnutrition among women is, therefore, likely to lead to under-weight childbirth. Undernourished mothers cannot be expected to provide nourishment to infants they nurse. As a consequence, hunger and malnourishment in women will result in a hungry and malnourished and unhealthy next generation.

Since women usually have the well-being of their children as a priority, 67 million children who are underweight or wasted is one measure of the effects of women's relative powerlessness. The deck is clearly stacked against these children before birth. Sixty per cent to eighty per cent of women of childbearing-age in the developing world do not receive the minimum caloric requirements for good health and as a consequence large number of babies born in the developing world are born underweight at birth (*Manuliak,* 1999). Those malnourished in their mothers' womb and hence born underweight, carry a higher risk of developing health problems such as diabetes and heart disease in later life *(Rogers and Nduta,* 2000). And according to one study, there are four hungry children for every woman suffering the pangs of poverty. Yet women are over-represented amongst poor, illiterate, hungry and sickly people.

Box 2.9

Household Work During One Week in Landless Indian Households

Tasks	Female per cent	Male per cent
Kolam*	38.5	—
Serving Spouse	40.4	17.6
Childcare	42.3	15.7
Shopping in City	44.2	47.1
Whitewashing	48.1	62.7
Collecting Firewood	65.4	47.0
Local Shopping	69.2	43.1
Wetting the Yard	78.8	05.9
Washing Clothes	82.7	25.5
Cutting/Peeling	88.5	11.8
Fetching Water	88.5	23.5
Cooking	90.1	11.8
Cleaning House	94.2	15.7
Washing Vessels	96.2	5.9

*Rice powder or powdered chalk is used to make drawing in front of the home

Source: Bread for the World Institute (1995)

Hunger, amongst women, persists on account of patriarchal practices that are still operative where the women eat last, the least and the "left-overs". There is inequity in intra-household distribution of power loaded against women, which adversely affects women's ability to access food. There is inequity in accessing education and health care facility, strongly disfavouring women, which works against food security of women. The employment opportunities available for women are also much more restricted and where available, compensation package enjoyed by women is less than men's. Women, on an average, receive about 30 per cent less than men in wages.

Box 2.10

The Hunter, The Gatherer, The Shopper, The Cook

But I have been cooking all day.
Standing over a hot stove.
Slaving over a hot stove.
Cooking.

I've been shopping for groceries.
Putting them away.
Setting the table.
Cooking the food.
Making this dinner.
Wracking my brains.

I've been wracking my brains over this meal.
What to buy.
How much to pay.
I've been budgeting.
Looking for sales.
I've been feeding this family on $ 6.00.
Making it do. I've been wracking my brains over this meal.

I have been cooking all day.
Shopping for bargains.
Hunting for bargains.
I've been hunting all day.

I've been up and down hundreds of aisles.
Hunting.
Hunting and gathering and cooking this food.
Loading my cart.
Carrying carcasses.
I have been hunting all day.

I have gathered this food from across the land.
I've been everywhere.
I've been everywhere.
I have made this meal.
I have created this food.
This is my time.
My thought.
What you have on your plate is my blood.
My brains.
I tell you I have been cooking all day.

What do you mean
you don't want it?

Sondra Segal and Roberta Sklar in *Women's Body and Other Natural Resources*, 1987

Box 2.11
The Hierarchy of the Chicken

The father eats the breast.
He only likes white meat.

The kids eat the drumsticks,
the thighs and
the wings.

The mother eats the neck,
the back,
the liver,
the gizzard,
the feet
and the heart.

Source: Segal and Sklar in *Women's Body and Other Natural Resources*, 1987

Property laws and laws of inheritance militate against women having the control over productive resources to grow food and play a decisive role in making decisions in matters relating to growing food, except where the households are woman-headed. In India only on 7th February 2000 did we see reports in the Press that the Central Government has directed the states to amend the law of succession so that women will also be a co-sharer in inherited property of the father.

There are an estimated 75 million women-headed households in 114 developing countries, in which these women provide food to almost 377 million people.

In India widows as a class in many places are the worst affected *(Chen,* 1999). The patriarchal practices that create problems for women in other areas, create more difficulties amongst the widows. They are required to cut down consumption of food and clothing. Widows in some states in India are ordained to live lives of austerity bordering on hunger. Widows of Varanasi and Vrindavan live under inhuman conditions, scorned by their families, deserted by their friends and uncared for by a society often dominated by patriarchal values. The Government Sponsored Widow's Pension is Rs. 1500 per annum. This paltry sum is no social security for these hapless people but whatever their worth, the value of these pensions is further eroded by the informal taxes they have to pay to petty officials to get the money, that is rightfully theirs.

Box 2.12

Crooks Wait on the Road to Widows' Pension

Vrinda Gopinath, Vrindavan, February 6

The bundle of papers wrapped in cloth and kept behind a curtain in Swami Vivekananda School is forever mocking at the bitter sacrifices made by the widows and abandoned women in Vrindavan.

The 50 odd old-age pension forms with photographs, thumb impressions and official signatures have been lying for over a year, forgotten and dusty. For the women of Vrindavan, however, the papers carry a fervent hope that one day they will receive their meagre pension of Rs. 1,500 a year, which they have been entitled to since a decade and more. Kamala Ghosh, the school's principal (sic) and mother to the *mais*, can only offer solace as she comforts the women with some optimistic cheer.

Says Ghosh, as she unwraps and displays the fraying papers, "These forms were filled after we organised a camp for the women to come and take what is rightfully theirs…they were not even aware that they were entitled to a pension. I got my students to help in filling forms and completing formalities but the officials have not bothered to forward them to the district headquarters". Ghosh adds that work gets done if the district magistrate (sic) is sympathetic as some of the previous efforts have been quite fruitful.

The procedure is quite straight forward if it is carried out willfully—a Health Officer from the State Social Welfare Ministry certifies the age, the SJM and DM attests their signature, it goes back to headquarters where a cheque is drawn and deposited in the bank. What could be an easy task—as there are about 2000 aged widows in this temple town—a whole corrupt network has thrown a ring around them, picking on their drying bones. There are several cases of cheques being issued in names of landlord, account books which are wrongly tabulated, pension forms which are suspiciously lost and, last year, 250 cheques were retrurned because the beneficiaries could not be traced for lack of incomplete forms.

Bhanu Ghosh, a 70-year-old widow, still clutches on to a cheque which has come in the name of Premlal, her landlord, despite the fact that her husband's name is Gurudas Ghosh. Says the frail, old lady, "We have to bribe the patwari to get our money from the bank, even the postman to receive the money order from home".

The Indian Express, New Delhi, Monday, February 7, 2000.

In the 1980s and even in the 1970s, the development paradigm was to achieve economic growth for developing countries, which was expected to integrate women into the mainstream economy and solve their poverty and hunger. In this scheme of things the women, and indeed all those who were hungry and poor, had no say in the policies, structures and processes which afflicted their lives so fundamentally. Around the mid-80s, women realised that with the global recession, their condition had deteriorated and they partook the role of marginalised pawns in men's world. More women became poor and feminisation of poverty was on the cards. Several women's movements started, such as Development Alternatives with Women for a New Era (DAWN) and a series of UN Conferences were held to change the process and cause feminisation of development. The International Conference on Population and Development, Cairo, 1994; The World Summit for Social Development, Copenhagen, March 1995; and the Fourth Conference on Women, Beijing, 1995 provided strong support for empowerment of women. But the actions expected out of the follow up on the decisions emanating out of these summits/conferences have not fructified. The Heads of Governments and Heads of States, including India, who endorsed the programmes of action, did precious little to alleviate the conditions of women. No wonder, on 23rd January 2000, the Committee on Convention on the Elimination of All Discrimination Against Women (CEDAW), which met at New-York, "raised numerous questions about the condition of Indian women. They wanted to know why the promise India had made at the Beijing Women's Conference, of earmarking six per cent of GDP for education has not happened, and why the promised Women's Bill was not passed"....If one wanted to know whether domestic workers in India were protected by social insurance, another demanded to be informed about why dalit women were being attacked in Bihar and yet another asked what was being done to protect women from the ravages of pan masala" *(Pamela Philipose,* 2000).

And feminisation of poverty continues unabated. Globalisation, that is currently on the rampage throughout the world, is expected to further entrench the process of poverty feminisation.

Age and Vulnerability

There are two age groups, which suffer more hunger than others, more so if they are poor. These two groups are the children and amongst them the younger ones, particularly the girl children, and the old who are long past their more productive years.

In India about 37 per cent of children of and below the age of 4 suffer from second degree malnourishment or "stunting", which is higher in Karnataka, Madhya Pradesh, Gujarat, Andhra Pradesh, Bihar, Uttar Pradesh, North Eastern States, Haryana and West Bengal, than in Kerala and Tamil Nadu. About 29 per cent of the children in the age group of 5-12 are stunted. And stunting is found almost across the board and has little to do with parental income, landholding pattern of the parents, occupation and social groups. Additionally, about 5 per cent of children below 14 years of age suffer from wasting, which is higher in UP, Gujarat, Karnataka and Andhra Pradesh (for children between 5 and 12 years of age). As in the case of stunting, differences in occupational status, landholding pattern of the households and social groups to which the children belong, had no bearing on wasting of children as well *(Shariff,* 1999). This despite the fact that India has run the Integrated Child Development Services (ICDS) since 1975, in 3702 Community Development Blocks, which is 70 per cent of the country *(VHAI,* 1997), providing a package consisting of supplementary nutrition to children, pregnant mothers (during the last trimester of pregnancy) and lactating mothers; immunisation, health check up, referral services, non-formal education, and nutrition and health education.

Children's needs and their voices are not always heard in developing countries, including India, despite the UN Convention on the Rights of the Child, to which most of these countries, including India, are signatories *(Goonesekere,* 1999). Within children, as a class adversely affected by food insecurity, the street children, single parent children and child workers are specially vulnerable groups.

And the girl child is even worse-off. Researches have shown that boys receive better treatment than girls: they get more medical attention, and more food than girls. And for somewhat the same logic, young adults have priority over the old. The classic logic being that the bread winner must be fed better. But in reality it is power relationships. Thus it has been rightly observed: "Intra-household resource allocation shows bias not only by gender, but also by age and by sibling hierarchy. The household power relations determine claims to consumption" *(UNDP,* 1999). There is need to disaggregate and look at the causes of their hunger, just as it is necessary to look at the disaggregated data to locate the causes of women's hunger, irrespective of their poverty status.

Hunger in children strike silently and it strikes silently because only upto 2 per cent of children exhibit visible signs of malnutrition, though in reality millions under the age of five suffer chronic malnourishment. This makes them vulnerable to illness and to physical as well as mental under-development.

And even in democratic countries like India, despite a free press, malnourished children largely go unnoticed. [2]. Neither the print nor the electronic media pick them up very often, barring honourable exceptions, like Star News Channel which projected hungry children during the aftermath of the Super-Cyclone that hit Orissa in 1999. It is often not realised that hunger amongst children leading to child malnutrition is one of the world's greatest problems in the 21st Century with one in every three children in the developing countries stunted physically and underdeveloped mentally, because of malnutrition. There is "global south", of sorts, in this regard as well, in that many children in the low-income households in the developed countries also suffer from malnutrition and consequent ailments.

While there is prevalence of malnourished children in poor households, who face food shortages before and during harvests and during natural calamities (earthquakes, flood, drought, epidemic, etc.), civil strife and war, many malnourished children are found in homes who do not suffer from food shortage. And this is particularly true for the girl child. The principal cause of this is illness, especially water borne diseases, notably diarrhoea, which afflicts poor households. This is also true of poor households throughout India. And it is more acute for the girl children because they have lower and fewer access to health care. These diseases in turn emerge on account of the fact that poor communities do not have potable water even in "normal times" and the condition of sanitation abysmal. In times of stress, they have even lower quantity of water and "contamination" several times more.

Globally, 1.3 billion people are deprived of access to safe drinking water. The situation in individual countries gives an even more difficult picture. For instance, in Mexico the richest quintile have almost cent per cent access to public water supply while the poorest quintile have no more than 50 per cent access to public water supply. In Peru, over 80 per cent of the richest quintile have access to public water supply as against only 30 per cent of the poorest quintile. In case of Cote d'lvoire a meagre 2 per cent of the poorest quintile of the population enjoy public water supply as against 70 per cent of the people in the richest quintile. In Delhi thousands of people who live along and around the river Yamuna, consume the highly polluted water from Yamuna, which is dangerous. Rakesh Mohan Committee Report had indicated that Rs. 27,000 crore to Rs. 28,000 crore are needed each year in order to provide safe drinking water and sanitation in all urban areas of the country alone. But the allocation is only to the tune of Rs. 5000 crore per annum. Thus a gap of around Rs. 22000 crore is added each year to the dismal water supply and sanitation scenario (*The Indian Express*, February, 9, 2000). If this is any indication, consumption of poor quality water will continue with all the concomitant consequences. The situation is pretty much the same for sanitation as well. 2.6 billion people world-wide are without access to sanitation facilities. In Mumbai half the total population is without sanitation facilties.

And then there is the rural-urban divide. The urban people have better access to safe drinking water than their rural counterparts. The sanitation facilities are also better in the urban areas, except the slums, than in the rural areas (*UNDP*, 1998, p. 52-53, particularly, the diagrams).

Poor sanitation and poor quality of drinking water are the principal causes of water borne diseases. Street children who are found at railway stations, bus terminuses, busy street crossings in cities and towns; children who are abandoned by their parents, destitutes, orphaned, kidnapped and made to beg, suffer additionally from more diseases. Respiratory infections, tuberculosis and leprosy diseases are common. Diseases not only eat up resources which could have been used to improve levels of consumption, but also prevent absorption of whatever food is consumed, in the body. Children cared for by single parent are often involuntarily neglected for a wide variety of factors: lack of resources (including time), energy and conflicting pulls. Consequently, their food need, as well as educational needs and their health care requirements suffer. This again not only leads to fall in food intake below the required level, but is also germane to lower food absorbtion, illness and disease.

Children who toil as child labourers are ironically a hungry class though they waste their childhood so that probably others may eat. There is no need to debate that the state of child labour, whose numbers vary from 70-80 million (Campaign Against Child Labour) to 17.36 million (*Planning Commission,* 1983) in India, is appalling (*Joshi,* 1999). Most of these children are not only denied their basic right to education but they also work under stress in agriculture, hazardous industries, domestic jobs, roadside stalls, brick kilns, asbestos factories, carpet industry, firecracker-manufacturing units, mines, quarries and so on. They are very often the victims of occupational diseases, especially silicosis, asbestosis, pneumonoconosis, tuberculosis, bony lesions, deformities and skin diseases. They suffer from repetitive impoverishment *(UNICEF,* 1995). And as already stated when disease strikes, nutrition suffers and the worst consequences of diseases are magnified.

Then come the ***aged and the elderly people.*** They suffer food security and hunger in silence. They are past their most productive years but face a bleak future *(Rajan, Mishra* and *Sarma,* 1999). The growth of the world's elderly and aged people, that is, people aged 60 years and above, has been identified by the WHO as one of the major challenges of the 21st century. "The persistence of poverty combined with ageing in countries still tackling basic problems of development has no precedent in the history of mankind" (WHO as quoted in *Ridge,* 1999).

The number of Indians over the age of sixty has increased dramatically to 70 million in 1999 from 20 million in 1948. It is estimated by WHO, that their number will rise to 142 million over the next twenty years and to reach nearly 200 million in the next 25 years *(Nath,* 2000). The progress in medical science and health delivery system (however much criticised) has resulted in the average Indian living longer. In demographic terms, this has resulted in more persons living not only to adulthood, but more persons surviving into old age. Life expectancy at birth has become 63 years *(UNDP,* 1999) from only 53 years in 1978.

Elderly people are highly vulnerable to hunger and malnutrition, just as they are liable to die due to non-communicable diseases such as cardiac diseases. It is sadly projected that the number of old people who are likely to die due to non-communicable diseases will double in India from 4.5 million a year in 1998 to 9 million a year in 2020.

There are two types of aging: biological aging and sociogenic aging. While biological aging has to do with the number of years that a person lives, sociogenic aging is dependent upon the role that society reserves for people as they progress in years. These two types of aging reacting with one another creates a reinforcing spiral of problems for the elderly.

The state of hunger and the nutritional status experienced by the elderly depends on the one hand on the cultural beliefs, practices, customs, age, degree of social integration, extent of physical well being, economic situation and mobility. On the other hand, public policies with regard to health, education and social security, greatly determine the food intake of the senior citizens. Thus the triumvirate of family, society and the government have their respective roles cut out in determining the status of food security of the aged and elderly. With increased life expectancy, food security of the elderly will assume even greater importance in the years ahead. Already the increased life-span of the public in general is clearly discernible.

Modernisation and technological advances have increased incomes for individuals and households but at the same time they have generated a craze for greater and even more productivity, which leave the older people by the way side. In an age where the market is supposed to do the trick, the rule is "survival of the fittest". The elderly people, like the poor, are not the fittest by definition and hence, they are excluded, like the poor, from the mainstream of life, by the excluding mechanism operated by the market. The growing participation of women in the workforce has made a dent into the traditional system of care for the elderly people.

Economic development has led to greater urbanisation. This has also created problems for the elderly and the aged, particularly so in the Indian context. People who leave their villages in search of a better life in the cities, leave the elderly behind, often to fend for themselves.

The breaking down of the joint family system and the decline of the extended family culture, have led to the emergence of the nucleus family, comprising husband, wife and their children. The old parents, and at times grand–parents, have all fallen off the picture. In this process of nuclearisation of the family, the elderly remain uncared for and hence they suffer from hunger, amongst other deprivations. Unless the couple is a working couple, with children to be cared for, parents are unlikely to be wanted in the household, get cared and looked after.

Life styles have also changed. Gone are the days when people pursued the profession of the father (mothers rarely worked), stuck to their family business and hung on to their ancestral place. Newer opportunities and newer range of careers have opened up for the lucky lot of educated Indians, like the educated elsewhere in the world, which take them to distant places in search of a job. For the unlucky majority, who are not educated (we are making a distinction between being literate and being educated), especially for those in the rural areas, their traditional family vocation/profession/land can no longer support them (there is already widespread disguised unemployment and open unemployment). They have to move out of their homes, villages and towns, to etch out a living, to distant places. The massive surge in rural-urban migration and growth of urban-slums all over India provide some pointers to this phenomenon. Thus in either case, people have moved out to distant places and cities in search of meaningful employment. It is even fashionable and necessary for the younger generation to go to schools at far away places. In this system of deciding to move out of their homes in search of livelihoods, the elderly remain a non-entity.

Even otherwise, with increases in industrial employment and growing population pressure, often the male and the able-bodied people move out of agriculture and come to urban centres for job, returning only during the cultivation and harvesting seasons. The thousands of people from Bihar and Uttar Pradesh, for instance, who come to work in other states, like Punjab and in cities like Mumbai, Delhi and Calcutta, return to their villages during the cultivation season. They leave the elderly people in the villages to fend for themselves and also to look after their property, home and hearth, without adequate command over resources. The elderly have little choice but to suffer in silence.

Social and professional life has so changed in a competitive environment that people have increasingly lesser and lesser time to look after the elderly people in the family. It is too well documented to be laboured here. Indeed, people have lesser and lesser time for their children as well. Most families suffer from a three-tier-generational trap, with deep chasms between each tier. The elderly belong to one generation (read the past generation!), the adults and able-bodied belong to the second generation (read present generation !!) and the children belong to the third generation (read the future generation !!!). The range of interest and the intensity of interest of the third generation are so varied and so fundamentally different from the interest of the first and the second generations, that there is no common ground. This has led to a general isolationism amongst the elderly, even where they live with the younger people. The everyday family dinners, where the whole family would meet and talk about their lives' joys and sorrows, are almost gone.

Inappropriate policies and inadequate implementation of some policies, and institutions also cause hunger for the senior citizens. In the developed countries the publicly funded social security benefits are the mainstay for the survival of the elderly, though there are also private pensions. However, in the developing countries these systems do not exist or do not work. For instance, take in India as much as g84 per cent of the labour force is in the unorganised sector. A Committee set up by the Government of India to look at the social security of the elderly came to a conclusion that the present pension provisions cover less than 11 per cent of India's workers. Out of a working population of 314 million, approximately no more than 28 million are employed in the organised sector. This means that about 286 million people must make do with old age pension of Rs. 200 a month plus whatever little provision they might have made out of their own savings during their productive years. Thus the pension scheme and the system of paying provident fund (only in the organised sector) in India covers only a very small segment of the Indian society. The Indian Government has just introduced a policy for the old, which includes plans for better legal help, homes and mobile health clinics for the elderly. But as with all policies for the non-vocal groups, the implementation and funding of the programmes under the policy, need to be seen. If experience is any guide, there seems to be no cause for cheers.

Even the implementation of the existing policies leave much to be desired. As we discussed in the context of the widows, elderly people find it difficult to derive benefits from the policies for the old. As Ridge notes the words of Kala Watti, 66, who says " I am too weak to spend three days arguing at the government offices and my son cannot go for me or he will lose his wages and we will have nothing to eat". And Maneka Gandhi, India's Union Minister for Welfare laments: "...the weakest go to the wall, no matter what we try" *(Ridge,* 1999).

War, civil strife and communal disturbances cause a range of special problems for the aged and the elderly, just as they do for the poor. They often flee to refugee camps and to displaced persons' shelters/homes or remain in their homes, in the belief that they will be spared by the intruders, without enough provision for food and health care facilities. When food arrive in the affected areas their physical condition and social standing prevent them from competiting for food, leaving them hungry. In the unfortunate event of the able-bodied members of the family being killed in such disturbances, the elderly are left to fend for themselves, because they can play an economically productive role only at the margin. The cases of parents of Jawans killed in the Kargil war in India during 1999 are examples in point.

The old and the aged are also susceptible to certain diseases that hit them most and knock them out of reckoning from the work force. Alzheimer disease is one example. Though its prevalence is less in India than in the developed countries but this data is suspect (as is many data) for people are reluctant to disclose these diseases. Old-age blindness (millions suffer from Cataracts); broken limbs, and failing general health are some crippling diseases for the old. The crippling effect of non-communicable diseases such as cardiac diseases (which as stated above, killed 4.5 million elderly a year in 1998 and may kill upto 9 million a year by the year 2020) is far reaching. This is particularly so, where the state of health care facilities for the non-rich is far from perfect *(VHAI,* 1997).

Box 2.13
Support for the Old

New Delhi
A group of frail and stooped figures crouch in the dust in a Delhi Slum. One by one, they stand to be examined by a doctor and then wait in line for a free medicine handout. "I have pain in both legs and my chest hurts", says 70 year-old Hardev Ram. "But without this medicine I would be in greater pain".
"My sight is failing", says Mungli Devi, a 65 year old labourer.
Ram and Devi represent a phenomenon that will soon have serious and far reaching effects: the ageing of India.

The Sunday Nation, July 4, 1999, p. A5.

Diseases have three-fold effect on hunger for the elderly. *One*, diseases reduce the earning capacity of the older people and hence, they have to suffer even more hunger. *Two*, the expenditure on treatment takes a heavy toll of the slender financial capacity of the old, which is often met by cutting down on consumption of food. *Three*, the diseased older people are additionally vulnerable to criminal attacks, robbing them of whatever assets they may have, thereby reducing their earning capacity and hence their capacity to have access to food. The newspapers in Metropolitan cities like Delhi which are replete with news relating to attacks on the elderly people, bear testimony to this.

In a rapidly changing world the elderly gét isolated. Changing value system, changing tastes, changing attitudes, changing lifestyles, changing social norms, changing religious percepts all leave the elderly people gasping for breath. In fact, diseases alone is one of the major causes of isolating the older people. Small wonder, *Times of India* in an *Editorial*, in December 1999 (exact date not known) wrote: "Among most Indian families a person suffering from disease would be treated much in the manner of an embarrassing eccentric to be bundled out of sight when guests come calling". A society unwillingly to look after its elderly arguably does not provide the best situation to prevent the old and the aged from starving. This isolation often leads to hunger and neglect of the old. The old and the aged eat alone and are neither visited by others nor can they visit others. Lack of motivation and cooking skills as well as mental and physical problems lead to malnutrition, especially those who live and eat alone. Inadequate food intake is not always a function of insufficient resources to do so. There are homes for the old and the aged, with medical and recreational facilities, but these are still restricted to the upper end of society [3] and are available only in bigger cities.

It is somewhat distressing that the hunger among the old and aged people has not received adequate attention of public policy. Policies cannot reverse the biological aging, like serious visual and hearing impairment, osteoporosis leading to broken hip bone, general debility, senility, reduced physical capacity due to affliction by Parkinson's and Alzheimer's disease. But public policies to address the consequences on hunger of sociogenic aging must be put in place. The provision for old age pension and widow's pension exists on paper but they leave far too much to be desired. Policies to foster family care have to be emphasized.

Box 2.14

Care for the Old in the Family

... Despite the difficulties of keeping our "loving, caring relationships when [one has] the emotions of hunger, anger and desperation", it is still possible to make a difference regarding our respect, love and care for the elderly (UNICEF, 1994). On All Souls Day, while I was lighting candles at my father's grave in Bangaldesh, a feeble voice surprised me by asking, "Could you please give me a candle?" I turned to see a boy who was about 10 years old. Following his eyes, I saw a grave, lying dark in the middle of hundreds of illuminated graves. What has the little penniless boy taught us? Is it not love?

Jushinta D'Costa in BFWI: *Causes of Hunger, 1995*

There is no substitute for family care of the old. There is no substitute for mother's milk for the infants.

III. The Nutrition-Poverty Trap

Having discussed the causes of hunger, it is important to discuss the nutrition poverty trap, shades of which were foreshadowed in the preceding section while examining the relationship between poverty and hunger.

It is important to define who all fail to enjoy the right to food. They are usually the poor *(Mukherjee,* 1999). There are fundamental issues in the economics of food deficiency flowing from inability to enjoy the right to food and the poverty traps. Those who cannot exercise the right to food are the ones who are undernourished, noting that undernutrition is not the same thing as starvation. Thus "the economics of undernutrition is not the same thing as the economics of famines. Famines are disequilibrium phenomena. They cannot persist, for the reason that their victims do not survive. In contrast, even a widespread incidence of undernourishment can persist indefinitely" *(Dasgupta,* 1997). The link between nutritional status and capacity to work imply that assetless people are simply assetless. Their only asset is potential labour power, but it is not necessarily an asset because if the poor have to convert their potential labour power over long periods of time, into actual labour power, they need adequate food and nutrition over that period of time as well. Because the poor are undernourished their capacity to convert their potential labour power to actual labour power is constrained and the quality of service they are able to offer in the market place is of inferior standard. The conversion of their potential labour power into actual labour power is inadequate and hence their capacity to obtain food to improve their nutritional status is low. The situation is even worse in case of early childhood undernourishment, which is damaging not only for well being but also for productive abilities and skills of the people involved, as there is a clear link between early childhood undernourishment and poor cognitive skills (*Sen,* 1997). Thus over time, undernourishment and ill–health can both be a cause and consequence of individuals' and households' falling in the poverty trap.

And such poverty can be inter-generational: once a household falls into a poverty trap, successive generations tend to remain trapped in poverty. Once a family gets into poverty, it can prove to be fairly hard for its descendents to emerge out of it, even if the economy in the aggregate were to experience growth in output for a while. The vicious cycle of undernourishment looks something like the following:

> Lack of nutrition→undernourishment→low capacity to convert potential labour into actual labour→inadequate capacity to provide quality work→inadequate capacity to obtain food lack of nutrition undernourishment, and the cycle starts all over again.

The inter-generational question of how undernourishment leads to perpetuation of poverty is easy to analyse in terms this flow-chart. It is well known that early childhood undernourishment causes long term damage to individuals (*Scrimshaw,* 1997). This is perpetuated from one generation to another. Consider the following:

> Lack of food→lack of nourishment of pregnant women→low birth weight→low ponderal index at birth→impaired glucose tolerance and non-insulin dependent diabetes millities/cardiovascular diseases/high blood pressure→low cognitive skills→low productive abilities and skill→low income→undernourishment and the cycle starts all over again.

Thus hunger and undernourishment in one generation sets a chain reaction that penetrates deep into the subsequent ones, especially in societies where there is inequality in intra-familial distribution of access to food and education, loaded against women.

In this nutrition-poverty trap, maintenance requirements of individuals take a severe beating. It has been long established that 60-75 per cent of the energy intake of someone in nutritional balance is expended towards maintenance and the much smaller 40-25 per cent is expended on "discretionary activities" such as work and play *(WHO,* 1985). Thus, those who are undernourished cannot provide nutrition for the maintenance function. They can work less and burn out early. Large maintenance requirements are a reason why in poor societies one can expect the emergence of inequality among people who may have been similar to begin with. At least one expert has estimated that during the great Industrial Revolution, 20 per cent of the population of England and France subsisted on diets of such low calorific value that they were effectively excluded from the workforce. Many of them even lacked the energy to stroll for a few hours *(Fogel,* 1994, quoted in *Dasgupta,* 1997).

Fogel uses his data to conclude that this was the reason why beggars constituted as much as 20 per cent of the populations of ancient regimes. "This picture of begging contains both physiological and behavioral adaptation with vengeance. It tells us that emaciated beggars are not lazy: they have to husband their precarious hold on energy". The theory outlined earlier makes sense "by showing how low energy intake, undernourishment and behavioural adaptation, that takes the form of lethargy, can all be regarded as being mutually reinforcing. In the extreme, these variables can feed on one another over time to reduce a person to a state of destitution" *(Dasgupta,* 1997, p. 6).

IV. How to Overcome Hunger?

An answer to the question is obviously not: produce more food. While increased food production is very important there is much more that needs to be done, if we are to get rid of hunger and food insecurity. These include, among other things, enhancement of general economic growth, expansion of employment and decent rewards for work, diversification of production, enhancement of medical and health care, arrangement of special access to food on the part of vulnerable people (including deprived mothers and small children), spread of basic education and literacy, strengthening democracy and the news media and reduction in gender–based inequalities. As Sen puts it

> "These different requirements call forth an adequately broad analysis alive of the diversity of causal antecedents that lie behind the many sided nature of hunger in the contemporary world. ....it calls for better integration of public policies in different levels, involving an active role for the public itself. The problem of hunger cannot be dissociated from these other deprivations and a broader approach is certainly needed" *(Sen,* 1997).

In order to achieve this broad based approach towards ensuring right to food, it is essential to recognise and manage several interdependencies. These interdependencies include:

> "interdependence between consumption and income, interdependence between distinct sectors, interdependence between different countries, interdependence between right to food and macroeconomic stability, interdependence between intra-familial distributional equity and sharing of food, interdependence between women's standing and fertility decline, interdependence between political incentives and public policies, interdependence between wars, military expenditure and economic deprivation, interdependence between early undernourishment and cognitive skills and finally interdependence between public activism and social policies" *(Sen,* 1997).

Failure to exercise the right to food and the problem of hunger is a problem of general poverty and of deprivation of food entitlements and adequate health and social care. Increase in income is, therefore, essential for guaranteeing the right to food. This is why, it has been noted that enhancement of general economic growth, expansion of employment and decent rewards for work are essential for guaranteeing the right to food.

We have also seen in Chapter 1 that people have command over food through both direct entitlements and exchange entitlements, that is through trade and exchange. Thus how favourably people can exchange their labour power and commodities will have a bearing on right to food. Similarly, public policy must pay attention to exchange between non-food and food commodities, given by general economic opportunities of production and trade. That is why, it is important to have diversification of production.

Like the spread of democracy, the emergence and spread of the global market economy, where "capitalism reigns uncontested", is a distinguishing feature of the post-cold war era, particularly after the conclusion of the Marakesh Agreement in 1994 formally establishing the World Trade Organisation from 1995. The global market economy interweaves with every part of our lives *(Hoehn,* 1999). In this increasingly shrinking world, the role of international trade in ensuring right to food has to be recognised. Though self-sufficiency in food is the optimum goal, even if not the most economic one, the need to resort to import food may arise. And that route needs to be kept open. But for that to happen, without let or hindrance, *inter alia,* wasteful consumption of the North at the expense of the South needs to be eschewed *(UNDP,* 1998). Such waste, not only in terms of quantity but also in terms of what is consumed, needs to be put an end to. There has to be a greater realisation of what Frances Moore Lappe said "...our global economic system actively creates scarcity from plenty" *(Lappe,* 1999).

Since the right to food requires that people have the capacity to buy the available food, keeping food prices in particular and overall price line in general, under leash is very important. High degree of macro-economic instability erodes people's capacity to buy food. In times of inflation, groups that fall behind in the inflationary race, typically the wage earners, for wages always lag behind price rise, become select victims of starvation. As we saw earlier in this Chapter, increases in wages are lagging behind increases in food prices throughout the nineties in the Indian Economy. During the Bengal Famine of 1943, millions perished as they could not access food because of its rising prices. The Great Bengal Famine has, thus, been also called a "boom famine", an example of inflation driven decline in food entitlement (*Sen*, 1981).

There is considerable intra-familial inequality in power status structure within households, particularly in patriarchal social arrangements in North Africa and Asia. This gets translated into disparity in accessing food and health care facilities, within the households. Women often eat last, leftovers, least and frequently eat nutritionally deficient food. The economic empowerment of women, (See *Mukherjee,* 1999 for a definition of empowerment) employing women in remunerative jobs, redefining property rights and spreading female education are crucial elements in this scenario. This explains why there has been so much stress on the spread of basic education and literacy as vehicles for guaranteeing the right to food.

Spread of basic education, especially female literacy and right to food, are also connected through an alternative channel as well. It has been well documented now that higher female literacy is associated with greater access to health care facilities and a consequent decline in fertility rates *(Murthi, Guio* and *Dreze,* 1995). As we noted in the earlier sections, no one is unduly scared of Malthusian doomsday prediction, nevertheless there is no denying that a decline in fertility rate is a big step towards guaranteeing right to food. This provides the rationale for gender based equity.

Some of the major trends affecting the global hunger scenario in the post-cold war world picture are the spread of democracy, the growth of civil society and its efforts to empower people. It has been the lesson from history that famines do not occur in democracies, with a relatively free media and active opposition parties. "There has never been a serious famine in a country—even an impoverished one—with a democratic government and a free press" *(Sen,* 1998).

Box 2.15

Peace—That is all Required of Africa...

My country is almost permanently drought-stricken, but because there is so much peace, so much democracy—and the government is one of the most in corruptible on the continent—no one has ever died from starvation.

Legwaila Joseph Legwaila, *Botswana's Permanent Representative to the United Nations*, Quoted in *Barbara Crossette,* 1998

On one plane, the prospects of returning to the electorate at regular intervals, public criticism and opposition within the legislatures, keep democratic governments alive of the need to ensure that people do not go hungry, as far as possible. There have been major famines in China over the last few decades but none in India, despite overall economic performance of the Chinese economy being consistently better than India's. "India has a remarkably effective record in preventing famines". On the other because of better communication in a democracy, when political executives know that others may suffer from hunger and even die of starvation and when they have the power to affect political outcomes, they do something about it. Spread of democracies and news media are, therefore, considered very important for enjoyment of the right to food. The emergence of the global electronic media, with all its pitfalls, has indeed enlarged the impact of media on hunger. "By focusing on the starving children in Somalia, a pictorial story tailor-made for television, TV mobilized the conscience of the nation's public institutions, compelling the [US] government into a policy of intervention for humanitarian reasons" *(Cohen,*1994). Small wonder that the then Secretary General of the United Nations commented that "CNN is the 16th member of the Security Council" *(Minear et. al.* 1996).

Box 2.16
Hunger and Democracy

Hunger is not caused by scarcity of food but a scarcity of democracy. Those who go hungry are those without voice in their societies.

Frances Moore Lappe

We have seen in Section-II, that military expenditures and wars have a big impact upon right to food, through destruction of assets, destroying incentives for investment and economic expansion, disrupting entitlements through war-induced inflation and eliminating political incentives in the direction of protecting the vulnerable. Cuts in defense expenditure can release funds for increasing food production, food imports where necessary, supplementing dietary requirements, basic education and primary health care. This is particularly so for the major powers in South Asia *(UNDP,* 1998). Ironically much of war and military build up are in the developing countries, whose people suffer the pangs of hunger most. South Asian countries, Indonesia, Sub-Saharan Africa, North Korea, China and Iraq are some of the names that come to one's mind immediately. Reduction in military expenditure and war preparedness is a variable that should attract considerable attention.

Public action, including what is done by the public at large, and the State have a bearing on right to food. What people can do is demand remedial action and make governments accountable.

> "This recognition demands that an adequate role be given not only to the protection of basic means of living and social security, but also.....to promoting the use of democratic rights of free elections, uncensored news reporting and unfettered public criticisms. The use of political and civil rights can make a radical difference to the problem of hunger... and its manifold consequences" *(Sen,* 1997, p. 23).

In the realm of public action the emergence of civil society actors and NGOs have assumed great importance. They are a force to reckon with and have made their impact in every major international policy making event since the Earth Summit in Rio in 1992 *(UNDP,* 1999). The impact that they can have in social mobilisation and in harnessing public opinion for eliminating hunger is enormous. Indeed, in countries where civil society movement is strong, the chances of famine and starvation are so much less. Promotion and nurturing of civil society organisations and community–based organisations have to be fully integrated into a strategy for dealing with hunger.

Endnotes

1. The discussion of this section is an adoption and extension of BFWI (1995) framework.
2. The exceptions being the International Funding Agencies, particularly the ones which run on Child Sponsorship money, who pick up areas where there are hungry children to impress upon the donor's, the need to have their contribution.

3. The old are now even isolated in their death. As Veena Das *(Das,* 2000) aptly observed: "Whereas in the pre-modern period, the picture of death was one in which the dying person was surrounded by family and friends, being offered the solace of ritual, the medicalisation of death" (an aspect of the present mind set) has completely changed the scenario. True "religious rituals did not offer the hope of cure, but they did offer the hope of redemption". Even that is no longer true.

3 The Theory of Hunger: The Social and Political Perspectives

I. Hunger as a Symptom of Poverty

Food is a basic human need and a human right. It has been so recognised in numerous instruments and declarations, including the Universal Declaration of Human Rights, adopted by the U. N. *General Assembly.* Human beings need food every day and as one farmer put it to me: "We need air every two seconds, we drink water every three hours and we food every eight hours". Small wonder that the need to ensure that no one goes hungry has been accepted with total unanimity throughout the world. But the need for food is so self-evident that most people who are well fed and well–nourished take it for granted. They hardly think about it, if at all except perhaps about its palate, variety and taste.

In a motivational framework Abraham Maslow classified human needs in terms of physiological and social parameters. He deduced that some needs are more basic than others and was thus able to construct a hierarchy of these needs and suggested that at least minimum satisfaction of one level of need is required before a person can move up to seek satisfaction of the next higher level of need. Beyond a minimum level of satisfaction needs may be met to a greater or lesser extent, and progress to the next level is still possible.

As the base of the hierarchy of needs visualised by Maslow are *survival* needs. Irrespective of the cultural variations in food usage, there remains one universal imperative: *food is fundamental for individual's survival.* "For the man, who is extremely and dangerously hungry, no other interest exists, but food. He dreams food, he perceives only food and he wants only food".

Box 3.1
Right to Food

Everyone has the right to a standard of living adequate for the health and well-being of himself and of his family including food, clothing, housing and medical care and necessary social services, and the right to, in the event of unemployment, sickness, disability, widowhood, old age or other lack of livelihood in circumstances beyond his control.

Universal Declaration of Human Rights, adopted vide United Nations *General Assembly Resolution No. 217 A(III)* dated 10th December 1948, quoted in *U.N. Document No. A/810, at 71 (1948).*

Once survival needs are assured people begin to think about securing food needs to be met. They start thinking about, not just what we will eat today, but also what shall we eat next week. *Security needs* can be met through storage of food. Once survival and security needs are no longer overriding concerns for people, food becomes a way of what Maslow thinks meeting *love, belongingness and affection* needs. *Self-esteem* is next in the hierarchy. Pride in food prepared may be reflective of this aspect of human behaviour and most people enjoy being praised for the quality of food they produce and prepare. Next in hierarchy of needs is *self-actualisation.* Whereas self-esteem is bolstered through the praise received for the quality of food, *self-actualisation* is expressed by the innovative use of foods, new recipes and food experimentation. Self actualisation only occurs if an individual has self-confidence and is ready to embrace failure. Self actualisers dare to be different. Food becomes a personal trademark—a source of personal satisfaction and achievement. Figure 3.1 is a depiction of Maslow's hierarchy of needs.

The lower order needs thus predominantly represent biological needs whereas the higher order needs are more obviously social in nature. In Maslow's hierarchy of needs, it is one of the lower order needs that individuals want to satisfy first. Most people under normal circumstances try to move up the hierarchy of needs and slipping down the ladder signifies a disaster situation, typified by conditions when natural disaster or famine strikes, as the one obtaining in Kendrapara and Paradip Districts of Orissa after the super-cyclone in October 1999 or by the near famines in Saurastra Region of Gujarat *(Chandra,* 2000; *Times of India,* 21st April 2000) and in Western Rajasthan in April 2000 *(Sinha,* 2000; *Indian Express,* 22nd April, 2000). Such slippage can also be seen during times of severe economic recession. Just as individuals satisfy their lower order needs first before moving on to satisfying the higher order needs, most subsistence economies also first direct their efforts at satisfying their basic needs, of which food need is central, on a nation-wide scale. It then directs its efforts towards dealing with other societal needs, such as education, health or growth, recognising nevertheless that all needs are inter-linked, one way or the other. It is often said that hunger is the threshold to poverty.

Indeed, hunger is closely inter-related with poverty. We have seen the hunger and poverty traps in Chapter 2. Poverty is often measured by the intensity and extensiveness of hunger. The Expert Group on Estimation of Proportion and Number of Poor of the Planning Commission of India, did consider (though it did not accept) the criterion of hunger as one of the methods to define those who are poor *(Planning Commission,* 1993). But hunger is not equivalent to poverty *(White,* 1972; *Planning Commission,* 1993) because people may be hungry, though not poor. And poverty is more than hunger because those who are in poverty may not only be hungry but they are also deprived of most human rights and freedom *(Mydral,* 1968, *Sen,* 1999a, 1999b; *World Bank,* 2000). The phenomenon of hunger is intricately interwoven with important aspects of poverty in society and, therefore, hunger has to be understood within the broader context of a theory of society.

Some Basic Concepts of a Dialectical Approach to a Theory of Society [1]

The development of society is determined by both the technical and material conditions, as also the social conditions of production *(Althusser,* 1965). Ideology, politics, culture, religion, customs, usage, social norms and practices, legal system, customary rights, system of justice, etc. all have a strong bearing on development. These are what economists have called the "non-economic" factors which interface with the economic factors to generate or retard development. [2]. In theory of society these "non-economic factors" of the economists are called the "*super-structure*". The technical and material conditions of production reflect the relationship between people on one hand, the means of production and nature on the other, where the means of production are identical with the existing tools, technology, ecology, environment, bio-diversity, etc. They are the objective elements in the conditions of production process.

But there are both objective and subjective elements in production process. And these subjective elements, which include, but not restricted to, technical knowhow, professionalism, imagination and ideas, skills, entrepreneurial spirit, risk aversion, spirit of adventure, willpower and cultural traits, even altruism, have as strong a bearing on production as the objective factors. The subjective elements as a basket of resources in the production process have been called "*potential resources*".

The social conditions of production, which reflect the interrelationship between people and the means of production, determine what is produced from a spectrum of goods and services that can potentially be produced. In this scheme of social conditions of production, the existing property relations are the critical elements, which admit of description in terms of ownership and control of, and access to, the means of production, the division of labour, the power-status structure, institutional arrangements, etc. This has been called the "*economic structure*" of society.

There is a relationship between the *potential resources* and the *economic structure* of society, a relationship of continuous interaction resulting in a certain mode of production, which is called the "*economy*". But the basic interaction between the *potential resources* and the *economic structure* of a society also influences people's perceptions, their culture, their beliefs and ideology. When contradictions are overcome or solved by changes in the *economic structure* of the society, then the *superstructure* (ideology, culture, etc.) will slowly change. Such a change will in turn affect the basic interaction between *potential resources* and the *economic structure*.

In summary, the economy and the political as well as ideological superstructure interact in every society. This interaction is represented schematically in Figure 3.2.

The interaction between the economy and the superstructure (politics and ideology) manifests itself in many different observable ways. One of the most important implications of looking at a society in this way is that, in the last analysis, production, distribution, and consumption are basically all determined by the economic structure of the society. Changes in any one of them will always be constrained by the existing structure. However, this analysis also implies that efforts to attempt a change in the pattern of production, distribution, and consumption can themselves change the economic structure in that technology by itself cannot be right or wrong. One cannot from first principles oppose food aid, or the use of chemical fertilisers to restore soil nutrition, or the use of high-yielding varieties of seeds to increase yield of foodgrains. Similarly, in principle use of computers to predict changes in soil chemistry over the next twenty years, or the use of nuclear energy to energise water pumps for irrigating land, and harnessing bio-technology to increase food productivity, all seem unexceptionable.

However, in a specific society, with a given social, politico-economic and natural environment, and at a given point of time, one can examine the consequences of these applications and predict the danger or the usefulness of such transformations of the potential resources. For instance, in parts of the Haryana and Punjab of 2000, use of any more chemical fertilisers in the form of NPK to replenish soil nutrition would be suicidal. This is so as the soil in Haryana and Punjab is highly chemicalised and yield from further use of chemical fertilisers would fall dramatically, apart from other harmful effects. The harmful effects of genetically modified seeds and genetically modified food are yet to be discovered. Food aid, capital-intensive technology, bio-technology and the rest of it, are all used in such diverse countries as the USA and Nepal, both developing and developed, with dramatically different effects. The basic dialectical relationship between technology and society, however, is hardly considered in any serious pubic policy debate on hunger and right to food. The dialectic relationship remains largely ignored in public policy formulation, in matters of adoption and transfer of technology as well.

One way of developing a theory of hunger and society can be through this dialectical model of society. However, before we do so and in order to place the discussion in a perspective, it would be rewarding to summarize some "mono-disciplinary" or reductionist approaches as well as political approaches, used to analyse hunger and formulate policy prescriptions emanating from these analyses.

II. Approaches to Tackle Hunger

Reductionistic Approaches

Like in all pastures of human endeavour, approaching any problem like hunger from an unidisciplinary perspective would yield solutions, which are, naturally enough, unidisciplinary in content and character. While such unidisciplinary approach may be appropriate in some cases, it is likely to yield partial remedies to a complex problem. This would render the remedies, in consequence, vulnerable to slippage. Let us take the issue of physiological dimension of hunger. Hunger certainly has, amongst others, a physiological dimension. Therefore, a medical practitioner may have important contributions to make, but a medical practitioner, in dealing with hunger, approaches it from the health and malnutrition perspectives, something like what Scrimshaw and others have done (*Scrimshaw,* 1997; *Osmani,* 1993). But hunger and food insecurity are beyond issues of health and malnutrition, though these may be parts of the total scheme. Each one of us has our own beliefs, biases and indeed convictions, as has the health expert. And, therefore, it is likely that the medical practitioner trying to deal with the problems of hunger and food insecurity, will tend to recommend health interventions only, because that is where her expertise lies and it is in that domain that she is at her best. A Demographer concerned with adverse impact of rapid population growth on hunger situation, like Wright, Snyder and Reeves (*Bread For the World,* 1994; *Dyson,* 1996, *Kumar,* 2000) might believe that hunger can be eliminated by a decline in fertility rate. Demographers are entitled to their view that if the rate, at which the number of mouths to be fed could be reduced, the chances are that the size of the pieces of the cake for all would either remain the same or increase. For the demographers the best course is to have in place an appropriate population policy to reduce population growth and ensure food security. One can cite more of such approaches, to which we will return later. Suffice it to say for the present, that the point we are driving at is that each of such reductionistic approaches and consequent interventions may be valid under specific circumstances and deserve serious attention. But they generally can offer only partial solution, unlikely to succeed in the medium and long run. The solutions emerging out of reductionistic approaches can lead us to holistic solutions only when conjoined with other interventions and are networked into a fabric of programmes. Hunger and food insecurity at the household, community and national levels are systemic problems and complex phenomena *(Sen,* 1997). Granted that, the problem of hunger deserves a characteristically multi-faceted remedy.

Some of the common reductionistic approaches seeking a solution to the problem of hunger are listed in Table 3.1.

All these approaches have made significant contributions towards understanding hunger and in taking us nearer to a hungerless world. They have a lot to commend but they will not tackle hunger on a sustainable basis. To approach the matter from the right perspective, examining each of the approaches, would be a rewarding exercise.

Let us start with the approach of the agriculturists, for they are concerned with food production that lies at the heart of the matter. The crux of this approach is that availability of food has to be increased either by increasing food production or by seeking and delivering food-aid. The importance of augmenting systemic food availability, as a means to solving hunger, has been examined, at length by a long chain of experts. Hence, it may not detain us for long. Suffice it to say for the present that even if agricultural production rises rapidly, people may still go hungry and people do die in front of granaries full of foodgrains. We did see in Chapter 1 that during the early years of Green Revolution, while food production increased, so did hungry people throughout the world. In case of India, though we produced over 204 million tons of food (in 1998-99) yet millions go hungry because either they could not access the available food or they had no purchasing power to take control over such food. Indeed, this has been convincingly demonstrated by Sen in a long series of authoritative work *(Sen,* 1981, *Dreze* and *Sen,* 1990) which we have discussed in Chapter 1.

Augmenting systemic food availability is important but it is one part of the story. We have to look at distribution of food. We need to look at the economic and physical access that people have to food, and this encompasses a whole range of issues, like acess to basic education and primary healthcare, gender justice and employment and fair wages.

Table 3.1. Reductionistic Approaches to the Problem of Hunger

Disciplinary Background of the Observer	Main Diagnosis of the Causes of Hunger	Typical Reductionistic Recommendations
Health	Nutritional disorder, environmental stress, disease.	Vaccination, Breast-feeding/weaning food, Environmental sanitation.
Agriculture	Poor yield and low food supply.	Increase in yield and food production; Food-aid, new-technology and Post-harvest technology, marketing.
Education	Ignorance, inappropriate food habits; lack of resources to access food.	Spread of basic education, nutrition education, mass communication.
Demography and Population sciences	High population density, high fertility rate and high rate of population growth.	Population Control, access to health and family planning facilities, resettlements.
Neo-classical economy	Non-availability of food domestically and mal-distribution of food.	International trade, changing fiscal policies, implementing income-generating projects and employment generation programmes.
Marxist/ Socialists economy	Capitalism	Changing the capitalist mode of production, collectivisation of agriculture, public interventions in food distribution.

Source: Jonsson (1984)

It is also necessary to see the structure of agricultural production. If the emphasis is on increasing production of export crops, food availability will not increase and hunger will not be less, unless the counterfactuals are such that they indicate the possibility of importing additional food grains resulting from the utilisation of export earning from export crops. In that event it is really import of food grains and not increase in agricultural yield which reduces hunger.

Box 3.2
Differentiated Consumption Levels

Average per capita consumption of foodgrains in India is 14 kg per month which corresponds to 467 gm per day. This varies from 9 kg in Kerala and 10 kg in Gujarat to 17 kg in Himachal Pradesh.

India Human Development Report, A Profile of Indian States (New-Delhi: Oxford University Press) 1999.

If we take the remedies suggested by the educationists, they are clearly important in themselves. Without spread in basic education and information on food and nutrition, it is not possible to eliminate hunger. Education is key to making people "capability-rich". Without spread of education, particularly women's education, women will not access health facilities at the warranted level, hampering use of family planning methods and hence cutting into one important element in a programme of tackling hunger, viz., controlling population growth. Basic education will empower people to earn wages to access food, and demand their right to food. Nevertheless, unless other conditions are present, capacity to buy food and awareness to demand of the State their rights to have food, may still leave hunger unchanged unless, *inter alia,* there is enough food in the system. The case of Kerala is an example in point. While its literacy rate is over 91 per cent, consumption of food is only 9 kg per month per capita as against 17 kg in Himachal Pradesh and 14 kg nationwide, despite literacy level being far less in Himachal Pradesh and only 60 per cent approximately in the country. This is the reason why the State needs to run a Public Distribution System to keep hunger for the vulnerable (read poor) sections of the people at bay (*Kannan,* 2000).

Thus, making people "capability rich" is one important part of the story, which must be added to other essential parts to complete the picture. This includes increasing their capacity to take decisions, their willingness to take decisions and an enabling environment where they can exercise their decision making capacity.

The neo-classical approach to solving problems of hunger and malnutrition has not solved the problem of hunger either in the developed world or in the developing world and certainly not in India. Even in the US there are estimates showing that the total cost of eliminating hunger and food insecurity in the short term is of the order of US $ 49.2 billion (*BFWI,* 2000). The reasons are not far to seek. The tonics and elixirs of the neo-classicists come in the garb of fiscal incentives to farmers to grow more food, income and employment generating schemes (like the Employment Assurance Scheme of the Government of India and Employment Guarantee Scheme of the Government of Maharastra) to provide purchasing power to the people to access food. These have been tested and tried out in India and elsewhere for decades. It has now been fairly well established that not all farmers respond to price incentives to increase foodgrains production as many other variables enter their decisions making process, including risk aversion, access to appropriate technology and availability of water for irrigation (*Dantwala,* 1967 and 1976; *Vaidyanathan,* 1999; *Mukherjee,* 2000). Income and employment generation schemes to provide purchasing power to the people have serious drawbacks in their implementation, and income generated from such programmes do not necessarily get expended on food, particularly so because of the inequity in intra-household distribution of food flowing from inequity in distribution of intra-household power. There is no debate that these approaches have provided relief and succour to millions of hungry. Yet many more millions suffer from chronic and transitory hunger and hunger stalks a huge chunk of our population, particularly in the states of Uttar Pradesh, Madhya Pradesh, Bihar and Orissa, and in different parts of the world in Africa and South East Asia in particular.

That trade can solve the problem of hunger is something which we are being boxed into believing by the neo-classicists just as the African countries were foxed into believing with disastrous consequences. Trade can only provide food, but it cannot give people the capability and capacity to access food *(Timberlake,* 1991). Secondly, through trade in an unequal world, the countries, which have hungry people, will be impoverished leading to general decline in prosperity with negative consequences on hunger. All the comparative advantage arguments do not work in an imperfect world market. Reliance on this route alone does not commend itself on economic grounds *(Lappe* and *Collins',* 1988). The vagaries of international politics are another set of matters that should bother policy makers and governments and must be factored into any policy aimed at eliminating hunger through trade, though keeping the option of meeting temporary food shortages through trade need not be foreclosed *(Das Gupta,* 1999). We should also not be oblivious of the fact that food in the world market is in short supply almost exactly when their scarcity hurts the domestic economy *(Mukherjee,* 1994).

If we take the route commended by the Socialists and Marxists, we would not travel very far either. Collectivisation of farming did not work either in the erstwhile USSR or in Communist China. Chinese had to dismantle their commune system and distribute their land to the people, on a long lease. People suffer from hunger and certainly the food consumed by the people lack nutrition and calorific value for a long and healthy life *(UNDP,* 1997; author's own observation). As a matter of fact such regimented governance has been thought of as being the cause of major famines in China over the last few decades. This has led to dismantling of the commune system in China and a return to private mode of production, where each person is given 2-3 "Mu" of land on a lease of 30 years initially. Lack of democracy and the non-existent free press are inimical to prevention of famines and hunger *(Sen,* 1999b), no matter which mode of production we opt to choose for the agricultural sector.

However, it has to be recognised that the essence of the Marxist-Socialists approach has a grain of truth as well. While it is nobody's case that there should be nationalisation of agriculture where the state gets into the act of growing "food for all" or collectivisation of land as a means toward eliminating hunger, land reforms are essential elements in a comprehensive scheme for food security. Equitable distribution and access to land, one of the fundamental resources for food production, is a must *(IFAD,* 1994). If there exists inequity in distribution of land and hence inequity in access to a basic resource for food production, food security is in jeopardy *(Barraclough,* 1996). Even in India, experience tells us that States where land reforms have been carried out, howsoever imperfect, the food security situation is much better. West Bengal is a case in point, which has recorded the highest rate of growth in agricultural production in recent years. Kerala is another example. The entire issue of land reforms in countries like India, where rural residents such as small-holders, tenants, squatters and landless workers depend on agriculture for livelihood, could have been solved, by nationalising all agricultural land and then redistributing the same in a transparent, just and equitable manner.

Those with demographic dispensation also have solutions, which yield only partial solution. Demographers would argue that the problem of food insecurity is best tackled by controlling population growth. The fruits of increased food output and better distribution of food get lost in the wave of rising population numbers. The key to solving the problem of hunger is to arrest population growth. Though there is no possibility of the Malthusian Doomsday visiting humankind, nevertheless a fall in the fertility rate is crucial for solving the problem of hunger. Feeding an ever-increasing number of mouths, most of which are in poor households or in poor countries, shifts the horizon of a hunger free world further and further away. There are elements of truth in such formulations. But the problem is that with best of efforts the rate of population growth may be just equal to replacement population, in the *very* long run, but even then there is need to have food security for those who are food-deficit in the existing population. Population control alone cannot deal with their hunger and food security. And then till such time we are able to achieve a rate of growth in population which is equal to replacement population, the number of people to be fed will rise both in the short run and the medium run. A solution to those who will be food-deficit amongst them (and most of them would be) has to be found in strategies, other than population control.

Similar is the case with the arguments set forth by the health expert, about which we have briefly mentioned above. These may, as in the other reductionist approaches, provide relief under certain given circumstances for a short period of time but they will not yield lasting solution. Thus while all the above reductionist approaches have strong elements of a comprehensive policy, they need to be joined with missing links for tackling the complexities of hunger.

The Moral Economy Approach

The moral economy approach to solve hunger problem is the first holistic approach we will discuss. In a moral economy approach, pre-capitalist rural communities are viewed as societies where social rights of minimum subsistence are secured to all members of society. The risk of hunger is in a sense insured collectively by the community and, hence, under exceptionally adverse circumstances, like a war or epidemic, would the traditional system of security against hunger collapse. Such a situation is germane to anarchy characterised by strategic behaviour on the part of the individuals as a matter of life and death, such as the ones described by Turnbill and Dirks (*Turnbill,* 1984; *Dirks,* 1980). Individuals, who elect to breech any customary rule in the process, are unlikely to retain their membership of the community and hence jeopardise their entitlement to the comfort of their traditional insurance against hunger, in a stochastic world. Individuals are by nature cautious and are keen to avoid the prospects of facing hunger in an environment fraught with serious uncertainties. And granted that it is always difficult, if not impossible, to get accepted in other communities, once driven out of one for breech of customary law or even otherwise, open violation of the customary law is the rarest of rare exception than the rule. This approach, thus, tells us that societal arrangements and economic institutions in traditional village societies have been designed to eliminate hunger and related contingencies, and hence the high incidence of retribution and reciprocity mechanisms, not excluding patronage relationships, must be taken cognizance of in ensuring that individuals do not go hungry.

Exchange at the market place, in this approach, is seen as a form of transaction at the margin only, restricted mostly to inter-community inter-relationships (and less so intra-community inter-relationship). Exchange at the market place is seen as restricted to exchange of goods without any special significance for physical or social survival. Indeed, the functioning of the market is unsympathetically viewed as a mechanism for endangering subsistence of individual members of the community by reducing their food entitlements and threatening the group's capacity to reproduce. This is so because the market mechanism is capable of driving a wedge of socio-economic differentiation in the community's societal behaviour, and of inducing class polarisation, which lay beyond the capacity of the traditional power-status structure of the group/community to deal with. In consequence, in terms of this approach, market forces cannot be allowed a free play inside the community space, and though market exchange is seen as restricted mostly to relationships between communities, these market relations are not the standard "Economic Textbook" general equilibrium framework that we read about.

Box 3.3

Community and Food

"No community intent on protecting the fount of solidarity between its members can allow latent hostility to develop around a matter as vital to animal existence, and, therefore, capable of arousing as tense anxieties as food. Hence the universal banning of transactions of gainful nature in regard to food and foodstuffs in primitive and archaic society. The very widely spread ban on higgling-haggling over victuals automatically removes price-making markets frcm the realm of early institutions"

Karl Polyani, 1957

An intra-community subsistence ethic prevails to guarantee subsistence as a moral claim or as a social right to food that all members of the community are entitled to, which is manifested in the "patterns of social control and reciprocity that structure daily conducts" *(Scott,* 1976). This subsistence ethic being talked about here is not tantamount to an egalitarian utopia. "Village egalitarianism in this sense is conservative not radical: it claims that all should have a place, a living, not that all should be equal"

(Scott, 1976). That is, food is guaranteed but there will be differentiation according to some agreed criteria, for there is none of an automatic distribution of food equally amongst all the members of the community.

The Moral Economy Approach to Hunger tells us that non-capitalist rural societies are largely organised around the problem of food contingencies and other subsistence hazards. These rural societies tend to act as guarantors of minimal subsistence for all their members. In this pursuit, traditional village societies aim to achieve a high level of self-sufficiency in food and other essentials at the village and household level. Thus, the approach is categorical about the necessity of ensuring food security at the household and community levels. Nevertheless, in terms of the Moral Economy Approach, *total* self-sufficiency in food cannot be achieved at the household level, and household food supplies are vulnerable to wide fluctuations. To that extent, failure or non-existence of institutional arrangements, other than the market mechanism, backed by value system and moral codes that emphasize co-operation amongst members *inter se,* to see that food security is ensured for all the members of the community at all times, causes hunger.

Where food exchanges within the community cannot ensure food security for all its members, it will be necessary to carry out trade with partners located outside the community space, or else hunger will ensue. However, socio-political mechanisms have to be in place to control the free rein of the market forces and ensure orderly exchange in a predictable manner. In the absence of such mechanisms, as we stated earlier, societal arrangements will break down because trade in food will drive a wedge of socio-economic differentiation in the community and induce class polarisation.

The Political Economy Approach (PEA)

The MEA is not without its critics. Popkins and others have emphasized that traditional village institutions, arrangements and norms have neither been motivated nor been effective in guaranteeing the subsistence needs of the community *(Hayami* and *Kikuchi,* 1981) and hence in preventing hunger. "Insurance welfare and subsistence guarantees with pre-capitalist villages are limited" and "the calculations of peasants driven by motives of survival in a risky environment led not to subsistence floors and extensive village-wide insurance scheme, but to procedures that generated and enforced inequality within Villages" *(Popkin,* 1979).

The Political Economy Approach starts from the premise that household-level strategies for avoiding hunger are much more common than village or community-level schemes designed for the sharing, pooling and shifting of household risks. In a community facing hunger, such as the one now afflicting the people of Orissa after the super cyclone of late 1999, household level coping mechanisms are commonly sighted, but community or village level strategies are not much in evidence. Thus for example, the household-level strategy of scattered fields illustrates the "conflict between individual and group rationality whereby each individual, following a safety-first strategy, ends up with less production than he would if the village as a whole could follow an aggregate safety-first strategy" *(Popkin,* op.cit). Indeed "consolidated fields with higher average output and higher variance from year to year would be a better strategy for peasants to follow if the village could provide insurance for farmers to compensate for increased variance of consolidated fields" *(Popkin,* op.cit). This, according to the PEA, would be one case where actions taken by rational peasants individually, in both market and non-market situations, do not aggregate to an action of a rational village. Thus, sum of the parts is not equal to the whole.

PEA argues that since villagers do not adopt village-level and/or community-level strategies for avoiding risks of hunger, any assumptions about the behaviour of the peasants in the matter of ensuring food security is not correct. The assumptions that peasants behave as ultruistic actors or passive subjects, willing to subject themselves and their households, to societal norms of conduct and moral principle of reciprocity, is contested by the protagonists of PEA on the ground that peasants in non-capitalist societies are egoistic and calculative, who are inclined to derive maximum personal benefits from all actions that they get involved in, and they do not necessarily work for the "greatest good of the greatest number". Because many villagers exhibit opportunistic behaviours, community level strategies and collective action to prevent hunger will not carry the people very far, on account, *inter alia*, of the "free rider" phenomenon widely prevalent in individual behaviour. People like to get the benefits for themselves of the availability of anything that partakes the nature of a public-good without they themselves making any significant contribution towards its obtention. Hence, insurance or welfare schemes for avoidance of hunger are among the collective goods which may thus never be produced. In so far as societal norms are concerned, they will fail to mitigate the "free rider" phenomenon by instilling altruistic preoccupations into the internalized value system of the individuals, or by holding their most dangerous opportunistic proclivity in hold. Norms in society are never cast in stone. They are dynamic, continuously negotiated and renegotiated and shifted according to considerations of power and strategic interactions among individuals change. Thus societal norms as a guarantee against hunger are often found to be inconsistent or prone to conflict so that they "cannot directly and simply determine actions". Thus according to PEA individual's proclivity not to behave towards a societal action, for insuring against hunger, leads to hunger.

Both the MEA and PEA give us insights into how organising the community for preventing hunger through enforcement of self-proclaimed norms can contribute to eliminating food insecurity. The MEA approach does foreshadow what roles Gram Sabhas can play in tackling food insecurity at the community level. The importance of self-sufficiency in food is amply demonstrated and these approaches foreshadow the potential dangers of allowing "others" (whoever they are) to trade in food in any attempt to tackle hunger. They tell us where individual interest may come in conflict with group interest and jeopardise schemes to eliminate hunger, because of either strategic behaviour or "free-rider" principle. But these approaches cannot by themselves provide for policy prescriptions to tackle hunger in the medium and long run.

The Gender Approach

The Gender Approach to solve hunger problem is of recent origin and emanated out of movements for the rights of women. The nineties saw a shift in the development paradigm. The earlier approach to development and hunger problem, viz., through the service delivery approach, came under severe scrutiny. The SAARC Independent Commission on Poverty Alleviation came to the conclusion that the entire approach—the service delivery approach—is far too inflexible and inefficient to make a significant difference. Because the service delivery approach misidentifies the most important resource for development—the creativity and productivity of the poor themselves, where the poor were treated as mere passive recipients. Hunger persists because hungry people lack the opportunity they need to bring their own hunger to an end. The reality is that hungry people not only lack the opportunity but are denied the opportunity to end their hunger and in the process of denying the opportunity to the hungry people to overcome hunger, the subjugation, marginalisation and disempowerment of women is the key factor.

On the one hand our society holds women responsible for all key actions required to end hunger: ensure household nutrition, health care, education, food production, food gathering and collecting, food processing and cooking, and augment family income to bolster food security of the households. On the other hand subjugation and marginalisation of women through laws, customs, traditions, practices, religious mores and social relationships, are matters of public history. Women are systematically denied the resources, the information and the freedom of action they need to have, in order to carry out their responsibilities.

Box 3.4

Incongruity in the Language of Development

"Subservience and resistance, strength and submission form part of the paradoxial nature of women's experience in India...The language of development does not reflect the grit, reality and sparkle of these women's lives".

Sonali Sathaye, *The Hindu,* April, 1999.

Though Indian women provide one-half of the country's labour in rice cultivation; 51 per cent in forest based small scale enterprise and 93 per cent in dairy production, there are 8 elements which marginalise Indian women and hence cause hunger:

- Women are disorganised and are prevented from being organsied. For instance, there was a law in Bihar which barred women from forming fishing co-operatives *(Holmes,* 2000).
- Women are not recognised and supported as producers. Women work in disagreeable conditions with dangerous machinery and work for unusually long hours. They are almost always paid lower wages than their men counterparts for the same amount of work.
- Women do not have access to credit. Organised sector credit outlets, more often than not, deny credit to women. One reason for this is that women fail to meet the requirement of providing collateral to credit granted to them, because either by law or by practice or by some combination of the two, they do not own and inherit property from their parents, particularly inherited property.
- Women are often discriminated against even in matters of accessing primary health care and basic education. "Discrimination against women and girls is an important basic cause of malnutrition. The very high rates of malnutrition and low birthweight throughout much of South Asia are linked to such factors as women's poor access to education and their low levels of participation in paid employment" *(Manuliak,* 1999). UNICEF came to the same conclusion a year earlier as well *(UNICEF,* 1998), despite the overwhelming evidence that basic education and access to health helps reduce fertility rates dramatically and thus ease the hunger problem *(Sen,* 1999).
- Women are denied any voice in decision making. Democracy, as a way of life, is key to ending hunger *(Sen,* 1997). The faux pass in the Indian Parliament over the Reservation Bill for Women in the Lok Sabha is just one example of how systemically we are inclined to see that women are denied a voice in decision making.
- Laws that provide for women's equality are not implemented.
- Violence against women is rampant in all societies. Subjugating women through violence and threat to violence militates against ending hunger. Crimes against women prevent girls from going to schools and violence against girl children prevents them from getting health care. Thus, women cannot access basic health and primary education, which are fundamental to ending hunger.

- Attitudes, beliefs and traditions, which obstruct women's social, economic and political progress, bar them from being full participants in society.

Thus, the answer to the problem of hunger is empowerment of women. And this requires the transformation of social conditions that prevent women from being full participants in society. "Fundamentally, what needs to be understood is that the women's struggle is not only a struggle to transform the position of women in society, it is a struggle to transform society itself" *(Holmes,* 2000).

That women–centred development is critical to solve the problem of hunger is not debatable. It tells us what has to be done. But the "how" of it has not been spelt out clearly. In order to achieve what the Gender Approach to Hunger prescribes for tackling hunger, it is necessary to have a broad and systematic strategy to deal with the problems at hand. Whether attempting at transforming the position of women in society or of transforming society itself, so that the forces that inhibit women from participating in solving the hunger problem, strategies that empower women and strategies that transform society have to be worked upon. The elements of such strategies have been discussed in the Chapter on Theory of Hunger elsewhere in this book.

The Social Approach to Hunger

A. Depth of understanding: Analyses of hunger for designing and implementing public action and public policy can best be undertaken on the foundation of a deep understanding of the hunger as a problem confronting society. While some of the simpler approaches discussed above commend themselves to formulating short term and very often uni-directional course of action, but these actions do not necessarily lead to lasting solutions. A deeper analysis than what is commended by the simpler approaches is necessary for a lasting solution. It is true that a deeper analysis will increase the complexity of the analysis. We are often reminded that too much analysis leads to paralysis. Nevertheless, the fact remains that a deeper analysis will also generate a larger number of options for long-term solutions.

It is possible to distinguish four general levels of depth of analysis *(Ljunqvist et. al.* 1980), viz., symptoms or signs, immediate causes, underlying causes and basic causes. Basic causes themselves can take many forms and are of different kinds. Generally, the immediate causes and the symptoms and signs attract far more public and media attention than the underlying or basic causes. This is, in part because the symptoms or signs are visible, immediate and dramatic, and in part because the public outcry is directed towards dealing with the immediate causes than meeting the underlying or basic causes of hunger. For instance, environmentalists and civil society actors were crying hoarse over mismanagement of water resources in Rajasthan, Orissa, Gujarat and Andhra Pradesh in India, and its dire consequences. It attracted scant notice, if at all, but now that these States are in the grip of drought and famine leading to dying cattle and migrating emaciated humans, both print and electronic media have taken up the cudgels with religious ferocity. Additionally, in a democracy like ours, the political compulsions of dealing with the symptoms and immediate causes of hunger bring into play state action fairly swiftly (their effectiveness notwithstanding). However, to tackle hunger on a comprehensive scale, it is important to deal with all of the causes and not symptoms only. It would be best to first describe, in brief, the different kinds of causes and then deal with the basic causes in greater detail.

A.1 Symptoms or signs: Symptoms are the direct observable manifestations of hunger in a society. They could be emaciated beggars on the streets, they could be grossly undernourished children with bulging bellies or they could be anemic pregnant women. Symptoms could also be low ponderal index at birth or they could be large scale migration of human beings in search of food and employment (irrespective of whether these expectations are met or not), such as the ones we see from Eastern Orissa or what is called the KBK Area (Koraput, Bolangir and Kalahandi Area) of Orissa. These are mainly deficiency symptoms and are usually not specific and may have been the result of a number of different causes, including lack of access to food, nutrient deficiencies or diseases in combination with other factors. Planning any policy and developmental interventions on an assessment of these symptoms only would yield unsatisfactory result. Because these symptoms are so visible and the spread of the electronic media make them so horrendous right inside everyone's home, there usually is public outcry to tackle these first. In a democracy like India, policy planners, often guided by political correctness, deal with these symptoms more aggressively than the basic causes. The underlying causes and the basic ones as well do not, in the process, get the consideration that they deserve.

The symptoms themselves, however, taken one with the other, indicate that a problem of hunger exists, they should be taken as barometers of a hunger situation. They are certainly warnings of an impending crisis. In that perspective identifying the symptoms has to be taken as the first step towards a comprehensive attack on hunger for guaranteeing right to food.

A.2 Proximate causes: The causes of hunger are diverse. There is no one undifferentiated cause for hunger. Causes of hunger are usually of three types—the *proximate* causes, the *underlying* causes and the *basic* causes. The proximate causes of hunger are inadequate intake of food, inadequate intake of calories and consequent inadequate nutrition and sudden onset of diseases *(Call and Levison,* 1973) like Cholera, Malaria and Dengue Fever, diseases which are common in India. The interaction amongst these factors *inter se* is important and well known *(Gordon* 1976) and the interaction of these factors on the one hand with other factors such as inadequate economic and physical access to health facilities, inadequate supply of drinking water and poor (read absence of) sanitation, have deepening effect on hunger and food insecurity. Thus, interventions for elimination of hunger based on an understanding of only the proximate causes can be misleading. For instance, interventions for elimination of hunger, based on an understanding that there is a shortage of food supply, may result in operationalising a Public Distribution System (PDS) or in opening the floodgate of food aid drowning the food deficient areas. But the fundamental reasons why the area is food deficient will remain unattended. If it is detected that hunger is caused by the outbreak of a particular disease, there could be rapid action or tasks force set up to deal with it. The crash programmes undertaken to deal with Malaria in 1995 in Rajasthan and Assam are examples in point. But the root cause leading to the outbreak of the diseases leading to hunger will remain in hybernation. While interventions designed in the light of the proximate causes may be important to provide immediate relief to the hungry, they do not give the lasting solution for guaranteeing right to food.

However, this in no way diminishes the importance of knowing the proximate causes. If patterns of food consumption, nutrition intake and onset of diseases are mapped out, the picture of hunger becomes clearer. It is possible to design several measures that can improve food and nutritional intake and augment promotive, preventive and curative health care for a long term solution.

A.3 Underlying causes: The underlying causes of inadequate intake of food, nutrition and affliction of diseases are many and complex *(Gravioto,* 1970; *Dandekar and Rath,* 1971; *George,* 1976; *Sen,* 1981 and 1990; *Planning Commission,* 1993). But most of the factors are a result of unequal and inadequate access to, for example, goods, services and other resources such as food, housing, basic education, potable water and primary health care, among individuals or groups of individuals. The production, distribution and consumption of all these goods and services are determined by the socio-economic structure of the society, including its political and ideological superstructure.

A.4 Basic causes: There are several contradictions and the interrelationships in society that have bearing on hunger through development of a society. The contradictions and interrelationships within the economy *inter se,* between the economy and between the economy and the political as well as ideological superstructure are the ultimate determinants of the development of a society. The basic causes explain how the potential resources of a given society are mobilized for production of goods and services and how these are distributed. The different categories of causes are shown in Figure 3.3.

To deal with the problem of hunger, it is essential to understand the links between the different levels of causes. We, therefore, now turn to a discussion of the basic causes of hunger.

B. Types of basic causes: The basic causes could be historical, ecological, technological, economic, ideological, cultural and political. We will elaborate them briefly on these.

B.1 Historical causes: There is a formidable literature demonstrating that imperialism, colonialism, neo-colonialism, slavery, exploitative intermediation, division of labour, laws of inheritance, iniquitous intra-familial distribution of power, religion, wars, technology, etc. all have their impact in causing and perpetuating hunger. For instance, the Zamindari, Mahalwari and Jagirdari Systems of land tenure, established by the Colonial British power in India in the 19th century, have made significant contributions towards initiating the processes and structures that have caused and perpetuated hunger for a long time thereafter. Similarly, the laws of inheritance denying women a share in inherited property of her father are distressing and do cause destitution and hunger *(Agarwal,* 1994). The historically iniquitous distribution of power within households, wherein the women eat last, least and after all others have eaten, leaves women members of the household hungry within households, even if the household *per se* may not be in the grip of hunger *(Mukherjee,* 1999). Similarly for the other components of the historical causes of hunger. These causes can be understood by analysing the socio-economic milieu in terms of the types of basic causes detailed in sections B.2 to B.5 below.

B.2 Ecological and technological causes: All our societies and economies are endowed with near unique sets of natural resources, climatic conditions, soil fertility, knowledge and technical knowhow. These operate on the problem of hunger through the technical and material conditions of production (potential resources). For example, in the deserts of Western Rajasthan, the technology of food production is dependent heavily upon water stored by harvesting every drop of scant rainfall that they receive and not on either rainwater per se or on surface water, for there are very little of these. The technology for storing food and the kinds of food stored are also very different in that part of the country from what people generally find in the rain-rich areas of Assam, West Bengal and Bihar. The dependence on food gathered, hunted and collected from CPRs/micro-environments for tackling hunger in the arid and semi-arid areas of India *(Jodha,*1991) and in tribal areas of West Bengal, Bihar and Orissa as also the technology for processing such food, *(Beck,* 1994) are unique. These have to be taken into consideration in any approach to understanding and tackling hunger.

B.3 Economic causes: Property relations, ownership of or access to means of production, division of labour, power-status structure, exploitative inter-mediation, etc. operate on hunger through the social conditions of production (economic structure of a society). The system of money lending in rural areas throughout India best illustrates the case of exploitative intermediation. It is not denied that these institutions of money lenders play an important role in our society in the delivery of much needed credit and in time, but the rates of interest, formal and informal, that they charge are killing and the process which they set in motion to disposes poor debtor's assets, demeaning *(Jazairy,*1992). The system, where ownership of land is concentrated only in a few hands who grow food through leasing out their landholdings to *tenants-at-will*, creates an environment wherein investment for long term improvement in land is an exception, particularly so where distribution of produce of land on a fair basis is not possible. In such conditions it is reasonable to expect that hunger is lurking round the corner.

B.4 Ideological and cultural causes: Ideology, religion, opinions, customs, usages, practices, values, mores, beliefs habits, traditional laws, etc. all have been long associated with causing or otherwise perpetuating hunger. These ideological and cultural causes are related to hunger through the superstructure of a society. Let us take the case of religion to illustrate how it relates to hunger. Religious practices in some religions and sects prohibit consumption of meat or poultry. People belonging to such religion will exclude, in the light of their faith, these items from their consumption basket and include only a vegetarian diet. In countries like India, where agriculture depends on rainfall, a failure of monsoons would lead to a fall in availability of vegetarian food. Those dependant on vegetarian diet for their sustenance would suffer hunger, even when meat and poultry products go abegging. In traditional societies, it is considered dishonourable if women step out to work for others. Women are thus disempowered and made to suffer the "unfreedom" of choosing their food and the capacity to access food *(Sen,* 1999).

B.5 Political causes: The prevailing power structure, military and police, law and the courts, democratic rights, fiscal policy, free press, employment policy, organization, etc., mainly related to the structure and function of the state, have critical roles in perpetuating or eliminating hunger, as the case may be. Wars always take away resources, which could be used to feed people or produce more food. Democracy, multi-party politics and elections at regular intervals provide political incentives to Governments to act responsibly in preventing hunger, for governments otherwise would stand exposed by the opposition and both the print and electronic media, which could spell disaster in returning to power the next time around. Lack of democracy leads to hunger, as is exemplified by the fact that democratic countries rarely face famines, as we have discussed earlier.

The role of the fifth estate is not merely to act as a watchdog but also to act as a channel of communication and transmitting information about the dangers of potential hunger and details of impending hunger. It has been our experience that when a calamity like drought and famine strikes, lack of information acts like a double barrel gun. On one hand, it leads to wild rumours that exacerbate the hardships people face, by such events as speculative hoarding, and on the other, those responsible for mitigating hunger, in the absence of information, do not respond as fast as they could have, if they had the information. If the free flow of information that the fifth estate facilitates and which has traditionally played a very important part in preventing further hardships and tackling hunger, is disrupted or non-existent, dealing with hunger and food insecurity becomes so much more difficult.

Employment policy has similarly its part to play: where employment creation through newer investment in industry, trade and business is hamstrung by a myriad of licenses, approvals and controls, employment is not created faster, giving people lesser power to access food. It increases the "unfreedom" of people to choose the food they wish to consume. Worse still when programmes for employment generation are designed and implemented, women are generally invisible. And where "projects are implemented specifically for women, they are most often formulated from limited, stereotypical and essentialist notions of feminity" (*Beneria* and *Bisnath,* 1996). Hunger ensues.

B.6 Natural causes: Nature plays a crucial role in preventing and causing hunger, particularly in the context of an economy dependent on nature for food production. Droughts, floods, earthquakes, landslides, hailstorm, frost, fog and thunder and indeed any form of natural disaster can cause hunger. For the last nine years in a row India had a fairly good series of monsoons and barring a few aberrations (such as the conditions in Koraput, Bolangir and Kalahandi Districts of Orissa) there has been no famine and acute shortage of food to which people have no economic and physical access in the country. But in 2000, with the onset of summer as surface water has started vanishing and ground water tables falling due to poor rainfall, at least five states are in the grip of near famine situation: Gujarat, Rajasthan, Orissa, Andhra Pradesh and some parts of Maharastra. Millions are in the grip of hunger.

C. Level of incidence of the causes: The third dimension to be considered is the level of society at which the causes of the problems exist. Let us take an example of inadequate access to food by an individual leading to hunger as caused by maldistribution of food, an underlying cause. The maldistribution of food may exist at many different levels. There are at least five levels at which maldistribution of food and hence hunger may exist. These are: (i) at the *international* level, i.e., maldistribution of food among countries, evidenced by wastage and pomp in North and starvation and death in the horns of Africa (see Box 3.5); (ii) at the *national* level, i.e., maldistribution of food among regions/areas of a country, evidenced by plenty and plethora in Punjab and Haryana on the one hand, and near famines and forced migration of the rural people from Bolangir in Orissa and Western Rajasthan, every year, on the other hand; (iii) at the *area* level, i.e., maldistribution of food among villages (or localities of urban areas); (iv) at the *village* (local) level, i.e., maldistribution of food among households *inter se*; such as more food being available in Upper Caste Muhalla (Wards) and hunger in Scheduled Caste Muhalla of village Tikri, Kashi Vidya Peeth Block, Varanasi District *(Mukherjee,* 1999) and (v) finally, at the *household* ievel, i.e., maldistribution of food among household members particularly women and girl children, on which volumes have been documented and written.

Box 3.5
Who Consumes What?

Wealthy people in the industrial countries make about one-fifth of world's population, yet they consume 45 per cent of all meat and fish, while the poorest fifth consume 5 per cent. They account for 86 per cent of total private consumption expenditure

Human Development Report, 1998.

The incidence of hunger is always on the individuals, where the symptoms manifest. We see emaciated men, we see anemic pregnant women, we notice men struggling to get out of the drought affected districts of Rajasthan like Jodhpur *(Sinha,* 2000). We see on our Television sets pictures of famished children in Ethiopia, beamed by BBC World Service in its BBC World News, throughout the week preceding the Easter-week of 2000. We cannot see famished villages or countries, though we may see famished groups of individuals. We don't see pictures of "anemic regions", though we see parched land and burnt out vegetation. But the causes of hunger can be located at different levels. Causes that lead to hunger, whether underlying or basic, may work at any, or all, of the five levels, either severally or jointly. Elimination of symptoms of hunger, that manifest in individuals and many of which are visually perceivable, requires elimination of hunger itself. This warrants interventions at those levels where the causes are situated. If hunger is perpetrated due to working of international forces, such as a free trade regime without quantitative restrictions and with zero tariff barriers, (a prospect faced by our milk producers), interventions may have to be make at the WTO level, for instance, or at the level of other international forums *(Outlook,* 2000). There could also be a need to deal with issues at the national level concurrently such as reduction in budget deficit of the government (by reducing wasteful expenditure) to prevent macro-economic instability, which eats into the capacity of the people, particularly the non-food producers, to access food. This is what makes a strong case for a total approach. Such an approach will be complex but a complex problem of hunger does not have a simple solution.

III. Some Conclusions

Hunger manifests itself at the individual or household level as inability to access food, undernourishment, malnourishment, nutrient deficiency, metabolic disorders, loss of weight, apathy, entitlement failure, etc. and even loss of dignity as in the case of a beggar, illustrated by Dasgupta *(Dasgupta,* 1997). Hunger thus is a symptom of a complex economic and social disorder, where the causes are to be traced via immediate and underlying causes to the basic causes. The basic causes can only be understood in relation to the specific historical, ecological, economic, cultural, and political contexts in which the hungry people, their economy and society are situated. The basic causes have to be contextualised and categorized according to the foregoing dimensions, to arrive at an appropriate response to deal with it.

A total or integrated response to hunger problem can be based on a Jonsson's Matrix of Levels and Kinds of Causes, an illustrative sample of what is possible is shown in Table 3.4. The historical cause can of course be any combination of the causes mentioned in the columns for ecology, economy, politics, etc. But the matrix helps to systematise our thinking and marshalling of facts for interpretation of all possible types of causes, where each type is related to the socio-economic structure of the society. One can also combine the dimension of the depth of the analysis and the dimension of the level of the society.

As we mentioned earlier, the *symptoms* of the problem of hunger manifest themselves in different ways at different levels. At the individual and household levels the manifestation of hunger is most obvious, and in most cases visually apparent. In case of a village or of an area above the village, such manifestations may not be so obvious and hence other indicators have to be used to gauge hunger. For instance, at the village level anthropometric variations or poderal index may be easier to observe whether the village suffers hunger, apart from using participatory methods to determine the presence or otherwise of hunger such as the ones used in Chapters 4 to 7 in this book. At the national level the age-specific mortality rate or the extent of anemia prevalent in pregnant women may be the more valid parameter reflecting hunger. The same is true with the ***underlying causes***. Inadequate intake of food at the household level may be a manifestations of low food availability at the household level, lack of extension/education services at the village level, or inadequate production of agricultural output at the national level. In Table 3.3 an example of the different manifestations of symptoms and the immediate, underlying and basic causes of hunger at different levels of a society are shown. The Table should serve merely as an example of this approach. With the matrix of some methods of identifying hunger at different levels of society shown in Table 3.4, it should be possible to identify the most valid and appropriate methods by which the problem of hunger may be dealt with.

If we now compare the economic theory of hunger discussed in Chapter 2 and the Social and other theories of hunger in this chapter, several important elements come out. In both the economic theory and social theory of hunger, its complexity is well recognised. In consequence whether one is approaching hunger from the social perspective or the economic perspective, an integrated, as opposed to a "mono-directional" approach, is commended. The problem of hunger is too complex to be treated on one single plane. The need to look at hunger at different levels is brought forth and, therefore, a differentiated approach is warranted to eradicate hunger from different levels, starting from the individual to the national level. This foreshadows the fact that if hunger is to be attacked, and food security ensured at different levels, starting from the individual (especially the women and girl children), then people have to play a crucial role.

Finally, in whatever theory we are seeking answers, the role of democracy and media in tackling food insecurity comes out in bold relief. There is need to vigorously strengthen democracy and democratic values as ways of life, from the household to the national level to guarantee a right to food. This is not only necessary for creating political incentives for political executives in power to prevent hunger but also as a means to empower people to take decisions regarding their lives and bring people at the centre-stage of "public action", to see none goes hungry. And similarly, there is the need to strengthen media as a watchdog and as a source of vital information. Information to the public and to those, who are entrusted with the task of creating an environment that will enable people to eliminate hunger, hold critical places in any scheme to ensure food security at all levels, particularly at the household levels.

Box 3.6
Achieving Food Security: Whose Responsibility?

"Who is responsible for food security?
I would imagine that many of you ...would probably say that Government is responsible. ....
I am personally of the view that Government's responsibility for food security is both less than we think, more than it actually is, and certainly different than the way it is now met.
Food is either grown, or grown and processed in one way or the other, or is grown, then fed to animals or poultry, who produce eggs, milk, meat and what have you. To grow crops we require land, water, seed or other planting material, warmth to some degree. If soil is poor, we have to add nutrients—either natural or manufactured. Then there is the need for money to buy some of the ingredients. Last, but not least, is "knowledgeable care"....... the one ingredient that helps to ensure that all the others are brought together in a way that produces the desired result. That is the role of the farmer. And as far as I am aware, Government isn't a farmer.
So who then is responsible for food security.....? Ultimately there can be only one answer: our farmers, the women and men who live in our rural areas and who produce food, fibre and forest products that we use.

V. Kurien, "*India's best-known Milkman*"
7th March 2000, at Vigyan Bhawan, New-Delhi. .

Table 3.2 A Suggested List of Types of Basic Causes of Hunger at Different Levels of Society

Level	Historical Causes	Ecological/ Technological Causes	Economic Causes	Political Causes	Ideological and Cultural Causes
Inter-national	Ecology/ Techno-logy. Ideology & culture. Economy.	Natural Resources. Soil fertility and climatic conditions. Technology.	Imperialism and Neocolo-nialism. Trading Laws.	Wars and threats of war. Poli-tical orga-nization. Government	Ideology. Religion. National ethics. National laws.

Level	Historical Causes	Ecological/ Technological Causes	Economic Causes	Political Causes	Ideological and Cultural Causes
	Folitics.	Knowledge Base.	International division of labour. Exploitative intermediation.	Organization. Existence of democracy	
National	Ecology/ Technology. Ideology. Culture. Economy. Politics.	Natural Resources Soil and Climate Technology Knowledge and wisdom	Ownership of or access to the means of production. Division of labour. Power structure. Centre-periphery relationships. (exploitation)	Political organization. Government organization. Degree of Democracy. Fiscal policy. Power structure.	Ideology. Religion. Beliefs. Traditional laws.
Region	Ecology/ Technology. Ideology. Culture. Economy. Politics.	Natural Resources Base. Soil fertility and Climatic Conditions. Technology Knowledge and wisdom	Ownership of or access to the means of production. Division of labour-power-Status structure. Centre-periphery relationships. (exploitation)	Political organization. Government organization. Degree of Democracy. Fiscal policy. Power structure.	Religion. Beliefs. Traditional laws.

Level	Historical Causes	Ecological/ Technological Causes	Economic Causes	Political Causes	Ideological and Cultural Causes
Vill-age	Ecology/ Techno-logy. Ideology. Culture. Economy. Politics.	Knowledge and wisdom.	Ownership of or access to the means of produc-tion. Division of labour. Power structure. (exploita-tion)	Political organization. Government organization Level of democratis ation. Fiscal policy. Power structure.	Religion. Beliefs. Traditional laws.
House Hold	Ecology/ Techno-logy. Ideology. Culture. Economy. Politics.		Division of labour	Fiscal policy. Power structure.	Religion. Beliefs. Traditional Laws. Habits, practice and custom.

Source: Same as Table 3.1.

Table 3.3 Some Symptoms and Causes of Hunger at Different Levels of Society

Level	Symptoms	Immediate Causes	Underlying Causes	Basic Causes
Natio-nal	High level of in-fant unde-nutrition as the cause of deaths.	Disease pattern. Food intake pattern.	Accessibility of health services, drinking water and education services. Produc-tion of fertilizers.	Imperialism & neo-colonialism. Power structure. Political organization. Soil and climate Technology. Historical Causes.

Level	Symptoms	Immediate Causes	Underlying Causes	Basic Causes
Area	Low weight/age, etc. Low birth weights High infant mortality Malnutrition as the cause of deaths	Disease pattern Food intake pattern	Accessibility of health services Water and education services	Divisional of labour Exploitation Fiscal policy Political organization Soil and climate Historical Causes
Village	Low weight/age, etc. Clinical signs of nutrient deficiency Low birth weights High infant mortality	Disease pattern Food intake pattern	Accessibility of health services Water and education services	Division of labour Exploitation Fiscal Policy Political organization Knowledge & wisdom Historical causes
House-hold	Clinical Signs of nutrient deficiency Metabolic disorders Weight loss Apathy, etc.	Disease pattern Food intake pattern	Accessibility of health services, Sanitary conditions, Educational, Access to water	Division of labour, Fiscal policy, Power structure, Religion Habits, Traditional laws

Source: Same as Table 3.1

Table 3.4 Some Methods of Identifying Causes of Hunger at Different Levels of Society

Level	Symptoms	Immediate Causes	Underlying Causes	Basic Causes
National	Mortality data Birth weights Hospital records.	Health statistics. Food balance sheets	Distribution of health institutions, health workers, schools, etc. Food distribution pattern Income distribution, etc.	Import/export pattern, Corruption, Political oppression, Technology, Land ownership.
Area	Age-specific mortality Birth weights Hospital records	Health statistics Food balance sheets Household budget surveys	Distribution of health institutions, health workers, schools, etc. Food distribution pattern Income distribution, etc.	Land ownership, Social stratification, Soil quality, Rainfall.
Village	Clinical and biochemical assessment Anthropometry	Clinical screening for disease Rapid diet evaluations Food production and sales	Distance to health centre, water, etc. Food distribution pattern Income distribution, etc.	Land ownership, Social stratification, Educational level,
Household	Clinical examination for deficiency signs Biochemical assessments	Clinical examination for disease Individual diet examination for dietary intake	Distance to health centre, water etc. Income Food production	Time budget for mothers, Accessibility to land, Employment, taxes, Food habits, Education.

Source: Ljungqvist et al. (1980)

Endnotes

1. Sub-sections IB, II.1 and II.5 are extensions of Jonsson (1984).
2. Two distinguished early writers in development wrote: *The basic determinants of economic growth are non-economic.*

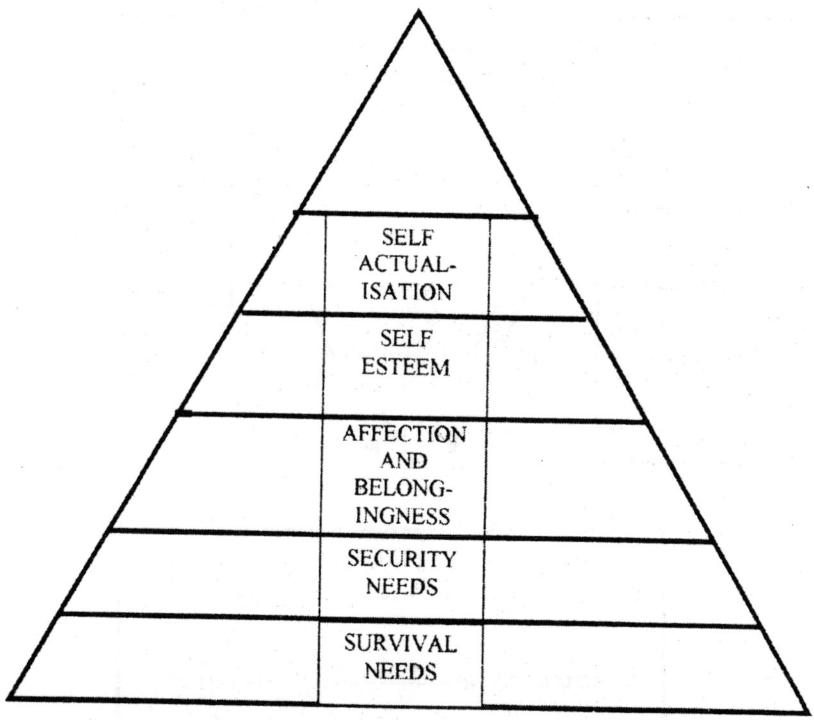

Figure-3.1: Maslow's Hierarchy of Needs

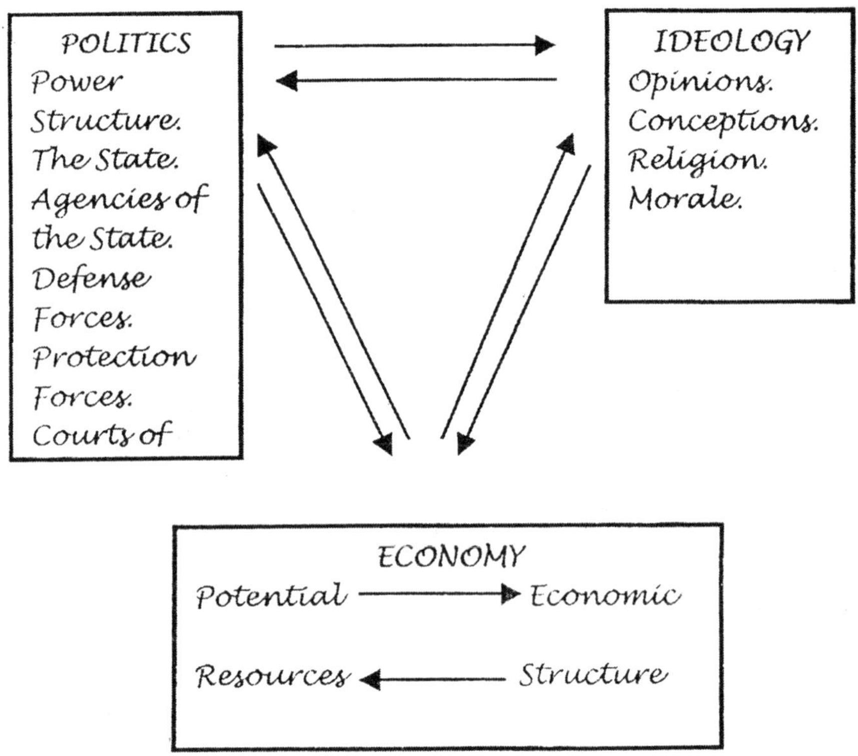

Figure-3.2 : Interaction of the economy, political and ideological infrastructure

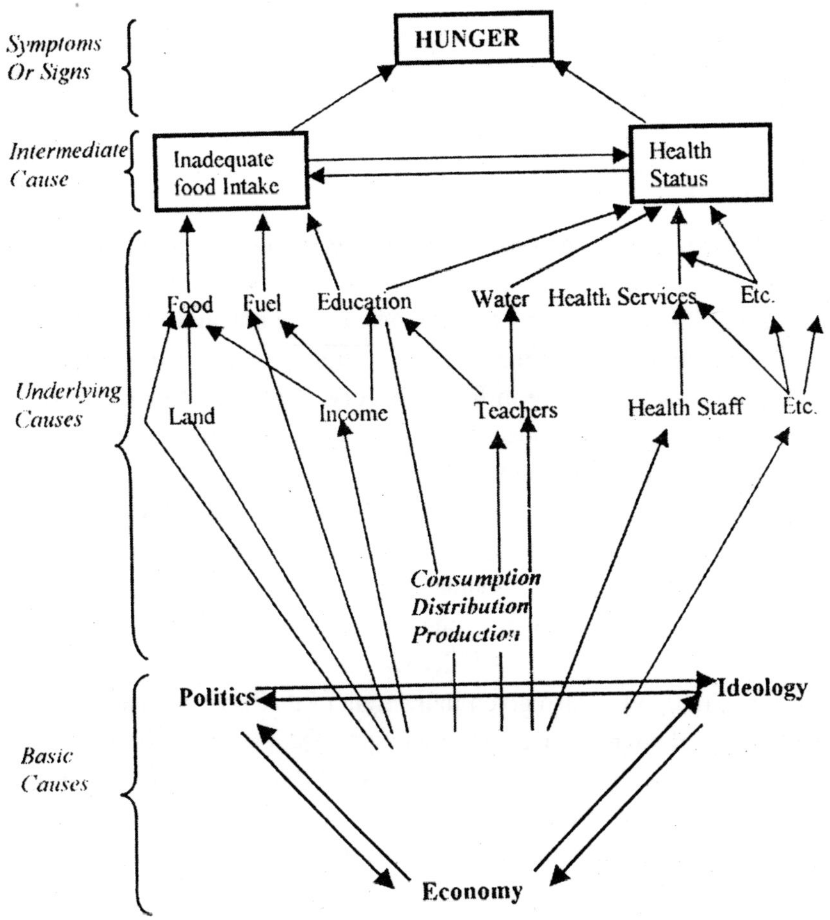

Figure-3.3 : Categories of causes of hunger

4 Community Perspective on Hunger from a Backward State, Village Chandpur, Varanasi

I. Introduction

Chandpur village lies in the district of Varanasi, which is the home of the ancient and holy city of Banaras, known in ancient literature as Kashi, venerated and inhabited by the Hindus, Muslims, Jains and the Buddhists alike. In education, art, culture, religion, trade, crafts and commerce, Varanasi holds a special place in Indian history. It has a commanding view of the mighty Ganges, on whose banks the city of Banaras and the district of Varanasi have thrived for centuries.

Varanasi lies in the eastern part of the State of Uttar Pradesh, known for its role in Indian political history, size (if it were to be a country, it would have been the seventh largest country in the world), richness of culture, history and of course, poverty. It is one of the states which have seen a rise in poverty levels during the last decade (*Sen and Patnaik,* 1997; *Sen* 1996). Uttar Pradesh has also given India eight of its Prime Ministers.

The principal sources of employment and occupation of the people in Varanasi are agriculture, medium and small scale industries, diesel locomotive works of the Indian Railways and a spattering of heavy industries such as the Bharat Heavy Electricals, agro-processing units and agro-based industries.

The following landholding pattern in Varanasi gives an impression of the situation at hand.

Landholding Pattern in Varanasi

Size of Holding	Number of Holdings
Less than 1 hectare	5,52,565 holders
1 to 2 hectares	47,619 holders
2 to 3 hectares	11,608 holders
3 to 5 hectares	7,276 holders
More than 5 hectares	2,627 holders

Thus 89 per cent of the farmers hold 1 hectare or less of land, and 96.5 per cent of the farmers own 2 or less than 2 hectares of land. There are two main cultivating seasons, Kharif and Rabi, with a relatively insignificant winter season.

The total area of Varanasi district is 4035.01 sq. kilometers, having a population of 3,7,82,949. The literacy rate is 65.36 per cent, which is higher than the national average and much higher than the State average of 41.6 per cent. The district is divided into four Blocks, viz., Harhua, Araji Lines, Chirai Gaon and Kashi Vidyapeeth. *Chandpur village*, which is the subject of our study, falls within the territorial jurisdiction of Kashi Vidyapeeth Block.

Kashi Vidyapeeth

Kashi Vidyapeeth consists of around 129 villages of which 122 are inhabited, and they are organised into 13 Panchayats, the smallest unit of governance (Local Self Government). The occupational structure of the inhabitants of the block exhibits an overwhelming preponderance of labourers, agriculturists and agricultural labourers: 49 per cent of the total population is main workers, 14 per cent are cultivators and about 6 per cent are agricultural labourers. Most of the farmers are small and marginal farmers.

Chandpur is a large sized-village situated in Kashi Vidyapeeth Block in the District of Varanasi, which forms part of Eastern Uttar Pradesh. It lies on the north west corner of the Block, situated to the north of the famous Grand Trunk Road connecting Calcutta to Delhi and then to Pathankot (and earlier to Peshawar, now in Pakistan) and to the south of the main Railway trunk route, connecting Calcutta with Delhi. The influence of these major transport systems on the village is significant.

It is also eight kilometers from the holy city of Varanasi and only one km. from the Block Headquarters.

II. General Information

Chandpur has a population of 5332, with 49 per cent females and 51 per cent males. The sex ratio in Chandpur compares favourably with the sex ratios in Uttar Pradesh and India, which are less flattering. The literacy rate is 60 per cent for males and 30 per cent for the females. That is, of the total population of 4700, about 55.5 per cent are literate, which is slightly below the national average, though the state average is 47 per cent. The disaggregated litercay rate for the state is 62 per cent for men and 28 per cent for women. This is somewhat surprising given that the village has a primary school, a co-educational school and two Junior High Schools, one for girls and the other for boys. Being near a major urban centre, the villagers have access to a Post Office, modest healthcare facilities, a Kisan Kendra, State Agricultural Farm and Bank.

The village has several sources of water, including 10 hand pumps, two wells and two pump sets for irrigation. Despite these sources of water, dependence on rain for agriculture seems to be very high.

There are several industrial establishments in and around the village. It has biscuit factories, saree printing firms, confectioneries, Banaras Beeds Factory and the Agra Fan Factory. Some of these firms are not strictly polluting but all cause some disturbance or the other to the social, economic and ecological environment of the village. The Lahartara industrial estate, situated to the east of village with over 100 factories, has considerable influence on the mind set of the villagers, on the ecology, environment and economy of the village.

The village, like many Indian villages, particularly the large ones, is divided into separate hamlets: there are five such Hamlets (called Bastee in local parlance). The distribution of population amongst different caste groups is as follows.

Caste	No. of Families	No. of People
Patel	182	3932
Scheduled Castes	8	150
Harijans	20	250
Yadavs	45	1000
Total	255	5332

In the context of Chandpur, the Patels (the majority population) can be divided into two groups. One, the group of Patels (about 62 per cent) who are engaged in agriculture and vegetable cultivation as their primary means of livelihood, having animal husbandry and wage employment as their secondary means of livelihood. Two, the remaining 38 per cent or so of Patels have wage employment as their primary source of livelihood, and engage themselves in agriculture and casual labour as the secondary sources of income. Villagers belonging to Scheduled Castes have vegetable vending and daily wages as their means of livelihood. Those belonging to the Harijan community work both as daily wage earners and as agricultural labourers. Daily wage earners suffer from instability of wages they receive for most of the time they are not the "price setters"; they are wage takers: they have to work for whatever is on offer. They suffer all the disadvatages of the informal sector (*Mehta, 1997*). The Yadavs are the ones primarily engaged in animal husbandry, mostly bovine wealth.

Farming and livestock rearing, services, daily wage labour, agricultural labourers and in-home activities like saree printing, processing of Rudraksh, making Birdi (local variety cigarettes made of leaves) etc. are the main occupation in the village.

III. The Food Production pattern

Since, irrigation is limited and there is dependence on rains for agriculture, the cropping pattern is guided by the rainfall pattern. During Kharif season, the monsoon months starting from end June, cultivation of paddy is evident. This is followed by maize. Generally, these two crops are grown concurrently on different kinds of land depending on moisture retention:

paddy in low lands which retains a lot more moisture, and maize in uplands that retain less of moisture. During Rabi Season, wheat is cultivated, along with vegetables and green gram/green peas. In both the seasons, there is a mixture of food crops and cash crops, with food crops occupying a larger share of cultivable land.

Only one principal food crop is harvested in each of the two seasons: paddy in Kharif and wheat in Rabi. Except for cauliflower, all other crops/ vegetables (radish, spinach, fenugreek, green grams, green peas, potatoes, brinjals, onion, garlic, lentil) grown are seasonal, which indicates that the inhabitants of Chandpur depend more upon the bounties (or niggardliness!) of nature than on new technology for their output. The villagers are satisfied with one crop per season (Kharif and Rabi) from their agricultural lands, with vegetable production on a limited scale during the intervening winter. Cultivation during the winter season is limited. But while in the 1940s, the 1950s and the 1960s as well, farmers were happy cultivating only during Kharif and Rabi seasons when they ploughed with bullock and the hoe, now with the introduction of tractors they have begun cultivating in the winter as well. The frequency of cultivation has increased, because the farmers explained, it was no longer necessary to rest the animals.

Different crops are grown but the practice of cultivating the same land several times over does not seem to have caught on. This has as much to do with poor state of extension services and incentives to produce more of agricultural crops, as to the fact that alternative means of livelihood elsewhere are available. The nearness of the village to a major urban centre of Varanasi and the industrial estate has helped in the process, which somewhat reduces the importance of agriculture as a source of livelihood.

IV. Changes in Cropping Pattern and Agricultural Practices

The kinds and number of crops grown have been fairly dynamic. Over the years, there have been significant changes. While in the forties, the principal crops were barley, bare, sawa, sugarcane and vegetables, during the fifties wheat, paddy, peas, bengal gram, maize and red gram began to be cultivated, and cultivation of *barley* and *sugarcane* was *discontinued.*

That is, there was a diversification in production, between the 1940s and the 1950s. From the 1960s, this diversification lost its sway and the number of crops being cultivated got reduced to paddy and wheat, besides vegetables. The trend continues till today, through the 1970s and 1980s. The cropping pattern has, therefore, seen substantial changes over the years but has stabilized during the 1990s. The Historical Transect that the group of villagers gave us with Mohan Patel, Rajendra Prasad, Dhanilal, Shyamdayal Patel as Table 4.1 is revealing.

Interestingly, the Historical Transect reveals that two concurrent processes were in operation. One, the *cropping pattern* was changing and two, the *yield* was also changing. If one looks at Table 4.1, the yield increased quite dramatically during the 1960s and then again fell during the 1970s, and continued at that level throughout the 1980s and 1990s. In 1988 there was a sharp drop in yield both for paddy and for wheat. Though the yields in the 1988 were higher than those obtaining in the 1950s, it is a cause for concern, unless one is prepared to treat it as an aberration. This is significant and needs further investigation.

The village has partially mechanized its cultivation. Whereas in the 1940s, 1950s and 1960s, ploughing was predominantly with bullocks and hoe, in the 1970s and thereafter, use of tractor became the norm. As a consequence, the number of animals owned by the farming community has dwindled significantly, which contributed to a reduced need for fodder and hence a negative preference for crops which yielded high percentage of fodder, namely, barley. The use of tractors has also contributed to the noticeable increase in frequency in cultivation. While in the 1940s, land was cultivated only once, during 1950s and 1960s it went up to two: once, during the monsoons and then again during winter. However, after tractors entered the fray the cultivators tilled their land thrice: during Kharif (the monsoons), winter and Rabi (the post-winter season).

Table 4.1 Historical Transect of Main Crops and their Yield in Naipurwa Hamlet, Chandpur Village by Men's Group

Decade	Principal Crops	Yield (Quintal/ acre)
1940s	barley, bare,	04
	sawa,	0.5
	sugarcane,	
	vegetables.	
1950s	wheat,	3.5-4
	paddy,	3.5-4
	peas,	2.4-2.5
	bengal gram,	2.4-2.5
	red gram,	3.5-4
	maize	2.4-2.5
	barley discontinued.	
1960s	wheat,	16-18
	paddy,	16-18
	vegetables.	
1970s	wheat,	10
	paddy,	10-12
	vegetables.	
1980s	wheat,	10
	paddy,	10-12
	vegetables.	
1990s	wheat,	10
	paddy,	10-12
	vegetables.	
1998s	wheat,	10
	paddy,	08
	vegetables.	

Village Analysts: Mohan Patel, Rajendra Prasad, Dhanilal, Shyamdayal Patel.
Facilitator: Ms. Meera Jayaswal.

The substitution of animal power by mechanical power (Tractor) in agriculture has not been uniform all through the period from 1940s to 1990s. Mohan Patel, Rajendra Prasad, Dhanilal Singh and Shyamdayal Patel told us that there had been a gradual and steady increase in the rate of substitution of bullock power by tractor power. Thus, households of Chandpur have reduced their Bovine wealth from 10 pairs in the 1960s to a meagre 1 pair in the 1990s. Villagers of Naipurwa Hamlet, Chandpur village gave us the following Historical Transect at Table 4.2, to summarise the position.

Table 4.2 Historical Transect of Farming Systems and Livestock in Chandpur Village: Men's Group

Serial No.	Decade	Method of Ploughing	Frequency of Cultivation	Kinds of Livestock	No. of Bullocks
1	1940s	Bullock	One	bullock, cow, goat, buffalo.	5-6 pairs per family
2	1950s	Bullock	Two: Winter and Rainy	bullock, cow, goat, buffalo.	7 pairs per family
3	1960s	Bullock	Two: Winter and Rainy	bullock, cow, goat, buffalo.	10 pairs per family
4	1970s	Tractor	Three	bullock, cow, goat, buffalo.	6 pairs per family
5	1980s	Tractor	Three	bullock, cow, goat, buffalo.	2 pairs per family
6	1990s	Tractor	Three	bullock, cow, goat, buffalo.	1 pair per family

Village Analysts: Mohan Patel, Rajendra Prasad, Dhanilal Singh, Shyamdayal Patel.
Facilitator: Ms. Meera Jayaswal. Date: 11.11.99.

V. Why Have the Changes Taken Place?

We are reviewing a period in our economic history, which saw rapid changes in every direction. Changes were many and some with quite far reaching consequences, such as mechanisation of agriculture and the introduction of "new technology", to which we made a brief reference above. A tentative answer to the questions relating to changes in cropping pattern and yield in Chandpur is best provided by Time Line drawn by the senior citizens of Naipurwa Hamlet of Chandpur village which bears repetition here in Table 4.3.

In the 1960s, new variety of seeds came, improved varieties of wheat were introduced, lift irrigation through pump sets and electification of the pump sets commenced. There was a sharp rise in productivity in wheat and paddy as we have seen in Table 4.1 earlier. This sharp rise in productivity in wheat and paddy during the 1960s was clearly due to the introduction of new varieties of seeds as also due to the introduction of pump sets for irrigation. This also marked a significant change in the mind set of the people, depending on the sky for succor. Thus, not only did they resort to improved varieties of wheat and paddy seeds, as opposed to traditional varieties of seeds, but also shifted their dependence from "Raingods" to their own ingenuity of making water available through pump irrigation. The use of chemical fertilizers also started (*Joshi and Bisht,* 1999). However, after the initial spurt in yield due to "new technology" in the 1960s, the yield fell as the chemical composition of the soil changed, no further improved varieties of seed were introduced and the extension work could not keep pace with changing times. The initial spurt during 1960s in much higher yields was lost during 1970s and in the subsequent decades. The use of HYV seeds, chemical fertilisers and pesticides, etc. has adverse consequence which has been noticed in several parts of the country. The adverse impacts of Green Revolution have been called the "Yellowing of the Green Revolution" or classified as the "Violence of the Green Revolution" (*Shiva,* 1991).

Table 4.3 Time Line: Historical Events as Recalled by the Senior Men of Naipurwa Hamlet of Chandpur Village

Decade	Year	Events
1940s	1942	Food in river Baruna; bridge washed away
	1947	India wins Independence
	1947	Single stage coach started from Vitari to Morai
1950s	1950-51	Locust attack
	1959-60	Transportation by truck started.
	1959-60	Birdi making unit started
	1959-60	Reinforced Concrete Construction (RCC) of houses started
1960s	1962	New varieties of seeds introduced
	1964	New wheat variety (RR21) started
	1969	Electric supply started. 2-3 pump sets introduced.
1970s	1972-73	Tractor introduced
	1975	Four new pump sets introduced
	1975	Sardar Ballab Bhai Cross Road (Chaumahani) constructed
	1976	Torrential rain leading to damage of crops (in November-December) which lasted for 7 days
1980s	1981(?)	Rudrax garland making unit started
1990s	1990	School constructed

Village Analysts: Mohan Patel, Rajendra Prasad Singh, Dhanilal, Shamdayal Patel.
Facilitator: Ms. Meera Jayaswal. Date: 12.11.99.

The decision of the farmers to discontinue cultivation of barley and sugarcane was mostly economic. In case of barley the farmers found that the proportion of chaff was very high, which had no use as the number of cattleheads with the farmers had dwindled, culminating in the substitution of draught power by tractor power in 1972. There was also a change in the taste of people: they no longer liked the taste of barley and the new taste of wheat allured the people to make a shift in favour of wheat. As regards sugarcane, the farmers decided generally to discontinue its cultivation because of a large variety of reasons. Firstly, the production cycle is such that land apportioned to sugarcane got occupied throughout the year, disabling the farmers from using the same land for a second or third crop, such as wheat or green grams. Secondly, there is an increase in pest attack. 'Deemak' in local language, or whiteant, infestation has increased resulting in loss of crop yield. And then, since the village is near or on a main road, theft of sugarcane was a common phenomenon, causing substatial losses to sugarcane growers.

It is worth noting that the variety in principal crops grown has come down to three or so, because of major shifts in yields in other crops. The production of jowar has stopped because it has been replaced by a cash crop, namely, cauliflower. Jowar gets ready for harvest in October-November, if it is sown in August, whereas cauliflower seedlings have to be planted in September-October. Since income from growing cauliflower is much higher than what jowar can provide, villagers have opted for the former. This trend has been buttressed by the fact that people no longer like the taste of jowar. Cultivation of lentil (arhar) has been almost abandoned since last 10-12 years because it is highly vulnerable to pest attack and also because the same land on which arhar used to be cultivated competed with wheat as a crop. Given that people have a preference for wheat as a staple food crop, vis-a-vis arhar which is not a staple, arhar got pushed out. This may have adverse effect on nutritional security as well as the palate and variety in the diet of the villagers, but that is another matter to which we shall come later in the study.

If we see the changes in farming in Chandpur over the years, it is clear that agriculture has tended to move from Zero External Input Agriculture (ZEIA) in the 1940s to Low External Input Agriculture (LEIA) in the 1960s. And then, it is now tending towards High External Input Agriculture (HEIA) beginning in the 1980s through the1990s. As farming in the 1980s and 1990s has tended to become more dependent on sourcing from outside Chandpur, farming has tended to use resources that are not always renewable. Internal resources are "inherently renewable and thus have the potential to be used on a 'sustained' basis indefinitely through ecologically sound methods of farming" (*Conway and Barbier,* 1990). For instance, electric pump (as opposed to traditional irrigation systems) to irrigate fields does not use a renewable resource and does not have the potential to be used on a sustained basis.

Since agriculture in Chandpur has tended to become more dependent on external resources, much of the resource is also not provided as a "free good". Internal resources partook the nature of "free goods". Manure from animal dung and agricultural wastes, family labour, seeds saved (often) from the last harvest, irrigation using traditional harvesting structures and traditional irrigation methods, etc. did not require the farmers to spend money. Inter–cropping helped to replenish soil nutrients automatically and helped ward-off pests and insects. External resources, in contrast, have to be purchased from "outside". Chemical fertilisers have to be purchased at a price. Pump sets require capital outlay and entail running cost, even if power is "obtained" for free, formally or infermally. And so on. This implies that the farming households must buy such of these that they use and hence must generate a surplus of production, cash or whatever else of value, to exchange for external resources. And the cost of acquring these resources and their supply channels are rarely controllable by the farming households. For instance, HYV seeds, insecticides, pesticides and irrigation pumpsets are purchased by the farming houesholds of Chandpur at prices dictated by the market. Farmers are, in these matters, almost always price takers. This has atleast three cost implications in terms of *open costs, hidden costs* and *real costs*.

The tendency in Chandpur to make agriculture move from ZEIA to LEIA and eventually to HEIA, has shifted agriculture towards a high *open* cost activity because the farmer has to buy more of the inputs than what they were required under LEIA. There is little of the external resources required which is free of charge. Thus the cost of farming operation is seen as gradually going up so much so that it has made sustainability of agriculture doubtful.

Many of the traditional activities were not only processes which involved more of free goods but also acted as employment creating systems, particularly for women. Weeding is an example in point. Deweeding not only provides women with employment but it also helps them gather fodder for their cows and buffaloes for free and this helps them make savings, howsoever small, from buying feed for their animals. If farmers in Chandpur start using weedicides, it will not only take away the employment opportunities from women but also force them to buy fodder from their scarce resources for their animals. From these perspectives, using chemicals for deweeding is against food security, as it cuts into economic access to food.

The transition from ZEIA to HEIA has also made a noticeable impact on the *hidden* cost of operation. The increase in fossil fuel use to keep outputs high also means more energy consumption. Shift from ZEIA to HEIA has led to substitution of manual labour and animal power by tractors and pump sets (either diesel or electric) that we saw, which implies that external energy sources have substituted energy sources found in the household and the community. All this along with the tendency to increasingly use chemical fertilisers, which is mostly NKP, agriculture has become more energy intensive in Chandpur than before. We have no estimates of how much has been the increase in the total energy input to agriculture due to the use of fertilisers (NKP), pump sets and tractors in Chandpur. However, for India as a whole there is one estimate that 10-20 per cent increase in yields following mechanisation, costs an additional 43-260 per cent more in energy consumption.

In high external input agriculture entails a lot of *real costs*. Even where there is no direct monetary outgoing to acquire a resource, there may be real cost incurred by the farming household. The most obvious examples, of real costs, are time expended in obtaining seeds and other inputs from local distributors in Varanasi or Block headquarters, time expended in fetching diesel for pump sets (in case the pump sets are not electricity operated), chasing the State Electricity Board employees for various reasons and loss of crops when any of the inputs is either not available or not available in time.

VI. Changes in Yield of Crops.

If we look at what villagers like Mohan Patel, Rajendra Prasad Singh, Dhanilal and Shamdayal Patel of Naipurwa Basti had to say as at Table 4.1, it would be apparent that there is a historical trend. From column 3 of the Historical Transect, it seems that productivity was quite modest in the 1950s and then came in the 1960s, the era of improved variety of seeds, use of chemical fertilizers and irrigation water. In the 1960s, yield per acre of wheat jumped from an estimated 4 quintal per acre to 16 quintal per acre. Similar is the case with paddy. The yield in case of vegetables also increased quite dramatically in the period under review but how much from the earlier base is not clear. After the initial jump in yield for wheat, paddy and vegetables in the

1960s, the yield showed considerable decline in the 1970s: yield for wheat per acre came down to 10 quintal per acre, and yield per acre of paddy came down to 10-12 quintal per acre. Thereafter, the yield seems to have stabilized as a plateau at the 1970s level, barring that in the year of investigation, 1998, when yield of paddy had declined further due to bad weather. This decline in 1998 has to be treated as an one-off aberration for the present. If one were to draw a graph of the yield of Chandpur, the trend is of an inverted 'V', with a longish flat portion attached to the right hand segment of V.

If we look at what villagers of Patel Basti told Ms. Sunita Bist and Hema Joshi, as at Table 4.4, we get some idea of yield in Patel Basti which is more or less in the same vein as trends in yield noticed in Naipurwa Basti depicted in Table 4.1. In Patel Basti though we have no timeline data, yet the yield reached its peak in the 1960s, and then in 1998 it shows a marked decline. For instance from an yield of 37.5 quintals of wheat per acre, the yield fell to 12 quintal per acre. The story is the same for maize and green peas and for all other crops that continued to be cultivated in 1998.

Table 4.4 Cropped Area and Yield in Patel Basti of Village Chandpur

Crop	1960 Area Under Cultivation (Bigha)	1960 Yield Per Acre in Quintals	1998 Area Under Cultivation (Bigha)	1998 Yield Per Acre in Quintals
Wheat	10	37.5	25.0	12.0
Barley	25	12.0	-	-
Sugarcane	20	600.0	-	-
Green Gram	5	12.0	-	-
Green Peas	15	13.5	0.05	1.5
Paddy	10	6.0	15.0	15.0
Jowar	20	3.0	5.0	1.5
Arhar(Lentil)	10	6.0	0.5	3.0
Maize	10	18.0	1.00	9.0

Source: Primary Data collected by Ms. Hema Joshi and Ms. Sunita Bisht as reported in *Report on Impact of Air Pollution on Agriculture In Urban and Peri-Urban Areas*, NIUA, New-Delhi, 1999.

VII. Cultivation Processes

The cultivation process is different for the two main seasons. For Kharif, the principal crop is paddy with which we shall deal in a bit of detail.

- The process starts in *May-June* every year. A small piece of land (called *Beehingardhi)* is chosen as a nursery in which paddy seedlings are grown. Farmers generally grow their own seedlings.
- In *June-July* once the monsoons set in, cultivation starts and by and large the farmers concentrate solely on paddy. It is a multiple step operation. First the fields are ploughed, usually twice or thrice. Farmers have found that yields are better in fields which are repeatedly ploughed. Then the lumps of earth that ploughing yields are broken down, called "Karha". This is followed by "Kurhol" for puddling. Once this is completed, the paddy seedlings are uprooted from the "Beehengardi" and transplanted on to the fields. The ridges of all the fields are repaired. The first dose of fertilizers and/or some manure is applied. As a secondary activity, the farmers plant brinjal, tomato, bottlegoud, pumpkin and "Seeam", a kind of beans, mostly in kitchen gardens.
- In *August and September* deweeding becomes necessary, usually more than once depending on the need. These are the months most appropriate for the second/third doses of fertilizers and limited amount of manure, after deweeding is completed, depending upon the capacity of the farmers to bear the expenses.
- During *October-November,* we have the big harvesting season. paddy is harvested and post harvest operations like threshing, winnowing, dehusking and pounding follows.
- Once the harvesting of paddy ends, green grams are sown in *October-November*. Now is the time for the farmers to sow potato, radish and cauliflower.
- During *November-December*, potato fields are tilled and readied for sowing vegetables. Cauliflower seedlings are transplanted and radish is harvested. This is the period when early variety wheat is

sown. A moderate quantity of green peas is also sown and seedlings of onion are planted. Generally farmers procure onion seedlings from outside their farms.

- *December-January* are the months when attention is concentrated on wheat just as undivided attention is given to paddy cultivation during June-August. The wheat fields are tilled once again, deweeding is carried out and fertilizers are applied. Fields are irrigated.
- During *January-February*, a second round of irrigation is applied to the *early-variety* wheat. This is also the time when *late-variety* wheat is sown. The second dose of fertilizer is applied to *early-variety* wheat fields. Green peas, sown in the months of November-December, are now harvested. The first harvest of potatoes (sown in *October-November)* is reaped.
- *February-March* is the time for the third round of irrigation to be provided to the *early-variety* wheat. In case flowering starts, another round of fertilizer is applied. A second round of green peas is harvested. Irrigation is applied to onion fields.
- *March-April* is again harvesting season. Wheat is harvested. Onion and garlic are harvested. Green gram is also harvested.

During all these months, some minor vegetables are also grown. Since they are very small in quantity, no significance is attached to them, except that such crops are for sale in the market and not for self-consumption at the household level. The cultivation process is involved for paddy and wheat cultivation, requiring tilling, weeding, applying irrigation and fertilizers and a lot of incidental activities in keeping the fields intact and protecting the crops from damage due to animal and human trespassing.

There is no significant use of herbicides, insecticides or pesticides. While deweeding is done to obviate the need for use of herbicide, no apparent steps are taken to take care of the problems of either pests or insects, except for minor applications of Gamaxine *(sic)* and Dalidal *(sic).* The practice of soil testing is non-existent and there is no technical way of deciding both on the quantum and kind of chemical fertilizers that need to be used for different crops in the different fields during different seasons.

Since the number of animals has dwindled over the last few years, availability and hence application of manure from animal dung and compost are limited. This could possibly have led to an imbalance in the chemical composition of land leading to a fall in yield during the 1980s and 1990s, after the initial spurt in the 1960s. This requires further investigation. Though improved varieties of seeds have been introduced, the agricultural processes remain the traditional ones, except for the substitution of animal power by mechanical power in ploughing the agricultural lands, limited use of pumps for irrigation and the beginning of the use of chemical fertilisers.

VIII. Agricultural Inputs and the Economics of the Input

From the cultivation process discussed above the inputs into agriculture sought by the farmers of Chandpur can be easily deduced. Clearly, the inputs would come in the nature of "public" good or "free" good, such as soil fertility, sunshine, rains and some in the nature of purchased inputs: be they seeds, fertilizers/manure, water and water lifting devices, labour and tractor. The nature of agricultural inputs has changed over time, which is consistent with various trends we have noticed earlier. As agriculture moved from greater diversification to lesser diversity (refer to Table 4.1) and as Chandpur saw the introduction of "new technology" in a limited way, agriculture has started moving from LEIA (Low External Input Agriculture) to HEIA (High External Input Agriculture). What impact this movement had on sustainability, one cannot say for sure, but agriculture in Chandpur has become more dependent on outside sources for its continuance.

In the 1940s, the inputs in agriculture were livestock dung and green manure, bullock available in the village, irrigation by the wheelbarrow, traditional variety of seed saved from earlier year's harvest and local, mostly family labour. There was no use of insecticides, herbicides and pesticides as there were none of the pests, weeds and diseases found now, or at least the villagers did not perceive their presence. In the 1950s, the same trend continued except that some chemical fertilizers (Chand Brand) came into use.

In the 1960s, green manure and animal dung got (at least partially) substituted by calcium, ammonia (urea), potash dye, ammonium chloride, and irrigation by bullock drawn wheel burrows was replaced by pump sets and in came Gamaxine as a few insects were noticed. By the time Chandpur came in the 1970s, use of local seeds literally vanished and improved varieties of seeds came in: Jaya, Mansuri, Saket and P-4 in the case of paddy, and RR-21, K-68, Kalyan-2003, MRP-102 and UP-262 in the case of wheat. These were all imported varieties. The incidence of insects increased significantly and application of Dalidal *(sic)* started.

As Chandpur entered 1980s, inputs to agriculture remained unchanged from the ones used in the 1970s, except that amongst the varieties of paddy cultivated, Jaya was discontinued due to its long gestation period and Pant-4 introduced. In case of wheat, Meelwi 37, 34 and 6, supposedly "disease resistant", came into use along with the other varieties. The infestation of insects increased even more. An insecticide called Roger *(sic)* came into use along with *Gamaxine* powder (*sic*). In the 1990s the position remained unchanged.

It is significant that over the years, not only did Chandpur start 'import' of seeds, fertilizers and insecticides from outside, but it even started hiring labourers from Mahuadih, and tractors from Kiraktarpur. Diesel had to be brought from nearby towns for the diesel pump sets and electricity was tapped from the rural electrification programme of the Uttar Pradesh State Electricity Board. It is also significant that as agriculture became HEIA from LEIA, the vulnerability of the farming system in Chandpur increased significantly. The dispersal of risks due to a diversified cropping pattern was no longer available.

With a higher level of external inputs, cost of production in agriculture has risen very significantly and at times it may even be not enough for the farming family to be above the poverty line defined as Rs. 11500 per annum per household (of five members). The economics of agriculture, in one of the hamlets (Yadav Basti) of Chandpur worked out by the villagers is shown in Table 4.6.

In Column 13 of Table 4.6 the net returns are per season. Since cultivation and harvesting of several crops/vegetables overlap, it is difficult to calculate the net return to the farmer per month. If we look at the size of holdings, small farmers are no longer viable. The landholding pattern in Patel Basti, a typical Hamlet of Chandpur is as in the table that follows:

Table 4.5 Landholding Pattern

No. of Families	Landholding
10	Landless
8	Less than 0.16 Acre
9	0.16-0.33 Acre
4	0.33-0.5 Acre
0	0.5-0.66 Acre
8	0.66-1 Acre
2	1-2 Acre(s)
1	2-2.66 Acre(s)

Notes: The above table has been drawn up from the primary data collected by Ms. Hema Joshi and Ms. Sunits Bisht and reported in *Report on Impact of Air Pollution on Agriculture In Urban and Peri-Urban Areas*, NIUA, New-Delhi, 1999.

Clearly, the landholdings are very small and hence agriculture as a source of livelihood all by itself is ruled out. Then significantly enough the cultivation of cash crops is far more profitable than cultivation of food crops (paddy and wheat in particular) which partly explains why people are shifting from food to cash crops. Because of small size of landholdings, diseconomies of scale operates in the cultivation and harvesting of food crops and hence they are not as profitable as one would have liked them to be.

In Table 4.6, it may be mentioned, villagers did not show credit as an input separately. Credit is used by villagers in different amounts and doses, and hence cost of credit should be added to reflect true cost of cultivation, which has not been done.

Table 4.6 Agricultural Return per Acre in Yadav Basti, Chandpur

Crop	Cost of preparing land	Quantity of seed	Cost of seed	Quantity of fertilizers	Cost of fertilizers	Person days of labour	Cost of insecticide and irrigation	Other costs such as transport cost	Output per acre	Total cost	Return per acr~	Net profit
1	2	3	4	5	6	7	8	9	10	11	12	13
Wheat	Rs. 850	50 kg	Rs. 400			30 day @ 30/ day= Rs. 900	Rs. 80 plus cost of 21 hours irrigation = Rs. 315	Rs. 150	12 quintals	Rs. 2645	Rs. 700 per quintal which is Rs. 8400	Rs. 5755
Paddy	Rs. 1000	25 kg	Rs. 200	DAP 100 kg & Urea 200 kg	Rs. 900 plus Rs. 800	46 days @ Rs. 30 per day = Rs. 1380	25 kg = Rs. 250	Rs. 150	15 quintal	Rs. 4680	Rs 800 per quintal = Rs 12000	Rs. 7320

1	2	3	4	5	6	7	8	9	10	11	12	13
Maize	Rs. 200	18 kg	Rs. 100	Urea 50 kg	Rs. 200	10 days @ Rs. 30 per day = Rs. 360		Rs. 100	10 quintal	Rs. 960	RS. 200 per quintal = Rs. 2000	Rs. 1040
Bajra	Rs. 200	5 kg	Rs. 30	Urea 30 kg plus DAP 50 kg	Rs. 200 plus Rs. 450	15 days @ 30 per day= Rs. 450		Rs. 50	1.5 quintal	Rs 830	Rs 600 per quintal = Rs. 900	Rs. 70
Cauli-flower per 5 Biswa	Rs. 1050	100 gm	Rs. 80	Urea 10 kg and DAP 10 kg	Rs. 130	18 days @ Rs. 30 per day = Rs. 240	Rs. 15 plus Rs. 450	Rs. 200	4000 pieces approxi-mately	Rs. 2165	Rs. 4 per piece = Rs. 16000	Rs 13835 per Biswa
Radi-sh per 5 Biswa	Rs. 1235	250 gm	Rs. 100			10 days @ Rs. 30 per day = Rs. 300	Gam-axin Powder = Rs. 50 plus irrigation cost of 20 hours = Rs. 300	Rs. 200	500 kg	Rs. 1735	Re. 6 per kg = Rs. 3000	Rs. 1215 per Biswa

Table 4.7 Scheduie of Wages Payable

Wages per Day	**Rs. in Village**	**Rs. in Town**
For Men		
On daily wages in construction activity	70	80
Mason	110	110
Saree weaving*	60	
Stitching	50	
Transport sector work: driver etc.	100	
Auto rickshaw driving	100	
Vegetable vending	50	
Working in petty village shop	50	
For Women		
Agricultural labour	30	
Deweeding	30	
Paddy harvesting	30	
Threshing	30	
Wheat harvesting	30	
Transplanting	30	
Birdi making**	8	
Rudrax garland making***	15	

* Wage received per Saree is Rs. 600 and it takes 10 days to weave one Saree. ** Women are paid on piece rate basis. For 100 Birdis, Rs. 16 is paid and it takes a person a day to make 50 Birdis. *** For 90 Garlands, the total wage payable is Rs. 50. It take about three days to make 90 Rudrax Garlands.

Village Analysts: Nawarangi, Budhram, Ramjatan Patel, Santlal.
Facilitator: Ms. Meera Jayaswal.
Date: 13.11.98.

IX. Food Security

Take the case of Patel Basti hamlet. Wheat produced in the hamlet meets the requirement of wheat for the villagers for 4-5 months in a year. Paddy harvested can meet the needs of paddy of the villagers in the hamlet for 3-4 months. Maize and bajra produced is enough to meet the needs of the villagers for 8-10 days and 1-2 months respectively. And all the villagers do not grow all the crops. Thus, the food produced meets about half the quantity of food necessity. For the rest of the food needs people buy food from the open market. Food produced in the village is culturally acceptable and given the employment opportunities outside of agriculture, available in and around Chandpur. The people have the requisite purchasing power to access food.

Apparently, people do not suffer starvation but existence of relative hunger is discernible. Take the case of Naipurwa women as revealed by the food calendar produced by the women of the hamlet such as Rampati Devi, Dhandai Devi and Rita Devi as is reproduced in Table 4.8. If we look at table 4.8, it is significant that the women like Rampati Devi, Dhandai Devi, Rita Devi and others have started the food calendar from the month of June-July (Ashar) and ends it in May-June (Jeth). This is because June-July is the month when the main cultivation season (Kharif) starts and it is associated in the psyche of the people as being the start of the process of food production.

If we look at column 3, it manifests that the women suffer from various degrees of hunger throughout the year. In Baisakh, Jeth, Ashar, Sawan and Bhado, for five months they have to survive just on one meal of chappatis and chilly paste and some inexpensive vegetables. That is, their hunger is at its peak during the very hot summer and wet monsoon months, namely, Baisakh (April-May), Jeth (May-June), Ashar (June-July), Sawan (July-August) and Bhado (August-September). Women survive on one unwholesome meal for 5 months. Only with the advent of Kuar (September-October), once harvesting of some pulses start, and the poor earn some wages, they have some nutrition and palate in the food intake by way of pulses and vegetables and this lasts for the five months from Kuar to Magh (mid-September to mid-February). During Fagun and Chait (mid-February to mid-April) pulses become scarce in the diet of the poor, until it vanishes in Baisakh (mid-April to mid-May).

Table 4.8 Food Calendar Prepared by the Women of Naipurwa Hamlet, Chandpur Village

Months	Financial Condition	Food Intake	Serial Number
Ashar (June-July)	Loan for purchasing seeds from the village headman or the money lender.	One meal of few chapatis and salt or chilly paste or some inexpensive vegetables.	1
Sawan (July-August)	Take loan for purchasing food.	One meal of few chapatis and salt or chilly paste or some inexpensive vegetables.	2
Bhado (August-Sept)	Take loan for purchasing food.	One meal of few chapatis and salt or chilly paste or some inexpensive vegetables.	3
Kaur (Sept.-Oct.)	Income starts from sale of vegetables and from working as agricultural labourers.	The same diet as in Bhado but intake of pulses and vegetables start.	4
Kartick (Oct.-Nov)	Income from vegetable sale and birdi/rudrax garland making.	The same diet as in Kaur.	5
Aghan (Nov.-Dec)	Income from vegetable sale and birdi/rudrax garland making.	Milk supplement is added to diet.	6
Poosh (Dec.-Jan)	Income from vegetable sale, work in fields and birdi/rudrax garland making.	Same as in Aghan	7
Magh (Jan-February)	Income from vegetable sale and birdi/rudrax garland making,	Same as in Poosh.	8
Fagun (Feb.-March)	Reduction in income from vegetable sale, income from birdi/rudrax garland making is sustained.	Same as in Magh but intake of pulses get reduced.	9

Months	Financial Condition	Food Intake	Serial Number
Chait (March-April)	Income from non-agricultural work, income from wages earned in harvesting wheat.	Same as in the month of Fagun but the intake of pulses gets further reduced.	10
Baisakh (April-May)	Income from non-agri-cultural work, income from wages earned in harvesting wheat.	One meal of chapatis and salt or chilly paste or inexpensive vegetables.	11
Jeth (May-June)	Take loan for food at 10 per cent per month.	One meal of chapatis and salt or chilly paste or inexpensive vegetables.	12

Village Analysts: Rampati Devi, Dhandai Devi, Rita Devi.
Facilitator: Ms. Meera Jayaswal.
Date: 12.11.98.

If we take a total view of the hunger situation, women suffer acute hunger for five months (Baisakh to Bhado), less acute hunger for two months (Fagun and Chait) and some hunger for five months (Kuar to Magh). Practically, at no point in time during the year, are they totally free from hunger. And their food intake is at its worst, during the summer and monsoon months (Baisakh to Bhado) when they have to work the hardest. For these are the months when they get to work in their own fields as also on wage employment in others' fields. These are also the months when the women expend a lot of energy in taking care of the sick, for during summer and monsoon months various kinds of diseases afflict the poor, to which we will come later.

If we look at Columns 2 and 3, then a high degree of correlation between income and food intake is apparent. During the months of Jeth, Ashar, Sawan and Bhado (mid-May to mid-September) the women survive on loans for their food intake. Only when their income from sale of vegetables and wage earnings improve, do they include pulses and even milk in their diet.

On the whole then, people do not have food security all through the year, though they do not suffer from chronic hunger. Under nutrition and malnutrition, of women are clearly made out. That the same holds true for the men cannot be inferred straight away, because of the social fact of gross disparity in intra-familial distribution of food, flowing from disparity in intra-familial distribution of power, where the male member(s) dominate. However, given the wage rates, the employment rates and yield from agriculture, as we have discussed earlier, it is unlikely that men would have food security throughout the year, though they would probably be better-off than women. This is particularly so when about 25 per cent of total village income is expended on consumption of liquor.

Additionally, Chandpur does not have access to much of common property resources, "micro-environments" (See Chambers for definition) and forests to support their food consumption. Food gathered from forests and CPRs have played a dynamic role in reducing hunger during hunger periods (See *Jodha,* 1990; *FAO.,* 1983, 1984, 1986). Unfortunately, the villagers of Chandpur did not have that benefit and whatever food producing CPR they had in the village were destroyed to produce commercial crops.

In terms of importance of agriculture as a source of income, Table 4.9, reconstructed from a Pie-Chart prepared by the villagers of Chandpur, provides some confirmation of our inference.

Table 4.9 Agriculture as a Source of Income

Sources of Income	Percentage of Income
Agriculture	30 per cent
Wages as casual labourers	25 per cent
Trade/Business	35 per cent
Regular Employment	10 per cent
Total	*100 per cent*

Source: Villagers of Patel Basti as shown to Ms. Hema Joshi and Ms.Sunita Bist.

If we go by the percentage of people who are engaged in agriculture, which is about 80 per cent, the fact that agriculture is the source of only 30 per cent of income, indicates, *prima facie*, that in terms of income generation, agriculture is not a very profitable venture. This is true even in case of agricultural labourers. The local people come to work as agricultural labourers only as a second choice, because wages in this sector is lower than in alternative avenues of employment. Whereas in factories in the adjoining industrial estate, in Saree printing and in construction work, a male worker makes Rs. 50, Rs. 100 and Rs. 100 per day, respectively, he earns no more than Rs. 40 per day in agriculture. Similarly, women folk, who earn Rs. 35, Rs. 50 and Rs. 100 per day from factory work, Saree printing and construction work respectively, can earn no more than Rs. 25 per day in cash and in kind in the fields during cultivation and harvesting operations. Importance of agriculture, however, in the lives of the people of Chandpur, lies in that it not only provides employment opportunities but also makes valuable contributions towards food security for the people (may be for part of the year), cash income, as also fodder for their livestock.

Of this income, expenditure looks astonishing: 25 per cent is spent on food, 25 per cent on consumption of liquor, 15 per cent on health, 10 per cent on education, 15 per cent on litigation and 10 per cent on others. This pattern of expenditure has serious implications for the village including its impact upon the social capital, state of health, literacy and food security of the villagers.

X. Summary and Conclusions

The villagers of Chandpur depend on agriculture. They produce food both as owner-cultivators and as tenant cultivator, with the former the dominanat feature. Both kinds of people suffer hunger and food insecurity throughout the year. Women face acute hunger for five months and hunger for two months in a year. Practically, at no point in time they are free from hunger. Men also suffer from food insecurity and hunger throughout the year, but they suffer less because of the employment opportunities they have, which help them in their exchange entitlements. Nevertheless, the wage rates and employment rates are far below levels, which would guarantee them food security and freedom from hunger for all thc twelve months in the year. The movement from growing a large number of crops to only a few have contributed to increasing food insecurity, though we cannot say whether same holds for increasing hunger as well.

Food security of the people could have been better ensured if the expenditure on health (15 per cent) and education (10 per cent) could have been more, and expenditure on liquor and litigation been less. The unusually high appropriation of household income for liquor and litigation has made serious inroads into food security of the poor households, both by diverting resources which could have ben used to buy food and by reducing money available for basic education and primary health care of the families. Food security depends a great deal upon not only food production, distribution and access to food, as also nutrition of food, but on general access that people have to basic education and primary health care *(Sen,* 1995).

5 A Second Perspective on Hunger in a Backward State, from Villagers of Tikri, Varanasi

I. Introduction

Tikri village lies in the district of Varanasi, which is the home of the ancient and holy city of Banaras, known in ancient literature as Kashi, venerated and inhabited by the Hindus, Muslims, Jains and the Buddhists alike. In education, art, culture, religion, trade, crafts and commerce, Varanasi holds a special place in Indian history. It has a commanding view of the mighty Ganges, on whose banks the city of Banaras and the district of Varanasi have thrived for centuries.

Varanasi lies in the eastern part of the state of Uttar Pradesh, known for its role in Indian political history, size (if it were to be a country, it would have been the seventh largest country in the world), richness of culture, history and of course, poverty. It is one of the states which have seen a rise in poverty levels during the last decade (*Sen and Patnaik,* 1997; *Sen,* 1996).

The total area of Varanasi district is 4035.01 sq. kilometers, having a population of 3,7,82,949. The literacy rate is 65.36 per cent, which is higher than the national average and much higher than the state average of 41.6 per cent. The district is divided into four Blocks, viz., Harhua, Araji Lines, Chirai Gaon and Kashi Vidyapeeth. *Tikri Village*, which is the subject of our study, falls within the territorial jurisdiction of Kashi Vidyapeeth block. Agriculture in Varanasi is mostly peasant agriculture.

Almost 89 per cent of the farmers hold 1 hectare or less that 1 hectare of land, and 96.5 per cent of the farmers own 2 or less than 2 hectares of land. There are two main seasons, Kharif and Rabi, with a relatively insignificant winter season. The villagers of this village, like villagers of Chandpur, generally seemed content with two principal cropping seasons. We will revert back to the subject again later in this chapter.

II. General Information

Tikri village is situated on the banks of Ganges, at a distance of 12 kilometers from block headquarters, Kashi Vidyapeeth and 6 kms from the Banaras Hindu University. It has a total population of 3400, with an unusual sex ratio of 1:1.

Tikri is organized into 13 Bastis or wards: Mahato Basti, Yadav Basti, Chowdhurian Basti, Dherabir Basti, Malah Basti, Tisra Basti, Sato Patti Basti, Brahmin Basti, Maurya Basti, Telyiyan Basti, Atari Basti, Naale Par Basti and Bari Basti. The names of the Bastis indicate that most of the Bastis are organised more or less along caste lines: Harijans (Chamars, Lohars, etc.), Mauryas, Mahatos (predominantly vegetable growers), Yadavs (Milkmen), Chowdhury, Malah (Fisherfolk), Bhumiyars, Brahmins, and Telyia (Oilmongers) live in separate Bastis of their own. (Bastis are also called Pattis). The village is decidedly a Hindu village. Tikri has been declared as an "Ambedkar Village" and hence has at least 50 per cent of the people belonging to Scheduled Castes.

The total area of the village is 1300 acres, of which 100 acres is under orchard, 50 acres is waste land and 50 acres is covered by human habitation. The area under orchard is significant since Varanasi and its adjoining areas are famous for fruits, notably, Mangoes and Guava. The area under waste land is also alarming, because Tikri is situated right on the Ganges, which makes the soil extremely fertile as the river brings alluvial soil from the higher reaches of the Himalayas. However, the villagers explained that 50 acres of land has become barren because of repeated attacks by nilgais and hence the villagers have abandoned the land, leading to barrenness and degradation.

The village has four Primary Schools and two Middle Schools. The literacy rate is 40 per cent, which is way below the national average of 60 per cent.

It has a Health Sub-centre in addition to a Mother and Child Centre ("Jachcha Bachch Kendra"). It has a branch of a bank, and a Kisan Sewa Kendra is also located in the village. There is also a Post Office. In terms of social overheads, therefore, Tikri is relatively well endowed (See *Shariff,* 1999 for a comparative picture). This does not, however, seem to have any impact on the village: the literacy rate is only 40 per cent though the state average is 47 per cent, 62 per cent for men and 28 per cent for women. And the average number of children per households is 4-6, which indicate non-accessing of health facilities for family planning in general.

III. Livelihood Pattern for Accessing Food

Though Tikri is a large village and is near the urban agglomeration of Banaras, the means of livelihood available to the villagers are limited mainly to agriculture, employment either as agricultural labourers or as employees in the service sector and as milk vendors. The traditional professions in which specific groups specialised are on the decline. The distribution of the population of Tikri amongst various means of livelihood is given in Table 5.1.

Table 5.1 Livelihood Activities of Village Tikri

Serial No.	Livelihood Activities	Population Involved (per cent)
1.	Agriculture and Milk Vending	10
2.	Agriculture and Labourer	20
3.	Agriculture and Services	10
4.	Agricultural Labourers	30
5.	Out Migrated (Emigrants)	30

Village Analysts: Sushil, Uday Nath, Murli Singh, Meera, Phulwati.
Facilitator: Sudipta Roy
Date: 2.11.98

The number of inhabitants dependent on agriculture, partly or wholly, is a hefty 70 per cent, which is a shade above the national average of 69 per cent for the country as a whole, according to the last Census Operations. Incidentally for India, around 70 per cent (give or take 2 per cent) of the people in India have been dependent on agriculture throughout the 20th century, since the 1901 Census, though there is a noticeable declining employment intensity of agriculture (*Singh and Dash,* 1999). In Tikri the picture is same with the additional feature that except for the agricultural labourers (30 per cent of the villagers) others who depend upon agriculture as their primary source of livelihood, all have a secondary means of livelihood as well: either as milk vendors, or as labourers or as providers of services. As a matter of fact only 5 per cent of the villagers have only one source of livelihood, 26 per cent have two, 32 per cent have three, 26 per cent have 4 and 11 per cent have 5 means of livelihood. Within the system of adopting multiple means of livelihood, some people pursue several of these options concurrently while a handful are pursued consecutively at different times in the year. Thus, purchasing power to access food does not *prima facie* seem to be a problem.

The landholding pattern for Tikri looks like Table 5.2 as narrated by Kanhaiya Lal, Mangal Singh and Channa.

Table 5.2 Landholding Pattern in Tikri

Landholding size	per cent of Population	Definition
Nil	15 per cent	Landless
Less than 1.5 Bigha	40-45 per cent	
1.5 to 3 Bighas*	30 per cent	Small and Medium Farmers
Above 3 Bighas*	10-15 per cent	Large Farmers

*1 Acre is equal to 1.5 Bighas.
Village Analysts: Kanhaiya Lal, Mangal Singh and Channa.
Facilitator: Sudipta Ray.
Date: 2.11.98

The picture depicted by villagers as in Table 5.2 is clearly a picture of a village of small and marginal farmers. The number of landless in Tikri compares favourably with the macro picture, the percentage of landless people in India being 11 per cent and in Uttar Pradesh (U.P.) being 4.9 per cent. The number of marginal and small farmers in U.P. stands at 68.01 per cent and 18.52 per cent respectively according to NSS of the 48th round *(NSSO,* 1997). The general situation of landholding in Tikri is, therefore, little worse than in U.P. as a whole.

Except for the inhabitants of Telıyan Basti, all other Bastis have cultivators. Farmers of Sato Patti, Tisra Patti, Chowdhurian Patti and Dherabir Basti are large or "middle-sized" farmers. The remaining cultivators are small and marginal farmers. Significantly, only 25 per cent of the cultivators are owner-cultivators. The rest 75 per cent of the cultivators are either owner-tenants or pure tenants and the systems of landlordism and absentee landlordism are fairly widespread. The Malahs, Harijans and Yadavs are generally all tenants. This is consistent with the fact that 30 per cent of the inhabitants of Tikri have migrated out of the village. Land belonging to the emigrants (some of them) are cultivated either by the landless as pure tenants or by small and marginal farmers (who have 'spare capacity') as owner-tenants. And people belonging to upper castes, namely the Mauryas of Mauryan Basti, Bhumiars of Tisra Patti, Bhumiyars of Sato Patti, Brahmins of Brahmin Patti and Chowdhurys of Chowdhurian Patti, also do not cultivate their landholdings themselves and lease out their land for cultivation to tenants of both varieties.

The tenancy in Tikri is either on fixed cash rent of Rs. 100 per Biswa per annum, or on share-cropping basis. In case of share-cropping, the produce is shared in the ratio of 50:50 between the landlords (owners) and the tenants, with landlords providing no input, save the temporary usufructory rights on the land to the tenants. All tenants are *hidden tenants* because, as we mentioned in case of Chandpur, by law tenancy is forbidden in Uttar Pradesh, whether on the basis of share-cropping or fixed cash rent or fixed output rent (*Kripa Shankar,* 1999).

The total livestock population in Tikri is about 4000, of which majority are owned by the Yadavs. Of these 60 per cent are buffaloes, 30 per cent are cows/oxen and 10 per cent goats. Each Yadav family owns about 20-25 buffaloes. The Yadavs are the ones who sell milk in partial fulfillment of their livelihood needs, which also explains the large size of the herds they own. The large animal population in Tikri, the villagers indicate, is explained by the fact that cultivation is still only partly mechanised and animal power provides the bulwark of energy required in farming.

Milk vending is also important for the Yadavs as it is their traditional occupation handed down to them for generations. Sale of milk is also part of the livelihood of the Chowdhurians, the difference being that they, unlike the

Yadavs, they do not sell milk in the nearby township but sell it to the Yadavs who in turn sell the milk to retail buyers in the city. The Yadavs are thus both milk producers and milk traders.

The price of milk charged by the Yadavs is constant at Rs. 10-11 per litre in the town throughout the year. The Chowdhurians sell the milk at differential rates: Rs. 14 per litre inside the village and Rs. 22 per litre in the town during *summer* months and at Rs. 12 per litre inside the village and at Rs. 18-20 per litre during *winter* months. That is, the Chowdhurians modulate the prices of milk according to its supply gyrates: when supply is higher during winter (due to various reasons, including higher productivity and greater availability of green fodder) the prices are lowered, when supply shrinks during the blistering summer months, the prices are hiked. Buyers are prepared to pay a higher price (100 per cent more in case of town) for the milk supplied out of Chowdhurian Basti than that supplied by the Yadavs. The price differential is on account of higher fat content of milk from Choudhurian Basti, making it more suitable for commercial use such as churning butter, manufacturing Ghee or making sweatmeats. The milch animals in Chowdhurian Basti are stall-fed. This explains the higher fat content in milk from milch animals of Chowdhurian Basti.

Women work as agricultural labourers, birdi makers and bead necklace makers. Some of these women, especially from the Harijan Basti, are also into flesh trade. These women prefer to work inside their homes in case their menfolk have sufficient income to take care of the families' needs. Men prefer to work outside the village, in the towns. Working with contractors is the preferred option for those offering their services for a wage because of continuity of service and stability of income. Daily wage earners feel hamstrung by the inflexibility in working environment in jobs available on daily wages and suffer from instability of wages they receive, for when they get to negotiating their daily wage, they are wage takers most of the time. They suffer all the disadvantages of the informal sector (*Mehta,* 1997). Wages earned by different classes of workers are given below in Table 5.3.

Table 5.3 Schedule of Wages Payable

Wages per Day	**Rs. in Village**	**Rs. in Town**
For Men		
On daily wages	40	80
Mason	100	120
Service	200	
Artificial pearl making	Rs. 2 per dozen. Per day Rs. 4-6	
For Women		
Kordai	20	
Deweeding	20	
Paddy harvesting	7-8 kg paddy plus a frugal lunch	
Threshing	Rs. 20 p.d.	
Wheat harvesting	Rs. 20-25 7-8 kg wheat plus frugal lunch	
Transplanting	Rs. 30 p. d.	

Men are generally in semi-skilled work (such as masonry, driving auto-rickshaws) whereas women are in unskilled jobs (like kodai, deweeding, harvesting). And where men engage in unskilled work, such as artificial pearl making, their wage earnings fall dramatically.

The difference in work done by men and women, and the employment structure *per se* of the village mirrors the traditional "inside-home" and "outside-home" syndrome. Most of the employment opportunities for the women are inside their homes whereas most of the employment opportunities for the men are outside their homes. The wage differentials between men and women, as also between work in the village and in the towns, are significant. The wage rates are more during Rabi season than in Kharif, because, *inter alia*, during Rabi the farmers grow potatoes and with the soil being sandy, the labour input is significantly higher and consequent demand for labour is higher.

Additionally, during Rabi, because land brought under wheat cultivation is much higher than in Kharif when the farmers cultivate paddy, demand for labour is pushed up and with it wages rise.

There has been a dramatic change in the livelihood pattern over the last few decades. While in the 1940s, Tikri was a predominantly an agrarian society, in the late 1990s, there is a craze for service sector: the less educated seek blue-collar jobs on daily wages, the relatively well educated seek jobs with the Government. A section of the Harijans, like the Chamars (Cobblers), are no longer interested in their traditional profession as it lacks social respectability. Though Malahs would still like to persist with their traditional profession of fishing as a secondary source of income, they fail to do so as the increasing pollution of Ganges has reduced fish breeding. In consequence the Malahs face secularly declining diminishing returns from fishing. The Lohars (blacksmiths), however, continue to practice blacksmithy.

There has been a significant change in the labour market as well. In the 1940s, bonded labourers were a common sight in Tikri, and the Harijans were mostly confined to working within the confines of the village. The situation has changed since. In the 1970s, more particularly during the latter half of the decade, Harijans started moving out of the village in search of work. By 1980s men stopped working as agricultural labourers, leaving the field for the women only. The attitude of the upper caste has also changed, as they could no longer find all the labourers to complete their tasks and the practice of hiring labourers from lower castes slowly got acceptance.

IV. Food Production Pattern

There are three cultivation seasons, two major and one minor:

(i) Summer season from Baisakh to Sawan (mid-April to mid-August) is a minor season,

(ii) Kharif (the monsoon season) running from Bhado to Kartik (mid-August to mid-November) is one of the major seasons, and

(iii) Rabi season from Aghan to Chait (mid-November to mid-April) is the most important agricultural season for Tikri.

The principal crops grown during Kharif are paddy, bajra and fodder at the margin. During Rabi, the principal crops cultivated are wheat, vegetables and spices such as ginger, garlic, chili, fenugreek and coriander. The summer season is of no major significance since only some sundry vegetables are grown such as "ninwa" (snake gourd), bitter gourd, bottle gourd, cucumber, kakri (another species of cucumber, longer and thinner in shape with a thick outer skin) sugar baby, kohra (pumpkin), lady's finger and moong (a kind of lentil).

The principal crop during Kharif is paddy and the principal crop during Rabi is wheat. The area-wise cropping pattern is as in Table 5.4.

Table 5.4 makes an interesting reading. First, Rabi is the major season for the villagers in terms of the area cultivated: only 5 per cent remain fallow. During Kharif as high as 30 per cent of the land is left fallow. Second, in a predominantly rice eating area, wheat is the major crop being cultivated on 90 per cent of the land. Paddy, being the second principal crop, is grown on only 30 per cent of land under the plough. Maize, jowar, and bajra are the other coarse cereals produced, but on less than 20 per cent of land. Third, agriculture in Tikri is dominated by food crops and the concept of cash crops has caught on only in the 1990s: potatoes, cauliflowers, tomatoes, etc. are grown for sale in the market during the winter season (Rabi) and that too on only 5 per cent of the land with other vegetables notably brinjals. The villagers pointed out that cultivation of peas and maize in particular have lately increased because of a reduction in the predation by nilgais (an endangered species of large deer).

The economy of Tikri mirrors a curious phenomenon. While it receives most of its rain during Kharif (monsoon) season, its major cultivation season is Rabi, when wheat is grown. One explanation for this paradox is the food habits of the people influenced by the industries near Varanasi, which attract lot of outsiders.

Table 5.4 Area-wise Food Production Pattern in Tikri

Kharif (Monsoon) *Crop*	**Kharif (Monsoon)** *per cent of Area*	**Rabi (Winter)** *Crop*	**Rabi (Winter)** *per cent of Area*	**Summer** *Crop*	**Summer** *per cent of Area*
Paddy	30	Wheat.	90	Vegetables	10
Bajra	20	Vegetables: cauliflower, potato, brinjal and spinach.	5	Fallow	90
Maize, Jowar, Bajra, Peas, Sesame	20	Fallow.	5		
Fallow	30				

Table 5.5 Time Line: Historical Events as Recalled by Men of Mahato Basti Hamlet of Tikri village

Period	**Events**	**Cropping Pattern**	**Agricultural Practices**	**Crop Care**	**Agricultural Constraints**
1940s	Flood in the village.	Bajra, barley, paddy (in limited quantity), wheat (in limited quantity, gram, peas, and chili (as speciali-sation).	Ploughing by oxen, irrigation by moat, organic manure in use, tradi-tional seeds used.	Yield 4-5 maunds per bigha.	Flood from the Ganges.

Period	Events	Cropping Pattern	Agricultural Practices	Crop Care	Agricultural Constraints
1950s	Middle School started.	Same as in 1940s.	Aluminum sulphate introduced, tubewell installed for irrigation.	Yield 8-10 maund per bigha.	*Tirri* pest attack on jowar, *Kanduwa* attack on wheat, flood caused damage.
1960s	Brick houses constructed.	Increased wheat and paddy, cultivation of vegetables like potatoes started.	Irrigation by pump sets, fertilisers, new hybrid seeds and pesticides introduced, tractors came.	Same as in 1950s.	*Gurchawa* disease in chilies.
1970s	Irrigation canal constructed, washed away by floods.	Moong, barley, peas, grams, chilies, pigeon peas, bajra and sunui dominated cultivation, wheat as second fiddle.	Same as in the 1960s.	Same as in 1960s.	*Gurchawa* disease in chilies forced farmers to stop its cultivation.
1980s	Outbreak of measles, increase in fertiliser use, famine.	Intensive wheat cultivation overtakes all other	Same as in the 1970s.	Yield 10-15 maunds per bigha.	Nilgais damage crops, rats damaged crops.

Period	Events	Cropping Pattern	Agricul-tural Practices	Crop Care	Agri-cultural Cons-traints
	in 1986-87. Bank opened.	crops. cultivation of moong, barley, gram, peas and chili reduced.			Diseases like *Hardwa, Jhulsa* and *Gurchawa* affecting crops
1990s	1995: vaccination on mass scale, girl's school started, 1997: metaled roads laid.	Wheat, peas, potatoes, paddy, ninua (snake gourd), cauliflower, tomatoes etc., jowar cultivated for fodder only.	Same as in the 1980s, weedicides introduced in the farming of wheat.	Yield 12-14 maund per bigha for wheat and 10-12 maunds per bigha for paddy.	Nilgais and rats dama-ged crops, diseases like *Hardwa, Jhulsa* and *Gurchawa,* as also pests like *Dhola* and *Hazari* affecting crops**.
1998	Hails before Diwali.				

**Note that these are the major constraints indicated by the farmers. There are other constraints which they narrated during the analysis and prioritisation of agricultural constraints.

Village Analysts: Pratap Narain, Hiralal, Radheysham, Ramesh Kumar Patel, Bahadur Patel, Munnalal, Ashok, Krishan.

Facilitator: Sudipta Roy.

V. Changes in Food Production Pattern and Agricultural Practices

It is important to put in perspective the general socio-economic and political changes that have been faced by the villagers in Tikri, to better appreciate the changes in pattern of food production and agricultural practices. The villagers of Mahato Basti, viz., Pratap Narain, Hiralal, Radheysham, Ramesh Kumar Patel, Bahadur Patel, Munnalal, Ashok and Krishan, give us through the Historical Transect prepared, reproduced here as Table 5.5, a graphic account of these changes.

In the sixty years covered by the Historical Transect, Tikri has seen major changes in general and in the agricultural sector in particular. In this changing scenario, there are *four* landmarks in the flow of agricultural history: *one*, the introduction of Aluminum Sulphate in 1950s and the installation of Tubewells for irrigation in the same period, *two*, the commencement of mechanisation of ploughing and irrigation through use of tractors and pump sets respectively, introduction of hybrid variety seeds and the beginning of extensive use of fertilisers and pesticides in the 1960s; *three*, for two decades, the 70s and 80s, there has been no change in farming systems, and *four*, in the 1990s the substitution of manual weeding by weedicides and proliferation of crops which are highly saleable.

1940s was a decade of indigenous system of farming of zero external input agriculture (ZEIA). The 50s was still low external input agriculture (LEIA). Come the 60s, the romanticism of the "new-technology" swamps Tikri, and the entire farming system becomes driven by external inputs: the farmers of Tikri arrived at the age of high external input agriculture (HEIA). And it continues to be so since then until the 1990s, when HEIA was further intensified with the introduction of weedicides. This has also meant that over the years as Tikri migrated from ZEIA to HEIA, the cost of cultivation has gone up perceptibly: whereas in the 40s and a good deal in the 50s, much of what was necessary for farming was supplied by the resources of the farmers and by community/ common property resources, by the time Tikri stepped into the "new-technology" era of the 60s, most agricultural inputs used in Tikri had to be bought by the farmers (at prices determined by the market forces) from outside the village.

The agricultural practices have had significant influence on the food production pattern. Because agriculture became HEIA, yield, income and cost of cultivation became the dominant determinants in deciding what crops would be chosen for cultivation; not taste, not cultural acceptability, not nutritional value, not staying power, not even tradition. There are five phases in the cropping pattern:

- Through most of 1940s and 1950s a wide range of food crops were grown: bajra, barley, paddy, wheat, grams, chilies, peas and the like. There was an unfailing sign of poly-culture and crop diversity.
- In the 1960s, the "new-technology" in agriculture had its influence on Tikri and cultivation of wheat and paddy was increased, and other crops slipped down the ladder of importance. Vegetable cultivation was carried out for sale in the adjoining towns and not for consumption at the household level.
- Then came the 1970s, when again a wide variety of crops (barley, chili, pigeon peas, gram, pea, bajra and sunui) came to be cultivated. Wheat was cultivated but on a limited scale. Again productivity remained at about the same level as was the case in 1960s.
- By the time we come to the 1980s, intensive cultivation of wheat had begun and cultivation of barley, chili, peas and gram fell considerably. This was so, the villagers explained, because the use of fertilisers rendered the soil unsuitable for cultivating these crops. The non-existence of improved varieties of seeds in some of crops, such as barley, led to a reduction in farming them. And then the predatory attacks by the nilgais made life for those farmers who cultivated these crops somewhat more difficult.
- In the 1990s, wheat became the dominant crop and those vegetables, which had higher commercial value such as cauliflowers, potatoes, onion and ninwa, came to be included in the farmer's agenda, to the exclusion of others. Jowar was still cultivated, not as food crop but for fodder. The yield of wheat increased to 12 maunds per bigha and that of paddy was recorded at 10-12 maunds per bigha.

This chronology of events also indicates that after the seventies, agriculture made a shift towards greater market orientation and less towards meeting household needs.

Why have the changes taken place?

Implements: The most significant change seen by the villagers is the use of implements for ploughing. The introduction of tractors for cultivation was a big change, but farmers still prefer the good old oxen and wooden plough, though it costs more to plough the fields that way. The primary reason being the old combination of oxen and plough constitute an appropriate technology for Tikri, with most of its cultivators classified as small and marginal farmers, since they enable the farmers to cultivate smaller plots, where tractors cannot be operated.

Agricultural Practices: The observed changes in agricultural practices have been caused by several factors. First was the technological change. As supply of improved variety seeds (wheat and paddy) was made possible, lift irrigation became available and use of chemical fertilisers was encouraged, the farmers responded to these moves, though not necessarily with higher yield. The farmers apparently did respond to incentives and to technological breakthrough. The use of chemical fertilisers in a village with nearly 4000 animals and the consequent availability of free manure in large quantity, was a surprising change. However, the villagers explained, the use of fertilisers was also "needs driven" because animal dung which used to be available as manure was diverted to alternative use as fuel. The shortage of fuelwood, consequent upon loss in bio-mass production and deforestation, had the ultimate effect of diverting animal dung from manure to fuel. Second, the practice of growing of a large number of crops was abandoned because of degradation of soil caused by over/wrong use of chemical fertilisers. The use of fertilisers was not scientifically administered and without support of extension services, which adversely affected soil fertility. Third, the decrease in the forest cover, which led to shortfall in supply of fuelwood, also forced the farmers to change the cropping pattern. With the decrease in forest cover, nilgais lost a better portion of their natural source of fodder and therefore intruded into human habitations in search of food. This brought the predation of the nilgais to the doorsteps of the farmers, who could not deal with these animals the way they would normally deal these predators, because these were amongst the endangered species and killing nilgais is banned.

VI. Changes in Yield of Crops

Looking at Table 5.5 one gets an idea of the changes in yield, indicated by the villagers, of their principal crop, namely, wheat. During the 1940s, the yield was unusually low at 4-5 maunds per bigha. It rose during the 1950s to about 10 maunds and it remained at that level during the next two decades. In the 1980s there was a jump to 10-15 maunds per bigha and remained at more or less that level during the 1990s. In the Historical Transect in Table 5.5, since people were trying to portray a whole range of changes, they restricted the information on yield to their principal crop, wheat. A better picture emerges from the Historical Transect of Yield drawn up by Pannalal, Kanhaiyalal, Laxman Mourya, Musseram and Chhatanki of Tirki, which is reproduced as Table 5.6 read with historical transect of vegetable yeild in Table 5.7.

If we compare Historical Transects at Tables 5.6 and 5.7, clearly there has been changes both in terms of diversity and yield. The number of Rabi crops got reduced to 2 in the 1990s, from 7 in the 1940s, 1950s and 1960s. It came down initially to 3 in the 1970s and then from the 80s it got to 2. Similarly in case of Kharif crops, from a basket of 8 crops grown in 1940s, by the time Tikri reached the 70s, the basket had only 4 crops, a pattern that continues till today. Similarly with vegetables, as only potatoes are grown as the main vegetable. Reduction in crop diversity means that distribution of risk has also shrunk and the vulnerability of the farmers to natural or man made calamity has increased. It has led to the abandonment of several time–tested practices known to the community such as crop rotation which is possible when a large number of and different kinds of crops are grown, for restoration of soil vitality and to reduce the risk of failure (*See Murakami,* 1991; *Wijewardene* 1994).

Prior to 1960s (pre-new-technology or "Green Revolution" days), the villagers explained that they practiced *crop rotation, field rotation, mixed cropping, rotational grazing* and applied *green manure* to ensure better yield from farming. Field rotation and rotational grazing were complementary activities: fields were left fallow deliberately for restoring nutritional strength of the soil and allowing animals to graze on fallow fields, a process which also naturally manured the fields from animal droppings. Depending on the nature of the crops, farmers cultivated crops in a series sequence to ensure that subsequent crop replenished nutrients used by the earlier one. And in some cases, crops were cultivated concurrently in the same field for reasons similar to crop rotation. For instance, mustard and wheat were farmed concurrently. Grass was grown in the arable areas to be ploughed back into the same fields to manure them. After the 1960s (post-new-technology or "Green Revolution" days), these systems lost out to the use of chemical fertilisers, improved varieties of seeds, etc. They had several adverse consequences in several parts of the country classified as the "violence of the Green Revolution" (*Shiva,* 1991) though they were not mentioned by the farmers of Tikri.

Table 5.6 Historical Transect of Main Crops and Their Yield (Maunds/Acre) in Tikri Village

Main Crops	1940s	1950s	1960s	1970s	1980s	1990s
Monsoon (Kharif) crops						
Paddy	10	10	20	40	45	50
Maize	30	40	40	50	50	40
Pearl millet (bajra)	10	10	20	25	20	15
Red gram (arhar)	12	12	12	6	3	1
Green gram (moong)	5	5	10	—	—	—
Urad	5	5	10	—	—	—
Kodo	5	5	10	—	—	—
Utalia	5	5	—	—	—	—
Winter crops (Rabi)						
Wheat	10	10	20	45	45	50
Barley	10	10	5	—	—	—
Bengal gram	10	10	5	—	—	—
Bare	10	10	5	—	—	—
Peas	10	10	5	2	—	—
Alsi	2	2	2	—	—	—
Mustard	3	3	3	2	1	0.50

Village Analysts: Pannalal, Kanhaiyalal, Laxman Mourya, Musseram and Chhatanki.
Facilitator: Meera Jayaswal.

Table 5.7 Historical Transect of Vegetable Yields (Maund*/Acre) by Men of Tikri

Main Vegetables	1940s	1950s	1960s	1970s	1980s	1990s
Potatoes	150	150	150	200	200	250
Chilies	5	5	5	—	—	—

* A maund is roughly 36 kilograms.
Village Analysts: Pannalal, Kanhaiyalal, Laxman Mourya, Musseram and Chhatanki.
Facilitator: Meera Jayaswal.

Nevertheless yield of foodgrains did show distinct changes. Take the case, of paddy. With the onset of new-technology in the 1960s, the yield jumped by 100 per cent and then again by another 100 per cent between 1960s and 1970s: paddy yield increased from 10 maunds per acre in the 50s to 50 maunds per acre in the 1990s. Thereafter, the increase in yield has been more modest. In case of wheat the pattern is similar. Yield jumped up from 10 maunds per acre in the 1950s to 20 maunds per acre in the 1960s and then to 45 maunds per acre in the 1970s and then it, more or less, stabilised at that level till date. In this case too, yields seem to have responded to the introduction of new-technology. As a matter of fact all food crops grown during Kharif have recorded remarkable growth in yield. For Rabi, it is different. Except for wheat, which has shown remarkable increase in yield as well, all other crops have recorded a secularly falling yield, with decline in yield from pea being most dramatic: from 10 maunds per acre in the 50s, it has come down to 2 maunds per acre in the 1970s.

The variation in yields has also been influenced by the variations in the quality and kinds of agricultural inputs applied by the farmers. A detailed discussion of this aspect will not be made here. Suffice it to say for the present that farmers of Tikri indicated that prior to 1960s yield was low because there was total dependency on monsoons for water, which often betrayed the farmers. After the introduction of the pump sets, water supply was guaranteed through assured irrigation. The system of field rotation prior to 1960 also meant that some fields would be deliberately left uncultivated, which resulted in lower returns to the farmer from agriculture per year. The older system of farming may have been more sustainable but was poorer in terms of yield per acre.

VII. Agricultural Inputs and the Economics of the Inputs

The agricultural inputs being currently used by the farmers as they were used over the years, are described in the Historical Transect of inputs as reported in Table 5.8. The economics of agricultural inputs would be different for different crops. For the sake of brevity, we will discuss the economics of agricultural inputs in relation to paddy and wheat, the principal crops of the Kharif and Rabi seasons, of milk vending and vegetable cultivation. Reference is invited to Historical Transects and Time Lines given by the villagers of Tikri reproduced as Tables 5.8 to 5.11. If we summarise these tables, it is apparent that:

(i) Return per annum from paddy farming is Rs. 1145 per biswa, from wheat farming it is Rs. 949 per biswa, from vegetable cultivation it is lump sum of Rs. 6000 per annum on an average.
(ii) For those engaged in dairy business, they earn Rs. 480 per month per buffalo, without taking into account their labour cost.
(iii) For those engaged in Artificial Pearl Making, they earn Rs. 1800 per year.
(iii) Assuming that a person is employed for 15 days a month, the earnings from daily wages for men is Rs. 7200 per year, whereas women would make about Rs. 3600 per year.
(iv) If a person is gainfully employed with a regular employer the person earns Rs. 6000 per month or Rs. 72000 per year.

From the cultivation process discussed above the inputs into agriculture sought by farmers of Tikri can be easily deduced. Clearly, some inputs would come in the nature of "public" good or "free" good, such as soil fertility, sunshine, rains, and some in the nature of purchased inputs: be they seeds, fertilizers/manure, insecticides, pesticides, water and water lifting devices, labour and tractor. The nature of agricultural inputs have changed over time, which is consistent with various trends we have noticed earlier. As we have noted earlier, agriculture moved from greater diversification to lesser so, and as Tikri saw the introduction of "new technology", agriculture in Tikri moved (like in Chandpur) from ZEIA (Zero External Input Agriculture) to LEIA (Low External Input Agriculture) and then to HEIA

Table 5.8 Historical Transect of Agricultural Inputs in Tikri

Decade	Wheat Seeds	Paddy Seeds	Potato Seeds	Fertilisers/ Manure etc.	Irrigation	Disease	Medicines
1940s	Local	Local	Local	Dung, green (savai)	Bullock	No	No
1950s	Local	Local	Darjeeling	Dung, green (savai)	Bullock	No	No
1960s	Imported (Mexico)	Imported	Darjeeling	Chemical (Chand Brand-sindri)	Pump set	Very few	No
1970s	Imported Malwi 34 Malwi 36 RR 21	Pant 4 Saket 4	Local	Aluminium Sulphate, Zinc and Potash	Pump set	Increased	Yes. Gamaxine *(sic)*
1980s	Imported Malwi 34 Malwi22 RR 21 RR 2003	BHU	Local	Aluminium Sulphate, Zinc and Potash	Pump set	Increased	Gamaxin & Dalidal *(sic)*
1990s	Imported Malwi 234, 236, 2003 and Malwi 2285	BHU	Imported	Urea, Dye, Potash, Calcium, Sulphate, Zinc	Pump set	Very high	Gamaxin & Dalidal and Roger *(sic)*

Village Analysts: Pannalal, Kanhaiyalal, Laxman Maurya, Musseram, Chhatanki.
Facilitator: Meera Jayaswal

(High External Input Agriculture). In the process, agriculture in Tikri, like in Chandpur, has become much more expensive. In the 1950s, the inputs in agriculture were livestock dung and green manure, ox available in the village for ploughing, irrigation by the wheelbarrow and harvesting rainwater, traditional variety of seed saved from earlier year's harvest and local, mostly family labour.

Table 5.9 Return from Agricultural Operation Per Biswa Paddy: (1 Biswa = 0.16 Acre)

Inputs	Rate or Cost Per Unit	Quantity Used	Total Cost
Seeds	Rs. 100 per kg	1 kg	Rs. 100
Fertilisers			
Dye	Rs. 40 per kg	1 kg	Rs. 40
Potash	Rs. 5 per kg	5 kg	Rs. 25
Urea	Rs. 4 per kg	15 kg	Rs. 60
Deweeding	Rs. 20 per day per person	6 labourers for 1 day	Rs. 120
Harvesting	Rs. 20 per person per day	5 labourers for 1 day	Rs. 100
Threshing	Rs. 20 per person per day	3 labourers for 1 day	Rs. 60
Kutai (Dehusking)	Rs. 25 per quintal		Rs. 60
Total Cost	—	—	Rs. 555
Yield	2 quintals paddy = 1 quintal rice	Rs. 1700 per quintal of rice	Rs. 1700
Net Return	—	—	Rs. 1700-Rs. 555 = Rs. 1145

Note: This table does not include the cost of ploughing as it is provided by family labour.

Village Analysts: Amarnath Morya, Ashok Morya and Pannalal Morya and others.

Facilitated by: Ms. Meera Jayaswal.

Date: 3.11.98.

Table 5.10 Return from Vegetable Production

Net Return	Period	Total Net Return
Rs. 1000 per month	Six months	Rs. 6000

Village Analysts: Amarnath Morya, Ashok Morya and Pannalal Morya and others.
Facilitated by: Ms. Meera Jayaswal.
Date: 3.11.98.

Table 5.11 Return from Food Production Per Biswa: Wheat (1 Biswa = 0.16 Acre)

Inputs	Rate or Cost Per Unit	Quantity Used	Total Cost
Seeds	Rs. 12 per kg	3 kg	Rs. 36
Fertilisers			
Dye	Rs. 8 per kg	5 kg	Rs. 40
Urea	Rs. 4 per kg	5 kg	Rs. 20
Potash	Rs. 5 per kg	3 kg	Rs.15
Ploughing	Rs. 20 per ploughing	4 times	Rs.80
Harvesting	Rs. 30 per person per day	5 labourers for 1 day	Rs. 150
Threshing	Rs. 25 per maund	6 maund	Rs.150
Irrigation	Rs. 10 per hour	8 hours on three occasions	Rs. 240
Total Cost	—	—	Rs. 731
Yield	6 quintals of wheat	Rs. 700 per quintal of wheat	Rs. 1680
Net Return	—	—	Rs. 1680 – Rs. 731 = Rs. 949

Note: This table does not include the cost of ploughing as it is provided by family labour.
Village Analysts: Amarnath Morya, Ashok Morya and Pannalal Morya and others.
Facilitated by: Ms. Meera Jayaswal. *Date:* 3.11.98.

There was no use of imported seeds, chemical fertilisers, insecticides, herbicides, weedicides and pesticides, or at least Amarnath, Ashok and Pannalal Morya and other villagers did not perceive their presence. But as the external content of agricultural inputs increased so did the cost of operation. A comparison of the net return from growing paddy and wheat and milk vending with the wages earned and the salaries received made by Kusum Devi, Anita, Urmila, Jali, Amarnath, Ashok and Pannalal and others (as set forth in Table 5.13), gives an indication of why the younger generation moves out of the village and absentee landlordism is on the rise. Indeed, according to some estimates the return to the farmers is negative in agriculture *(Shiva,* 2000).

The movement of agriculture from ZEIA to HEIA also means that the vulnerability of the farmers of Tikri to external shocks has increased, and their and their community's control over the supply of quality agricultural inputs has been nearly extinguished. The increased vulnerability of agriculture to eternal shocks could play havoc with the lives of farmers. Farmers are already experiencing constraints to agriculture on account of poor supply of electricity, adulterated fertilisers and spurious insecticides. The farmers have become dependent on outsiders for their inputs, as we have seen in case of Chandpur. If the current phase of globalisation is taken to its logical end, which probably will happen, farmers in Tikri will be rendered dependent upon transnational companies and their dealers for supply of many more of their inputs, adding to not only costs but other externalities associated with such dependence. When we add to the picture, facts about dwindling diversity of crops, any hope of preventing Tikri farmers from widely diffusing risks of farming is likely to be turned into a nightmare. Farming is not only more risky but also more open to disturbance due to external shocks.

As farming in the 1980s and 1990s has become more dependent on sourcing from outside Tikri, farming has come to use resources that are not always renewable. Internal resources are "inherently renewable and thus have the potential to be used on a 'sustained' basis, indefinitely, through ecologically sound methods of farming" (*Conway and Barbier,* 1990). Seeds saved from earlier harvests, manure from animal dung, irrigation by

Table 5.12 Return from Dairying Milk per Buffalo

Expenditure Head	Rate, Sale/Purchase Price	Total
Fodder 6 kg per day	Rs. 3 per kg	Rs. 3 times 6 times 30 = Rs. 540
Grass/oil cakes etc.	—	Lump Sum Rs. 300
Total cost	—	Rs. 840
Milk yield 4 liters per day	Rs. 11 per litres.	Rs. 11 times 4 times 30 = Rs. 1320
Net return		Rs. 1320 less Rs. 840 = Rs. 480
Imputed labour costs	Rs. 20 per day for 20 days	Rs. 600
Final net return		–Rs. 120 (Net Loss)

Village Analysts: Amarnath Morya, Ashok Morya and Pannalal Morya and others.
Facilitated by: Ms. Meera Jayaswal. *Date*: 3.11.98.

Table 5.13 Schedule of Wages Payable

Wages per Day	Rs. in Village	Rs. in Town
For Men		
On daily wages	40	80
Mason	100	120
Service	200	
Artificial pearl making	Rs. 2 per dozen per day Rs. 4-6	
For Women		
Kordai	20	
Deweeding	20	
Paddy harvesting	7-8 kg paddy plus a frugal lunch	
Threshing	30	
Wheat harvesting	7-8 kg wheat plus a frugal lunch per day	
Transplanting	30	

Village Analysts: Kusum Devi, Anita, Urmila, Jali, Amarnath Morya, Ashok Morya and Pannalal Morya and others.
Facilitated by: Ms. Meera Jayaswal. *Date*: 4.11.98.

moat and harvesting rain water, ox and the wooden hoe for ploughing, and of course family labour are all renewable and have the inherent property of being used on a sustainable basis through ecologically sound methods of farming. This is not the case with HEIA currently practiced.

Since agriculture in Tikri has become dependent on external resources, much of it is not provided as a "free good", implying that the farming households must buy them and hence must generate a surplus of production, cash or whatever else of value to exchange for external resources. And the cost of acquiring these resources and their supply channels are beyond the control of farming households. This has, like in case of Chandpur, increased open costs, hidden costs and real costs.

The transition from ZEIA to LEIA and eventually to HEIA, has made agriculture a high open costs, hidden costs and real costs. The reasons and cosequences are the same as in case of Chandpur, and discussed in Chapter 4, to which reference is invited.

The increase in fossil fuel use to keep outputs high also means more energy consumption. Shift from ZEIA to HEIA has led to substitution of manual labour and animal power by tractors, threshers and pump sets (either diesel or electric) that we saw, which implies that external energy sources have substituted energy sources found in the household and the community. All this along with use of fertilisers, which is mostly NKP, agriculture has become very energy intensive in Tikri. Although we have no estimates of how much is the total energy input to agriculture due to the use of fertilisers (NKP), pump sets and tractors, in Tikri but in third world countries these amongst themselves consume more than 90 per cent of total energy inputs for farming. For India as a whole there is one estimate that 10-20 per cent increase in yields following mechanisation, costs an additional 43-260 per cent more in energy consumption. In Punjab, farms in a class 14-25 hectares use three times as much direct energy per hectare as farmers smaller than 6 hectares (*Singh and Miglani,* 1976).The following Chart is interesting.

Chart 1 Energy Intensity of Food Production

Low Input comparison	High input comparison	Amount of extra yield for high input	Amount of extra energy consumption for high input
State of West Bengal, in Eastern India			
Bullock, rice	Power tiller, rice	+ 8 per cent	+ 200 per cent
Bullock, rice	Tractor, rice	+ 13 per cent	+ 43 per cent
Bullock, wheat	Power tiller, wheat	+ 12 per cent	+ 74 per cent
Bullock, wheat	Tractor, wheat	+ 6 per cent	+ 89 per cent
State of Uttar Pradesh in North India			
Bullock, rice	Mechanized rice	+ 20 per cent	+ 45 per cent
Bullock, wheat	Mechanized wheat	+ 29 per cent	+ 138 per cent

Source: Singh and Singh, 1976.

VIII. The Landowning and the Landless Groups

The pattern of settlement in the village is a clear indication of landowning and the landless classes. Tikri is a multi-caste village and caste composition of the village gives a fairly good approximation of the landless and landowning groups. In Tikri, generally, the Telys, Harijans, Chamars, Lohars, Malahs and the Yadavs comprise the landless people and many of them are hidden tenants. As mentioned above, about 15 per cent of the people in Tikri are landless. They are the people who are categorised as belonging to Scheduled Castes (SC) and other backward castes (OBC). The upper castes comprising the Brahmins, Bhumiars, Mauryas, Chowdhurians and inhabitants of Dherabir Basti are the landowing classes. Many of the emigrants also own lands but do not till their own lands. Tenants cultivate landholdings of emigrants.

With such a neat classification of landless and landowning classes, it is easy to see that there is some overlap between landownership and produce ownership. The landowning people do not cultivate all the land they own and they lease out their land. It may be recalled that 75 per cent of the people in Tikri are some form of tenants and, only 25 per cent of the population are owner cultivators. There are five kinds of tenancy systems and land-produce ownership pattern found. *Firstly*, those who own and cultivate their land fully, have a complete overlap between landownership and produce thereof. They have in Amartya Sen's terminology endowment entitlements. *Secondly*, those who own land but have leased it out on share cropping ("Bataidari"). These people have exchange entitlement. In this case there is 50 per cent overlap between landownership and produce, because under the tenancy agreement, output is shared between the tenants and landlords (read landowners) on a 50:50 basis. *Thirdly*, we have those who own land but lease it out on fixed cash rent. There is, in these cases, no overlap between landownership and produce because the landowner is only entitled to an agreed fixed rent specified in monetary terms. In the *fourth* category we have included those who own land but lease it out on fixed rent expressed as a fixed quantity of the produce ("Dana Bandi"). Here the overlap between landownwership and produce is only partial. The *fifth* category would have been the bonded labourers, who cultivated their own land without any right to the produce. Thus in Tikri, there are a large number of people who produce food but are not legally entitled to that food. They at best have legal right to only one portion of the food they produce.

IX. Gender Equity

That both men and women work hard in villages is a reality. Nevertheless, the tasks performed by the two are different. We will discuss this issue here only in relation to increasing household's purchasing power to access food and food production.

The division of work is clearly demarcated. Mason's work, work in the service sector, Pearl making etc. fall in the domain of male work. Ploughing of fields, applying of fertilizers, irrigation,, "karha", "khurhol", repairing of ridges, carrying harvested crops from the field to the granary ("Khalihan") and preserving seeds for next year's cultivation, etc. are all primarily the work of men. As against this, kodai, transplantation of seedlings, deweeding, paddy harvesting, wheat harvesting, threshing, winnowing, par boiling paddy, paddy husking and paddy pounding lie in the women's domain. In addition, they work for supplementary income in Tikri on garland making etc., often late into the night. The figure (Figure 2.1) drawn by the villagers of Morya Basti of Tikri, depicting the length of working hours for men and women separately, clearly bears this division of activities. The diagram brings home the fact that all our village folks are early risers: their day begins at about 4 A.M. and then for men it ends at sundown at about 6 P.M., but women work till almost midnight. Within this working day men have rest in the afternoon and then recreation and leisure during the evenings, but women have none of it.

X. Significance of Agriculture and Food Security

The capacity and potential of agriculture to provide employment and hence access to food, are unmistakable, given the composition of the village population, notwithstanding that 30 per cent of the people seek employment outside the village.

In the circumstances of Tikri where people lease-out and lease-in land, *ipso facto,* all inhabitants cannot be food insecure. The poor people would be the ones who would probably be the real sufferers. It would be useful to refer to the classification provided by the villagers of Morya of those who were poor and those who were non-poor. They used five criterias to classify people as falling in three socio-economic strata (SES): *Garib* (Low SES), *Kamate-Khate* (Middle SES) and *Amir* (High SES): size of land holding, condition of house and its physical facilities, economic status, facilities provided to their children and capacity to meet the expenses for "social function". Based on the above criteria the villages arrived at the classification of the inhabitants of Tikri as in Table 5.14.

We need not labour the point that the issue of food security concerns people belonging to Lower SES. Food Security will neither bother people belonging to Middle SES nor to Higher SES. We would, therefore, examine the issue of food security in the context of people belonging to Lower SES only. This does not, however, mean that all people belonging to Middle and

Higher SES are food secure. Because of disparity in intra-familial distribution of power and because of traditions and customs, in many households categorised as falling in Middle SES and Higher SES, there would be women and girl children suffering from food insecurity. For want of data from the villagers' perspective we are not pursuing here that line of investigation.

Table 5.14 Characteristics of Low, Middle and High SES in Morya

Criteria	Low SES	Middle SES	High SES
Landholding	Less than 5 biswa	5 biswa to 1 acre	More than 1 Acre
Condition of the House	clay built. Single storied. No toilet, no latrine and bathroom. Only one room for one family. No source of drinking water.	Cemented. Single storied with latrine and source of water: well. Separate guest room ('Baithak') and chauki (wooden cot).	Cemented. Well maintained, double-storied or more, house with hand pump, well, etc. for drinking water, toilets, latrine, bathroom and 'Baithak'.
Economic status	100 per cent dependent on daily wages to arrange for food	Do not have to strain resources for meeting daily needs.	Economically very sound. Money lenders for Middle SES and Low SES people.
Employment	Daily wage earners. Agricultural labourers.	Cultivators, daily wage earners and milk vendors.	In service and/or in business
Facilities for children	Cannot afford to send children to school. Children start working at an early age and help parents in their work.	Children are enrolled in local school.	Children are enrolled in "good" schools.

Criteria	Low SES	Middle SES	High SES
Capacity to bear expenses to meet social obliga-tions	Cannot afford to bear expenses to meet social obligations associated with birth, marriage, death etc. Survive on borrowings and charity during emergency such as illness, death, etc.	Can partially bear expenses to meet social obligations out of own resources and partly out of borrowings.	Spend ostentatiously during social occasions.

Village Analysts: Indubala, Kamala, Urmila and Iali.
Facilitator: Meera Jayaswal. *Date*: 4.11.98.

The role of food production in food security is important but not overwhelming. Take the case of Morya hamlet. Wheat produced in the hamlet meets its requirement for 4-5 months in a year. Paddy harvested can meet the needs of paddy of the villagers for 3-4 months. Maize and bajra produced is enough to meet their needs for only a few days. And as in the case of Chandpur, all the villagers do not grow all the crops. Thus the food produced meets only a part of the quantity of food necessary for food security. For the rest of the needs people buy food from the open market.

There is no question that food produced in the village is culturally acceptable and given the employment opportunities outside of agriculture, available in and around Tikri, people do have the requisite purchasing power to access food. Apparently, people do not suffer starvation but existence of differentiate hunger is discernible.

The facts revealed to us by Indubala, Kamala, Urmila, Jali and other women, in terms of the Food Calendar of Morya hamlet as in Table 5.16 are instructive. If we look at column 2, it is manifest that the women and men suffer from various degrees of hunger for a considerable part of the year. But their hunger is at its peak during the very hot summer and humid monsoon months, namely, months of Jeth (May-June), Asharh (June-July), and Sawan (July-August). That is, the women, men and children survive on one unwholesome meal for 3 months. As Bhado (August-September) comes, the nutritional value of food intake increases due to inclusion of vegetables harvested from their own fields. With the advent of Bhado (August-September), harvesting of some pulses also start, which enables people to have some pulses as well which further increases the nutritional content and palate in their food intake. The pattern of food intake in Kuar (mid-September to mid-October) is generally a continuation of the pattern obtaining in Bhado.

For the four months from Kartik to Magh (mid-October to mid-February) people earn handsomely, as this is the principal farming season, which they use in good measure to buy food. Thus daily intake of vegetables, bi-weekly or tri-weekly intake of pulses and some amount of milk, poultry, meat and fish, at least once a month, make the diet best during this part of the year.

During Fagun and Chait (mid-February to mid-April) though people still manage two meals, the nutritional content of the food and their palate are considerably diminished as the quantity of pulses, vegetables and milk steadily become scarce in their diet, until it vanishes by the end of Baisakh (mid-April to mid-May). Jeth, Ashar and Sawan are the real "hunger months" for the villagers. Through Table 5.14 read with Table 5.15, the villagers, particularly the women, tell us that food intake is at its worst during the months when all of them have to work the hardest, namely, the summer and monsoon months. For these are the months when not only do they get to work in their own fields as also find wage employment in others' fields, but also work hard at home to deal with disease and sickness that visit the people during this part of the year.

Savita Devi, Rita Devi, Shanti Devi, Saraswati Devi, Urmila devi, Shakuntala Devi, Dhanra Devi, Kumari Devi, Satti Devi, Sangeeta Devi, Phula Devi, Chnmna Devi, Bindo Devi, Chandrawati Devi, Sacho Devi, Rama Devi, Meena Devi, Arti Devi, Seema Devi, Prabha Devi and Kalawati, all inhabitants of Bari Basti, village Tikri also gave us their food calendar in terms of a Seasonality Analysis. They divided the year not in terms of months but in terms of farming seasons, viz., summer, rainy and winter. Table 5.15 is what they said in a nutshell:

Table 5.15 Seasonality Analysis by Women's Group in Bari Basti, Tikri Village

Season	Livelihood	Constraints to Livelihood	Consumption Pattern
Summer (Chait, Baisakh, Jeth)	Work as agricultural labourers during harvesting of wheat and planting of onion seedlings.	Work under scorching sun leads to heat stroke ("Loo"), fever, boils and malaria.	One meal of pulses, rice, chappati, and vegetable every alternate day.

Season	Livelihood	Constraints to Livelihood	Consumption Pattern
Rainy (Asharh, Sawan, Bhado)	Some women work as agricultural labourers during paddy sowing. Women also work for 8 days in deweeding. They get employment for about 10 days in paddy transplantation. Some crops are also harvested which help women get jobs for 15-20 days.	Swelling of hands and feet due to work in paddy fields, in rain. Suffer from cold. These are the worst months as only females earn, while men sit at home as they find no employment in the towns.	Pulses, rice, chappati, and vegetables every alternate days. Meat/fish/eggs once in two months. Two meals a day.
Winter (Kuar, Kartick, Aghan, Poos, Magh and Phagun)	Men get more work in towns during early Kuar to end Kartick, which are considered as the best months of the year. In the beginning of winter employment is available in harvesting paddy and bajra. Women go out to sell vegetables in the village and in the neighbouring villages.	In Magh, men do not work due to a social custom called "Bhenv". Expenditure increases due to use of warm clothes and detergent. Cold and cough are major health problems. Difficult to work in the fields for weeding in cold as the body starts aching.	Bajra chappati, rice, pulses and vegetables every day. Sometimes eat Kichri (a kind of porridge) made of bajra.

Village Analysts: Savita Devi, Rita Devi, Shanti Devi, Saraswati Devi, Urmila Devi, Shakuntala Devi, Dhanra Devi, Kumari Devi, Satti Devi, Sangeeta Devi, Phula Devi, Chnmna Devi, Bindo Devi, Chandrawati Devi, Sacho Devi, Rama Devi, Meena Devi, Arti Devi, Seema Devi, Prabha Devi and Kalawati.

Facilitator: Sudipta Roy.

Date: 31.1.99.

They also told us that children upto 2 years of age are fed milk. Consumption of fruit (like banana, apples etc.) is rare unless it is available in the village CPR or some guests bring them. Guava is plentiful in village orchards. In addition to the work that women do in the field, 50 per cent of the women make necklace of beads since mid-1980s through the assistance they get from IRDP, which helps them to supplement their income to buy food by about Rs. 25 per week.

During summer months a typical food basket of the villagers in Bari Basti contains pulses, chapatis and rice. They would have vegetables every alternative day. During the rainy season, their food basket improves and includes pulses, rice, chapati, vegetables every alternate days, and meat, fish or poultry once in two months. Every household would have two meals a day. When winter sets in, rice, pulses, vegetables and sometimes "Khichri" (a kind of heavy porridge) make their meals. Though the food calendars of Morya and Bari Bastis are not comparable because different time frames have been used, nevertheless the general trends from both the food calendars have considerable congruence. The "hunger months" are almost the same and the hunger months correspond with the period when the women have to work the hardest.

Interestingly, the villagers tell us is very many words that there is a high, degree of correlation between income and food intake. Let us look at what the villagers in the company of Amarnath Morya, Ashok Morya, Chatanki Morya, Panchan Morya tell us about the income and expenditure of people in Morya hamlet, summarised in Tables 5.17 and 5.18. Starting from Jeth (mid-May to mid-June), when the income is at the lowest, Amarnath and his friends tell us that income starts rising from Asharh (mid-June to mid-July), when cultivation starts and employment opportunities expand for them. It peaks in Magh, they tell us and then it starts falling again to reach a fairly low level in Baisakh (mid-April to mid-May). This income comprises income from agriculture, sale of milk, daily wages earned by men and women separately and from artificial pearl garland making by women, of which income from agriculture is the *smallest* component and daily wage is the *largest* constituent. Of these, while daily wages earned by women remain virtually constant throughout the year at Rs. 200 per month, daily wages earned by men remain at Rs. 400 per month for 6 months from Jeth to Kartick and then jumps up to Rs. 600 per month in Aghan, to remain at that figure till summer sets in, in Baisakh when it falls back to Rs. 400 per month. Income from garland making out of artificial pearl remains at a low ebb from Jeth till Bhado at Rs. 120 per month, and then picks up to reach Rs. 180 per month in Kuar and stays at that level till Baisakh.

Now look at Table 5.18 to see what villagers like Amarnath Morya, Ashok Morya, Chatanki Morya, Panchan Morya say on expenditure. Their aggregate expenditure, they tell us, is made up of expenditure on basically three items: food, miscellaneous and social visit. Of these, expenditure on food is by far the largest chunk of the expenditure. It is about 66 per cent for Jeth and Asharh; 80 per cent for Sawan, Bhado and Kuar; 96 per cent for Kartick; above 80 per cent from Aghan to Chait and above 76 per cent in Baisakh. Expenditure on food rises in absolute terms also from Rs. 600 per month in Jeth to Rs. 1300 per month in Poosh, only to marginally decline in Chait and Baisakh. Thus the pattern of expenditure exhibit a copybook case of an under-developed economy, where expenditure on food consumption is unusually high. This rise in expenditure has a high degree of correlation with the incremental variations in income. Compare now what villagers say in terms of columns 7 and 1 of Table 5.17, read with columns-1 and 5 of Table 5.18 and the picture will be clear. If we also compare last column of Table 5.17 with column-5 of Table 5.18, we see there is excess of expenditure over income during the summer months of Baisakh and Jeth and the wet month of Asharh. This is the time when people get into debt.

Table 5.16 Food Calendar Prepared by the Women of Morya Hamlet, Tikri Village

Months	Food Intake	Serial Number
Asharh (June-July)	One meal of few chapatis and salt or chilli paste.	1
Sawan (July-August)	One meal of few chapatis and salt or chilli paste. Towards the end of the month, two meals are possible.	2
Bhado (August-Sept)	One stomach filling meal of chapatis, vegetables and rice. Pulses very rarely	3

Months	Food Intake	Serial Number
Kuar (Sept-Oct.)	The same diet as in Bhado.	4
Kartick (Oct-Nov)	Stomach filling meal of chapatis, vegetables and rice. Two meals.	5
Aghan (Nov-Dec)	Stomach filling meal of chapatis, vegetables and rice. Two meals.	6
Poos (Dec-Jan)	Same as in Aghan.	7
Magh (Jan-February)	Same as in Poosh.	8
Fagun (Feb-March)	Same as in Magh but intake of pulses and costly items get reduced. Two meals.	9
Chait (March-April)	Same as in the month of Fagun but the intake of pulses gets further reduced.	10
Baisakh (April-May)	Same as Chait.	11
Jeth (May-June)	One meal of chapatis and salt or chilly paste.	12

Village Analysts: Indubala, Kamala, Urmila, Jali.
Facilitated by: Meera Jayaswal.
Date: 11.11.98.

Table 5.17 Monthly Income of Low SES Family in Morya Hamlet, Tikri

Months	Daily Labour (Men)	Daily Labour (Women)	Garland Making	Selling Milk	Agricul-ture	Total
Jeth	400	100	120	100	—	620
Asharh	400	100	120	200	—	820
Sawan	400	200	120	300	50	970
Bhado	200	200	120	300	100	1120
Kuar	400	200	180	500	250	1330
Kartick	400	200	180	500	250	1530
Aghan	600	200	180	500	250	1530
Poos	600	200	180	400	250	1630
Magh	600	200	180	400	250	1630
Fagun	600	200	1809	400	100	1480

Months	Daily Labour (Men)	Daily Labour (Women)	Garland Making	Selling Milk	Agricul-ture	Total
Chait	600	200	180	300	100	1380
Baisakh	400	—	180	300	—	1280
Total	5600	2000	1920	4200	1600	15320

Village Analysts: Amarnath Morya, Ashok Morya, Chatanki Morya, Panchan Morya.
Facilitator: Ms. Meera Jayaswal
Date: 5.11.98

Table 5.18 Monthly Expenditure of Low SES Families in Morya Hamlet of Tikri

	Expenditure				
Months	Food	Miscellaneous	Social Visit	Total	Loan
Jeth	600	200	100	900	500
Asharh	600	200	100	900	200
Sawan	1000	100	100	1200	200-
Bhado	1000	100	100	1200	—
Kuar	1000	100	100	1200	—
Kartick	1200	100	150	1250	—
Aghan	1200	100	200	1450	—
Poos	1300	100	200	1500	—
Magh	1300	100	200	1600	—
Fagun	1300	100	200	1600	—
Chait	1200	100	100	1400	—
Baisakh	1000	150	150	1300	—
Total	12700	1500	1700	15900	900

Village Analysts: As in Table 5.16.

XI. Summary and Conclusions

The people of Tikri, especially the women, suffer hunger during large parts of the year, particularly during summer. Barring the five months from Kuar to Magh, the people do not have enough to eat. The question whether households had two square meals a day asked by the 38th Round of the National Sample Survey Organisation of the Government of India (*Planning Commission* 1993) would have definitely evoked a response of no in this village. For seven months they suffer from hunger and for the three summer months of Chait, Baisakh and Jeth, they suffer acute hunger. And as in case of Chandpur, women in Tikri suffer more from hunger than men do.

There is a high degree of correlation between income and food intake. Thus, there would have been greater hunger had there been no employment opportunities provided by the industrial estate near Tikri. That is, diversification of the economic activities has given the people economic access to food. The poor households also borrow considerable sums of money to keep their consumption levels from falling further to push them into starvation. The supplementary income, earned by the women by working late in the nights, plays a crucial role in reducing hunger.

On the whole, people do not have food security throughout the year, though they do not suffer from chronic hunger. Undernutrition and malnutrition of women is clearly made out. Incidentally, in many parts of the country people, who suffer from food insecurity of the variety we see here, resort to satisfying a part of their hunger by collecting, gathering and hunting food from secondary sources of food (*Mukherjee,* 1994, 1997; *Mukherjee and Mukherjee,* 1997, 1999) viz., common property resources, forests, and "micro environments" *(Chambers,* 1993). In case of Tikri that option is also closed. There is none of that present here. The guava orchard and the mango orchard in the village have been cleared to raise crops etc., because apparently yield from these trees had declined so sharply that retaining them was of little value.

6 Community Perspective on Hunger from Vegetable Producing Farmers: Village Uncha Gaon, Faridabad

I. Introduction

Uncha Gaon is situated approximately 4.3 kms south east of Faridabad old industrial area and 1.34 from Ballabgarh industrial area. Uncha Gaon is spread over a very large area. It is exposed to vehicular traffic and dust pollution due to its location right on the road. Uncha Gaon has the look and feel of a town as well as of a village. On both sides of the road you have rows of shops including liquor shops (called wine shops), hotels, chemists and studios. Most of the people living in Uncha Gaon proper are engaged in non-agricultural occupations, largely ignorant of what goes on in the various hamlets around the township. Most of the houses in Uncha Gaon are more than one storied, and are brick houses.

The inner area of Uncha Gaon is called *Gola Neem*, resembles a village and is divided into smaller hamlets. The inhabitants have knowledge of agriculture and many of them are agriculturists and have considerable experience of cultivation. Uncha Gaon is divided into five hamlets or Muhallas. Inhabitants of Ahir, Saini and Sahupura Roadside Muhallas have agricultural lands and cultivate their own land. Quite a few of the inhabitants work as agricultural labourers. Generally the *Malis* of Saini hamlet grow vegetables and the *Ahirs* of Ahir Muhalla cultivate wheat during Rabi season and jowar during Kharif season.

The participatory sessions began in a small teastall where a few elder citizens of the ward were sitting. The senior citizens gave some idea about Saini Muhalla: there were about 500 people in 150 households and around 80 per cent of whom were engaged in agriculture. Subsequently, younger people joined the group and this helped. The group was divided into two: one of the groups sat in the teastall and the other went out to the fields. Both the groups had a mixture of young and old alike, though the number of people participating in the discussion kept on changing, with fresh entrants and exists.

Livelihood Systems

The groups were separately led into discussing their livelihood systems, through seasonality analysis. Since the group inside the teastall had difficulty in discussing a month-wise seasonality analysis, as they thought it was boring, the group decided to change their discussion to per annum basis from the month-wise analysis. The method was also changed from verbal (group discussion) to visual. The group was, thus, provided with postcard sized 'flash' cards, with a request to note down the names of months separately on the cards provided. The group wrote down the names of the months, according the lunar calendar, and then arranged them on the floor, starting with Baisakh (the first month in the lunar calendar). They then recollected the livelihood they pursued in each month, wrote them separately on another set of cards and placed them alongside the name of relevant month. They were then requested to write down the constraints they faced in the pursuit of their livelihoods, against each month, on another set of cards and place them against the livelihood to which the relative constraint was most relevant. This was executed with precision.

The group also indicated the nature of agricultural work done by them during these months and the constraints they face in agriculture in different months. They then wrote down these two sets of information on two sets of cards and placed them against the name of the month to which they relate. The "document" that was generated on the floor, was then "interviewed". In course of the interview the group brought live pests/ insects (such as *gandars, lalrii, locust)* from the fields to explain the nature of the constraints faced. A similar exercise was carried out with the women group as well. The resultant output is transcribed as Table 6.1 and 6.2.

The women's group mentioned that agriculture, selling milk, working as labourers and working in industry provided them with purchasing power throughout the twelve months. And the constraint that they faced was repayment of loan in Baisakh.

Tables 6.1 and 6.2 indicate that the main occupation of the inhabitants of Uncha Gaon is agriculture. A much smaller number of people are self employed in small business and petty trade, employed in government service, and working as labourers. Selling of milk is a secondary occupation of a large number of villagers. The exact livelihood structure of Uncha Gaon in 1990s consists of 80 per cent agriculturists, 60 per cent milk vendors, 7 per cent private small businessmen and petty traders, 2 per cent government employees and 5 per cent labourers. There are no visible variations either on a month to month basis or seasonally, in the nature of "employment" available to the people.

The present livelihood structure has evolved over the years. From a purely agrarian economy in 1940s, when 100 per cent of the people were agriculturists, Uncha Gaon had experienced a 5 per cent reduction in the number of people dependent on agriculture in 1950s and then another 5 per cent reduction in the number of people dependent on agriculture during the decade of the 70s. Between 1980 and 1990, agriculture lost another 10 per cent people embracing agriculture as their source of livelihood. Thus in 1990s, 80 per cent of the inhabitants of Uncha Gaon are agriculturists. At least 60 per cent of villagers generally pursue more than a single occupation.

Table 6.1 Seasonality Analysis of Livelihood and Constraints (Men's Group, Saini Muhalla) Uncha Gaon

Months	Means of Livelihood	Constraints Encountered
Baisakh	Agriculture, private and government service, selling milk, labourer, trucker, petty business like brokerage, shops.	Stomach ache and diahorrea due to consumption of new wheat. Milk yield declines, prices increase marginally, hence net loss. Repayment of loans to money lenders.
Jeth	Same as in Baisakh.	Acute shortage of water, irregular power supply, extreme heat, increase in mosquitoes, milk yield falls, prices rise marginally, hence total loss.

Months	Means of Livelihood	Constraints Encountered
Asharh	Same as in Jeth	Fever and malaria. Threat of Cholera. Farmers and daily wage earners find it difficult to go out for work.
Sawan	Same as in Asharh	Fever and Malaria. Threat of Cholera. Farmers and daily wage earners find it difficult to go out for work. Forced to cut expenditure. No income from agriculture. Excess humidity. *Gulguta* in buffaloes due to eating new grass.
Bhado	Same as in Sawan	Fever and malaria. Threat of cholera. Farmers and daily wage earners find it difficult to go out for work. Forced to cut expenditure. No income from agriculture. Excess humidity. Insects attack foot of buffaloes. Burning sensation in eyes from thermocol factories' smoke. Allergy due to Congress Grass.
Kuar	Same as in Bhado	Same constraints as the ones faced in Bhado.
Katak	Same as in Kuar	Getting loans. Cough, cold and headache. Repayment of loans..
Aghan	Same as in Kartick	Same as Kartick.
Poosh	Same as in Aghan	Pneumonia in children.
Magh	Same as in Poos.	Same as Poos.
Fagun	Same as in Magh.	Repayment of loan. Cold and fever (no serious health problem). Milk yield starts falling, resulting in loss.
Chait	Same as in Fagun	Same as in Fagun.

Village Analysts: Balbir, Bansi, Harish, Omprakash, Bhagawat, Krisen, Mahesh, Babloo.
Facilitator: Sudipta Ray

Table 6.2 Seasonality Analysis of Agricultural Activities and Constraints (Women's Group)

Months	Livelihood	Agricultural Activities	Constraints
Baisakh	Agriculture, selling milk, working as labourers and in industry.	Harvesting wheat and threshing. Selling lobia (beans), ridge gourd, radish and brinjals.	Power shortage. Hailstorm. *Lalrii* eats leaves of vegetables.
Jeth		Irrigating vegetable fields. Sowing bajra, jowar, chilies, bottle gourd etc. Selling lobia, bitter gourd, onions, lady's finger, bottle gourd etc.	Power shortage.
Asharh		Sowing bajra & jowar., seeds of cauliflower, lady's finger, bottle gourd, spinach. Selling pumpkins, green chilies, onion, lady's finger.	Locust on jowar. Low rainfall. *Moriya* in chilies. Chitli in young vegetable plants.
Sawan		Paddy transplantation. Applying fertilizers. Transplanting spinach and cauliflower seedlings. Selling bottle/ bitter gourd, onion, lady's finger etc.	Same as in Asharh.
Bhado		Selling spinach.	Same as in Sawan.
Kuar		Planting cauliflower, radish and potatoes.	
Kartick		Harvesting paddy. Planting cabbage and cauliflower. Selling cauliflower, brinjals, spinach, chilies and radish.	*Sundi* infestation in vegetables.

Months	Livelihood	Agricultural Activities	Constraints
Aghan		Sowing wheat. Sowing potato. Selling carrot, cauliflower, lobia, chilies, gourd, lady's finger.	Same as in Kartick.
Poos		Irrigate wheat fields. Sow onion and chili seeds. Sell carrot, cauliflower, lobhia, potato (earlier stored), cabbage.	
Magh		Irrigate wheat fields (twice). Apply fertilizers. Sell brinjal, carrot, lobia, cauliflower. Sow bitter gourd, cucumber, onion, ridge gourd, chily, radish etc.	
Fagun		Irrigate wheat fields. Selling chily, potato, cabbage, cauliflower, spinach. swing seeds of lobia, ridge gourd, bitter gourd.	Rust in wheat.
Chait		Harvesting and threshing of wheat. Selling of bitter gourd, onion, cucumber, brinjal. sowing spinach.	

Village Analysts: Tarawati, Kamala, Lali, Sarbir.
Facilitator: Ms. Meera Jayaswal.

The landholding pattern in Uncha Gaon is as follows:

Table 6.3 Landholding Pattern in Uncha Gaon

Category of Villagers	Landholding Pattern
Landless	5 per cent
Less than 1 acre (marginal farmers)	60 per cent
Between 1 and 3 acres	35 per cent

Clearly most of the inhabitants of Uncha Gaon have some land except for the 5 per cent landless. Generally speaking, in the ecology and natural resources base that the area has, any land holding below 1 acre is worse than, or at best no better, than the landless. The village is predominantly a village of the agriculturists.

Tables 6.1, 6.2 and 6.3 show that within the agriculturists class there are two notable features. One, there is a great deal of emphasis on growing vegetables, large in variety and significant in the number of times they are grown, and not on food crops like wheat and paddy. Two, the agriculturists primarily comprise of only small and marginal farmers, there being very few large or medium sized farmers. The urban base of the village and the nearness of the industrial areas of Ballabgarh as well as Faridabad, provide the vegetable growers good access to a market for vegetables, all round the year, not just in any particular season. And secondly, the small pieces of land owned by the villagers make growing of paddy and wheat less feasible than growing vegetables. Thus the composition of agricultural produce is determined by the size of landholdings, availability of markets and the economics of growing vegetables vis-à-vis growing foodcrops like paddy and wheat (the last we will discuss later in this book).

If we take all the livelihood systems pursued in Uncha Gaon, they form part of the larger hierarchy of agro-ecosystems shown and the villagers gave us an account of the agro-ecosystems from village level and below. Villagers in Uncha Gaon are not generally engaged in gathering-hunting and handicraft manufacture, only a few are in off-farm employment and trading systems. Agriculture remains at the heart of the livelihood system in Uncha Gaon, though a fairly large section of the population has more than one source of livelihood. Within the farming system, the inhabitants rely partly on livestock system and more fully in cropping system, involved in the field and growing crop.

However, farmers in Uncha Gaon grow primary commodities, mostly vegetables, for sale. These commodities may be eaten, used in preparing drinks, turned into paper or clothes or used as drugs. The farmers are unconcerned. Only a portion of what these farmers grow is used to feed themselves and their family. Agricultural trade (read vegetable trade) is a significant factor in the trading system of Uncha Gaon. Thus food is available to the farmers of Uncha Gaon primarily through exchange entitlements. But in this game the farmers are price takers, not price makers, which makes their life a little more insecure and uncertain.

General Problems

A village comprising landless people, marginal and small farmers, is likely to have several general problems. The women among the group volunteered to sit down to isolate their "best problems" and then rank them in descending order of their severity. This was agreed. The women listed their best problems first and then indicated the severity of general problems faced by the community, by placing rajma seeds against each of the identified "best problems". The principle followed is larger the number of seeds placed against a "best problem", the more severe it is, 10 indicating the severest problem and 1 indicating the least severe problem. The outcome of the exercise is in Table 6.4. The group also indicated the hardship caused by each of their best problems.

Table 6.4 Scoring and Ranking of Problems of Ahir Muhalla of Uncha Gaon by Women's Group

Problems	Hardships Caused	Rank/ Score	Since How Many Years
Power shortage#	Fodder cutting and irrigation hampered.	Score: 6 Rank: 4	5-6 years
Land acquisition by Govt..	With limited employment opportunity, households threatened by land acquisition face prospects of starvation	Score: 10 Rank: 1	Anticipated from 1999
Unemployment	Poverty in households.	Score: 7 Rank: 3	10-12 years
Drinking habit of men	Loss of household, income, violence and spousal battery.	Score: 8 Rank: 2	5-6 years
Poverty#	Cut in consumption of essential commodities	Score: 6 Rank: 4	6-7 years
Outsiders employed in local industry*	Local persons get displaced from the labour market. Increased theft, robbery etc.	Score: 4 Rank: 5	10-12 years
No training centre for women*	Women remain unskilled.	Score: 4 Rank: 5	—

\# Power shortage and poverty ranked at par as the 4th severest problem.

* Outsiders grabbing employment opportunities and lack of training centre ranked at par, as the 5th severest problem.

Clearly acquisition of land by the Haryana Urban Development Authority is ranked as their foremost problem. It foretells the pains of impending hunger. For the farmers, growing crops is the source of life itself. Even a small piece of land, with the irrigation potential and the suitability of growing and marketing vegetables help people avert the pangs of starvation. Thus a legal action by the state, apparently in public interest, is about to push the farming households of Uncha Gaon to starvation. This seems to be a vindication of what Sen beautifully wrote, nearly two decades ago, as the concluding line of his famous work, *Poverty and Famines* (1981):

"Starvation deaths can reflect legality with a vengeance". Alcoholism is ranked only next tc land acquisition as a general problem of Uncha Gaon. It is as much a social problem as it is an economic problem. Recognizing the problems created by alcoholism, the Government of Haryana had in 1996-97 imposed prohibition in the State along with other States like Andhra Pradesh. However, in a patriarchal society, where higher echelons of Government and bureaucracy are dominated by men, prohibition was repealed in 1998, on the ostensible grounds that it was difficult to implement the prohibition, leading to illicit brewing and "smuggling" of liquor, and that the State exchequer was losing out valuable excise revenue, which could have been utilised for development projects. Whatever happened to the revenue from sale of liquor one is not sure, but the villagers, particularly women, know what consequences flow from abolition of prohibition, namely, domestic (and social) violence and loss of peace. It has a more severe implication. Alcoholism is not only an evil in itself but it also causes loss of household (scarce) income, indicating that irrespective of who creates household income, or the how of it, the end control is with the male members of the household. It sadly mirrors an iniquitous distribution of intra-familial power, loaded against women.

Villagers comprising landless people, 60 per cent marginal farmers and 30 per cent small farmers, where men revel in expending scare resources on alcoholism, the experience in suffering poverty is telling. And their sense of deprivation is much more painful as they are exposed to and aware of the luxuries enjoyed by the 'haves', due to the nearness of Uncha Gaon to much richer urban areas of Ballabgarh and Faridabad, and access to TV programmes crammed with crash consumerism. This pain of deprivation is heightened by the reality that the employment opportunities created at considerable cost to the villagers, subserve the interest of outsiders, most of whom are not the 'have nots'. Thus the villagers faces, the twin realities: of land, the vital source of life itself, being taken away by the State (which ironically is supposed to protect them) and of employment opportunities being taken away by outsiders, not infrequently, the 'haves'. The resultant scenario is increase in theft, robbery and spousal battery. How much of alcoholism is on account of social pressure and how much of it is on account of habit, could not be determined but both have their own roles to play.

II. Crops Grown and the Cropping Pattern

There are two kinds of crops grown: food crops and cash crops. Jowar (in Kharif season) and wheat (in Rabi season) are the principal food crops grown. The cash crops are vegetables: during Kharif, tomato, brinjal, lady's finger, spinach, field-ridge, ghiya and cucumber are principally grown. During Rabi potato on the one hand and cauliflower, mustard "Saag", cabbage, spinach, bitter gourd and bottle gourd etc., on the other, are the principal crops grown. It is pointed out that with improved varieties of seeds, some of the vegetables like cabbage and bottle/bitter gourd are beginning to be grown round the year. However, food crops are grown on a much smaller scale than cash crops in both absolute and relative terms.

The cropping pattern of Uncha Gaon is fairly straight forward: a wide variety of vegetables, jowar and wheat are grown. The researchers in fact saw numerous vegetable crops at various stages of their maturity: untied cabbage, prematurely dried onion leaves, ready and healthy vegetables like brinjal, tomato, cucumber, spinach, young vegetable seedlings, which are also sold for profit. The distribution of wheat, jowar and vegetables is best described in Table 6.5, prepared by women of Sahupura road side Muhalla.

Land is partitioned into two sectors: the food crop sector and the cash crop sector, each occupying approximately 50 per cent of cultivable land.

Table 6.5 Cropping Pattern in Uncha Gaon

Months	On 50 per cent of Cultivable Land	On 50 per cent of Cultivable Land
Jeth	*Land Preparation*	Cultivation of tomatoes, brinjal, lady's finger, spinach. cucumber, ridge gourd, bottle gourd etc.
Asharh	Jowar cultivation	Same as Jeth.
Sawan	Jowar cultivation	Same as Asharh.
Bhado	Jowar cultivation	Same as Sawan.
Kuar	Jowar cultivation	Same as Bhado.

Months		**On 25 per cent of Land**	**On 25 per cent of Land**
Kartick	***Land Preparation***	Vegetables like cauliflower, spinach, cabbage, radish, chily, onion, bitter gourd, etc.	Potato
Aghan	Wheat cultivation	Same as Kartick.	Potato.
Poos	Wheat cultivation	Same as Aghan.	Potato.
Magh	Wheat cultivation	Same as Poos.	Potato.
Fagun	Wheat cultivation		Potato, vegetables.
Chait	Wheat cultivation		Potato, vegetables.
Baisakh	Wheat *harvesting*		Potato, vegetables.

Village Analysts: Amarwali, Bhagwati, Umraon and others.
Facilitated by: Ms. Meera Jayaswal. *Date*: 27.3.1999

In the food crop sector jowar and wheat are the principal crops grown. The entire land earmarked for food crops is utilised for jowar cultivation for 5 months, from Jeth to Kuar, including land preparation in Jeth and harvesting in Kuar, or may be in some years spilling into Kartick. The same land is utilised for the next 7 months, from Kartick to Baisakh for growing wheat, including preparation of land in Kartick and harvesting of wheat in Baisakh. Almost 80 per cent of the wheat sown are late varieties, viz., 1553, 2339 and 2338.

In the cash crop sector, the principal crops are vegetables of every description and potato. During the 5 month period (from Jeth to Kuar) when jowar is grown on the land earmarked for food crops, on the entire land earmarked for cash crops, vegetables like tomato, brinjal, lady's finger, spinach, gourd of various kinds and cucumber are grown.

During the 4 month period of Kartick, Aghan, Poos and Magh, only 50 per cent of the land set apart for cash crops (that is, only 25 per cent of total cultivable land) is utilised for growing vegetables like cauliflower and cabbage etc., and on the balance 50 per cent of the land set apart for cash crops (that is, 25 per cent of total cultivable land) potato is cultivated. In the following three months of Fagun, Chait and Baisakh, the segmentation of land between growing vegetables and raising potatoes, seen in the earlier four months is done away with. The entire 50 per cent of cultivable land, meant for cash crops, is devoted to growing vegetables of all kinds.

Table 6.6 Seasonality Analysis of Agricultural Activities and Food Consumption (Men's group Saini Muhalla)

Months	Food Consumption	Agricultural Activities
Baisakh	Chappatis with pickle or Chili chutney. Vegetables from their own fields.	Harvesting of wheat and selling the produce. Brinjal, melon and onion sold. Sow seeds for lady's finger, bottle gourd, toraï, chili, pumpkin, cucumber, bitter gourd. Income from agriculture is 50 per cent.
Jeth	Chappatis with pickle or Chili chutney. Occasionally vegetables, fruits, dalia, lassi or milk and tea. 3 meals plus an evening meal of tea/ milk.	Irrigation and weeding in the fields. Collection of fodder, like cutting grass and harvesting jowar. Sowing of jowar and maize seeds. Selling cucumber, kakri and melon.
Asharh	Same as Jeth.	Irrigating fields. Cutting fodder. Selling vegetables sown in Baisakh. Income 25 per cent. Sowing bajra.
Sawan	Two meals of chappatis with pickle or chili chutney. Home grown vegetables. **H**	Seedling of cauliflower and brinjal raised. Cutting some jowar for fodder.
Bhado	Same as Sawan **H**	Cutting jowar. Sowing radish, carrot, spinach cabbage seeds. Transplanting cauliflower brinjal seedlings.
Kuar	Two meals of chappatis with pickle or chili chutney. Some vegetables. **H**	Irrigating and weeding fields. Cutting some jowar.
Kartick	Chappatis with pickle or chili chutney. Occasionally vegetables, fruits, milk tea. 3 meals plus an evening meal of tea or milk	Harvesting jowar and bajra. Selling spinach, cauliflower, fenugreek, coriander, brinjal, radish. Income is upto 20 per cent.

Months	Food Consumption	Agricultural Activities
Aghan	Same as Kartick.	Sowing wheat seeds. Selling spinach cauliflower, coriander, brinjal, radish, cabbage. Income upto 40 per cent.
Poos	Bajra chappatis with sarson da saag, pickle or chili chutney. Occasionally vegetables. 3 meals plus an evening meal of tea/milk.	Irrigating land. Selling spinach cauliflower, fenugreek, coriander, brinjal, radish, cabbage. Income upto 45 per cent.
Magh	Same as Poosh.	Selling spinach cauliflower, fenugreek, coriander, brinjal, radish, cabbage. Income upto 40 per cent. Irrigating fields. Sowing cucumber and melon seeds.
Fagun	Same as Magh.	Selling cauliflower, potato, brinjal, fenugreek, spinach, carrot, radish. Income is 45 per cent. Irrigating and weeding fields.
Chait	Same as Fagun.	Fenugreek, spinach, coriander, carrot and sarson da saag sold. Income is 35 per cent. Irrigate fields.

H indicates hunger periods.

Village Analysts: Balbir, Bansi, Harish, Omprakash, Bhagawat, Krisen, Mahesh, Babloo.
Facilitator: Sudipta Ray.

In the process farmers practise crop rotation: land on which jowar is grown in the first instance is then utilised to grow vegetables and potatoes. And land on which vegetables are grown in the first place is then devoted to growing wheat. This means that the same plot of land is cultivated alternately for growing jowar and wheat on the one hand, and vegetables and potatoes on the other. Such rotation, the villagers perceive, replenishes soil nutrients and residues from one kind of crop helps manure land for growing the other kind of crop. It is pointed out that in Table 6.5, though the villagers have shown that they grow vegetables on all the 12 months, yet the nature of the activities varies from month to month. This is made clearer in the Seasonality Analysis done by men in Saini Muhalla, which is presented in Table 6.6. Attention in particular is drawn to Column 3.

There is in virtually all the months of the year something to harvest/gather/collect, something to sow, something to transplant and something to sell. It absorbs the energy and resources, including time of the farmers and their households all through. The farmers' households are in the field from 7.00-8.00 in the morning till 6.00-7.00 in the evening (with a margin of about an hour or half an hour on either side to make adjustment for sunrise and sunset during winter and summer months) with an hour of break in the afternoon for midday meals. This is one reason why apart from selling milk, the farmers in Uncha Gaon have no secondary occupation.

III. Intensity of Cultivation

From the discussion we had with the villagers and from what is articulated in Tables 6.5 and 6.6, the intensity of cultivation is fairly high. Each plot of land is cultivated several times over. And there are several doses of fertilisers applied, and pesticides used, for each round of crops grown. If we see column 3 of Table 6.6 and read it with Table 6.5, it clarifies that the same land is cultivated several times in a year. Though in Table 6.5 the villagers have shown that they grow tomato, lady's finger etc. from Jeth to Kuar (four months) it does not mean that the crop cycle of each of these crops is of four months duration. There is a good mix of fast growing and late varieties of vegetables. Cauliflower has a longer gestation period while spinach and cabbage yield crops faster. They also pointed out that they grow some vegetables once, but reap harvest several times over. For instance, spinach can be harvested upto 7 times. If they find that due to excess supply a vegetable is unlikely to fetch a good price, they do not harvest it at all and leave it to flower, so that they can gather the seeds and sell them instead or plough them back into the fields as manure. Similarly for ridge gourd, bitter gourd and bottle gourd: the creepers are raised once and the fruits (for want of a better word) they bear are plucked several times.

All farmers also do not grow all the vegetables concurrently: different farmers grow different vegetables, with considerable overlaps as well. Similarly, farmers grow various combinations of early and late varieties of several of these vegetables in order to ensure that there is something to sell all the time and the cash flow of the household is maintained in all the months. As one farmer poetically told us: "Wheat is like the moon: it vanishes after some time. Vegetables are like streams, always flowing". Similarly, it does not take 7 months (from Kartick to Baisakh) to grow cauliflower, spinach etc. For instance the land on which potato is cultivated (between Kartick and Magh) is used for vegetable cultivation from Fagun to Baisakh (see Table 6.5, last column).

The facts that most of the farmers are small and marginal farmers, and are owner cultivators, also contribute to increase the intensity of cultivation. This is particularly so because the farmers have their small and marginal farms as their basic (and in many cases, the only) source of livelihood. The amount of labour applied to land is another indication of a high level of farming intensity. There is no data, however, to exactly pinpoint and say precisely how many times the farmers cultivate their plots of land.

IV. Changes in Agricultural Practices that Have Taken Place

The group of men, who went out of the teastall to tell us the story of their livelihood system, was asked by the facilitator if it is possible for them to provide some insight into the story of the livelihood pattern as it has evolved over the years, now that they have told us what their agricultural practices are at the current point of time. The facilitator first prodded them to recall the significant events of their lives over the last 50 years or so. The group responded remarkably well and told us that in the 1940s the wells were *Kuccha* (unbricked), India won independence and Punjabi Refugees from Pakistan were allotted land in Faridabad for resettlement and rehabilitation. In the 1950s, they recalled, the *Kuccha* wells were all brick laid as the government gave incentives for so doing and Bata Shoe factory came to be established. In the 1960s, tractor and electricity were first used in cultivation, and fertilisers were used too. It was not until the 70s that the HYV seeds came to Uncha Gaon. This was the historic decade when the state of Haryana was curved out of Punjab. The group recalled that in the 1980s, Uncha Gaon became a part of Nagarpalika (municipality). They then went about drawing the Historical Transects as at Tables 6.7 and 6.8.

Table 6.7 Historical Transect of Farming System and Crops (Male Group, Saini Muhalla, Uncha Gaon)

Decade	Occupation	Cropping Pattern	Farming System	Constraints
1940s	100 per cent agriculture.	Wheat, jowar, bajra, barley, gram, maize, moat, henna.	Irrigation by rehant and rains. Organic manure. Seeds from previous year's harvest. Ploughing with bullock. Cart for transporting produce.	None
1950s	95 per cent Agriculture. Rest in industry, government and labourers.	Same as 1940s.	Same as 1940s.	None
1960s	95 per cent Agriculture, 2 per cent labourers, 3 per cent service and 50 per cent milk.	Same as in 1950s but pulses reduced.	Late 60s HYV seeds intro-duced. Tractor for ploughing. Electric pump for irrigating.	Increase in Nagfal (weed).
1970s	90 per cent agriculture, 55 per cent milk, rest as in 1960.	Vegetables started to be grown on a commercial basis.	Hybrid seeds in full force. Pesticides. Tractor for Ploughing. Electric pump	*Jai* and *Mundi* appear in wheat field. *Kanduwa* in wheat fields.

Decade	Occupation	Cropping Pattern	Farming System	Constraints
			for irrigation. fertilisers are in thing.	
1980s	Same as 1970s except 60 per cent in milk	Onion added to the list of items grown on a commercial basis	Same as 1970s	Termites emerge. Nilgais start grazing crops
1990s	80 per cent agriculture, 60 per cent milk, 5 per cent private service, 7 per cent petty trade/business, 3 per cent labourer and 2 per cent in government	Wheat, jowar. mustard, cauliflower, potato, cabbage, brinjal, chili, gourds of all varieties.	Same as 1980s	Termites increase. Nilgais continue grazing. Weeds: doob grass, motha, zinzri, makra, sati and congress grass. Green tidda in lobhia and cauliflower. Increase in incidence of Gandar (Caterpillar). Water level has gone below 85 feet. Moriya in chilies.

Facilitator: Sudipta Ray

Table 6.8 Historical Transect of Changes in Farm Produce (Male Group) Saini Muhalla, Uncha Gaon

Decade	Yield of Wheat	Size of Wheat Grains	Colour of Wheat Grains	Industrial Growth
1940s	3-4 quintals/acre	Long and fat	Golden	Nil
1950s	3-4 quintals/acre	Long and fat	Golden	Bata and Escorts came.
1960s	16 quintals/acre	Relatively small and thin	Orangeish red	Steel factory opened
1970s	16 quintals/acre	Relatively small and thin	Yellow	Ajit Rubber & Thermocol Factories opened
1980s	13 quintals. Yield started falling in late 80s	From late 80s less grain per ear of corn and small in size	From the late 80s, creamish	Khanna Thermocol Factory opened
1990s	Wheat yield 13 quintals/acre. Yield of lady's finger, cucumber, small melon and onion falling since last 4-5 years.	Small in size and less grain	Creamish. Height of standing wheat crop has declined. Wheat corn size has fallen by 1 per cent.	

Notes: The villagers also indicated that bottle gourd no longer tastes as good as it used to be. Cauliflower since last 10-12 years develop black stains, which when washed turns creamish, spoiling the white colour of cauliflower, considered a mark of its good quality.

Facilitator: Sudipta Ray

By examining Tables 6.7 and 6.8, one could read a few general trends indicated by the villagers:

Agriculture, which absorbed 100 per cent of the total population of Uncha Gaon in the 1940-50, has gradually lost its pre-eminence. It now supports no more than 80 per cent of the population, though it is above the national average of 70 per cent.

As agriculture declined in importance, selling milk gained in prominence: from none in the business of selling milk in the 1940-50, it now engages almost 60 per cent of the total population of Uncha Gaon, as a secondary source of employment and a supplementary source of income.

With the flux of time as new industries moved into the vicinity of Uncha Gaon, people to some extent diversified their livelihood pattern: from a purely agrarian economy in the 1950s, Uncha Gaon has moved into an economy where service sector has gained in importance, small industry and petty business have given livelihoods to quite a large number of the people, and demand for pure labourers has increased.

This diversification in livelihood and demand for labourers as also services could not absorb all the additional hands that were added to the labour force, because the villagers perceive that outsiders have come in to fill in the job vacancies created. The mechanisation of agriculture also prevented these people being absorbed into the agricultural sector. This shows up as 5 per cent of the people being unemployed.

Having summarised the general trends indicated by the villagers, we might now turn to what villagers perceive as changes in food grown, agricultural practices and yield as well as crop quality. Let us take the decade of the 40s as the point of departure and Tables 6.7 and 6.8 as reference data. Refer to first column of Table 6.7 and last of Table 6.8. In that decade, a large number of food crops were cultivated, though it is difficult to reconstruct the exact percentage of arable land on which each food crop was grown. The crops were a mixture of staples, coarse cereals and pulses and Henna for use as cosmetic, usually worn as intricate designs on palms/hands and feet during weddings. The main crops were coarse grains (barley and bajra) and cereals (wheat, jowar and maize). All the food crops grown were for household consumption in the village. Farming was both subsistence and sustenance activity. The variety of food crops grown gave the farmers not only the opportunity to diffuse their risks of failure due to pests, insects, droughts, floods, disease or whatever, either singly or in some combination, but also ensured that consumption basket of the households had a combination of foodgrains which contained fibre, nutrition and protein. In the 1950s the position remained largely the same.

In 1960s, winds of change began to sweep Uncha Gaon. Pulses were reduced. By the time Uncha Gaon reached 1970s, vegetable was introduced as a commercial crop and it is important to recognise this fact. In the next decade, as HYV seeds took ground, wheat remained the only main Rabi crop and bajra held on as the main Kharif crop. Cultivation of gram stopped. In the 1980s mustard and onion took roots as a cash crop in the hope of high return.

As of now (1990s) farmers in Uncha Gaon are left with wheat and jowar as principal Rabi and Kharif non-commercial crops respectively, with a sprinkling of bajra. Food crops are grown in 50 per cent of the gross cropped area of the village. Wheat is grown for household consumption as also for sale in the market.

Cash crops are grown on the other 50 per cent of arable land, which are mainly vegetables and grown, in the main, for sale. Amongst the vegetables now grown, in Rabi, potato is by far the most important and is grown on 50 per cent of the land which is earmarked for cash crops, or 25 per cent of the total arable land of Uncha Gaon. The variety and diversity, therefore, of food crops grown are markedly reduced.

As we move from the 1940s into the last decade of this century, Tables 6.7 and 6.8 bring us near the truth that the mosaic of food crops grown in Uncha Gaon is also becoming boring in terms of nutrition and palate: from several crops of different values, uses and nutrition, the present days crops grown are basically three: vegetables, wheat and jowar (as fodder). This reduction in diversity of crops signals a movement away from poly-culture *towards* standard mono-culture. It signals reduction in palate and nutritional value of the food consumed in farm households of Uncha Gaon. The crop grown in the farms can provide basically only carbohydrates and a modicum of fibre in terms of some vegetable, as most of it is for commercial purpose. Additionally, whereas in 1950s and 1960s much of agricultural operations were for ensuring self-sufficiency in *food*, in 1990s the emphasis seems to be on generating *income for self-sufficiency in income*. There is a movement from growing crops for meeting the food requirements of households and of the community, to growing crops for consumption of outsiders, who can buy in the market and for money. Thus, in a sense and certainly partially, production in Uncha Gaon has shifted from catering to the needs of the "have nots" of the village to the needs of the "haves" outside the village, by exhausting the natural resources meant to serve the essential needs of the "have nots". This has serious inter-generational questions and somebody needs to address them. Indeed, the villagers have mentioned the falling of the water level to below 85 feet which makes irrigation difficult. This may be interpreted to mean that water resources are being used up beyond sustainable (read replenishable limits), to cater to the current needs of "haves" outside the village at the expense of conserving resources for future generations.

V. Changes in Agricultural Practices and Reasons for the Changes

With the changes in pattern of food production witnessed by Uncha Gaon, there has been other changes as well, some influenced by it, others influencing it. A chain of dynamic changes in farming practices has influenced the changes in cropping pattern shown to us by the villagers. In 1940s and 1950s, we were told agriculture was wholly rainfed. Agriculture in Uncha Gaon was all about traditional practices in regard to seeds, water harvesting structures, soil nutrients and implements. It was a family affair. The farmers and the community were in total control of the inputs, barring rains where they depended on nature's bounties.

During 1960-70 mechanization of agriculture started taking roots: tubewells and tractors came to their own. In 1970-80, we see agriculture in Uncha Gaon adopting "new technology" in its full form: hybrid or HYV seeds replacing traditional varieties, chemical fertilisers crowding out manure, insecticides and pesticides put in operation in place of seeds known to be naturally pest and insect resistant and tractors substituting for the bullocks and the wooden plough. The last remnants of the traditional practice is crop rotation: land on which bajra/wheat is grown in one round is then used to grow vegetables and vice-versa. Dependence on rains for water is eliminated as pump sets provide water for farming, but the farmers have at once surrendered their independence from the clutches of the powerful elements in the economy. The farmers are dependent upon seed companies/farms, pesticide and insecticide companies through their dealers, Haryana State Electricity Board for their power and hence for irrigation tractor companies and the fertiliser companies. The control of the farmers and the community on inputs vital for their survival is out of their hands.

This shift in farming practices for food production also means that farming in Uncha Gaon, as in Chandpur and Tikri, is now a High External Input Agriculture (HEIA) from Zero External Input Agriculture (ZEIA) during 1940-50 and then Low External Input Agriculture (LEIA) in 1960-70, as we travel through time. In the 1940s and 1950s food production was based on what the farmer and the community had: seeds, labour, bullocks, plough and the wooden hoe, manure and rains. In the 1980s and 1990s, food production has come to be based on inputs more from outside the households and the community: HYV seeds, pesticides, insecticides, chemical fertilisers, electricity, tractor power, tubewells and pump sets. Thus, whereas in the 40s and 50s the farmers could be comfortable in cultivation and farming, buying virtually nothing from outside his/her household or at best the community, in the 1990s we are in Uncha Gaon where farmers buy virtually everything except family labour from outside the household. This transition from ZEIA to LEIA and eventually to HEIA, that the villagers of Uncha Gaon show us through Tables 6.7 and 6.8, is a copy book case confirming the framework of "internal resources vs. external resources" provided by Francis and King (*Francis and King,* 1988).

Except for energy required for photosynthesis drawn from sun, in the 1980s and 1990s, farming in Uncha Gaon relies primarily on external sources for accessing inputs for food production including knowledge. Water, nitrogen, other nutrients, seeds, machinery, weed and pest control, extension and credit are all accessed, in the main, from outside. Accessing inputs from outside the households and community results in a net outflow of resources from the households/community. In a sense, increasing agricultural activity could be a mechanism for immiserisation of farmers. For a more definitve assessment of this dimension, we need to work out the terms of trade faced by agriculture which is beyond the scope of this book.

A concommitant development is unsustainable use of resources. When food production in the 1980s and 1990s has become more dependent on sourcing inputs from outside Uncha Gaon, food production has come to use resources that are not always renewable. Internal resources are "inherently renewable and thus have the potential to be used on a 'sustained' basis, indefinitely, through ecologically sound methods of farming" (*Conway* and *Barbier,* 1990). Water, nitrogen, other nutrients, seeds, machinery, weed and pest control are made available by using resources that are no longer renewable.

Since food production in Uncha Gaon has become dependent on external sources for inputs into farming, much of it is not provided as a "free good", unlike growing food crops in the 1940s and 1950s. This implies that the farming households in Uncha Gaon, like those in Tikri and Chandpur, must now buy the required inputs and hence must generate a surplus of production, cash or whatever else of value, to exchange for external resources. And because the cost of acquiring these inputs and their supply channels are rarely controlled by the farming household, the farmers are most of the time "price-takers". This has at least three cost implications in terms of direct costs, hidden costs and real costs. We will analyse the monetised impact of these on the economics of agriculture later and concentrate now on the dynamics that this cost escalation has created, to which we shall now turn.

The transition from ZEIA to LEIA and eventually to HEIA has made agriculture a high direct cost because the farmer has to buy the inputs. There is little of the agricultural inputs required which is available free of charge. Farmers have to buy seeds, fertilisers, tractors, threshers, pump sets (or hire them), weedicides, pesticides, capital and so on. Thus, the cost of farming operation has gone up. It is reasonable to expect that with globalisation and full implementation of the TRIPS Agreement of the WTO, which is lurking round the corner, the cost of these inputs will rise further *(Sharma,* 2000). Under the new Patent Laws, a patent holder will have patent rights over new technology/chemicals for 20 years. Imitation and adoption of such technology will attract payment of royalty to the patent holder, making dissemination of technology and its local adoption a much more expensive venture now than before. Additionally, those firms who would take out patents will not change the technology for as long as they could and this bodes ill for the farmers so keen to adopt new technology: technology will remain stagnant for a long time. The several fold increases in yield seen in the 1970s by changing technology at a small incremental variation will no longer be possible.

The transition from ZEIA to HEIA has also made a noticeable impact on the *hidden* cost of operation. The increase in fossil fuel use to keep outputs high also means more energy consumption. The hidden costs rise as a result. Shift from ZEIA to HEIA has led to substitution of manual labour and animal power by tractors, threshers and pump sets (either diesel or electric) that we saw, which implies that external energy sources have substituted energy sources found in the household and the community. All this along with use of fertilisers, which is mostly NKP, agriculture has become very energy intensive in Uncha Gaon. Although we have no estimates of how much is the total energy inputs to agriculture due to the use of fertilisers (NKP), pump sets and tractors in Uncha Gaon, but in third world countries these amongst themselves consume more than 90 per cent of total energy inputs for farming. For India as a whole there is one estimate that 10-20 per cent increase in yields following mechanisation, costs an additional 43-260 per cent more in energy consumption. In the neighbouring State of Punjab, farms in a class 14-25 hectares use three times as much direct energy per hectare as farmers smaller than 6 hectares *(Singh and Miglani,* 1976).

The indication is that as farming moves from traditional methods of cultivation to mechanised or partially mechanised agriculture, yield increases, but the increases in energy consumption are steep. In percentage terms, the increases in energy requirements far outstrip the increases in yield. The differentials in yield increase and extra energy requirement depend on local conditions and micro-level environments. Since we do not have data specific to Uncha Goan, we can only draw a general conclusion that the movement from ZEIA to HEIA has increased the energy intensity of farming.

High external input agriculture entails a lot of *real costs*, in addition to direct and hidden costs. Even where there is no direct monetary outgoing to procure an input, there may be real cost incurred by the farming household.

The farmers also pointed out that the smaller farmers are constantly squeezed in a cost-price wedge. It is a squeeze that encourages farmers to be the first to maximise production from their resources. This promotes higher production using more and more of external inputs and encouraging part-time farming.

True in all these developments output has also increased but costs have also increased. And as we shall examine a little later, the increase in cost has outstripped the benefit of increased output. Small wonder, the villagers assigned high cost of agriculture as a reason why they want to migrate out of the sector. In such a situation, HEIA always puts sustainability of agriculture in doubt.

VI. Changes in Yields and the Reasons Thereof

Have such dramatic shifts in practices for growing food had any impact on yields? We have to return for a while to Table 6.8 once again. Since wheat is the principal food crop grown since 1940s, it is best to discuss variation in the yields in terms of how yield of wheat has varied for a temporal survey of yields. During 1940s, wheat output per acre was 3-4 quintals only. During 1950s the yield remained the same. In the late 1960s, the yield increased to about 16 quintals per acre, once tubewells and tractors came into use and HYV seeds replaced the traditional ones. That is, within a decade, yield jumped from 3-4 quintals an acre to around 16 quintals an acre, a jump of 400 per cent. In the 1970s this increase in yield got entrenched with "new technology" coming full circle: fertilisers and pesticides being the latest addition to the basket of agricultural inputs. The decade marks the advent of the high noon of the Green Revolution, when HYV seeds, fertilisers, other chemicals, pesticides and assured irrigation are seen as doing the trick. It is also the time when Government of India started providing price incentives to farmers of wheat (and paddy) in terms of *minimum support price*. Thus yield increase was responding to change in technology and to the price incentives offered by Government of India. And it remained at that level in most of 1980, but during the late 1980s yield started falling. It came to 13 quintals per acre and remained at that level in the 1990s. In effect, the high yield per acre, of the 1970s and early 1980s was not sustained in the late 80s and 1990s. Yield per acre fell by almost 19 per cent, to reach about 13 quintals per acre during the current decade. During the years under review, not only did the villagers perceive yield change but the intrinsic quality of the produce itself is perceived to have changed (for the worse) in look, shape, size and taste.

VII. Economics of Agricultural Operations with Special Reference to Food Production

The Inputs to Agriculture and the Cultivation Process

It is best to start with the cultivation process and then summarize the inputs to agriculture. Reference is invited to Seasonality Analysis of agricultural activities done by villagers in Uncha Gaon. Table 6.9 is generated out of the same. From Table 6.9, the basic inputs to agriculture are: ploughing (tractor time), seeds, fertilisers, irrigation in several rounds and pump sets, labour and of course land.

The process of agriculture, in a normal year, that is, a year not hit by disease and pests etc., is fairly straight forward, as is evident from a remark made by Umbrao to one of the researchers, whose English translation is: "Wheat cultivation is simple. Only west wind, if blows early, harms it".

Let us look at wheat cultivation first. It all starts in the months of Kartick and Aghan (mid-October to mid-December) when land is ploughed for five times, of which two are wet ploughing, and then leveled, followed by successive steps that go on for 6 months in a row. Land is then irrigated during the same months and puddles made. Aghan (mid-November to mid-December) is for fertiliser application and seeds to be sown. For four months thereafter, from Poos to Chait, wheat fields receive five rounds of irrigation, at the rate of one round per month except the month of Magh when fields are irrigated twice. Each of the first three rounds of irrigation is accompanied by a dose of fertiliser. In Baisakh (mid-April to mid-May), wheat is harvested and bundles made. Threshing occupies farmers for most of Baisakh. Jeth (mid-May to Mid-June) is the month for storing wheat and the surplus taken to the market (called "Mandis") for sale either to the government at the procurement prices declared, or to other buyers and traders at the going market price.

Growing cauliflower and potato is different and less organised, in that it does not follow a calendar of months. Let us take up cauliflower. First a nursery is raised, for which a nursery bed is prepared of rows and either 1 kg of Kisan Khad or manure (costing Rs. 250 per 50 kg) is provided as additional nutrients. Approximately 1 kg. of seed (bought at a price of Rs. 1000) is sown, out of which only 500 grams germinate. As a second step,

Table 6.9 Agricultural Process and Involvement of Men and Women

Agricultural Operations	**Months**	**Tasks handled by Men**	**Tasks handled by Women**	**Time taken (Days)**
Ploughing and leveling (Mej and Jot)	Kartick–Aghan	Plough by using tractors	Supervision* and help	Week to ten days
Irrigation and puddling (Palewat)	Kartik–Aghan	Irrigate with pump sets	Supervision	6 days or so
Apply fertilizer. Sow seeds	Aghan	Apply fertilisers	Supervision	4-5 days
First irrigation at 6 inch plant	Poosh	Irrigate with pump sets	Supervision	4 days or so
Second irrigation	Magh	Irrigate with pump sets	Supervision	4 days or so
Third irrigation on ear of corn coming out	Magh	Irrigate with pump sets	Supervision	4 days or so
Fourth irrigation on grain formation	Fagun	Irrigate with pump sets	Supervision	4 days or so
Fifth irrigation on grains maturing	Chait	Irrigate with pump sets	Supervision	4 days or so
Harvesting week	Baisakh		Harvest	All Week
Making bundles	Baisakh		Make bundles	2
Threshing	Baisakh	Using tractors		4-5
Transporting to home and market	Jeth	Using tractors		1

* Supervision means making sure that irrigation water reaches all parts of the field.

deweeding is done and at intervals of 10 days, the nursery bed is watered either manually by sprinklers or by rain. The third step is to plough the field where the seedlings are transplanted. A minimum of five rounds of ploughing are essential, at a cost of Rs.1000 per round. It takes the seedlings about 4-6 weeks to be ready for transplantation. The fourth step is to apply DAP (costing Rs. 150 per 50 kg) to the fields and then transplant the seedlings. As the fifth step, between 2 to 3 weeks, deweeding is essential and after another 2-3 weeks first round of irrigation is due. The fifth step is to deweed the fields again, before the next round of irrigation.This is followed by another round of deweeding. The sixth step is application of fertilisers, which in Uncha Gaon is Kisan Khad. The seventh step is irrigating the land again and for the last time. The flower are ready for sale within the next 2 weeks or so.

In order to keep the pests at bay, at intervals of every 15 days, "Trigen" *(sic),* as pesticide is sprayed. Trigen costs Rs. 50 per 50 kg.

VIII. The Economics of Input for Food Production

With all these inputs, cost of agriculture is fairly high. The economics of the inputs can be worked out by comparing the yield mentioned in Table 6.6 with the price of inputs. The villagers provided estimates of returns from wheat, mustard and potato, which influenced their decision on the choice of crops. Their estimates are in Tables 6.10 and 6.11.

Through these Tables the villagers clearly tell us that cultivating cash crop is far more profitable that cultivating their land for growing food crops. The tables also tell us how returns will behave if farmers grow only the particular crop per acre throughout the year. The costs of cultivation is not in the above Tables inclusive of the cost of credit. Farmers borrowed money, particularly during the months of Bhado, Kuar and Kartick, for sowing of winter vegetables (Rabi), preparing land for cultivating wheat, mending "animal shelter roofs", treatment of illness, etc.. Loan upto Rs. 5000 is borrowed from friends, relatives and local businessmen (money lenders) if it is to meet expenses for treatment, to defray costs of meeting social obligations like marriage in the family, etc. Loans for agriculture, buying buffaloes, tractors and threshers are availed of from the Gurgaon

Grameen Bank and the local land mortgage bank. For loans which cannot be backed by collateral security, resources are raised from informal sources at very high rates of interest; for loans which can be backed by collateral security, credit is sought from formal purveyors of credit, who charge regulated interest rates. That is why though the gross return from farming is very high, the monthly net income is modest. The villagers gave us the data in Table 6.12 to illustrate the point.

Table 6.10 Return from Agriculture in Rabi Season Per Acre (In Rupees)

Wheat	3000	8000	5000
Vegetables	12000	34500	22500

Table 6.11 Return from Agriculture in Kharif Season Per Acre (In Rupees)

Spinach	8000	50000	42000
Cauliflower	6000	50000	44000
Cabbage	6000	50000	44000
Cucumber	4000	30000	26000
Brinjal	8000	50000	42000
Potato	6000	50000	44000

Notes: Prepared on the basis of semi-structured interview with the villagers of Uncha Gaon.

Facilitators: Meera Jayaswal and Sudipta Ray.

Date: 27. 3. 1989

Table 6.12 Cost and Returns from Agriculture to Households Per Acre (in Rupees)

Months	Income	Input Cost	Savings
Baisakh (Veg)	6000	1500	4500
Jeth (Veg)	4500	3000	1500
Asharh (Veg)	6000	3000	3000
Sawan (Veg)	6000	3000	3000
Bhado (Veg)	6000	3000	3000
Kuar (Veg)	7500	4500	300
Kartick (Veg)	6000	4500	1500
Aghan (Veg)	4500	1500	3000
Poos (Veg)	4500	1500	3000
Magh (veg)	4500	1500	3000
Fagun (Veg)	7500	3000	4500
Chait (Veg)	7500	3000	4500
TOTAL from vegetables per annum (p.a.)	70,500	33000	37500
TOTAL from wheat p.a.	8000	3000	5000
TOTAL from jowar p.a.	3000	1000	2000
TOTAL from sale of milk p.a.	86400	24000	62400

The craze for vegetable cultivation is for its commercial value. Wheat is cultivated as a food crop and jowar is grown for fodder. The cropping pattern is so devised that agriculture provides food, cash and fodder. In Sen's terminology, for wheat farmers have endowment entitlements and for other consumption needs including other kinds of food, the farmers depend on trade entitlements (*Sen,* 1981). The returns from vegetables incidentally are reaped over a period of 12 months, whereas returns from wheat and jowar are reaped after putting in 6 months of labour.

Of the three main occupations (growing vegetables, growing wheat and selling milk) apparently selling milk is most lucrative and is assisted by farming for it provides fodder and labour, managed by household labour perceived as free. The villagers explained that profitability of the three livelihoods needs to be qualified. With the flux of time, the value of land increases, their asset appreciates in value and the farmers do not have to worry about its replacement cost, or provide for depreciation. In case of selling milk, on the contrary, the value of their bovine wealth gets depleted every year and replacement cost often becomes relevant. Loss of assets due to death of buffaloes has to be taken cognisance of as well, which is not the case with land. Hence, the return from selling milk requires mid way corrections. According to the farmer's perception, cultivating vegetable is their best bet.

The villagers in working out the economics of farming and agriculture did not factor in the imputed cost of labour of the household. Assuming that only adults work, a minimum of 2 adults spend one year in generating the income. If we assume that they are required to put in only 180 days of work and the wages they could earn in the next best alternative employment is Rs. 60 per day, they would have earned Rs. 21600. If we notionally deduct this cost from the net returns from agriculture seen in Table 6.12, the picture becomes less cheerful.

IX. Who Supplies the Inputs for Food Production and Who Provides the Extension Services Regarding New Seeds and Fertilisers

As we discussed above, agricultural inputs for cultivating wheat are tractors, seeds, fertilisers, irrigation in several rounds, and therefore water and pumpsets, family labour, outside labour, and of course land. As we saw, the year long agricultural operations are carried out by family labour. Tractors, and pump sets are owned by farmers, and there is inter-household hiring of tractors. In some rare cases generators are also used to energise the pump sets for irrigation, which is also accessed from the market. Farmers access other inputs from the open market. The existence of extension service is weak which is why farmers do not respond to a host of constraints though they are aware of them, which reflects absence of extension support. The steady decline in and ultimately breaking down of extension service is particularly felt.

In Uncha Gaon, we are talking about a community comprising Jats, where women's and men's domains are clearly demarcated. Jats are a community of farmers, generally landowning class and politically exceptionally vocal. Jats have been classified, by Government of India, as belonging to other backward castes (*Times of India,* 22nd October 1999). The dichotomy of "inside-home" and "out-side home" jobs, in this scheme is distinct.

The picture is the same as we found in other villages. The tasks cut out for men and women are well demarcated. Let us take the case of wheat cultivation. Women supervise ploughing, leveling and puddling and several rounds of irrigation. Everything relating to harvesting and making bundles from harvsted crops for threshing are under the charge of women. Even when men are engaged in threshing with machines, the women make the smaller bundles to facilitate the process.

The next picture is also familiar. Tasks entrusted to women's care in Uncha Gaon are in addition to their traditionally assigned responsibilities, viz., fetching water, collecting fuel and fodder, feeding animals, cleaning and washing, bearing and rearing children, processing and cooking food for the households. They have to deal with their men folk, in some cases in drunken state. In case of men, for irrigating their land they work additional hours at night but for other operations like for threshing and for taking the produce to the *Mandis* (markets), they take leave from their normal routine. If one were to compute the workload of men and women on a comparative basis, women are obviously overloaded.

Most of the tasks assigned to the women in Uncha Gaon require them to work with their hands (as they can only be manually performed, using simple implements like a sickle for harvesting) starting from supervising irrigation to harvesting and making bundles. Women in the village have to soil their hands. The only aids and implements they use are the sickle and ropes. The tasks performed by men on the contrary, viz., ploughing, irrigating, threshing and transporting are all mechanised. Tractors, pump sets and threshers are their aids. Thus if we now compare the two sets of activities, it further reveals that most of what women do is confined within the household and their fields, and most of what men in Uncha Gaon do require them to interface with the outside world: arranging tractors, looking around for pump sets and transporting the produce for sale. In terms of effort and disagreeableness, therefore, women in the village face a more arduous set of tasks.

That men of Uncha Gaon sell vegetables and crops produced by the entire farming household has a serious economic implication. Without any disparity in intra-familial disparity in power-relationship, the proceeds out of the sale of the produce should ideally be distributed amongst all members of the "production team", on the basis of some principle of allocation, such as proportion of labour contributed. However, in case of Uncha Gaon, because men *sell* the produce created out of family resources, the proceeds of the sale from such produce go to men. Though in Uncha Gaon, women, men and children all conjointly participate in generating the output, custody of income arising out of such output eventually rests with the men. And decisions regarding appropriation of the household incomes also rests with men, which gives them the extra room to maneuver the pattern of expenditure, including the capacity to accommodate the cost of their drinks.

X. Food Security

The importance of agriculture for food security in a poor agricultural society, cannot be overemphasized. Food security means that there is enough food in the system, that people have the purchasing power to access the food so available, that people have the ability to access such food, that the food available is culturally acceptable and that the food so available has adequate nutritional value for a healthy life.

The data in terms of the Problem Prioritization in Table 6.4 do not indicate availability of food as a problem or as a constraint to livelihood. Even the historical transects of the village nowhere indicate that insufficient food or hunger ever visited the community. However, from the Seasonal Analysis of agricultural activities by men's group in Saini Muhalla, reproduced in Table 6.13, elements of food insecurity are clear. We reproduce in Table 6.13, the food consumption pattern as depicted by the said Seasonality Analysis.

Sawan, Bhado and Kuar are hunger months for the people at large. We have marked Column-1 of Table 6.13, with the letter 'H' to denote months, which could be hunger months. During these three months the typical diet of a farm household consists of chappatis and pickle or chili chutney,

Table 6.13 Seasonality Analysis of Agricultural Activities and Food Consumption (Men's group Saini Muhalla)

Months	Food Intake	Activities
Baisakh	Chappatis with pickle or chili chutney. Vegetables from their own fields.	Harvesting of wheat and selling the produce. Brinjal, melon and onion sold. Sow seeds for lady's finger, bottle gourd, torai, chili, pumpkin, cucumber, bitter gourd. Income is 50 per cent.
Jeth	Chappatis with pickle or chili chutney. Occasionally vegetables, fruits, dalia, lassi milk and tea. 3 meals plus an evening meal of tea/ milk.	Irrigation and weeding in the fields. Collection of fodder, like cutting grass and harvesting jowar. Sowing of jowar and maize seeds. Selling cucumber, kakri and melon.
Asharh	Same as Jeth	Irrigating fields. Cutting fodder. Selling vegetables sown in Baisakh. Income 25 per cent. Sowing bajra.
Sawan **H**	2 meals of Chappatis, pickle or chili chutney. Some vegetables.	Seedling of cauliflower and brinjal raised. Cutting some jowar for fodder.
Bhado **H**	Same as Sawan	Cutting jowar. Sowing radish, carrot, spinach, cabbage seeds. Transplanting cauliflower and brinjal seedlings.
Kuar **H**	Same as Bhado	Irrigating and weeding fields. Cutting some jowar.
Kartick	Chappatis with pickle or chili chutney. Occasionally vegetables, fruits, milk tea. 3 meals plus an evening meal of tea or milk.	Harvesting jowar and bajra. Selling spinach, cauliflower, fenugreek, coriander, brinjal, radish. Income is upto 20 per cent.

Months	Food Intake	Activities
Aghan	Same as Kartick	Sowing wheat seeds. Selling spinach, cauliflower, fenugreek, coriander, brinjal, radish, cabbage. Income upto 40 per cent.
Poos	Bajra chappatis with Sarson da Saag, pickle or chili chutney. Occasionally vegetables. 3 meals plus an evening meal of tea or milk.	Irrigating land. Selling spinach, cauliflower, fenugreek, coriander, brinjal, radish, cabbage. Income upto 45 per cent.
Magh	Same as Poos	Selling spinach, cauliflower, fenugreek, coriander, brinjal, radish, cabbage. Income upto 40 per cent. Irrigating fields. Sowing cucumber and melon seeds.
Fagun	Same as Magh	Selling cauliflower, potato, brinjal, fenugreek, spinach, carrot, radish. Income is 45 per cent. Irrigating and weeding fields.
Chait	Same as Magh.	Fenugreek, spinach, coriander, carrot and Sarson da Saag sold. Income is 35 per cent. Irrigate fields.

H indicates hunger periods.

Village Analysts: Balbir, Bansi, Harish, Omprakash, Bhagawat, Krisen, Mahesh, Babloo.
Facilitator: Sudipta Ray

twice a day. The story is about the same in Baisakh, with addition of vegetables from their own fields, which would be some brinjals and onions. Though people at large do not face starvation, there is hunger and the variety and palate of the meals very boring. The nutritional component of food intake is suspect. During the remaining 8 months people are less in distress and the consumption basket is little more varied. It has cereals, some fibre, protein and occasional dash of dairy products. Generally, people do not face acute hunger for 8 months in a year but they face food insecurity. Their consumption basket indicates that they eat three meals a day but the quantity and quality of food consumed leaves the villagers much below the desired level.

Because farmers of Uncha Gaon have migrated from agriculture for sustenance and subsistence (in their broadest connotation) and from food self–sufficiency to income self-sufficiency, hunger stalks the villagers whenever income dips. If we see Column-3 of Table 6.13, in all those months where the villagers have something to sell, they eat well. In the three months of Sawan, Bhado and Kuar the farmers have nothing to sell, and hence are cash-strapped. They, therefore, hack back consumption. This is also the period, the villagers explained, when diseases are at their full fury: malaria, diarrhea and dengue, apart from the chronic ones in the form of najla, headache, gastritis and white discharge amongst women. This means that farmers are forced to spend sizeable portions of their income on curative health during these months, making further inroads into their resource base for accessing food and forcing them in turn to cut their consumption basket. Food security for Uncha Gaon is, thus, a function of cash sales and incidence of disease. Uncha Gaon's food security is jeopardised, for at least three months, because the farmers have migrated from endowment based entitlement to food in favour of exchange based entitlement.

The redeeming feature is the cropping pattern. Though cash crops have the primacy, wheat as a food crop is still cultivated. The cropping pattern also indicates that despite Uncha Gaon having migrated from ZEIA to HEIA and the diversity of crops is on the decline, nevertheless, a variety of vegetables are grown. And there are overlaps. This helps in distributing the risks that farmers face. In the event of one crop failing, for whatever reason, they can fall back on the other vegetables that they grow. As a village women Umraon remarked: "The price of carrots fell tremendously. As a result, we did not dig out the carrots. Instead we ploughed the land. But potato and cauliflower saved us". Thus exchange entitlements have saved the villagers of Uncha Gaon from falling into deeper hunger.

Agriculture as a profitable venture is in no doubt in the villager's perception. However, instability and uncertainty of assured prices for their crops are in doubt. The stability of prices for wheat is imparted by the *Minimum Support Price* and *Procurement Price* for wheat (and paddy) declared by the Government. This helps reduce risks involved in farming. There are thus two kinds of agricultural produce: vegetables which are more profitable and food crops which are less lucrative. But the crops, which are more lucrative are the ones with higher risks of price volatility, and the ones which are less lucrative are the ones that have price stability. Stability and returns are the two opposing objectives that a wise farmer must reconcile.

Since 80 per cent of the people in Uncha Gaon depend on agriculture, it is one of the principal sources of income. The other principal source is sale of milk. From one acre of land, the total return from agriculture per household is about Rs. 44,500. That is, the income of the household is about Rs. 3700 per month. Tables 6.10, 6.11 and 6.12 give an idea of the kinds of money that farmers make from agriculture in Kharif and Rabi respectively. It will be seen from Table 6.11 that except for cucumber, the returns from all other vegetables in Kharif are about the same. But farmers grow potatoes on 50 per cent of their land under vegetables, because potatoes have a long self-life and can be stored for almost a year, obviating the need to sell them off when the prices are lowest immediately after the harvest. This is not the case with other vegetables. In Rabi, though vegetables give a far better returns than wheat and the other crops grown during the season (Rs.22500 as against Rs. 5000), yet farmers grow wheat along with vegetables, to make sure that they have enough of staple foods in their granary without depending on the market. There is an attempt to have partial self-sufficiency in food at the household level. Thus, wheat production gives the villagers direct entitlement to food and growing vegetables gives them exchange entitlements.

XI. Summary and Conclusions

From the above discussion what clearly emerges is that the people of Uncha Gaon have elected to grow vegetables in the hope of using the marketing opportunities available at the nearby industrial township of Ballabgarh. They have realised that growing vegetables for the market primarily does not solve their problems of hunger. People still face severe hunger over a period of three months every year. During other months they do not face hunger but are certainly confronted with food insecurity. The fact that these farmers are mostly small and marginal farmers, makes them vulnerable to vagaries of nature and price fluctuations and are doing the balancing act all the time. Price volatility makes their livelihood and food security so much uncertain. The entire food security of the community revolves around producing vegetables, with which they acquire exchange entitlement to food. With high levels of unemployment, people of Uncha Gaon have little hope of securing exchange entitlement to food through selling their labour and earned wages. The gender disparity within the households, leading to utilisation of household income for indulging in alcoholism, makes serious inroads into the ability of the households to access food. Then finally, the fear of hunger that stalks the people of Uncha Gaon due to anticipated acquisition of their agricultural land by the state is oppressing. The fact that the community suffers serious hunger is evident since the mere thought of loosing their source of food makes them so desperate.

7 Perspectives of Rural Women on Food Security from a Tribal Village (in West Bengal)—1993 to 1998

I. Introduction

What food and what kind of food the poor women and men and children consume to fill their stomach to get rid of their hunger? What food relieves them from the pangs of hunger in times of stress, caused by natural or man made calamity? In a patriarchal society with gender discrimination as a matter of public history, who decides on intra-household allocation of food everyday? Do the poor people find out every day the amount of food shortfall they face? And if yes, how do they do so? What coping mechanisms do they adopt to make good the shortfall or survive with the food shortages? These are some of the question we will try to address presently here from the perspective of tribal women in West Bengal.

Any discussion on issue relating to food and hunger (read starvation at times!) with poor people who silently suffer the pangs of hunger almost as a matter of routine, by outsiders who are well fed, is not easy. It requires a lot of tact and effort. In a society where food consumption and self-respect are interwoven, not all people are willing to participate in a session to discuss what they thought about such questions (*Rao, et. al.* 1999). "They often use interrogative form when replying, showing a mock contempt of the person making the inquiry, a common practice in India. In addition, estimates below of food consumption should be taken as such. As one man put it: 'we don't measure how much food goes into our stomach" (*Beck,* 1994).

Generally, it is believed *a priori* that if both husband and wife get work, the women earn less than the men do, but the household would have enough to meet their daily needs. However, because employment is available for only half the year at most, the poor people have to resort to cuts in consumption. On an average, people are said to face food shortages, of upto 25 per cent, except during certain months. The general nutritional pattern has shown that poorest people spend 80 per cent or more of their income on food but still only meet 80 per cent of their nutritional needs (*Lipton,* 1983).

This then is the background with which we proceed with the discussion of the issues in this study.

II. The Village

Krishna Rakshit Chak is in Midnapore District in West Bengal. It is in Arjuni Mouza in Kharagpur Block-I of Midnapore. It is one of the backward districts of West Bengal. It is also a district, which has been declared as fully literate district by the government according to its norm, having been covered under the total literacy mission. The district is predominantly an agricultural district, with very little industry. There are two agricultural seasons: *Aman* from Asard to Kartick, and *Boro* from Magh to Baisakh.

Box 7.1

Months of the Year in Bengali Calendar

Vernacular Month	*Corresponding Period in Roman Calendar*
Baisakh	Mid-April to Mid-May
Jaistha	Mid-May to Mid-June
Asard	Mid-June to Mid-July
Sraban	Mid-July to Mid-August
Bhadro	Mid-August to Mid-September
Ashwin	Mid-September to Mid-October
Kartick	Mid-October to Mid-November
Aghrayan	Mid-November to Mid-December
Poush	Mid-December to Mid-January
Magh	Mid-January to Mid-February
Falgun	Mid-February to Mid-March
Chaitra	Mid-March to Mid-April

Krishna Rakshit Chak was visited in 1993, in an attempt to study the dynamics of the rural economy in a tribal village in a leftist ruled state, through the eyes of the villagers. In the process of so doing, a Food Calendar prepared by the people (the women) of the village emerged, which provided valuable insights into the different dimensions of food (in)security and hunger, as portrayed by poor tribal women. Women are traditionally responsible for harvesting and gathering food, for processing and intra-household distribution (read serving) of food, consuming left-overs in the process and often suffering hunger themselves.

The village was visited again in May 1995 and then again in April 1998 in an attempt to discern and discuss with the villagers the changes in food (in)security and hunger that may have occurred for the poor households of the village between 1993 and 1995, and between 1995 and 1998. A second Food Calendar was prepared in 1995 and a third one, in 1998. An attempt has been made here to present our findings and a brief analysis of the findings during the three visits under reference.

III. The Methodology and the Process

The Context

We have described here three food calendars made by rural women in 1993, 1995 and in 1998, referred to earlier and have analysed the same to get an idea of what the women have to say on food security in Krishna Rakshit Chak. This has given us a ringside view of three aspects of village life. First is the view of the knowledge-base of rural women in gathering food from forests, common property resources (CPR) and micro-environments (See *Chambers,* 1990 for a definition of micro-environment). Second, a glimpse of their role in such procurement and third, the seasonality of food availability, its shortage and dependence of villagers on food from common property resources, forests and micro-environments.

In *Mukherjee and Mukherjee* (1994), the details of the process of preparing the Food Calendar in 1993 have been discussed and are, therefore, not discussed here again. Reference is invited to that paper. The processes of preparing the Food Calendars of 1995 and 1998 have been similar, except that the women were already in the know of the "technology". And there was no need to build rapport afresh with the villagers, especially the women, as the earlier visits and communications had already established a good deal of understanding with them, which persisted.

The Community

The inhabitants of Krishna Rakshit Chak are poor and they belong to the Lodha Tribe, who were given by the colonial rulers the appellation of a "criminal tribe". The village has 49 households as per the villagers, which figure may be at slight variance with the 1991 Census figures. Most of the households are landless.

A review of the secondary data and discussion with the people generally disclosed that poor people accessed food mainly from wages they get for the labour they sell, and they buy food from the local shops and from the local markets. Food was purchased generally on a daily basis, as the poor households did not have surplus cash to hold a stock of food they consumed. There is a ration shop to which the poor households are attached and rice from the ration shop was cheaper than rice brought locally from the market with cash. Almost all the households access the ration shop one time or the other depending on whether their cash flow coincided with the day of opening of the ration shop. The supplies from the ration shop were erratic and the quality of rice supplied was not very good for what the ration shop sold was, in government's terminology, of "fair average quality" or FAQ. Whatever little else the poor households consumed had to be brought on the open market, barring wages received in grains in the village.

In the three repeated exercises, we encouraged the women to prepare food calendars, as a part of the process of participatory learning to learn more about their food security situation. At the beginning, in 1993, women were hesitant and shy, but once prodded, they soon were able to engross into intricate details of food consumption, procurement and intra-household distribution of food. Using various locally available material like stones, pebbles, leaves, etc., and traditional knowledge of time and space, women drew on the ground 12 months (as per the Bengali Calendar) and identified various parameters related to food (in)security.

Across different months and between different commodities, the women of Krishna Rakshit Chak have only indicated relative changes in consumption and not absolute quantity of food consumed during the different months of the year. For instance, each column in the Food Calendars has to be read as "stand alones", indicating the relative amount of the particular food item (named as the Column Head) that is consumed in the different months. In Table 7.1, Column 1, the women depict the pattern of rice consumption through the twelve months of the year. The numbers 15 against Magh and 9 against Phalgun (in Column-1 of Table 7.1) show straight away that consumption of rice in Magh was higher than in Phalgun. Similarly, the number 2 against Poush indicates that the consumption of rice in Poush was even lower than in Phalgun. And so on. These numbers do not, however, indicate the absolute quantities of rice consumed during these months, such as 15 kg in Magh, 9 kg in Phalgun and 2 kg in Poush. Additionally, numbers across the columns are non-additive and non-comparable. Thus the number 15 under rice against Magh and the number 13 under Potatoes against Magh, does not indicate that the consumption of rice was higher than the consumption of potatoes in Magh. This is the schema followed in all the Tables showing the Food Calendars.

IV. The 1993 Food Calendar

The 1993 Food Calendar was prepared in the month of Magh, corresponding to mid-January to mid-February 1993 and hence starts with Magh. The Bengali Calendar year starts in Baisakh, corresponding to mid-April to mid-May. The 1993 Food Calendar is reproduced in Table 7.1.

The Two Food Systems

The Food Calendar shows two food systems. The kinds of food consumed by the poor people come from two sources. People consumed rice, potatoes etc, which is food produced on cultivable land by the application of technology in the economic sense. People also have access to fish, fruits, honey, gums, small animals, birds, tubers, snails, leaves, leafy vegetables, etc. which they collect from the common property resources, micro-environment and forests, and from gleaning and collecting them from lands belonging to richer, relatively well-off farmers, in neighbouring villages. The former we may call as food derived from the "primary food system". The second category of food that villagers eat, we would call, food from the "secondary food system". In case of food consumed by people from the primary food system, food does not generally regenerate once harvested unless there are specific interventions from human beings, whereas much of the food from the secondary food system is regenerated in most cases without human interventions (*Mukherjee, A.*, 1993 and 1994).

Thus, the concept of the *secondary food system* is slightly different in case of Krishna Rakshit Chak because the concept of CPR is different. The secondary food system includes food from the CPRs, forests and micro-environments. There are two ways in which the CPRs can be defined. There is the traditional definition of CPRs which includes common grazing lands, perambokes, sacred groves, village ponds, rivers and rivulets, etc., whose ownership is not recorded in the name of any individual private institution or private individuals. Ownership of these properties is vested in the state or its agencies. There is a "broader definition" of CPRs, which includes the elements of the "traditional definition" of CPR, and also the rights available to the community to use the usufructs of resources owned and possessed by individuals. Such access could be the outcome of a process of negotiation, bargaining or conflict between poor villagers and the relatively richer *de jure* owners of resources such as farmers. Examples of the latter are drinking water drawn from privately owned wells, ripe fruits that fall from fruit trees in orchards owned by individuals, herbs collected from ponds owned by others, and crops and vegetables gleaned from lands owned by individual farmers. *The CPR in Krishna Rakshit Chak is as delineated by the "broader definition" of CPR.*

The poor villagers of Krishna Rakshit Chak, therefore, not only collected, gathered and hunted food from the CPRs, forests and micro-environments, but also gleaned food from the land of richer farmers. The cabbage, pumpkins,

Jhinge, papaya, green banana, radish, tomato, brinjals, etc. that the poor villagers collected from other farmers' lands and gardens as part of the produce of CPRs) were the crops which the well-off farmers did not harvest from their lands. These products were the ones, which had little commercial value and were of inferior quality either because these were damaged by pests or insects, frost bitten or hit by hailstorm, or diseased, deformed and discoloured for some reason not known to the villagers.

Both systems of food play critical roles in providing food to the villagers of Krishna Rakshit Chak. The importance of the two kinds of food lies not only in the nutritional aspects of food consumed but also in the time when such food is available and the variety and palate that they add to the villagers' diet.

Seasonal Variations from Primary Food System

Not only does the food calendar reveal that there are two systems of food which sustain the villagers but also that there are seasonal variation in availability of food from both the systems. Let us divide the food consumed from the two systems of food as *principal food items* (rice, potatoes, pulses, etc.) and as *secondary food items* (consumed fish, fruits, honey, gums, small animals, birds, tubers, snails leaves, leafy vegetables etc.).

If we look at the principal food items, then rice consumption reaches a peak in Magh after which it declines until Chaitra, to remain stationary through to Ashwin (mid-September to mid-October) following which it further declines by almost half of the earlier period in Kartick. Rice consumption picks up in Agrahyan. Thus consumption of rice, the principal staple food in Bengal, reaches lowest level of consumption during the hot summer months of Chaitra, Baisakh and Jaistha, and then continues to be low throughout the monsoon season of Asharh, Sraban and Bhadra, when people have to work the hardest. Consumption of rice is thus the lowest when the work-load is the highest.

Levels of consumption of potatoes follow approximately the same pattern as the levels of consumption of rice for the months of Magh and Phalgun. Potato consumption then declines sharply and stays at a lower level during the entire period from Chaitra to Agrahyan, to pick up again in Poush.

The consumption of the third element in the basket of principal food items, viz., pulses, also shows variations. Intake of pulses touches an "all time" low in Baisakh and rises in the months of Sraban, Agrahyan and Poush. Consumption of pulses is, therefore, also low during the summer period and the beginning of the monsoon months. This is the time when energy requirements are about the highest, both to stave off the harsh climate, collect fuel, preserve fuel for the rainy season and meet energy needs of working for cultivation processes that are vital during these months.

Seasonal Variation from the Secondary Food System

Some vegetable from the CPRs and forests, and food of one kind or the other from the secondary system, are consumed almost all through the year except in Aswin. Fruits, namely, mangos and jackfruit, from CPRs are available only on Baisakh and Jyaistha. Fish, snails and wild water-plants are consumed in Chaitra, Baisakh, Jyaistha and Bhadra only. Wild rabbits are hunted in the two winter months of Poush and Magh. There are some other food, not shown in the Food Calendar but consumed by all households for different reasons, notable amongst which are drumstick (*Sojnae* in local language), mohua and kundru or kundree. .While mohua flowers are collected during the winter months and stored for later use, kundru and drumsticks are available as vegetables almost round the year.

Availability of fish from CPRs increases significantly during summer in Chaitra, Baisakh and Jayaistha, and then again during Bhadra, towards the fag end of the rainy season. The increased availability of fish during the summer months, the villagers explained, was on account of the heat itself. The water bodies, ponds, rivulets, etc. all dry up and the catch becomes easier. Hence the availability of fish increases. And concurrently it is also the lean period which leaves the villagers with enough slack time to venture into fishing and collecting snails and water weeds, which not only provide the poor with food but also money from that part of the "catch" that they sell. This shores up their sagging income, which in any case is low. As Asharh sets in, the water bodies swell and fishing becomes more ardous and time consuming whereas the people get busy working in the fields for cultivation for it starts in Ashar. They have less spare time to go out fishing.

Fishing and collecting snails start in Bhadra, when after two months of rain, in Asharh and Sraban, the rivulets, ponds and other water bodies start overflowing and flooding nearby fields and meadows. (The rainfall pattern in Midnapore district is that the month of Bhadra experience generally sharp showers on certain days, unlike in Asharh and Sraban, during which Midnapore usually receives heavy rainfall for days on end). With such overflowing comes fishes and snails into the meadows and fields.

The water recedes after the rain stops (or sometime thereafter) leaving in the mud and in small puddles, scattered all over the place, fishes and snails for the villagers to catch. This jacks up the amount of fish and snails in the secondary food basket of the villagers. Bhadra is also the month when agricultural activity is on a low key, leaving the villagers of Krishna Rakshit Chak with spare time to indulge in gathering activities. Thus, in Bhadra the consumption of fish is higher than in most other months.

Unlike the primary food system, the secondary food system cannot be analysed in terms of variations in individual items because most of the food from the secondary system are seasonal and vary from month to month. For instance cabbage is available in Magh, spinach in Phalgun and pumpkin in Chaitra. Similarly, radish leaves are available in Kartick, tomato in Aghrayan and brinjal in Poush.

There are nevertheless certain notable features which warrant comments. First, the secondary food system provides fibre and nutrition from green vegetables in the diet of the villagers of Krishna Rakshit Chak. This is an important function it performs. In the absence of the secondary food system, it would have left the quality of the food consumed by the villagers so much more deficient in nutrients and vitamins. Second, whatever animal protein, which inhabitants of Krishna Rakshit Chak consume also comes from the CPRs and forests. Had the people no access to the kinds of food they gathered and hunted from the CPRs and Forests, viz. wild rabbits, fishes and snails, the protein element in the villagers' diet would have been worse. Third, the number of foods, that the villagers accessed from the CPRs and forests, are more and higher when the basket of food from the primary food system is the lightest, viz., the months of Chaitra to Bhadra.

Table 7.1 Seasonal Food Calendar, 1993

Month	Rice	Potatoes	Pulses	Vege-tables@@	Fruits@	Food@@ from Water Sources	Others from Wild
1	2	3	4	5	6	7	8
Magh (Mid-Jan. to Mid-Feb	******* ********	******* ******	***	Cabbage	—	—	Wild borums and wild rabits
Phalgun (Mid-Feb.to Mid-March)	*********	**********	**	Spinach	—	—	Neem leaves
Chaitra (Mid-March to Mid-April)	****	****	**2	Pumpkin	—	—	Fish and wild water plants
Baisakh (Mid-April to Mid-May)	****	***	*	Pui leaves and herbs		Mango, jackfruit, fish, snails and wild water plants	—
Jyastha (Mid-May to Mid June)	****	****	**	*Lota,* leaves and herbs		Mango, jackfruit fish, wild water plants	—
Asharh (Mid-June to Mid-July)	****	***	***	Jhinge (nearer to sukini),	Green papaya	—	—
Sraban (Mid-July to Mid-August)	****	****	*****	—	Green papaya	—	—
Bhadra (Mid-August to Mid-Sept.)	****	***	***	Green banana	—	Fish and snails	

Ashwin (Mid-Sept. to Mid-Oct)	****	***	**	—	—	—	—
Kartick (Mid-Oct. to Mid-Nov.)	**	***	**	Radish, leaves		—	—
Aghrayan (Mid-November. to Mid-Dec.)	****	****	*****	Tomatoes	—	—	—
Poush (Mid-Dec. to Mid-Jan)	*****	*********	******	Brinjals	—	—	Wild fabits

(i) The number of "star" marks under column heads Rice, Potato, Pulses represent the number of stones used by the villagers to show the consumption of the relative item of food.

(ii) @Fruits from some trees growing near ponds and elsewhere in the village.

(iii) @@ From CPR and Forests.

Source: Prepared by Women's Group, Krishna Rakshit Chak, Midnapore, West Bengal. 4.2.93.

Facilitator: Neela Mukherjee

Table 7.2 Seasonal Food Calendar, 1995

Month	Rice	Potato	Pulses	Vegetables ###	Fruits ##	Fish ###	Snails ###	Others from Wild ###
1	2	3	4	5	6	7	8	9
Chaitra (Mid-March- to Mid-April)	*****	***	—	—	—	—	—	—
Baisakh# (Mid-April to Mid-May)	****	***	—	—	—	—	—	—
Jaistha (Mid-May to Mid June)	****	***	—	—	—	—	—	—
Asharh (Mid-June to Mid-July)	****	**	—	—	—	—	—	—
Sraban (Mid-July to Mid-August)	****	***	—	—	—	—	—	—
Bhadra (Mid-August to Mid-Sept.)	**	—	—	—	—	**********	—	—
Ashwin (Mid-Sept. to Mid-Oct)	****	***	**	—	—	**********	*****	—

Kartick (Mid-Oct to Mid-Nov.)	**	***	**	Radish, Leaves	—	**********	******	—
Aghrayan (Mid-Nov to Mid-Dec.)	****	****	*****	Tomatoes	—	—	—	—
Poush (Mid-Dec. to Mid-Jan)	*****	*********		******	Brinjals	—	—	—
Magh (Mid-Jan to Mid-Feb.)	**************		************		***	Cabbage	—	—
Phalgun (Mid-Feb to Mid-March)	***** ****	***** ******	** —	Spinach —	— —	— —	— —	Neem leaves

(i) The number of "star marks" under column heads rice, potato, pulses represent the number of stones used by the villagers to show the consumption of the relative item of food.

(ii) # This is the first month of the Bengali Calendar.

(iii) ## Fruits from some trees growing near ponds and elsewhere in the village.

(iv) ### From CPR's and forests.

Source: Prepared by Women's Group, Krishna Rakshit Chak, Midnapore, West Bengal.

Facilitator: Neela Mukherjee

Table 7.3 Rearranged Seasonal Food Calendar, 1995

Month	Rice	Potato	Pulses	Vegetables $	Fruits #	Fish $	Snails $	Others from Wild $
1	2	3	4	5	6	7	8	9
Magh (Mid-Jan to Mid-Feb.)	******* ********	****** *******	***	—	—	—	—	—
Phalgun (Mid-Feb. to Mid-March)	*********	****** *****	** —	— —	— —	— —	— —	Neem leaves
Chaitra (Mid-March- to Mid-April)	*****	***	—	—	—	—	—	—
Baisakh@ (Mid-April to Mid-May)	****	***	—	—	—	—	—	—
Jaistha (Mid-May to Mid June)	****	***	—	—	—	—	—	—
Asharh (Mid-June to Mid-July)	****	**	—	—	—	—	—	—

Sraban (Mid-July to Mid-August).	****	***	—	—	—	—	—	—
Bhadra (Mid-August to Mid-Sept.)	**	—	—	—	—	**********	—	—
Ashwin (Mid-Sept. to Mid-Oct)	****	***	**	—	—	**********	*****	—
Kartick (Mid-Oct to Mid-Nov.)	**	***	***	Leaves	—	**********	******	—
Aghrayan (Mid-Nov. to Mid-Dec.)	****	****	*****	—	—	—	—	—
Poush (Mid-Dec. to Mid-Jan)	*****	*********		******		—	—	—

(i) The number of "star" marks under column heads rice, potato, pulses represent the number of stones used by the villagers to show the consumption of the relative item of food.
(ii) @ This is the first month of the Bengali Calendar.
(iii) # Fruits from some trees growing near ponds and elsewhere in the village.
(iv) $ From CPR and forests.

Source: Prepared by Women's Group, Krishna Rakshit Chak, Midnapore, West Bengal.
Facilitator: Neela Mukherjee

Box 7.2
Nutrition from Wild Foods

Meat from Capybara, the world's largest rodent, and iguana can have similar protein, fat and energy content as pork, beef and chicken. Moreover, meat from Capybara is several times more efficient at converting food to meat than in domestic cattle. Rats have a nutritional score equivalent to beef or mutton (Kyle, 1987). Ants, grubs and caterpillars have similar energy protein and fat as goose liver, pork sausage and beef liver. Beetle larve eaten contain 23.3 g protein per 100 grams, while termites contain 58.9 grams of protein per 100 grams as compared to 43.4 grams per 100 grams for smoked river fish.

Paul Fieldhouse in *Food and Nutrition*, 1995 edition.

In terms of food security arguments, we outlined in Chapter 1 earlier, there are elements of food insecurity both from the perspective of food availability and quality of food. There is fall in food availability from the primary food system for the months of Chaitra, Baisakh, Jaistha, Aswin and Kartick. That is, people suffer hunger for at least five months in a year. The quality of food consumed also declines during this period, which is given by the consumption basket from the secondary food system. The fall in the consumption of rice, potato and pulses during these months indicate a lower intake of nutrition.

The Two Hunger Periods

The Food Calendar also reveals that people suffer differentiated hunger. They are hungry throughout the year but they are more so during some months. Let us look at columns 2, 3 and 4 of 1993 Food Calendar, as reproduced in Table 7.1. One can see that there are two "hunger periods" for the villagers of Krishna Rakshit Chak. The first hunger period occurs in the proverbial summer months of Bengal, namely, Chaitra, Baisakh and Jaistha (mid-March to mid-June) taken together, when availability of rice and potatoes come down to their lowest, and the availability and consumption of pulses reach rock bottom. These fall in availability of food, coupled with acute paucity of employment in the rural areas during this period (*Alagh,* 1999) which reduces the capacity of the poor to access food drastically, lead to entitlement failure. The food intake from the primary food basket of the poor villagers of Krishna Rakshit Chak reaches a very low level during the first hunger period.

"The second hunger period" occurs during the months of Aswin and Kartick (mid-September to mid-November) where again apart from lowest levels of consumption of rice (reaching 2 in Kartick), the availability and consumption of potatoes and pulses dip once again (the consumption of pulses being only 2 in Aswin). And as revealed by Table 7.6, this is also the period when employment availability is dismal as the harvesting season is yet to get underway and other economic activities are just not enough to provide income to the poor villagers. The power to access food is, therefore, also very low. There is a sustained entitlement failure during these two months as well.

During the first hunger period, the bounties of nature through the common property resources, forests, etc, come to the rescue of the villagers (see columns 5, 6 and 7 of Table 7.1). Fish, snails and water-weeds collected from the water bodies compensate at least partially, the loss in protein intake caused by a fall in consumption of pulses. The reduction in calorie intake, due to fall in the consumption of rice and potatoes, is partially offset by the consumption of fruits like jackfruits and mangoes from the secondary food system. Unlike during the first hunger period, there is no "safety net" provided to the poor villagers to tide over their hunger during second hunger period by the secondary food system. There is none of the vegetables available during the first hunger period. The fish, snails and water plants are all not there. There is none of small animals like rabbits to provide protein. This second hunger period is also the period which corresponds with the festival season of West Bengal, namely, Duga Pooja, Bhai Phonta (Bhatri Dwitiya) and Kali Puja (Deewali), all of which contribute to increasing the distress of the poor villagers, warranting "huge" social expenditures.

We will return later to a discussion on the role of CPRs in food security later in this chapter.

V. The 1995 Food Calendar

After about two years, in 1995, we returned to Krishna Rakshit Chak to meet the villagers. Nothing much had changed: the terrain, the landscape, the topography, the people, their poverty, their huts and even the vagaries of nature. The warmth, the forthrightness and the enthusiasm of the villagers remained undiminished. The women were as enthusiastic as they were in 1993 to work out the food calendar a second time over. There was only one difference: the rural women already had the "technology" to develop the food calendar. There was scant need to facilitate the production of the food calendar. The women used local materials like stones, leaves and sticks to produce the 1995 Food Calendar, with the same ease with which they cook food for their households, everyday, 365 days in a year. The 1995 Food Calendar is reproduced in Table 7.2.

Once the food calendar was ready, a discussion was held with the villagers with open ended questions to enliven the discussion and facilitate our understanding of their perspectives underlying the food calendar. The 1995 Food Calendar was prepared towards the end of Chaitra. Hence, the Food Calendar begins from the month of Chaitra, though the Bengali Calendar Year starts in Baisakh. However, in order to make the 1995 Food Calendar comparable to the 1993 Food Calendar, we rearranged only the months on the 1995 Food Calendar, so that the 1995 Food calendar may be read as starting (as in the case of 1993 Food Calendar) in Magh. The rearranged 1995 Food Calendar is in Table 7.3.

The 1995 Food Calendar reveals that the people of Krishna Rakshit Chak continue to depend upon both the primary food system and the secondary food system for their sustenance and subsistence. The 1995 Food Calendar exhibits very substantial variations in inter-month consumption of food, which reaches its lowest during the months spanned from Chaitra to Kartick, both months included. That is villagers of Krishna Rakshit Chak have very low level of consumption from mid-March to mid-November. This implies that people have enough food for approximately 4 months in a year. The dominance of rice and potatoes in the consumption basket of the villagers reflect the food preference of the people in West Bengal. Atleast one commentator has remarked that Bengalis believe that one cannot feel strong without eating rice (*Rizvi,* 1986). However, consumption of potatoes vanished during Bhadra, Aswin and Kartick. Columns 4 to 9 in Table 7.3 show that a large part of the diet of the poor households is made up of only rice and potatoes. The consumption of fish and snails is significant only during the months following the monsoons. Consumption of potatoes vanished, according to the villagers, during certain months of 1995 because the overall price increases did not allow them the luxury of consuming potatoes between Bhadra and Kartick.

The consumption of food from the secondary food system, to which we will again return later, deserves a few comments here. Firstly, the poor access virtually nothing of vegetables, fruits and other wild fruits from the CPRs, forests and micro-environments etc., unlike the 1993 Food Calender. Only fish continued to be available in Magh, Phalgun, Bhadra, Aswin and Kartick. The poor villagers did manage to have some snails in Aswin and Kartick. There was none of the fibre, nutrients and minerals that the secondary food system provided in 1993. And most importantly, the diet of the villagers of Krishna Rakshit Chak had become much less varied and lacked the palate, whatever its worth, depicted in the 1993 Food Calendar.

The variations in the levels of food consumed from month to month show a pattern. When more food is available (harvesting season) the consumption level goes up, when food availability goes down locally (cultivation season and the pre-harvesting season), inter month variation in the level of food consumption increases and the level of food consumption per se falls. It is important to recognise that variations in the levels of food consumption of the poor are brought about by both the "price effect" and the "quantity effect". The "price effect" and the "quantity effect" are more important in 1995 than in 1993, because the role of the secondary food system in providing food to the poor has been diminished in 1995 than earlier observed.

The villagers pointed out no limits to the amount of wild leaves that could be consumed. They added further that as a matter of routine food habit, they consumed tender *Neem*, whenever possible (which is rare) with brinjal.

VI. The 1998 Food Calendar

We returned to Krishna Rakshit Chak again in 1998, after three years and had a repeat of preparing the Food Calendar for 1998. The villagers, particularly the women, were ever so enthusiastic. A young lady came running exuding her enthusiasm to participate in one more participatory session by asking: *"Didi saye noksha gulo ki abar banabo*?" [Elder sister shall we prepare those diagrams (meaning the Food Calendars etc.) once again?]. The 1998 Food Calendar prepared is at Table 7.4. For the reasons mentioned for the 1995 Food Calendar, the 1998 Food Calendar was rearranged and the rearranged 1998 Food Calendar is at Table 7.5.

The picture emerging from the 1998 Food Calendar reveals a food security situation pretty much similar to the picture portrayed by the 1993 and 1995 Food Calendars.

In Aghrayan, Poush and Magh, the food intake from the basket, if primary food system is the highest, rice and potatoes being the major items consumed. That is immediately after the harvest people are generally well fed. During Phalgun and Chaitra, the consumption of rice and potatoes fall but the villagers still have substantial, relatively speaking, food to eat. By the time the Bengal summer is in full rage, in Baisakh, food consumption falls to a very low level, particularly so for rice and continues to be so till Kartick for seven months. The situation assumes extreme severity in the three months of Bhadra, Aswin and Kartick (mid-August to mid-November), when the only food that people have from the basket of principal food is rice, the consumption of potatoes vanishes and there are no pulses.

In 1998 Food Calendar we see a long hunger period from Baisakh through Kartick and there is a less severe hunger period in the months of Phalgun and Chaitra. Four clear phases are noticeable. The four phases are as follows. *Phase one*, runs from Aghrayan to Magh, when people eat the most. *Phase two* covers Phalgun and Chaitra, when people eat less and hunger sets in. *Phase three*, runs over the five months period from Baisakh to Bhadra, when the consumption level of the villagers is at a very low level. And *Phase Four* is of two month's duration between Ashwin and Kartick, when a typical diet of the poor households consists of only rice.

Food from the secondary food system provides some relief to the poor households. The majority of the vegetables from the secondary food system consist of leaves (called *Sak in Bengali)*. The one redeeming feature of the 1998 Food Calendar is that the quantum of food available from the water bodies has seen a dramatic upturn from what we saw in the 1995 Food Calendar. The availability from the secondary food system has been fairly high during the Baisakh to Bhadra and during Ashwin and Kartick, i.e., during the third and fourth phases of hunger identified above. This indicates that during the difficult hunger months Krishna Rakshit Chak would have suffered even greater hunger but for the food that they gathered and collected from the CPRs and forests. That is, when food from the principal food system declined and declined substantially, food from the secondary food system came to the rescue of the hungry. The range of vegetables, green banana, Sak (leafy vegetables), fish, snails and small animals, that the secondary food system provided, added variety and palate, apart from increasing the food value of the diet of the Krishna Rakshit Chak households.

Thus, the 1998 Food Calendar shows the same pattern as the 1993 and 1995 Food Calendars and the inter-month variations in food consumed in 1998 also seems to be a function of the availability of food in the system. However, the importance of food from the secondary food basket in eliminating hunger (or in reducing the severity of hunger) which had dwindled in 1995 vis-à-vis 1993, had returned. And this remarkably enough came about because, the villagers told us, a huge tank (called Rajbandh) which used to be auctioned by the Panchayat (elected local unit of self-governance), is under dispute now and it could not be auctioned. Right to produce of the tank remains disputed. As a result, no one has harvested and fished the produce of the tank and, thus, the villagers access the produce of the tank, which explains why the importance of food from the secondary food system has bounced back in 1998 to its level of criticality as was shown in the 1993 Food Calendar.

Table 7.4 Food Calendar, 1998

Month	Rice	Potato	Pulses	Vegetable From CPR	Fruits from CPR	Fish from CPR	Snails from CPR	Others from Wild
1	2	3	4	5	6	7	8	9
Baisakh** (Mid-April to Mid-May)	***	***	—	Brinjals	—	—	Snails, *Jal Geri*	*Jhinge*
Jaistha (Mid-May to Mid June)	***	***	Yes	*Kalmi Sak*, *Susmi Sak*, *Gim Sak*,	—	Fish	—	—
Asharh (Mid-June to Mid-July)	****	*	—	Wild potatoes, Mushroom	—	—	—	—
Sraban (Mid-July to Mid-August)	****	*	—	—	—	Weeds	Yes	—
Bhadra (Mid-August to Mid-Sept.)	***	—	—	—	—	*Laatha*, *Chang*, *Fusati*, *Magur*,	Snails, *Samuk*	—
Ashwin (Mid-Sept. to Mid-Oct)	***	—	—	*Jhinge*, *Borbotee*, Snake gourd,	—	*Punti*, *Magur*, *Chang*	—	
Kartick (Mid-Oct.	***	—	—	*Sak*, *Seem*, *Pui Sak*	—	Fish	—	

to Mid-Nov.)								
Aghrayan (Mid-Nov. to Mid-Dec.)	****** ******	**	—	—	—	Fish	—	—
Poush (Mid-Dec. to Mid-Jan.)	******* *****	**	—	*Sak,* radish	—	—	—	—
Magh (Mid-Jan to Mid-Feb)	****** ****	******	—	—	—	Some fish	—	—
Phalgun (Mid-Feb. to Mid-March)	********	****	—	Yes	—	Fish, *Jhinuk*	—	*Neem* leaves
Chaitra (Mid-March- to Mid-April)	*****	****	—	—	—	—	Yes	Rabits

(i) The number of "star" marks under column heads rice, potato, pulses etc., represent the number of stones used by the villagers to show the consumption of the relative item of food.

(ii) "Yes" means occasionally consumed in insignificant amounts, not worth quantifying.

Source: Preparec by Women of Krishna Rakshit Chak, Midnapore, West Bengal.
Facilitator: Neela Mukherjee

Table 7.5. Rearranged Food Calendar, 1998

Month	Rice	Potato	Pulses	Vegetable From CPR	Fruits from CPR	Fish from CPR	Snails from CPR	Others from Wild
1	2	3	4	5	6	7	8	9
Magh (Mid-Jan. to Mid-Feb)	****** ****	*****	—	—	—	Some fish	—	—
Phalgun (Mid-Feb to Mid-March)	********	****		Yes	—	Fish, *Jhinuk*	—	*Neem* leaves
Chaitra (Mid-March to Mid-April)	*****	****	—	—	—	—	Yes	Rabits
Baisakh** (Mid-April to Mid-May)	***	***	—	Brinjals	—	—	Snails, *Jal Geri*	*Jhinge*
Jaistha (Mid-May to Mid June)	***	***	—	*Kalmi Sak*, *Susmi Sak*, *Gim Sak*,	—	Fish	—	—
Asharh (Mid-June to Mid-July)	***	*	—	Wild potatoes, Mushroom	—	—	—	—

Srabon (Mid-July to Mid-August)	****	*	—	—	—	Weeds,	Yes	—
Bhadra (Mid-Aug. to Mid-Sept.)	***	—	—	—	—	*Laatha, Chang, Fusati, Magur*	Snails (*Samuk*)	—
Ashwin (Mid-Sept. to Mid-Oct)	***	—	—	Jhinge, Borbotee, Snake gourd.	—	*Punti, Magur, Chang*	—	—
Kartick (Mid-Oct. to Mid-Nov.)	***	—	—	Sak, Seem, Pui Sak	—	Fish	—	
Aghrayan (Mid-Nov. to Mid-Dec.)	****** ******	**	—	—	—	Fish	—	—
Poush (Mid-Dec. to Mid-Jan)	******* *****	**	—	*Sak,* Radish	—	—	—	—

(i) The number of "star" mark under column heads Rice, potato, pulses represent the number of stones used by the villagers to show the consumption of the relative item of food.

(ii) "Yes" means occasionally consumed in insignificant amounts, not worth quantifying.

Source: Prepared by Women of Krishna Rakshit Chak, Midnapore, West Bengal.
Facilitator: Neela Mukherjee

VII. Similarities in the Three Food Calendars

Having described briefly the three Food Calendars, it is possible now to compare them. Let us begin by identifying the similarities.

First, is the persistence of long hunger periods depicted by all the three Food Calendars. Despite all the talk of our national food security, Krishna Rakshit Chak remains a pocket of hunger for nearly a decade. This is worrisome, though the intensity and duration of the hunger periods may be different which we will deal with separately. This implies that despite there being no systemic shortage of food, reflected by the record harvest from the primary food system, and a burgeoning buffer stock with the government, hunger is a common feature in 1993 and is as much, if not more so, in 1995 and in 1998.

Second, the dominance of starch in the diet of the villagers remains unaffected in all these years. This is a cultural phenomenon. This is similar to what Beck (*Beck,* 1994) observed in respect of some other villages of Midnapore, studied by him around the same time, through the questionnaire method. He noted that during the discussion with the villagers in Midnapore, there was a common agreement that it was only rice, the staple grain that would make the stomach happy. "The stomach won't understand unless it get rice", as one villager put it, to him. Beck even notes that when sufficient quantity of rice was not available, many poor villagers with whom he interacted would take the water leftover from boiling rice (called *Bhater Phen*), which would fill the stomach and was usually fed to livestock in richer households [1].

The *third* similarity in the three Food Calendars is that for the poor households of Krishna Rakshit Chak the major source of protein nutrition remains the food collected from the CPRs, particularly water bodies, forests and micro-environments. More particularly, the relative dependence on food from the secondary food system, particularly for protein in 1998 and 1995 vis-à-vis 1993, has increased in good measure. However, it is not possible to identify whether the absolute amounts of protein intake from this source have actually increased or decreased either in 1995 or in 1998 from their earlier level.

Fourth, the consumption of food is the lowest during the summer months and rainy season, from Baisakh to Kartick, covering the summer months, the cultivation season and the harvesting season. Thus, food is consumed least during the period when the poor have to work the *hardest*: during Asard, Sraban and Bhadra they work in cultivation; during Aswin, Kartick and Poush when they work in harvesting operations as also gleaning from the paddy fields. This is also the period when the workload of the women increases on account of collecting fuel, making "cakes" and then storing them for future use. Poorest households meet their fuel for cooking from collecting fuel from the CPRs (collection of fuel is considered a traditional and unspoken right) which is mainly in the form of fallen leaves, animal dung, notably cow/bullock dung and dry branches. Crop residues and other forms of fuel are also gathered from homesteads, paddy fields, paths, area around ponds or wherever. *Gathering of fuel is the exclusive responsibility of women and girl children*. But collection of animal dung or other forms of fuel during monsoon or rainy season is not possible as leaves do not fall during the rainy season and cattle, goats/sheep are kept in the animal-sheds and stall fed. This is done to both protect them from rain and prevent them from trampling crops or grazing paddy crop, standing in the field. Poor households, therefore, store "cow/bullock dung cakes" made by the women out of dung gathered in the dry season. This increases the workload of the women in Krishna Rakshit Chak.

Finally, the consumption of food from the secondary food system increased during the months when the consumption of rice had to be curtailed. This means that much of the foods are gathered in the pre-*aman* harvest period when seasonal factors combined to the disadvantage of the poor and the price of rice highest. Thus, food from the secondary food system substituted food from the primary food system, particularly potatoes and rice, when these became too expensive for the poor villagers to afford. It also means that villagers in Krishna Rakshit Chak are saved from greater hunger during the summer months by food from the secondary food system, though they go still hungry.

VIII. And the Dissimilarities

If the three Food Calendars have similarities, they have dissimilarities as well. The dissimilarities are important and require some serious thought.

Firstly, pulses which were important components of the food basket of Krishna Rakshit Chak villagers as shown by the 1993 Food Calendar had vanished from the diet of the poor in the 1995 Food Calendar. Pulses, which provide essential nutrients to the poor households in our rural economy, were gone. The absence of pulses from the diet of the Krishna Rakshit Chak villagers indicates that the quality of food in terms of its nutritive value had deteriorated in 1995 vis-à-vis 1993.

Secondly, the intake of vegetables and fruits, which were significant in the 1993 Food Calendar, vanished in the 1995 Food Calendar. This also indicates that the quality of the food basket in terms of vitamins and fibre intake had deteriorated in 1995 as compared to 1993. In the 1998 Food Calendar we find a partial recovery of this, particularly in terms of food gathered from water-bodies.

Thirdly, the consumption of other kinds of food, herbs and leaves from common property resources, forests and "micro-environments", were almost gone in 1995 and limited to consumption of fish and snails over two and three months respectively. This means that elements of the consumption basket shown in the 1993 Food Calendar, which added palate, variety and nutrition to the food basket of the Krishna Rakshit Chak's poor households were gone in 1995. Because of the dispute over *Rajbandh* (a huge tank), the poor households of Krishna Rakshit Chak were again able to catch fish, and collect other food from the tank, which restored some of the loss in palate and variety in their food, noticed in the 1995 Food Calendar.

Fourthly, in the 1993 Food Calendar we had seen two hunger periods (from Chaitra to Jaistha was the first hunger period and Aswin to Kartick was the second hunger period) with some respite in between. From the 1995 and 1998 Food Calendars it is apparent that Krishna Rakshit Chak suffers one long hunger period from Chaitra to Kartick (both months inclusive), spanning almost eight months and increasing in intensity during the latter part of the hunger period, viz., from Bhardra to Kartick. The longer hunger period in 1998 Food Calendar, however, seems to be a little less painful vis-à-vis the long hunger period depicted by the 1995 Food Calendar, because of the availability of fishes, snails, etc. from Rajbandh, which were virtually missing in 1995.

The implications of the differences in the three food calendars deserve a few comments. It seems that in 1995 and 1998, the total food consumption *per se* of the poor households of Krishna Rakshit Chak had gone down, from an already low level. Concurrently, the quality of food in terms of fibre and vitamins contents had also deteriorated in 1995. Thus, the relative hunger had increased in 1995 vis-à-vis 1993. Additionally, the consumption pattern in 1995 was less varied and less palatable in 1995 than before. However, because of an exogenous factor, namely, dispute over use of usufruct of a water tank, there was some restoration in the palate and quality of food in 1998. In summary, if we compare the 1993, 1995 and 1998 Food Calendars, the picture remains the same: hunger has increased since 1993, but in 1998 due to greater availability of food from the secondary food system, the severity of hunger has been of lower intensity than 1995. The elongated hunger period of 1995, as opposed to two relatively shorter hunger periods of 1993, continues in 1998.

IX. The Probe

In keeping with the accepted practice of interviewing diagrams in order to have a right understanding of the community's perspectives, we had discussions with the villagers on the Food Calendars. We are restricting here to the discussions we had on the 1995 and 1998 Food Calendars. [2]. There were two components of the discussion. One component was on what food was available in 1993, 1995 and 1998 and the second component was on what was not available in 1995 though available in 1993 and what was available in 1998 but not available in either 1993 or 1995 or both.

Between 1993, 1995 and 1998 there has been no significant change in the dietary habits of the people in Krishna Rakshit Chak in so far as they continue to prefer and consume rice and potatoes as their principal food. The intake of rice, as seen in Column 2 of Tables 7.1, 7.3 and 7.5, roughly corresponds to a U-shaped curve with almost a flat bottom. It is relatively high in Magh and falls steadily to a lowest point in Ashwin and then again rises dramatically in the two months of Aghrayan and Poush. (Aghrayan,

Poush and Magh are the post harvest season in Bengal). Clearly, consumption of rice is higher immediately after the harvest and then falls steadily through the spring (called Basanta) and summer, to reach the lowest point during the cultivation season immediately preceding the harvesting of the next crop. That is, the consumption of rice apparently varies in direct proportion to its availability in the village: its availability is highest after harvesting in a season and lowest before the harvest in the following season.

The availability we are talking about here is not merely availability in the sense of rice being available for sale in the shops and rice being available to the poor as wages, but also availability in terms of what they can glean immediately after the harvests, from fields of farmers where they work as agricultural labourers. Since gleaning of paddy from paddy-fields recently harvested constitutes an important element of the sources of rice, it is highest in the months of Aghrayan and Poush, i.e., immediately after the harvest of *aman* crop, or Kharif crop. A woman can glean as much as 3 kg. of rice per day on the days when they glean. We will discuss more of this in a separate section on gleaning below.

We noted earlier that most of the villagers of Krishna Rakshit Chak are landless labourers belonging to Lodha Tribe. Basically they are not producers of rice and potatoes, their principal food. They buy these from the market for consumption by selling their labour or glean paddy and dehusk the gleaned paddy into rice by expending their labour. The villagers of Krishna Rakshit Chak explained that the level of rice and potato consumption was determined both by rice and potato being available (supply factor) which regulated the price of food in the market and the opportunity to glean, and availability of employment (power to access the available food). Nevertheless, the former was the dominant factor behind determining food consumption from the primary food system.

During Aghrayan, employment opportunities are available in the fields and farms for harvesting paddy both in the village and in adjoining villages. The average wage hovers around Rs. 30 per day together with a breakfast of puffed rice. Fortunately, both men and women find some work or the other. During Poush while men find work in threshing and winnowing paddy, women find some work in dehusking rice.

Finding work for the Lodhas is more difficult in Poush than in Aghrayan but the availability of rice is higher and hence the price of rice is relatively low. The villagers, therefore, not only consume more rice during the months of Aghrayan and Poush but are also able to buy rice for storing to meet future consumption during the next two months, Magh and Phalgun. This is part of their coping strategy to which we will refer again in Section XIII below.

During Magh and Phalgun, the on-farm activities virtually dry up and the villagers, therefore, make a living by selling fish, fuel and firewood they collect from the water bodies forests and common property resources respectively. Poor households of Krishna Rakshit Chak are able to maintain a certain level of consumption, both from these off-farm earnings and from stock of food they have from Aghrayan and Poush. From Chaitra onwards life becomes difficult as not only employment opportunities and off-farm incomes dwindle, the availability of their principal food (rice and potato) in the local market goes down, resulting in a rise in their prices. There are no fields to glean. In consequence, the poor households cut into their consumption of rice and successively reducing the intake of potatoes, until it becomes zero in Bhadra, Aswin and Kartick.

X. Food Insecurity in Terms of the ED Thesis

Let us now analyse the food insecurity situation in terms of the ED Thesis. In terms of the ED Thesis there could be food insecurity in the households of the village either due to direct entitlement failure or exchange or trade entitlement failure.

In 1993

If we examine the primary food system during 1993, the villagers being landless there could not have been any direct entitlement failure because they did not produce their own food. They have no production based entitlement. There is no transfer based entitlement, particularly with the collapse of the PDS. There is no trade based entitlement as the Lodha tribe do not have and do not trade their asset for food, except labour.

Table 7.6 Employment and Wages in Krishna Rakshit Chak (1998)

Month	Wages	Days of Employment (W)	Days of Employment (M)
Magh (Mid-January to Mid-February)	Rs. 30/- plus a snack of puffed rice.	10-15 days in winnowing	5-10 days earth work.
Phalgun (Mid-February to Mid-March)	Rs. 30-40/- per sq. feet of earth work	10-15 days carrying agricultural produce.	2-5 days work. Digging earth or stones.
Chaitra (Mid-March- to Mid-April)	—	Some work. Harvesting of Boro Paddy	Some work. Selling of Eucalyptus leaves etc.
Baisakh (Mid-April to Mid-May)	—	—	5-6 days
Jaistha (Mid-May to Mid June)	—	—	1-2 days in households of landlords/large farmers.
Asharh (Mid-June to Mid-July)	Rs. 30/- plus a snack of puffed rice.	Some work in the fields	1-2 days preparing fields of other farmers
Srabon (Mid-July to Mid-August)	Rs. 30/- plus a snack of puffed rice.	15-16 days work in paddy transplantation	15-26 days cultivation work

Bhadra (Mid-August to Mid-Sept.)	—	—	—
Ashwin (Mid-Sept. to Mid-October)	Rs. 30/-	4-5 days work in deweeding.	—
Kartick (Mid-October to Mid-Nov.)	Rs.30/- plus one meal (M) Rs 25/- plus one meal (W)	10 days work in harvesting.	10 days work in carrying headloads, storing grains etc. for women. 15-20 days for men.
Aghrayan (Mid-November to Mid-Dec.)	Rs.30/- plus one snack of puffed rice (W). Rs 50/- plus a snack of puffed rice (M)	15-20 days work	15-20 days
Poush (Mid-Dec. to Mid-January)	Rs. 30/- plus a snack of puffed rice	—	15 days

Source: Prepared by Women of Krishna Rakshit Chak, Midnapore, West Bengal
Facilitator: Neela Mukherjee. M denotes men. W denotes women.

Exchange entitlement of the Lodhas was determined by six factors. (i) Their ability to find employment and the duration thereof, which was highest in the months of Aghrayan, Poush and Magh, and moderate during Asharh and Sraban. Exchange entitlement failure faced by the poor households in Chaitra, Baisakh and Jaistha, and during Aswin and Kartick. (ii) The wages paid to them, which was around Rs. 30 per day plus a meal of "puffed rice" as reflected in Table 7.6. (iii) Their ability to exchange their labour with nature (embodied in the produce of the CPRs etc.) from which they acquired food. (iv) The cost of whatever food they brought during the months succeeding other harvests. (v) The indirect taxes that they are required to pay. (vi) The informal taxes that they are required to pay.

Their food security or insecurity was not dependent on security or insecurity arising out of endowment failure but entitlement mapping that they faced. In 1993 food insecurity (for five months) was due to reduction in employment opportunities and a rise in food prices. During the remaining seven months of the year, food security was ensured through trade entitlement, made possible by higher employment and higher availability of food due to harvesting of crops.

In 1995

In 1995, like in 1993, the food insecurity of the Krishna Rakshit Chak households in terms of the primary food system was due to exchange entitlement failure, caused by fall in employment and rise in food prices. The two hunger periods of the 1993 Food Calendar got enlarged into one long hunger period from Chaitra to Kartick because of the general rise in prices that had forced the villagers to forego consumption of potatoes and reduce the consumption of rice in Bhadra, Aswin and Kartick.

If we look at the secondary food system, depicted by the 1993 Food Calendar, poor households of Krishna Rakshit Chak had direct entitlement of food from the system. They could reduce hunger because their direct entitlement from CPRs and micro-environment was not jeopardised. As we come to the 1995 Food Calendar, there appears to be a direct entitlement failure in the secondary food system faced by the poor households. Such entitlement failure is caused both by a reduction in output of food in the system and by denial of access to such food by others, who owned some of these sources of food, whose effect partook the nature of alienation of land from the landowner, who puts his/her land to food production.

Significantly, direct entitlement of the poor of secondary food was reduced due to the emergence of a market for secondary food and a general decline in the conditions of a few of those who owned some of the sources of the secondary food system. Thus one can infer that, as in the case of the secondary food system described by 1995 Food Calendar, direct entitlement failure can occur where there is a change in the market for such goods. But access to the secondary food system improved in 1998, as the efforts at privatisation of CPR did not work out.

We can interpret the collection, gathering and hunting of food from the secondary food system as being exchange based entitlement, as the poor households exchanged their labour for the food they got from the CPRs, forests etc. In that event, one could have said that there was an exchange entitlement failure as the rate of exchange of food from the secondary system vis-a-vis labour moved adversely against the poor households of Krishna Rakshit Chak in 1995. But this may not be appropriate because though the poor households were exchanging labour for food, the CPRs, forests and micro-environments did not receive anything in exchange for the food they provided.

In 1998

If we now look at the 1998 Food Calendar, the situation of food insecurity from the primary food system was caused by a failure of exchange entitlement. The pattern was similar to what was seen in 1993 and 1995. However, the direct entitlement failure from the secondary food system, which increased food insecurity in Krishna Rakshit Chak in 1995, was eliminated, at least partially, in 1998. This was so because the poor villagers could exchange their labour for the food gathered and collected from Rajbandh (the tank) whose usufruct could not be auctioned and hence became available for the villagers' consumption. The dispute regarding ownership of the produce of Rajbandh turned out to be the saviour of the people of Krishna Rakshit Chak.

XI. Role of CPRs, Forests and Micro-Environments and Hunger Periods

The Literature

The role of forests as a source of food has been quite well known but not documented as much as it should have been. Recently, works by Shiva have attempted at documenting all the forest produce *(Shiva,* 1998a, 1997) and has provided their systematic classification. In the context of Orissa, Non-Timber Forest Produce (NTFP) is both a political issue and a livelihood issue: it is a political issue for the ruling-class and profit maximisers while it is a livelihood issue for the people dependent on forests for their survival such as the tribals, whose dependence on NTFP cannot be overemphasized (*Mallik,* 1997). Thus considerable attention has lately been focused on management of NTFP after long years of neglect. Not much work has, however, been done on the role of NTFP in coping with hunger, except perhaps the work of Jodha to which we will return later.

There is a growing literature on food from forests and common property resources in the international context (*Falconer,* 1989; *Falconer* and *Arnold,* 1989; *Food and Agriculture Organisation,* 1982, 1983, 1984, 1986, 1989).

In the Indian context, the literature on the role of common property resources in providing food and "hunger food" in particular, can be divided into two groups: one, dealing with the issue largely in the context of the semi-arid and arid parts of India and the hills and forest fringe regions (See *OFI,* 1991 for a review) and the other dealing with the issue in the context of Tribal Economy. Generally, it is estimated that 60 per cent of Non-Timber Forest Produce, also called Minor Forest Produce, are consumed as food or as dietary supplement by forest dwellers (*Khare et. al.,* 2000).

Jodha (*Jodha,* 1986) covers the semi-arid regions in seven Indian States and shows that in seven districts, for the landless and those with less than 2 hectares of land, income from the CPR accounts for 20 per cent or more of total household income. For the non-poor households, CPRs provide 9-13 per cent of income. Furthermore, he shows that the CPRs supplied over 90 per cent of firewood, between 64 and 88 per cent of all domestic fuel and 69 to 89 per cent of green fodder needs of the landless and land-poor. The NCAER (*NCAER,* 1981) study found that the dependence of the poor on the CPR for fodder and fuel was particularly high in the hills and desert areas of the North. And this has implications for food security: obtaining fuel from the CPR is tantamount to obtaining free good and hence it frees valuable scarce resources for accessing food, given that poor households spend upto 80 per cent of their income on food. An interesting study by Ryan, Bidiniger, Rao and Pushmpamma (1984) found that 8 to 9 per cent of dietary requirements of many of these villages are met out of CPRs.

Dasgupta (*Dasgupta,* 1987) reported that in the two villages studied by him, even in the heart of the green revolution belt of Delhi and Western Uttar Pradesh, 17 and 24 per cent of income respectively were derived from CPRs and free collections from other people's lands. According to this study the bulkwark of the dietary supplements to cereals were brought through wages or received as wages in kind. Poorer households in seven villages spread over four districts of Orissa derive as much as 50 per cent of their income from forests alone (*Saigal,* 1998). It has been found that in Andhra Pradesh as much as 58 per cent of Mahua flowers and upto 17 per cent of Tamarind are consumed by them. (*Khare et. al.,* 2000).

The discussion, however, on the role of CPR in the lives of the people and its utility as the source of providing food security to the poor in the eastern parts of India has been relatively less rich. This is true for the state of West Bengal as well, in which Krishna Rakshit Chak is located. And whatever discussion we have on the role of CPR in the lives of the people in West Bengal, it is very focused, largely concentrated on the role of forests or social forestry (*Shah,* 1987; *Nesmith,* 1990) in the rural scenario of the state. This is abundantly exemplified by the fact that in a survey of 216 households in Midnapore District, Jambone Range (*Mahlhaotra et al,* 1992) found that 44 of the plants listed by the people were used as food. This is so because, *inter alia*, in West Bengal very large areas do not exist as common property resources unlike in other parts of the country where the density of population is lower.

Box 7.3
Shrinking Land and Meals of Seeds…

By *Poornima Joshi* in Phulbani

"…of Badgaon's 585 inhabitants, 265 belong to the Scheduled Tribes (mainly Kandha) and 123 to the Scheduled Castes. The rest are upper caste and have built concrete houses in the nearby upcoming town of Baliguda, Orissa.

There is something static about Badgaon: in the broken plough propped against the cattle-sheds, in the algae-covered pond, in the women carrying pitchers on their heads, and in the resigned, almost numb expressions of village elder Sarveshwar Malik and his companion sitting in the afternoon sun.

In the "approximately 75" years of his life, Sarveswar has seen little change—besides the gradual slipping away of his land into the control of the money lenders who have settled in the nearby town. The single crop from his two acres of ancestral land cannot sustain Sarveshawar and his family through the year. So they depend on minor forest produce (which is difficult to obtain if the forest officials are not given their share).

Their meals comprise water boiled with rice and, when even that is not available, they boil mango seeds with water and drink the syrup residue. "We have a tradition of eating five meals a day. We never get that much food, so eat twice a day. When that also is difficult we make do with water", says Sarveshwar.

The Hindusthan Times, New Delhi, Sunday, February 6, 2000

The inter-class dimensions of the use of CPRs, particularly in the context of food security and hunger, are largely absent in the current analysis of the role of CPRs in the lives of the rural poor. World Bank Review (*OFI*, 1991), Jodha (*Jodha*, 1990,1986) and Chambers, Shah and Saxena (*Chambers, Shah and Saxena*, 1989) are examples in point. Beck (1994) is a notable exception. Class analyses have not looked at relations between differential access that different sections of the rural people have to CPRs.

Land, which exhibits very substantial variations in its access, is nevertheless recognised as a CPR in West Bengal. Of the total land in West Bengal, about 60 per cent is classified as cultivated, 25 per cent as wasteland and 12 per cent is forest area (*Singh and Bhattacharjee,* 1991). Given the political process of agrarian reforms in the state, which began in 1977, of whatever remains of the common land, the tendency is towards privatisation of land recorded in the name of the government. This happens through the land distribution programme pursued by the left-led government in the state, that allocates land held by the Government to the landless villagers. Thus, under the government's land reforms agenda, even in the western part of the State, comprising the four districts of Purulia, Bankura, Birbhum and Midnapore, which have relatively larger areas categorised as wasteland, land coming under common property resources is increasingly being allocated to individuals, the landless in particular.

In effect, common property resources in the State are not purely grazing lands and forests found in other parts of India but includes water bodies and access to usufruct of resources owned by others. Access to many such natural resources in villages in West Bengal is not in terms of any legally defined rights but is a result of the process of exercising rights as matters of : custom from one generation to the next, negotiation, bargaining and even conflict between resource-poor and resource-rich. Access to some resources is open, or what is called "open access", examples of which are the stubble left after harvesting of paddy or wild food that grow in drainage ditches, gleaned grains and vegetables, fallen fruit in orchards found mainly on private land, produce of river beds, produce of rivers and small ponds and rivulets. Access to produce of large ponds and tanks, controlled by large landlords and richer villagers, to which the poor have customarily negotiated access also partakes the nature of CPRs, but these are fewer, though there is a major one in Krishna Rakshit Chak to which we have referred.

Forests have a special place in the lives of the poor people, especially the tribal people. Even if we take no account of shifting cultivation (*Jhum* cultivation in local language) in which millions of people are involved in North Eastern States, Madhya Pradesh and Orissa, forests provide food, fodder and fuel to many more millions in North Eastern States, MP, Andhra Pradesh, Uttar Pradesh, Orissa, Bihar, Gujarat and West Bengal. Upto 38 per cent of tribal income in MP, 55 per cent of tribal income in Andhra Pradesh, 35 per cent in parts of Gujarat and 39 per cent of tribal income in Orissa comes from forests. Indeed the contracting of minor forest produce, (MFP) is a subject matter of considerable politics and controversy in Madhya Pradesh and Orissa. The criticality of the income from MFP in the lives of the poor people, and the related controversies and issues have been dealt with at great length by Fernandes and Menon. (1987, 1988).

Of course, the availability of MFP is subject to variations and seasonality (*Banerjee,* 1988; *Briscoe,* 1979). In central India, the tribal population derive 12 per cent energy during the pre-harvest period from food provided by the forests and CPRs, while they get only 2 per cent of energy intake in the post-harvest season. It is distressing that the productivity and production of food from CPRs and forests are on the decline (*Jodha,* 1985, 1986).

The Evidence with Special Reference to Other Parts of Midnapore

Crow (1984), Greenough (1982), Currey (1981) and Rahman (1981) found the consumption of *Kochu* by the poor families in famine conditions in Bangladesh and West Bengal as very common. Beck (1994) has reported that in the villages in Midnapore, West Bengal, during the three and half months of the rainy season (later part of Jaistha, Asharh, Sraban, Bhandra) when agricultural employment was limited, one person could gather or catch daily one or part combinations of the following food:

- 300 grams to 3 kg. of various kinds of fish, e.g., Puti (Barbus Sophora), Pekal (Clarius Batrachus), the market price for which varied from Rs. 4—Rs. 15 per kg.
- 200 grams of prawn, the market price of which is Rs. 30 per kg.
- 500 grams of jute leaves, not sold in the market.
- 1-2 kg of Kochu Stalk, not sold.
- 5 kg of watercess, market price of which is Rs. 2 per kg.
- 500 grams of drumsticks, market price of which is Rs. 8 per kg.

Beck (*Beck,* 1994) gives the table (shown here as Table 7.7) of the kinds of food collected by the poorest households.

Consumption of monitor lizard, or *goshap* as it is known locally, the skin and meat of which are sold, was reported as common by O'Malley in the early 1900s (*O'Malley,* 1914). This lizard is also hunted by the Hill Panadarams in South India (*Morris,* 1982) and by nomadic groups in Maharastra (*Malhotra and Gadgil,* 1988).

Davis (*Davis,* 1983) and Bhowmick (*Bhowmick,* 1963) mentioned the importance of CPRs to the Lodhas. Bhowmick (1963) also commented that access to farmer's fields by Lodhas for fishing was restricted. Such restrictions were not found elsewhere. Though not mentioned specifically, but used and collected widely were fruits which fell from trees, especially mangoes in the summer, plums and tamarind, which are collected in the main by children. Sengupta (*Sengupta,* 1978) noted how landless families lived on jackfruit and mangoes in Malda and Coochbehar districts during summer months. Some of these fruits such as figs and mangoes are being sold in the market now. Collection of snails from ponds as also from fields after monsoons is common.

A Digression on Gleaning

The poorest households also collect paddy grains that fall during harvesting after the *aman* harvest but access and type of gleaning can differ. A look at who gleans, when, how much and the restrictions imposed, an interesting spectrum emerges.

There are three categories of gleaning.

Category I, where gleaning is done whenever there is time and mainly the children actively carry it out. The amount that can be gathered depends partly on the overall yield of the crop and partly on the composition of the household and who have the time to glean. Where on an average children go out to glean for an hour a day in the 15 to 30 days when the crop is harvested, they have been found to collect in total between 10-15 kg. of paddy. The average collected by a household could be about 13 kg. per season and the highest per household per season can be upto 25 kg. Farmers refusing access to glean their field cannot be ruled out. *This is a case of negotiated access.* As one women said: "if the crop is good, the rich let us in, if not they don't."

Table 7.7 Food Collected by Poorest Households

Month[1]	Type of Food	Amount Gathered [2] (Kg/per day)	Market price (Rs/Kg)	Price of Rice
Baisakh	Mollusc,	1	7	3.50
Jaistha	Minor lizard,	1 Lizard is 10 kg	12*	4-4.20
	Bairon leaf	—	—	—
	[3], Sorrel,	0.25	—	—
	Mohua fruit	0.25	—	—
	[4], Mahua	?	?	—
	flower	20	1	—
Asharh	Bairon leaf,	0.25	—	4-4.20
	Sorrel,	0.25	—	—
	Sweet potato,	2	3*	—
	Prawns, various	0.3	10	—
	fish	0.5	5-10	—
		0.5-1	—	—
Sraban	Bairon Leaf,	0.25	—	4-4.20
	Sorrel,	0.25	—	—
	Sweet potato,	2	3*	—
	Prawns, various	0.3	10	—
	fish	0.5	5-10	—
Bhadro	Kudro [5],	0.2-0.5	8#	4.50
	Sweet potato,	2	3*	—
	Crab	2	8	—

Ashin	Sweet potato,	2	3*	4.50
	Crab	2	2	
Kartick	Churka Aloo [6],	—	—	3.50
	Sweet potato	2-3	—	—
		2	3	—
Aghrahan	Churka Aloo,	2-3	—	3.50
	Ikra rat	0.2-1	—	—
Poush	Churka aloo,	2-3	—	2.75
	Ikra rat	0.2-1	—	—
Magh	Shaluk[7],	10	—	2.75
	Ikra rat, pigeons	0.2-1	—	—
		0.25	3	—
Phalgun	Shaluk	10	—	2.75
Chaitra	Shaluk	10	—	3.50

1. Bengali calendar runs from 15th April, i.e., Boishakh month lasts from 15th April to 14th May. The main part of the rainy season is in Ashad, Srabon and Bhadro (i.e. 15th June to 14th September).
2. Average amount that could be gathered.
3. Not identified and eaten boiled.
4. Madhuka latifolia or Bassia latifilia.
5. Gourd, possibly Coccinia Cordifolia.
6. A kind of Yam, possibly Solesnostermon rotundiflius.
7. A kind of water lilly.

* Sold in village. # Exchanged for rice.

Category II, where gleaning is usually carried out by women and children. Estimates are that as much as 5 kg. could be gathered in a day per person. For the gleaning season as a whole, the estimates vary widely on the total amount gleaned per person, which can be anything between 15 and 80 kg. Most of the time gleaning is permitted as the poor households wished to glean, barring exceptions where the owners allow gleaning to only those who have worked to harvest the crop in the owners land. *This is also a case of negotiated access.*

Category III, where gleaning is done from rat holes. Lodhas are the gleaners. Rats make deep long holes under the narrow *"aals"* (or earthen ridges between fields). Rats have been found to store upto 100 kg. of grain in a single hole. Lodhas dig up rat holes and take the grains, in addition to killing the rats for their meat. The work is very hard and prone to snake bite, which means that those who can undertake this gleaning are limited in number. The average that two men can collect in could be about 6-7 kg. per day, and there would be days when there could be no gleaning at all. *This is a case of negotiated mutual benefit.* It is worth noting that Category III gleaning was helpful to both the farmers and the collectors, yet those wishing to glean are required to seek permission from the owners to do so, which is what makes Category III gleaning, an activity of negotiated mutual benefit rather than one of conflict.

Grains collected from all three forms of gleaning make substantial contribution to the poorest household's subsistence and there are households who can gather upto 100 kg. a season, which is the equivalent of wages from 30 days of male agricultural labourers.

There are cases where restrictions are severely placed by farmers, where the farmers themselves glean. Thus there can be situations of conflict in gleaning.

Beck found gleaning in Midnapore but he found that it is possible to glean after *aman* and not possible after *boro* harvest. The reason being that the HYV paddy husks, cultivated during *boro* season, did not fall as easily as those grown during *aman* season, which leaves the poor with little to pick up from the fields. Gleaning was possible from fields cultivated with HYV seeds only in case of hail or heavy rain. This is what has also been confirmed by Greely (1987). Greeley and Huq (1980) commented that it is the longer straw of *aman* paddy that ensures lodging, and therefore, more fallen grains as opposed to shorter statured HYVs cultivated during *boro* season. Given the importance of gleaned grains to the poorest, attempts to develop varieties of rice that drop less grain will "damage nutrition amongst the poorest gleaners" (*Lipton with Longhurst,* 1989).

The importance of gleaning in West Bengal and in a similar economy of Bangladesh has been the subject of a whole range of other studies as well. In Birbhum district, Sengupta and Ghosh (1978) found that landless labourer families resorted to gleaning immediately after harvests. "Children of their (landless labourers') families would rush to the fields and collect handfuls of grains that are left on the field. Each landless family could collect 30 to 40 kg in the process. Santhal (tribal) children are adept in collecting grains from rat hole where rats would store their days collection". Cian (1977) talks of opening of rat holes as an activity carried out by children in Bangladesh villages and Howes (1985) found that "children from poor households and the occasional widow, search for rat holes from which small quantities of grain may be retrieved".

In Birbhum there is an additional phenomenon called *Jhora,* involving the collection of unripened stands of unwanted paddy from the farmer's fields by poor people, usually found in places where the farmers wanted the poor quality stands to be removed so that the seed stock for the following year would be kept as "pure" as possible. *This is an example of negotiated mutual benefit between the landless and poor on the one hand and land owning farmers over resources on farmer's land.* The poor villagers, wishing to collect grains from other farmer's field, had to ask the farmer's permission to do so. This was more for the sake of ensuring that the collector did not damage the crop surrounding the stands to be collected, than an exertion to enforce rights.

In Bangladesh, Siddiqui (*Siddiqui,* 1982) also found that children, old men and women gleaned grains from fields upto 1 kg per head per day. Begum (1985) found that in Comilla district in Bangladesh, gleaning constituted upto 20 per cent of women's labour earnings, where it made no contribution in Modhupur. Blanchet also found that hundreds of gleaners worked during harvest in *haor* (or semi-permanently flooded) areas of Shylet in north eastern Bangaldesh.

Degradation of CPRs

Despite the importance and use of CPRs, they continue to be neglected and degraded. Poor upkeep and over use have been the principal causes for the physical degradation. Most of the CPRs are not subject to any regulation or user charge. For instance, there is no grazing tax or compulsory labour contribution for maintenance of CPRs or for fencing, desilting ponds, repairing woodlots, etc. These have been contributory factors towards mis-management or abandonment of CPRs (*Agarwal,* 1999; *Jodha,* 1985, 1991; *Brara,* 1987; *Chambers, Shah and Saxena,* 1989; *Singh, et. al.,* 1985; *Chopra, Kadekodi and Murthy,* 1990). In villages where the village elders have some informal authority, things are a little better (*Brara,* 1987). One of the principal sources of degradation has been the policy of the government to name a "monopoly contractor" to whom all produce from CPRs have to be sold. Take the case of Orissa where all NTFP have to be sold to a particular Company or in Madhya Pradesh, where all Kendu leaves collected from the forests have to be sold to a named authority. Chemicalisation of agriculture has contributed to fall in the quality of water in water bodies in many places (*Mukherjee and Mukherjee,* 1994).

XII. What Happened in Krishna Rakshit Chak?

Villagers of Krishna Rakshit Chak generally said that they gathered and collected food from the secondary food system as a way of coping with food shortages in times of stress, and such food was eaten regularly especially during rainy season when agricultural employment was limited and the price of food the highest. Gathering of food from the secondary food system is done whenever and wherever possible. We did not get any quantitative estimate of food gathered and consumed from the secondary food system, but the 1993, 1995 and the 1998 Food Calendars reveal that one kind of food or the other from the secondary food system is eaten in Krishna Rakshit Chak all round the year. The kinds of food from the secondary food system that the villagers of Krishna Rakshit Chak consumed were not, however, all the time "wild food" as found by Beck in other villages of Midnapore. Many of these foods were vegetables and "domesticated food". Wild food means food consumed by the poor but not cultivated by them. These are generally gathered from the sides of paths, ponds, swamps, the jungle and overgrown areas that are found in patches around the villages and accessible forests. They are, therefore, resources that could be gathered free and for the most part without restriction.

Notably enough, the villagers of Krishna Rakshit Chak, though they are Lodhas, did not make any mention of lizards (*Goshap*), minor lizards and rats as being parts of their diet, unlike what other researchers have found in Midnapore. Whether this omission is part of the phenomenon of hiding consumption of such meat, which is not consumed by the general public, or whether these were not abundantly available in Krishna Rakshit Chak are issues which require further investigation. The possibility of the former is somewhat bleak because of two reasons: one, there were repeated rounds of participatory sessions over a long period of time and second, the 1998 Food Calendar was prepared by the villagers, amongst whom there were non-poor participants as well.

We have seen earlier that whereas there were two hunger periods in the 1993 Food Calendar, the hunger period in the 1995 and 1998 Food Calendars runs almost eight months at a stretch. We also indicated that the peak segment of the hunger period of Bhadra, Aswin and Kartick, as also the earlier segment from Chaitra to Shraban, are more severe than the two smaller hunger periods shown by the 1993 Food Calendar. Look at columns 2, 3 and 4 of Table 7.1, and compare them with columns 2, 3 and 4 of Table 7.3. It will be apparent that the length of the hunger period in 1995 has increased by about 60 per cent between 1993 and 1995 and continues to be so in 1998.

A comparison of columns 5 to 8 of Table 7.1 with corresponding columns of Tables 7.3 and 7.5 reveal interesting features. Whereas in the hunger periods of 1993 Food Calendar, "hunger food" came from the CPRs etc., for the poor households of Krishna Rakshit Chak, which reduced the intensity of hunger, in 1995 the availability of such food was too little during the extended hunger period. Thus, not only has the hunger period been extended but also the depth of such hunger increased over the years. In fine then, the poor households suffered hunger in 1995 and in 1998 over longer periods than in 1993 and, at once, they were comparatively more hungry as well.

It was a rather distressing revelation that cabbage, pumpkin, spinach, Pui Saag, leaves, herbs, green banana, mango, jackfruit, wild water plants, etc. were all gone in 1995 and 1998. During and around 1993, the poor households of Krishna Rakshit Chak had negotiated access to sizeable amounts of these hunger foods from fields and tanks of relatively well off farmers. But from 1995 onwards, due to the relatively well-off farmers' inability to make both ends meet in the face of rising prices, they denied the poor access to these foods. There were two reasons cited. One reason was that because of the increasing difficulty faced by the farmers they had started selling these hunger foods produced in their fields in the local market to supplement their household income. The average "on going prices" (in 1995) of some of these food in the nearby Charkabani, Khemasuli, Tangra, Golbazar and Kalai Kunda Gate No. 2 markets were as follows: bitter gourd @ Rs. 1 for three pieces; Susmi Sak @ Rs.1 for three bundles; Kalmi Sak @ Rs. 2 per kg; Thanuni Sak @ Rs. 3.50 per kg and snails and fish at various prices. The second reason was, following from the first, people because of their economic difficulty started buying these poor quality food, which no one previously picked up in the market. Thus, the emergence of a market for poor quality food also contributed towards reducing the food availability from the secondary food system.

In 1998 the market situation remained the same but there was one significant change in the secondary food system scenario. The Gram Panchayat, as we mentioned before, within whose jurisdiction Krishna Rakshit Chak fell, could not auction the usufruct right of Rajbandh (the tank) in Krishna Rakshit Chak due to a dispute and hence villagers had access to its produce. Thus some food provided by the CPRs etc. was again available in 1998 for consumption, even after their sale.

The villagers pointed out though that in 1995 and in 1998 the total output of hunger food *per se* had also fallen on account of two factors. One, because of the use of chemical fertilisers and "medicines" in the paddy fields by farmers to deal with pests and insects, the run-off from these fields which flow into the small water bodies in and around the village, are fully chemicalised. In consequence, the water in these water bodies gets polluted, which has led to a fall in availability of fish, snail etc. from these sources. Second, the area under common lands (on which a portion of hunger food grow) is shrinking. Common lands are being privatised and diverted to other uses such as social forestry for timber. While no accurate figures for this diversion are available, the poor households did emphasize that it has been significant according to their reckoning in recent years. This is similar to what Beck found in other Midnapore villages and he noted that "wild foods available locally were continually declining as more land was put to agricultural use and the wild foods are either marketed or more villagers tried to collect them." As one villager remarked to him: "Ten years back all of the foods mentioned were found locally all round but now it's difficult to get them. We have to go a long way to get them now, going out in the morning and coming back at four or five in the evening" (*Beck,* 1994).

It is apparent as shown in the Food Calendars that in some seasons more food is available in both quantity and variety such as in the month of Magh as compared to say Aswin when not much food is available from the secondary sources as well. If we compare columns 2, 3 and 4 of the Food Calendars with columns 6, 7 and 8, we find that when food from the primary system is low, food from the secondary system rises. Thus, there is a complementary role played by the secondary food system, which is why it has been called "hunger food".

It has also been pointed out that collection of fuel, particularly twigs and wood, is becoming progressively more difficult which means that poor households are occasionally buying fuel. The outlay on buying fuel is not inconsequential in as much as the cost of three sack-full of dry leaves is Rs. 50, which is enough for three days fuel need of a household. The amount spent on buying fuel makes inroads into the level of consumption of the poor.

XIII. Coping Strategies in Krishna Rakshit Chak

Hunger is, therefore, a certainty which the villagers of Krishna Rakshit Chak endure every year. And it is increasing over the years. In such a situation, villagers of Krishna Rakshit Chak have only a few choices: regulate food consumption, to borrow food from neighbours/relatives, and take loans to buy food at the extortionist's high rate of interest. Villagers of Krishna Rakshit Chak exercise the last option cautiously, because of the triple burden it imposes: the monetary burden, the psychological burden concerning repayment and dependency on the money-lender, which is in many cases the shopkeeper.

The poor also adopted the strategy of curtailing consumption. They stayed indoors at home to save energy and fast, while sleeping or lying down, a phenomenon similar to what Lipton (1983) and Hartmann and Boyce (1983) found in other areas of Bengal and Bangladesh. The villagers of Krishna Rakshit Chak opt to spread their hunger rather than meet immediate hunger needs and they do so by making one meal stretch into two, or eat every alternate day, a phenomenon widely prevalent in South Asia (*Van Schendel,* 1989; *Dreze,* 1988; *Caldwell, et. al.,* 1986; *Jodha,* 1978). As we have noted in Section VIII earlier, villagers of Krishna Rakshit Chak would buy, earn or glean food in the months of Aghrayan and Poush and save the same in order to stave off hunger in Magh and Phalgun. The villagers tolerated some intensity of hunger at the present in order to safeguard against future hunger, probably even more severe, a strategy found in Howrah district of West Bengal as well (*Bharati and Basu,* 1988).

Reduction in consumption was, therefore, in the nature of attempting to stave off future hunger and circumventing the prospects of having to ιake loans from the moneylenders and the consequent increase in their dependency. Women were both mother and cook, who ate last and many a times only the leftovers. This practice of eating last and eating the leftovers, tied with the phenomenon of women themselves internalising the iniquitous norms set out by the custodians of the patriarchal system that operates in the rural areas of India (*World Bank,* 1989). Greenough (1982) remarked that "the patriarchal values of Bengali Hindu society required priority to be given to the feeding of the male members of the household so as to ensure the continuance of the make line". "Even in normal times men are fed first in peasant households. Women eat after the men, receiving a smaller and poorer share of food" (*Arnold,* 1985, p.89). And when food is in short supply, or when disease strikes, the male children get more attention and food resources.

Box 7.4
Food and Gender

If you're hunter and you have some camels, the small stock belongs to the women. If you're dairy farmers, the chickens belong to the women. If all you have are ducks, the ducks belong to the men.

Margaret Mead, the noted Anthropologist

Gleaning of food from the secondary food system that we saw is an important strategy of the poor in Krishna Rakshit Chak. Morgan's essay on the place of harvesters in nineteenth century village life indicates close parallels between gleaning as practiced in nineteenth century Britain and contemporary Krishna Rakshit Chak in Midnapore, West Bengal. "It is difficult to appreciate that the effort of so many days of back breaking work was thought worth while but to the gleaners the gathered grain represented one of the mainstays of the home—a safeguard against the threatened privations of winter. In the case of wheat, gleanings provided flour to the cottager's loaf. Barley gleanings were fed to the chicken or pig. For the family who were able to supply themselves with a winter's stock of flour, gleaning might be the most lasting of the harvest extra's" (*Morgan,* 1982).

Morgan gives an account of a dispute in Britain between property on one hand, supported by the State in the form of its courts, and common rights on the other. This involved, in case of Britain, infringements and encroachments from both sides. On the one hand, there are infringements by the poor on private property, and on the other, there are attempts at infringements of common rights (of the poor) by the rich farmers. An example of the former is farmers (mostly in neighbouring villages) prohibiting poor households of Krishna Rakshit Chak from gleaning of vegetables etc. from their land in 1995 when life became difficult for them, something still found in different parts of West Bengal.

Most significantly in Krishna Rakshit Chak, like in 19th Century Britain, gathering of CPRs is mainly the responsibility of women and children, especially girl children, whereas ownership of land is almost exclusively vested in men. It would be of interest to investigate whether the patterns of class and gender conflict seen in nineteenth century Britain can be found in contemporary rural West Bengal, but that is beyond the scope of this Chapter.

XIV. Conclusions

The story in brief is that there is hunger in Krishna Rakshit Chak. The fact that we produced 202 million tons of food in 1999/2000 and that the government holds buffer stocks far in excess of the warranted level may give the illusion of food security at the national level, but pockets of hunger persist. Despite huge strides made by West Bengal in increasing agricultural productivity (*Rogaly, Hariss-White and Bose,* 1999), despite establishment and successful functioning of the Panchayati Raj system, despite a PDS system, that we are told, "works" and despite significant land reforms measures taken to provide land to the landless and register the tenants *(Ghosh,* 1999), there are large sections of people who suffer hunger in rural Bengal. That is, ensuring a massive food output, a more than adeqaute food stocks as buffer, rapid rise in food output at the state level and at the national level, a functioning democracy at the local level and a PDS are not enough for elimination of hunger. Most of these are directed at ensuring food security at the supra-household level. We have to look for food security at a much lower level, that is, at the household level. Food security ensured at the household level is the only way to secure a hungerless society.

The nature and intensity of hunger varies from month to month. The situation is worst in the summer and monsoon months. Villagers face a long hunger period from Chaitra to almost Kartick. The consumption of food is thus lowest in the months when the energy needs are highest due to work-load on account of employment and harsh climate. The women face additional workload of maintaining supply of fuel during the period under reference, when particularly the latter part of the hunger period, fuel availability from "conventional sources" get reduced.

The way the poor households cope with their hunger leaves one wondering whether for the inhabitants of Krishna Rakshit Chak, their world is their village. For them local identity as people belonging to Lodha tribe is much stronger than any other identity or notion. As a result, the poor households try to deal with their lives as if they are circumscribed by only the village or villages they visit. There is no attempt at migration. There is no attempt (or may be better still, "failed attempt") to access food from the public distribution system. There is no attempt to seek any outside help to mitigate their suffering. Probably for them, as it has been found in a little village in Jhabua district of Madhya Pradesh, "the nation-state operates in an absent minded slow motion—if it does at all. And this is not an exotic example of backwardness" (*Chakravarty,* 2000).

The role of the secondary food system (common property resources, micro-environments, forests etc.) is critical in reducing hunger of the poor, all through the year but more so during the hunger period. Access to CPRs, micro-environments and forests plays critical roles in enabling the hungry villagers to obtain food, diversify income sources and increase the stability of the family livelihood systems. CPRs serve as a source of various kinds of food, the only source of animal protein, fodder, fuel, etc for household consumption and for sale to supplement income. Thus, the villagers depend heavily on the CPRs for sustaining them. There are two aspects of the dependency that warrants a few comments. First, the dependence on the CPRs and forests is not constant. It varies from season to season. It gets intensified during the slack season. Two, the availability of food and other resources from the CPRs and forests also varies but the slack season, as it were, for the output from the secondary sources is not co-terminus with the slack season for food availability from the primary food system. This helps the poor villagers to cope with reduction in food supply from the primary food system.

Box 7.5
The Hunter, The Gatherer, The Shopper, The Cook

But I have been cooking all day.
Standing over a hot stove.
Slaving over a hot stove.
Cooking.

I've been shopping for groceries.
Putting them away.
Setting the table.
Cooking the food.
Making this dinner.
Wracking my brains.
I've been wracking my brains over this meal.
What to buy.
How much to pay.
I've been budgeting.
Looking for sales.
I've been feeding this family on $ 6.00.
Making it do. I've been wracking my brains over this meal.

I have been cooking all day.
Shopping for bargains.
Hunting for bargains.
I've been hunting all day.
I've been up and down hundreds of aisles.
Hunting.
Hunting and gathering and cooking this food.
Loading my cart.
Carrying carcasses.
I have been hunting all day.
I have gathered this food from across the land.
I've been everywhere.
I've been everywhere.
I have made this meal.
I have created this food.
This is my time.
My thought.
What you have on your plate is my blood.
My brains.
I tell you I have been cooking all day.

What do you mean
you don't want it?

Sondra Segal and Roberta Sklar in *Women's Body and Other Natural Resources,* 1987

In the food systems of the village, the role of the women remains what they are traditionally required to do (*Jeffrey* and *Jeffrey,* 1999). They bear the burden of providing food to the households. They have a more detailed knowledge of food from the primary and the secondary food systems than men. This is consistent with what Boulding (*Boulding,* 1976) and Shiva (*Shiva,* 1988) found. More generally, the women in the tribal community of Lodhas in Krishna Rakshit Chak are the principal gatherers, collectors and gleaners of food from the secondary food system. They, therefore, have special knowledge of the edible produce of the secondary food system.

Collecting food from the secondary food system is time consuming and entails very hard work. Since there is a disparity in the intra-familial distribution of power, the task of collecting produce from the secondary food system falls on the younger women and girl children. This means that younger women and girl children in the poor households are forced to ensure that their future food security is jeopardised in the larger sense. Because they spend considerable time in collecting and foraging food from the secondary food system, they miss their schools. This is reflected in the poorer literacy rate among women in the village as depicted by the literacy map that the women have given us.

The concept of CPR as an element of the secondary food system itself has been distinctly different for Krishna Rakshit Chak. The women of Krishna Rakshit Chak consider negotiated rights, or their customary right, to collect and glean foodgrains and vegetables from the rich farmers' land, even in neighbouring villages, as part of their CPR. They are seen as CPR because the kind of foodgrains and vegetables collected and/or gleaned is utilised by the community in Krishna Rakshit Chak and no individual seeks to exert her right over them, to the exclusion of others, except the person who holds title to the land.

However, there is an upside to complement the downside of the phenomenon. Though the secondary food system robs the young women and the girl children of valuable opportunities to study in the village schools (and there is one in the village), yet its influence in providing women, girl children and even the aged with a independent source of subsistence, cannot be over emphasized. It eliminates the need for a mediated dependencey relationship on the able bodied (read younger) male adults. There is on the balance a need to look at food from the secondary as not merely helping in reducing hunger but also in empowering the women and the vulnerable groups in society.

XV. Policy Conclusions

There has to be a policy set in place to abate the deterioration and depletion of the CPRs, micro-environment and forests, noting that the CPRs are the only property that the poor people like the Lodhas of Krishna Rakshit Chak have.

While the distribution of land to the landless is unexceptionable, measure to protect the village commons and the micro-environment in the village must be put in place. If the run-off, for instance, from the fields of the better-off farmers pollute the water bodies, which cut off a vital source of food for the poor, the polluter-pays principle must be put in place. It could partake the nature of defraying the cost of detoxification of the water bodies. And distribution of land could be from land declared surplus, rather than from CPRs. This is not only because it provides food for the poor but also because it has a gender dimension. Because women and girl children are the principal foragers and gatherers of food from CPRs, they have access to food and to money to buy food by selling produce from the CPRs, it helps women and children to access food without the mediation of men. The dependency relationship with men, particularly the young male adults, is to that extent reduced.

There is need to design interventions to provide money to the poor during the hunger period not as dole, but as employment and as credit for self-employment. The record of the state in providing employment is not glorious and the record of the banking system (mass banking system, that is) is not exactly flattering. This is particularly so from the gender perspective. Some hope lingers in our mind that the success in preventing the Maharastra Drought of 1970-73 from escalating into a full blown famine provides clues to those in charge of statecraft with policy options that may help in reducing hunger in other states as well. But on the other, the abject failure of the State to prevent millions from migrating out of Koraput, Bolangir and Kalahandi (KBK) in Orissa, to prevent starvation, in successive years, is almost scandalous. The State in case of KBK not only failed to protect the entitlements to food for the most vulnerable households but also of the more vulnerable within these households such as women and children. Similarly, the Employment Guarantee Scheme (EGS) did precious little in Tamilnadu (*Guhan,* 1981). Thus, in States, where the leakages are less and governance is reasonably good, the Maharastra style EGS may work.

Dependence on the intrumentalities of the state alone may not have always been the best course. As it has been noted by commentators that even if the State has dealt with, efficiently enough, the threat of a full-fledged famines (*Sen,* 1982, *Dreze,* 1988), the Report-Card of the government in dealing with less acute situations, such as droughts, leaves much to be desired. There is need to look at alternative models, such as the SEWA Model for organising the poor and the Grameen Model (minus-the high rate of interest) for providing credit. The model pursued by several pioneering NGOs in India such as the Working Women's Forum in Tamil Nadu and Karnataka or Banco Sol in Brazil could also give some pointers for the answer. There is need to move away from the top down systems put in place for delivery of poverty alleviation programmes, which is self-serving and has run its course out.

It is not possible to have a long run solution to the problems of hunger unless we manage several other "dependencies", to use Sen's terminology. There is need to exert more emphasis on elementary education and basic health care. It is fashionable to talk of user charges and a reduced role of the State. But given the state of the hunger situation in particular and the poverty secenario in general, there is need for the role of the state to be entrenched in these areas. The answer to "bad governance" is not "no governanace" but better governance. If we cannot refrain from getting into the trap of thinking that market will do the trick, hunger will stalk us for a long time to come. Markets will not work in the social sectors in the poor rural areas. The example of "Orissa State Electricity" after the super cyclone that hit the State in 1999 should be enough of a reminder for us.

In the case of Krishna Rakshit Chak, at least the Summer Vacation could be made to coincide with the time when the women and the children are required to work most, in order to collect and gather food from the secondary food system. This will leave them time to maintain the food security status of their families and create space for them to attend school and be encouraged not to miss classes. Present concern for food security should not endanger their long run food security. This would help in building their future and contribute towards a long term solution of their hunger problems.

Organising the poor to assert their rights should have a high priority and State funded, if needed. It is not only important to have entitlements and rights but also to exercise those rights. The lessons learnt about the power of rural organisations in protecting the rights of the poor, from the Chipko Movement in the Garwal Himalayas is too well, known to be laboured here. The examples of what URMUL did in Lunkaransar, Bikaner to ensure water-rights to become inviolable, or what happened in Nepal where the poorest families in the village organised themselves in getting credit and grain, and in maintaining wage rates, or what Vidhayak Sansad did in Usgaon Thane district to secure minimum wages for the tribals, have all lessons in this regard.

Endnotes

1. Beck notes that during the Great Bengal famine of the 1943, hungry people went from house to house asking for *Phen* and Greenough comments that this has to do with the cultural significance of rice in Bengali culture, as *Phen* contains little of nutritional value. It may also have been connected to the fact that P*hen* appears to stave off hunger pains. The tactic of drinking *Phen* to stave off hunger was used by the poor rural families in Korea, during the Korean War.
2. For a report on the discussions we had on the 1993 Food Calendar see Mukherjee, Neela and Mukherjee, Amitava : "Rural Women and Food Insecurity", *Economic and Political Weekly*, March, 12, 1994. This Chapter is an extension of the paper under reference.

8 A Note on Force Field Analysis of Hunger in the Four Villages of Varanasi and Faridabad

I. Introduction

Having examined the food security situation in different villages, it is now appropriate to net out the findings. In all the village studied, people go hungry as they lack food security, at least during some months and they suffer from malnutrition. And it is apparent that there are a large number of factors that affect the food security and hunger situation in the villages. While *a priori* we do know that the factors that affect both Indian food production and the farmers, as also the food security situation that they and their community face, are many. The literature on the subject is formidable. What would be of interest to know is what do the farmers themselves and the communities in which they live think of their problems. What are their perceptions of the problems that adversely affect their food security status and exacerbate hunger? What are the forces that help them in improving the food security situation they face and in combating hunger, or at least in maintaining the status quo?

As far as some of the negative factors that cause or prevent betterment of the current state of the food security situation in the villages are concerned, the villagers have explicitly mentioned, scored and ranked the constraints that agriculture face as we have discussed in the earlier Chapters. But that is only part of the problem, against the backdrop of the definition of food security we have advocated in this book (See Chapter 1). There are other negative factors that the villagers and farmers have not ranked but have explicitly indicated, both in the context of food production and their well being. These factors have to be added on to the factors constraining agriculture which were ranked by the villagers, to have a full picture of what adversely affects food security and what helps them averting greater food insecurity in the villages.

As far as the positive factors are concerned, the matter is less straightforward. The factors that help the farmers in producing food and in accessing food have been mentioned and discussed at length at different places. For instance while indicating institutional mechanisms in place to support agriculture, they have worked out the Venn Diagrams where they have indicated which institutions are helpful and to what extent. However, though we have a set of factors that are supportive of improvements in food security, these have neither been ranked nor scored. And they have not been positioned against the negative influences. There has, therefore, been no "weighing" done by the villagers of the negative and positive influences in the context of their food security.

Thus, we do have a set of positive and a set of negative factors that affect food security in the villages studied. They now have to be put in an order of presentation to facilitate a graphic view of the forces that determine the state of hunger and food security in the villages under references. There are various ways in which this is possible. We would follow the Force Field method.

II. The Force Field Methods

As mentioned in the Chapter on Introduction, Kurt Lewin (*Lewin,* 1950) developed the Force Field Analysis (FFA). FFA is a way of looking at and analysing forces that have a bearing on any problem or situation (we prefer the word problem, because in the villages studied, we did find the villagers telling us that food security is a problem for them, only the degrees vary). This is seen as an aid to work out a course of action to bring about positive changes.

The FFA method views all situations under review as in a state of equilibrium, emanating out of two sets of forces working in opposite directions. One set of forces works to bring about change, while the second set tries to maintain the status quo. It is not necessary, though it is entirely possible, that for each force thare is a corresponding opposing force. It is also possible that any situation may have forces in only one direction, in which event the situation will be dynamic and there would be no equilibrium (*Kumar,* 1999). If we view the current status of food security as in a state of at least temporary equilibrium, we can use the FFA, noting that any consumption about food security being in a state of equilibrium may be contested. Those forces which help in improving the food security situation may be called the "Positive Forces" and those which hinder the improvement in the food security situation, are called the "Negative Forces". The conceptual model is at Figure 8.1.

Figure 8.1
Force Field Analysis of Food Security

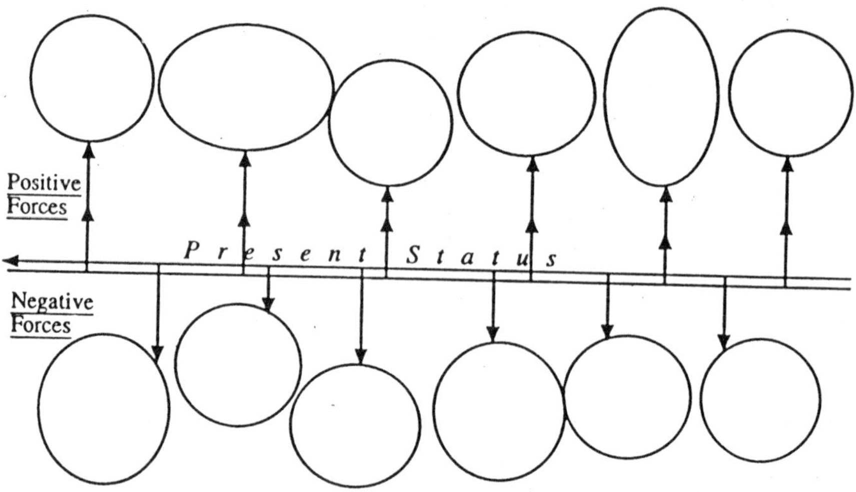

The distance of the circle or the ellipses from the bar at the centre of the diagram signifying the *present status* indicates the strength of the force. We have added a feature to the method in the sense that the diagram can be shown to identify those forces that are people friendly and those that are not or neutral. Thus, each of the forces can be put inside a "horizontal elliptical box" or in a "vertical elliptical box" depending on whether it is people friendly or people unfriendly respectively. Where the force is considered neutral to being people friendly or otherwise, it has been placed in a circle.

III. The Villages

We would examine the issues of Force Field analysis of food security in two clusters. First we will deal with two villages in Varanasi, Uttar Pradesh and then deal with Force Field analysis in Faridabad district in Haryana. Thus, it will give a contrasting view of Force Field analysis of food security in a backward State, still groaning under the sweaking wheels of the bullock cart, posited against Force Field analysis of food security in a developed State, in the heartland of Green Revolution. The villages chosen in Varanasi district are Tikri and Chandpur. The villages chosen in Faridabad are Uncha Gaon and Sagarpr. Let us begin by a brief description of the villages to put the discussion in perspective. [1].

Let us begin with the villages in Varanasi.

The first village is *Chandpur* in *Kashi Vidyapeeth* block in the district of *Varanasi.*

Socio-Economic Profile—Chandpur is a large sized village situated near Lahartara industrial estate. The village has a total population of 5682 with 255 households. 'Patel' is the dominant caste and the main occupations are agriculture and wage labour. The village has two junior high schools, a primary school, a bank, a post office, a Kisan Kendra, and a government agriculture farm.

Agriculture and Livelihood—In Chandpur livelihood comprises farming and livestock raising, services, wage labour including agricultural labour and non-farm activities such as saree printing, processing "Rudraksha" (a kind of "holy bead" made out of fruits of a tree), preparing "Birdi" etc. The villagers grow wheat, paddy, jowar, corn, etc. mainly for self-consumption. Some vegetables are also grown but are sold in the market. Around 30 per cent of total income is derived from agriculture.

Issues in Agriculture—Rise in incidence of pests and diseases in crops and vegetables in recent years, fall in crop yield with use of chemical fertilisers and 10 bighas of good agricultural land in the village being rendered barren due to flow of chemical water from industrial unit are the major issues. The running of brick kiln in the village has rendered some land uncultivable. The brick kilns have also affected horticulture and reduced yields of mango, jackfruit and guava. The fruits now suffer a high rate of termite attack. According to the villagers' estimate, at least 5 bighas of horticultural land have been converted into field for vegetable cultivation. Water bodies in the village have been adversely affected by pollutants and they do not grow 'singara' (a green coloured triangle-shaped fruit in water plant) any longer. These along with such other fruits were earlier grown and sold on a commercial basis.

Health Issues—Incidence of children falling sick has increased, the children tend to have prolonged cough. They also have problems with their eyes. There is now incidence of TB, which was not there earlier.

The second village is village *Tikri* also in *Kashi Vidyapeeth Block* in the district of *Varansi.*

Socio-Economic Profile—Village Tikri is 2.04 kilometres south-west of Banaras Hindu University (BHU). River Ganges is 2 kilometres east of the village, with a total population of 4,500 and total households numbering 450. It has a total number of 13 caste-based wards on a total area of 1500 acres. Nearly 40 per cent of population is literate in the village. The village has been recently declared as Ambedkar Gaon, since the scheduled caste population in the village is more than 50 per cent. The village has one senior secondary school, an agriculture cooperative society, one branch of the Union Bank of India and one health centre (which is non-operational). The village has no industries. Its neighbouring villages have several brick kilns.

Agriculture and Livelihood—In village Tikri, at least 70 per cent of population is engaged in agriculture and 50 per cent of agricultural land is irrigated. Selling milk is also one of the more important sources of livelihood. The total cultivable area is 800 acres. It has two types of soil-alluvial and *domat* and hence, the cropping pattern is also soil-specific. There are three types of cultivators in the village, the landowners doing their own cultivation, the sharecroppers and those renting land on an annual basis. In winter season, double cropping is generally practised with vegetables like potato in early winter for commercial production and wheat in late winter for self-consumption.

Issues in Agriculture—Some issues in agriculture for village Tikri are water shortage for cultivation, hailstorm, unseasonal rains, frost and fog, Nilgai (Blue Bull) and rat menace, plant diseases, pests and poor quality seeds. Smoke and heat from brick kilns of neighbouring village burn the mango flowers and affect mango yield. Dust from brick kilns falls on mangoes resulting in black spots and reduction in its size.

The third village for our study is *Sagarpur* in *Ballabgarh block* in the district of *Faridabad, Haryana.*

Socio-Economic Profile—The village is located approximately 7.5 kilometres south west of Faridabad Industrial Area and 5.4 kilometres south-west of Ballabgarh Industrial Area. It is an interior village with 6 wards. The village has a total area of 4500 bighas, total population of 3000 and 400 households. Jats have 170 households, Brahmins are in 50 households, backward castes have 80 households while Dalits have 100 households. The village has one Angadwadi, one middle school, one post office, one adult education centre, one Gram Sevak Samiti, one Nehru Yuva Kendra and one dairy.

Agriculture and Livelihood—The main source of livelihood in the village are agriculture and selling milk. The village has a total cultivable area of 800 acres. The soil is clay and sandy. Jowar, bajra, paddy, arhar, maize and dhencha are Kharif crops and Rabi crops are wheat, mustard and barsam. Some farmers have just started growing carrot, cauliflower and potato on a commercial basis.

Problems in Agriculture—Some agricultural problems for farmers are those related to short and irregular supply of electricity, pest attacks, high growth of weeds, crop damaged by Nilgais and irregular climatic conditions like hail storm etc.

Health Issues—All groups correlated health problems such as breathing problems and weakening of eye-sight to pollution from nearby factories such as gas plants and brick kilns. Apart from health, pollution from brick kiln had also affected wheat. To cope with pollution the village panchayat planted nearby 50,000 trees like Neem, Sesame, Pipal, etc. in the village.

The fourth area studied is *Uncha Gaon* which is in *Faridabad* Industrial Complex Area in the district of *Faridabad.*

Socio-Economic Profile—The village is located approximately 4.3 kilometres south-east of Faridabad Industrial Area and 1.3 kilometres south-east of Ballabgarh Industrial Area. It is a roadside colony. Uncha Gaon has a total population of 8000 with a total number of 800 households. Municipal colony of Uncha Gaon has one Government-run senior secondary school.

Agriculture and Livelihood—The main livelihood sources in the village are agriculture, livestock rearing and services. Uncha Gaon has a total cultivable area of 400 acres, in which vegetables are cultivated for commercial production. It has clay soil. Here, Kharif crops grown are jowar, bajra, maize and vegetables such as lady's finger, bottle gourd, chilli, pumpkin, cucumber, bitter gourd, *kakri* (a kind of longish cucumber) and melon. In Rabi, vegetables grown are brinjal, cauliflower, cabbage, radish, carrot, spinach, *methi* (fenugreek), coriander, *sarson ka sag* (mustard plants used as green leafy vegetables) along with wheat and mustard.

Problems in Agriculture—Some major problems in agriculture in Uncha Gaon are shortage of irrigation water, a problem which is increasing with water table falling, crops are becoming more prone to pest and weed attacks. Nilgais and stray cows graze or trample standing crops. Industrial pollution is damaging crops.

Black fumes from nearby thermocol factories get deposited on standing vegetables like cauliflower, tomato and spinach. Maximum impact of pollution is felt during the nights of October and November. Crop height and yield have been adversely affected for the last 4 to 5 years. Fumes waste the flowers of brinjal, tomato and chilly due to ashes falling on them.

There is an increase in health problems. Incidence of TB, asthma, heart attacks, cancer, cough and cold are common to the area.

IV. Force Field Analyses of Food Security

We will begin with Varanasi

Village Tikri

Reference is invited to Figure 8.2. The forces in the upper half of the figure are the forces that help the villagers in Tikri to maintain their food security.

The bank is considered an important factor though it is seen as the most unfriendly to the villagers. Thus, the justification for mass banking is demonstrated in some sense for real but the quality of assistance leaves much to be desired. That the pesticide and the seed shops are seen as favourable forces in maintaining the food security situation is not surprising. These shopkeepers not only supply to the villagers essential inputs for their agriculture but are also the only available source of guidance to the farmers on how, how much and when to use these inputs. The faux pass is a sad commentary on not only the state of sustainable agriculture but is indicative of the fact that food production in Tikri is moving toward high external non-free-goods input agriculture and at the same time there is a breakdown of extension service. The only free-goods that go into producing food is land and its fertility, and family labour. The somewhat horizontally elongated shape of the "boxes" also implies that the pesticide and the seed shopkeepers mean business: they are farmer friendly, they keep the farmers happy and have won their confidence, irrespective of the quality of the ware they sell.

Villagers maintain, as we have studied in Chapter 5, that 75 per cent of the cultivators in Tikri are tenants-at-will and are concealed tenants because by law in Uttar Pradesh, tenancy is banned and the systems of landlordism and absentee landlordism are fairly widespread. This is consistent with the fact that 30 per cent of the inhabitants of Tikri have migrated and lands belonging to the emigrants are cultivated either by the landless as pure tenants or by small and marginal farmers (who have 'spare capacity') as owner-tenants. And people belonging to upper castes, namely the Mauryas of Mauryan Basti, Bhumiyars of Tisra Patti, Bhumiyars of Sato Patti, Brahmins of Brahmin Patti and Chowdhurys of Chowdhurian Patti, lease out their land for cultivation to tenants of both varieties.

Thus, the tenant-landlord relationship is very critical for the livelihood of the villagers in Tikri and the landlords are perceived as a positive influence on food security for they elect to lease out their lands instead of leaving it fallow. There is a convergence of interest of both parties to the contract. The land-owners are either absentee-landlords or by custom (read caste!) they are unwilling to plough their land, and the landless and small and marginal farmers have either no land or own such a small parcel of land that they cannot sustain themselves without access to cultivating the big landowners' lands. As Kanhaiya Moira, father-in-law of the Pradhan, mentioned, the landlords also do not evict the tenants every year though several of the tenants are tenants-at-will. This provides stability to availability of food for the households of the landless and marginal farmers.

Figure 8.2
Force Field Analysis of Food Security in Tikri

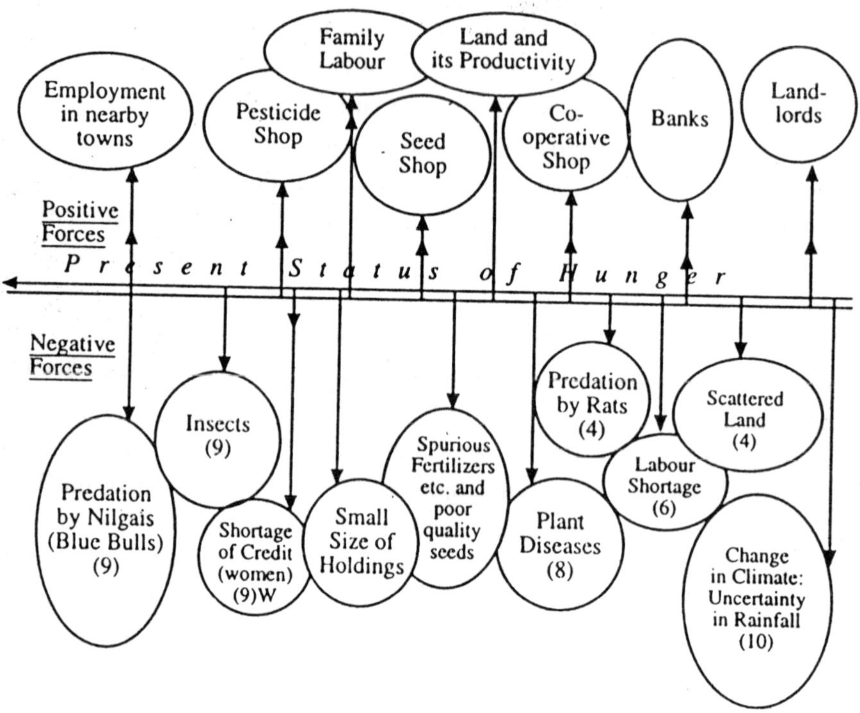

Those factors in our village life, viz., the pesticide dealer or the seed vendor or the landlord, who are viewed rather unsympathetically by *outsiders*, are viewed very differently by the villagers themselves. The landlord, the pesticide dealer and the seed vendor make important contributions to help the villagers have food security, howsoever fragile that may be. Not that the villagers are oblivious of the negative aspects that go with their services (this will be apparent from the discussion on the negative forces affecting food security in the village) and they are rated as the second best but that they are at least there, makes a difference. Employment is perceived as a positive force operating on food security in Tikri. Surprisingly, though the villagers are employed in a whole range of other income-earning activities (Rudraksha-garland making, daily wages earned, etc.), they only consider employment in the nearby towns as helping them in enjoying food security. By so saying, the villagers highlighted that they valued the continuity in employment and better wages that the neighbouring town offered.

Of the negative forces, the tyranny of both nature and human beings are viewed with alarm. The change in climate and the increased uncertainty of rain is rated, both by the men's and the women's groups, as the most intractable ones. While women thought shortage of credit was the next most important problem, men placed grazing of crops and fields by Nilgais, as their major problem after uncertainty of ranfall. The difference in perception stems from the fact that when the women talk of shortage of credit they talk about it in the generic sense. That is, shortage of credit for farming, for meeting social obligations, for meeting temporary shortfall in food availability assigned to women. When men highlight the problems created by Nilgais, they are highlighting their most arduous task of staying in the field during the chilly winter nights to keep the animals at bay.

Though the pesticide dealer plays a positive role in food security, the wares they sell land farmers in trouble. The spurious pesticides and fertilisers not only lead to lower productivity and loss of crops, but also inflate the cost of production, a phenomenon which is making farming less attractive for the small farmers. Most of the negative factors affecting food security in Tikri are nature driven. Only shortage of credit and spurious fertilisers and pesticides are man made. Interestingly since, all of agriculture in Tikri has not migrated to new technology, the impact of spurious pesticides and fertilisers in only partially felt.

Figure 8.3
Force Field Analysis of Food Security in Chandpur

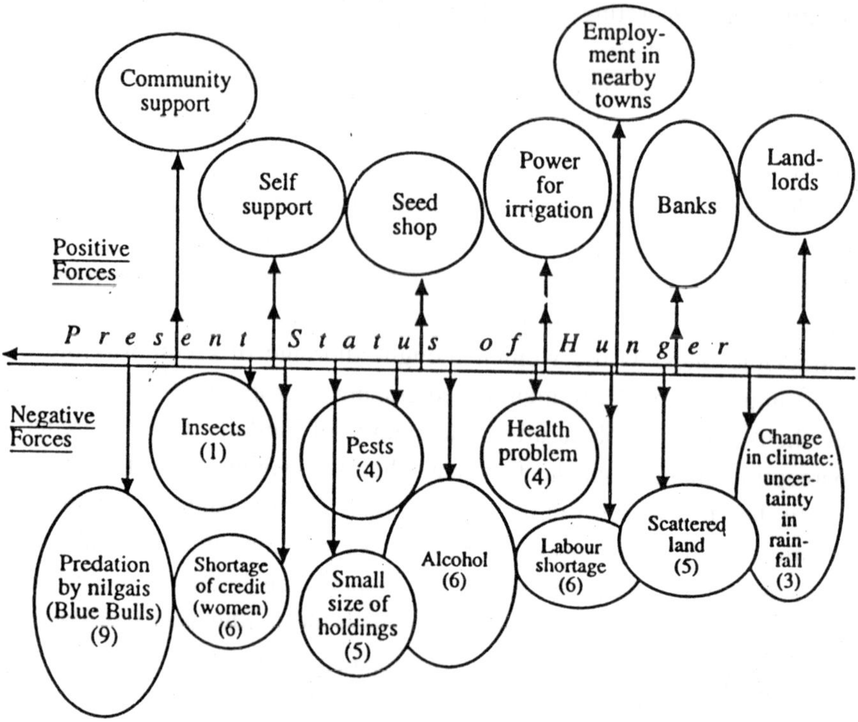

The perception in Tikri is that change in climate, the uncertainty in rainfall and predation by Nilgais are most unfriendly. These are factors, which are far beyond their control. Droughts, floods, untimely rain and mal-distribution of ranfall during the cultivation and harvesting season, all act against their food security. They explained that if it were only a question of shortage of water for irrigating fields, perhaps pump sets would have been the answer. That unfortunately is not the case. "Uncertainty of rainfall" takes many forms, of which shortage of water in some years is only one. The problem of attack by Nilgais is the other problem about which the villagers can do little for reasons we have discussed in Chapter 5 earlier on Tikri. The villagers perceive that pests and insects take their toll of food production and negatively impact food security. The negative factors, which the villagers perceive as being within their control, are scattered land and labour shortage.

On the whole most of the factors that villagers in Tikri consider relevant for food security are related to food production, except employment in the nearby towns which is related to access of food. The issue of distribution of food did not figure. Most of the forces which exert positive influence on food security in Tikri are friendly to the villagers, except the banks, but most of the factors that exert negative influence are generally issues about which the community could do very little.

Village Chandpur

The Force Field Analysis for Chandpur depicts a pattern similar to Tikri. Reference is invited to Figure 8.3. This is natural in one sense because both the villages fall within the same agro-climatic zone, have similar ecological base and have same bio-diversity. There are three banks in the village, viz., State Bank of India, Union Bank of India and The Banaras State Bank. There is concealed tenancy, as tenancy is banned by Law. The role of banks, landlords, seed shops and availability of employment have positive influence in Chandpur, as in Tikri. However, banks are considered as the most unfriendly amongst the forces that help food security. This is less comforting for the protagonists of mass banking.

There are some differences, which are important to recognise. The number of positive forces operaing on food security in Chandpur is more than in Tikri. Availability of employment and self-help and community support are the two major positive forces. An estimated 35 per cent of the village income ("Village Domestic Product" as it were) comes from either wage labour or regular employment. Employment in the terminology of the villagers includes income employment of printing sarees, making beads of Rudraksha, making birdis and working in the industrial estates where about 100 industrial units are established. The importance of self-help and community support, figure prominently in Chandpur because the community is better organised, given that there are more literate people in Chanpur than in Tikri and Chandpur is situated (unlike Tikri) right on the Grant Trunk Road, having greater interface with better organised people in cities, notably Varanasi. Since agriculture in Chandpur is more mechanised than Tikri, power for irrigation exerts positive force on food security. The existence of CPRs, which was not the case in Tikri, has helped people in improving their food security situation. This has been for two reasons. One, it provided supplementary food that helped people to cope with hunger. Secondly, the villagers view CPRs as a source of fuel and fodder, even if partial, that not only spares them of the burden of walking long distances to collect these but also saves money that they would otherwise have spent to buy fuel.

The negative forces having bearing on food security in Chandpur have a striking similarity to those working in Tikri. There is a slight change in some of the priority and social issues that are additionally noticeable. The impact of uncertainty of rainfall and climatic change has receded back in case of these villagers, because irrigation by energised-pump sets help them tide over some of the difficulties mentioned in this regard by villagers in Tikri. Like in Tikri, pests and insects take their toll of food production and negatively impact food security.

The two additional social problems in Chandpur, that exert negative impact on food security are unrelated to food production, are alcoholism and problem of health. Alcoholism among men not only lead to spousal battery but it also eats into the meagre resources of the poor households to buy food. The households spend 25 per cent of the income of Alcohol, which is equal to what they spend on food. Since food is consumed by all members of the household and alcohol is consumed by the male adults only, alcoholism has an adverse impact on the intra-household allocation of resources for accessing food. The problem of health negatively impacts on health from three different directions, despite the existence of the Government Hospital in Shibdaspur (only 1 km away) and health club in Mahuadih, which is 2 kms away. Firstly, the cost of treatment obviously makes a big dent on the household's budget for food. Secondly, the person days lost due to illness, cuts out the total income of the family and that again reduces the households' food budget and economic accessibility. There, when health problems afflicts children, it not only incapacitates the mother who looks after the sick children but also increases cost of the sick person's diet, leaving even less for the non-sick in the poor households to etch out a living. We are not going into the question of loss in food absorption due to illness, which reduces the nourishment level of people whose state of nourisment is at best of times only fragile.

Thus, if we look at the Force Field Analysis for food security in Tikri and Chandpur, it is apparent that most of the factors are related to natural forces affecting food production, that is those having bearing on food availability. There aren't many forces, which relate to economic or physical access to food, barring access to employment in both the villages and physical access to limited amount of food available from CPRs in Chandpur. This has serious implications for government programmes. The PDS has fallen off the food map of the people and the employment opportunities created under the Employment Assurance Scheme (EAS) etc. of the government apparently do not contribute much towards creating income for food consumption. They are not in the mental map of the people at all. Because much of poverty decline observed during the late eighties was on account of employment provided to the poor by employment generation programmes of the government, one suspects that reduction in poverty would abate with these programmes being on the wane.

Force Field Analysis of Food Security in Uncha Gaon

Now we shift our scene of review (Figure 8.4) to Faridabad, Haryana. Uncha Gaon is a municipal town in Ballabgarh block, in which most of the farmers are into cultivating their land for growing vegetables. It is located on a high way and is accessible to Ballabgarh's industrial township market. For the farmers of Uncha Gaon, the most important positive force impacting on food security is appropriate technology that they have of farming vegetables. Availability of power, irrigation facilities and suitability of land are important positive forces in favour of food security. These are all factors that do not directly help in the production of food. These factors help the farmers to produce vegetables, which they sell for money, with which they access food. Thus this is conceived at one level of forces. At the other level, availability of market in Ballabgarh helps them to sell their vegetable production at a better price than they would have otherwise succeeded. Employment opportunities in Ballabgarh industrial estate, help people, and the market for milk also at Ballabgarh industrial estate, help people have command over income with which to supplement their income from sale of vegetables and buy food with, amongst other items of consumption. It is now widely accepted that the per capita expenditure on milk and milk products is higher in Haryana, consideration, the roles of the seed vendor and the pesticide dealer are not seen as being of any consequence, either way.

Of the forces that exert negative impulses, hot westerly wind that hit their fields is considered the single most important negative factor. Termites, followed by weeds and high input costs, are the other important negative forces. As it is, vegetable cultivation is a high cost activity, and since agriculture in Uncha Gaon has moved from Low External Input Agriculture (LEIA) to High External Input Agriculture (HEIA), rising cost of inputs and cost of farming going up, exerts a negative impact on food security. Rising input cost has long term significance in this regard, including working out a system of fair returns to retain interest in agriculture, for those who rough it out there in the fields. Since Uncha Gaon is in the Green Revolution heart belts, the impact of rains is minimised through irrigation and quick growing variety seeds. The presence of weeds amongst the negative forces is a result of the use of what the farmers call "medicines" in the fields: weeds have multiplied in number as use of pesticides and fertilisers has increased.

On the whole, the forces that influence food security in Uncha Gaon have mixture of both factors that have a bearing on production of agricultural crops and on the capability of the people to access food. Of the positive forces, selling milk, employment opportunities in Ballabgarh, availability of markets for vegetables and milk, and the technology for growing vegetables that people use are considered as more villager-friendly. The power position is not perceived as villager-friendly. Of the negative forces, the hot westerly wind, weeds and uncertainty of rainfall are the ones over which the people have the least control. Smoke and falling vegetable prices are issues on which the villagers perceive they have some influence.

The Case of Sagarpur

Sagarpur is the second village in Faridabad we have examined through the Force Field analysis. Reference is invited to Figure 8.5.

The positive and negative forces that have a bearing on food security in Sagarpur has a striking resemblance to those in Uncha Gaon, just as there are similarities in the forces that affect food security in the two villages of Varanasi, Tikri and Chandpur. For instance, like in Uncha Gaon, employment is a major positive force in Sagarpur, where 43 per cent of the like in states of Punjab, Western Uttar Pradesh and parts of Andhra Pradesh and even Rajasthan than per capita expenditure on cereals. Thus in Uncha Gaon, the sale of milk has become over the years an important source of income. The forces that exert positive impact on food security, therefore, have to do with providing the villagers with the wherewithal to buy food. They have little to do with food production *per se,* except at the margin, because the farmers under study are not, in general, primary food growers.

Figure 8.4
Force Field Analysis of Food Security in Uncha Gaon

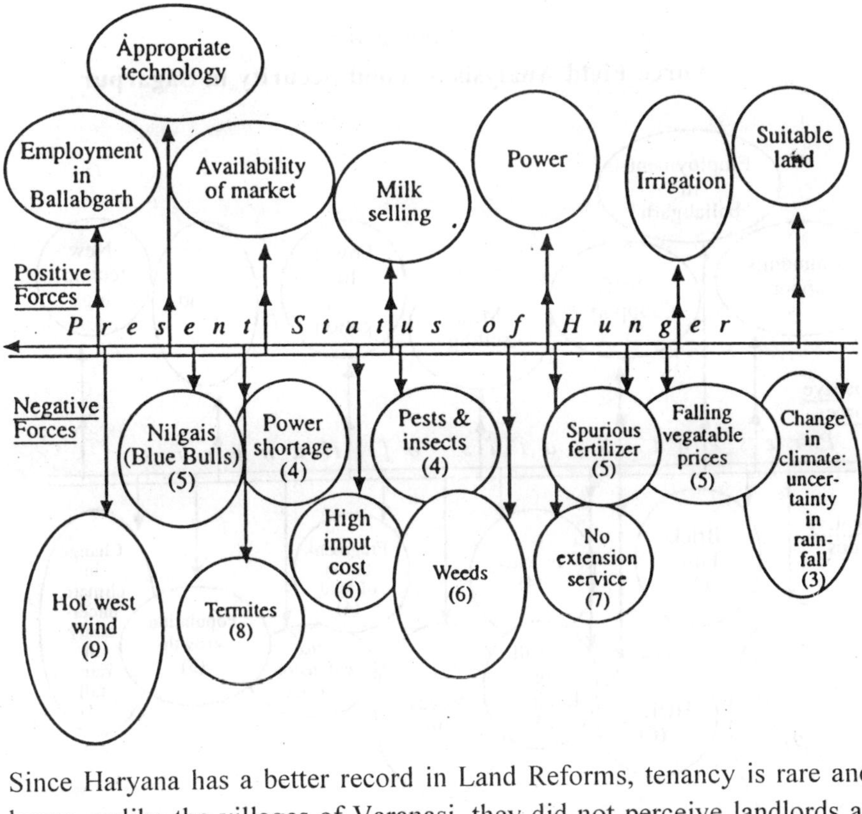

Since Haryana has a better record in Land Reforms, tenancy is rare and hence, unlike the villages of Varanasi, they did not perceive landlords as playing any positive role in the food security picture of Uncha Gaon. Because the literacy level is higher in the State, district and the village under people work in industry and government offices in Ballabgarh. In case of Sagarpur, the only major difference is that whereas in Uncha Gaon availability of market was a major factor contributing to food security, in Sagarpur it is not. This is very plausible because the villagers of Sagarpur do not meet most of their food requirements through purchase, by selling their output. They are mostly subsistence farmers and they access items of consumption, which they do not produce either by sale of milk and partial sale of their farm produce, or by the wages they earn in Ballabgarh and Faridabad. Hence, availability of market is not perceived as a critical, variable in maintaining food security. Instead, unlike in Uncha Gaon, self-support (meaning community support) is a very important positive force.

Figure 8.5
Force Field Analysis of Food Security in Sagarpur

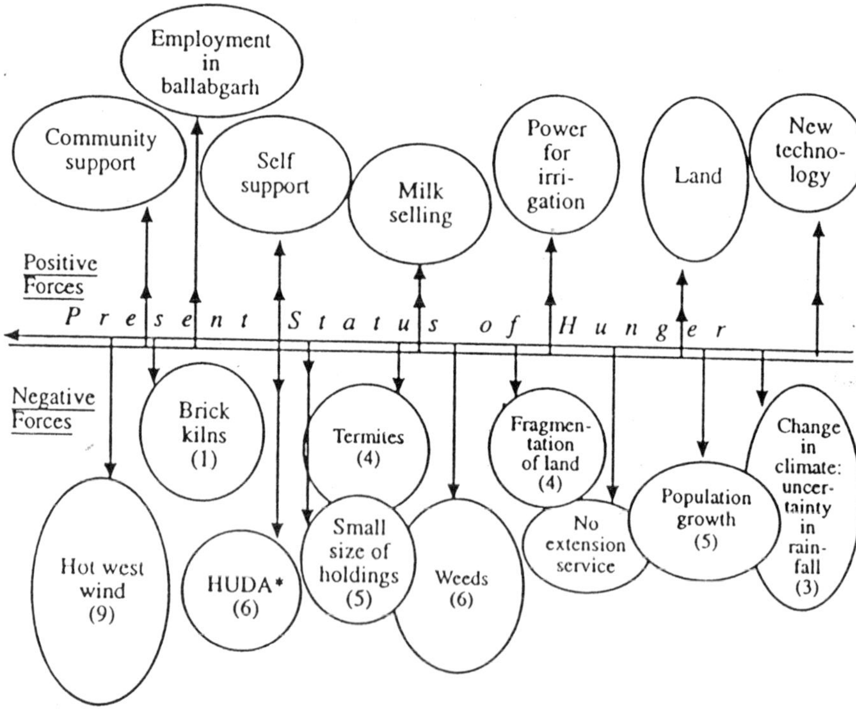

* *HUDA = Haryana Urban Development Authority*

Among the negative forces, the impact of hot westery wind, termites and weeds (mostly *Sati, Jai, Safed Mondi,* etc.) are acutely felt. This is on account of uneven distribution of rainfall because termites flourish in dry winter and in dry soil, receiving lower than normal rainfall. [*Indian Express,* 24th September, 1999]. Because these farmers grow food crops, which are better cultivated on relatively large pieces of land, fragmentation of land and small size of holdings are perceived as problem areas. The threat meted out by Haryana Urban Development Authority (HUDA) to acquire land for expanding the industrial township of Ballabgarh and the absence of extension services are felt as inimical to food security in Sagarpur. Because fragmentation and small size of holdings are seen to militate against food security, population growth (the average size of family is over 7 and it is even bigger amongst the Harijans and the backward castes), which has the potential of further sub-dividing the land that farmers put to cultivation, is seen as a negative factor. This is particularly important for a village in which 75 per cent of households have only 1 to 1.5 acres of land. Villagers are also aware that more mouths to feed means smaller size of meals, given that further dramatic increase in yield is not expected within their "expectational" horizon and actual yields have started falling from 16 quintals per acre in the 1980s to 14 quintals per acres in the 1990s.

Like smoke in Uncha Gaon, which causes deterioration in the quality of vegetables grown, brick kilns, which emit smoke and ash, reduce crop yields in Sagarpur. Thus, while air pollution in Uncha Gaon adversely impacts on food security by reducing the value of vegetables sold to buy food, in Sagarpur, air pollution directly reduces food availability.

Thus in Sagarpur and in Uncha Gaon, the variables considered critical to food security mostly relate to crop production, whether food crops or cash crops. The role of the PDS and of Government programmes for creating employment opportunities for increasing access to food are not in the picture. The supportive role of off-farm livelihood, like milk rending, in sustaining food security in Faridabad is worth noting. The absence of extension service in the villages of Faridabad as in Varanasi has negative impact on the overall food security situation in Faridabad villages.

V. Summary and Conclusions

Looking at the Force Fields Analyses of the four villages there are a few implications that are clear. The number of negative forces operating on food security situation in the villages under reference exceed the number of the positive forces and that too by a wide margin. That is why, one noted commentator remarked that if food production was seen as a chain of activities, then the Indian farmers were at the riskiest end of the chain. The negative forces affecting food security are unleashed by both men and nature, where natural forces are dominant. The villagers take little cognizance of the role of the state programmes in ensuring food security in their villages. Neither the PDS for supply of food nor the employment generation programmes to increase the accessibility of food find any mention in the food security mapping. Though we have not investigated the matter further, it seems that they are either non-existent or are only of consequence at the margin.

Though in both the districts, agriculture is the mainstay of the villagers, hunger persists and the response that the farmers can have is limited, given the structural and institutional problems, which bind the food security picture. In some cases, the villagers produce food for others but are themselves hungry. Irrespective of whether people are food-crop growers or cash crop growers, they all suffer from some food insecurity and hunger. Only the intensity varies. Irrespective of whether the green touch of green revolution, since turned yellow, have visited the village or not, hunger persists.

The nature of the negative and positive forces acting on food security in the villages of Varanasi and Faridabad also varies because the major crop in Faridabad villages studied are vegetables and wheat, whereas the major crops grown by the villages in Varanasi are rice, wheat and some vegetables. And then the major cropping season in Varanasi is Kharif whereas the major cropping season in Faridabad is Rabi.

Of the positive forces that have helped the villagers in all the villages, notably in Faridabad and Chandpur, to retain their food security, employment in the nearby industrial estates and township and sale of milk have played important roles. With the agreement, which came into force on December, 28th 1999, between Government of India and Susan Esserman that quantitative restrictions (QRs) on imports from 1429 items will be lifted, these sources of food security will be greatly reduced. The 1429 items on which QRs have been lifted include basic agricultural produce like wheat, rice, maize and all other cereals and dairy products. Fresh vegetables like cauliflower and cucumber and common fruits figure in the list. So do coconut, coconut oil and other edible oils, fruit squashes, pickles and chutnies. QRs from a wide range of finished products like footwear, fans, knives, inverters, sanitarywares, toilet papers, tooth brushes, pens, combs, ink, jute products and woven fabrics will have to go. From April 2000, QRs on 715 items and from 1.4.2001, QRs from the other 714 items will go. That will mean two things. The small and medium enterprises (SMEs) in the Industrial Estate near Tikri and Chandpur will get a beating. All the items which were produced by the SMEs have been freed from quantitative restrictions. This will mean a large number of people from Tikri, Chandpur, Sagarpur and Uncha Gaon, who get employment in the Industrial Areas of Varanasi and Faridabad, will be rendered unemployed.

Secondly, the removal of restrictions from imports of milk, cheese, butter, ghee, condensed milk, dried egg yolk and malted milk, amongst the hundreds of others, will mean that the sale of milk in Faridabad will nose dive. There is no way that the milk produced by the women of Uncha Gaon and Sagarpur, can compete with imported milk, which is heavily subsidised. Much of the demand for milk and milk products like ghee and cottage cheese will also go down. No less a person than Verghese Kurien lamented: "If a competitor has access to his government's exchequer and drives down our farmer's milk prices, in time we will have farmers reducing their investment in producing milk. If it continues, farmers will sell their milch cows and exit dairying. Our milk prices will rise and foreign milk will start coming at a much higher cost to our ... customers" (*Pillai,* 2000a). Thus, the supplementary income to support food security will be lost in the not too distant future.

This will have particularly damaging impact on the women and children. The employment that milk and milk products provide to the women will suffer. The process of empowering women will have a set-back.

With the abolition of the quantitative restrictions, import of agricultural products will rise dramatically. Free import of agricultural products, including rice, parboiled rice, broken rice, basmati rice, wheat, ragi, maize flour, rice flour, etc. (*Pillai,* 2000) will mean that our peasant agriculture will have to compete with foreign highly subsidised large farmers. According to WTO figures, the annual agricultural subsidies in OECD countries is a whopping $ 362 billion, while our farm subsidy bill which has been further reduced in the Budget 2000-2001, is a meager Rs. 4500 crores. Little wonder, the distinguished scientist-scholar M.S. Swaminathan noted with concern: "Import of raw foodgrain, pulses, fish and milk will badly hit farmers, fishermen....Food security is linked to national sovereignty" (*Pillai,* 2000a). Indian agriculture of peasant farmers will gradually die. With it there will be two critical phenomena: one, employment will fall because importing food into India is importing unemployment. And two, there will be a further onslaught upon dairying and animal keeping since there will be a reduction in availability of fodder. We are already a fodder-deficient economy and any further reduction in fodder availability does not augur well for us. And sadly enough, we do not have recourse to imposing high tarriff barriers because India has filed schedules to the WTO where the commitment is that the bound rate of duty has been fixed at a level for rice, including broken rice which provides little leeway. Milk, maize, jowar and bajra are also included in the category.

Villages like Uncha Gaon which survive on sale of vegetables and villages like Chandpur which partially survive from income from sale of vegetables will be doubly hit. They will not only not have the same market in Ballabgarh, if the SMEs close down as we discussed above but they will have to scout around for fresh pastures. Not a easy proposition. Secondly, with quantitative restrictions out from vegetables including on imports of ginger, edible roots and tubers (including Onion), cabbage, cucumber, sweet potato, cauliflower, etc., these small farmers will be called upon to compete with global players in selling their home grown vegetables. Even the most optimistic "free-trade-walla" will find it difficult to say that these formers will be happy and going.

Endnote

1. Description of villages obtained from Neela Mukherjee, *Alternative Perspectives on Livelihoods, Agricultue and Air Pollurion* (Aldershot: Ashgate, 2001).

9 A Note on Food Security in Villages of a Perpetually Hunger Stricken District, Bolangir

I. Introduction

The State of Orissa has a glorious history of religion, culture, art and statesmanship. It has been in the news near perpetually, of late, for all the wrong reasons: bad governance, droughts, super cyclones, backwardness and extremist movements. Some 60 per cent of its 31 million people live below the poverty line. 96 children die per 1000 live births (which is highest infant mortality rate for any state in India) and it has one medical doctor per 64000 people, which is the lowest number of doctors per capita among the states in India. Only 5 per cent of its population have access to Public Distribution System (PDS) and just 19 per cent of Orissa's rural households have electricity.

One of the reasons, which keep the state in the news at regular intervals, is the hunger that stalks the districts of Koraput, Bolangir and Kalahandi. These three districts have been separately identified as the KBK districts for special attention by the state in its development efforts. Thousands, nevertheless, migrate out of the districts every year in search of livelihood. In some of these cases migration is a coping mechanism adopted by the poor people to avoid hunger and privation. In this chapter, we would see how the picture of hunger looks like from the perspective of the poor people from the villages of one of the districts, Bolangir.

Bolangir is situated in western Orissa. It presents a mixture of curious paradoxes and peculiarities. The district normally registers a rainfall in excess of the state average, where average land holding size exceeds that of the whole state, and where per capita food grains production and availability exceeds the state figures, also happens to be the epicenter of poverty and disaster.

Historical Account

Bolangir was formed after independence, in 1948, by amalgamating the erstwhile states of Patna and Sonepur. Patna was under the Chauhans since 14th century AD. Sonepur, was carved out of Patna, as a separate state in the 17th century AD. The two states were under the occupation of the Marathas since 1755 till the beginning of the 19th century, when they came under the British rule. Under the Government of India Act, 1935, the two states were brought under the direct control of the Governor General of India, through a political agent based at Sambalpur. For administrative convenience, the district was divided into four sub-divisions, five Tehsils and seventeen police stations.

Physical Features

Bolangir lies on the western side of the state, having borders with the districts of Sonepur in the east, Nawapara in the west, Kalahandi in the south and Bargarh in the north. It also skirts the western tail of Boudh on its southeastern end. The district has an area of over 6569 sq. km with 14 blocks and more than 1700 revenue villages and many more settlements or habitations.

Bolangir falls under the dry and hot central tableland and has a low rain-factor of 50.8. The district comprises mainly of rolling uplands with height varying between 153 to 305 meters. The predominant soil-type is moderately acidic red, though patches of black soil are also found. Due to its unfavourable location, the groundwater potential of Bolangir is low and the yield prospects are less than 5 cubic meter per hour.

Though Bolangir is the ninth largest district, it is endowed with a little less than 3 per cent of Orissa's total forest cover, despite the district occupying 4.2 per cent of the total geographical area of the state. In absolute terms, the forest cover of Bolangir (inclusive of reserved, demarcated-protected, undemarcated-protected and unclassified forest areas) is 1647.49 square km, which is 25 per cent of its geographical area and is, therefore, less than the acceptable 33 per cent forest cover. This is a little distressing because many districts in Orissa have more than one third of their total geographical land under forest cover.

The forests in the district are of tropical dry variety and the main species include Sal, Kendu, Karada, Kurum, Teak and Bamboo. In addition to timber, Bolangir is one of the largest contributors to the total revenue pool of the state drawn from non-timber forest produce, amongst all districts in Orissa.

Table 9.1 is an overview of undivided Bolangir's relative position vis-à-vis other districts in Orissa:

Table 9.1 Bolangir in comparison to other districts

District	Rain factor	Percentage of highlands	Groundwater recharge potential
Baleshwar	60.8	15.97	247553 ha.mtrs.
Bolangir	50.8	40.51	187873 ha.mtrs.
Cuttack	55.2	25.91	465823 ha.mtrs.
Dhenkanal	54.8	51.39	175836 ha.mtrs.
Ganjam	48.1	29.41	255753 ha.mtrs.
Kalahandi	53.0	54.56	203590 ha.mtrs.
Keonjhar	63.3	45.60	137126 ha.mtrs.
Koraput	65.9	57.87	444836 ha.mtrs.
Mayurbhanj	60.8	45.12	215579 ha.mtrs.
Phulbani	64.3	64.44	129100 ha.mtrs.
Puri	53.4	18.51	292500 ha.mtrs.
Sambalpur	57.6	42.52	382947 ha.mtrs.
Sundergarh	60.4	51.91	154204 ha.mtrs.

Social and Demographic Features

The percentage of Scheduled Castes (SCs) and Scheduled Tribes (STs) in the total population of Bolangir are of the order of 15.39 and 22.06 per cent respectively. Of the tribal population, Gonds constitute the largest chunk (33.74 per cent), followed by Kandhas, Saoras, Binjhals, Lodhas, Dals, Mundas and Mirdhas. The groups prominent amongst the Scheduled Castes are the Gandas, constituting 85.1 per cent of total scheduled caste population in the district. The other SCs are Dhobis, Ghasias, Doms, Mehras, Barikis and Chamars, in addition to people belonging to the other backward castes, such as Agarias, Banias, Bairagis, Kalharas, Malis, Telis, Pudias, etc.

The higher castes in the district include the Brahamans, Karans, Khandayats, Chasas, Kultas, etc. Over 24 different languages (including many tribal languages) are spoken in Bolangir.

Hindus constitute 98.5 per cent of the total population, followed by Christians (0.925 per cent) and Muslims (0.386 per cent).

Economic Status

There are various estimates of the number of people living below the poverty line in Bolangir. According to Drought Mitigation Cell of Zila Swechchasevi Sangh, a local NGO, nearly 92 per cent of all the rural families in Bolangir live lives of penury, being below the poverty line. The last round of NSSO data reveal another picture. Of this chunk, almost 42 per cent are marginal farmers, 23 per cent are small farmers and 25 per cent are agricultural labourers.

While 4.75 per cent and 27.37 per cent of Orissa's population are classified as marginal workers and non-workers respectively, the corresponding figures for Bolangir are at significantly higher levels of 6.17 per cent and 59.25 per cent respectively.

In comparison to population pressure on land in Orissa generally, the average population pressure on cultivable land in Bolangir is less, due mainly to the low population density of the district, of only 183 persons per square km, which is well below the state density of 203 persons per square km. But the land distribution pattern in the district is highly skewed in favour of large farmers and the majority of the farmers only have a marginal share in the total land holdings and a small number of large and medium farmers occupy an abnormally high share of total cultivated land.

The average land holding in the district is 1.69 hectare, while that of Orissa is only 1.34 hectare. This is mainly due to the low population density of the district as we have mentioned above. In fact, in Bolangir the percentage numbers of marginal and small land holdings (44.54 per cent and

21.16 per cent respectively) are less than the corresponding figures for the state, which are 53.66 per cent and 26.22 per cent respectively. Similarly, the figures relating to percentage areas covered by marginal and small land holdings are 13.76 and 17.23 respectively for Bolangir, vis-a-vis 19.73 and 26.93 respectively for Orissa as a whole.

Livestock

The total cattle population in Bolangir was 3,21,707 in 1995-96, while the total number of sheep and goats was 4,31,392. Given that the poor people mostly own sheep and goats and that cattle are owned largely by the non-poor, the high concentration of poverty in Bolangir is empirically confirmed. Judged against the context of Orissa, where the total cattle population is almost double the total number of sheep and goats (14,765,996 and 7,276,831 respectively), the abysmal state of Bolangir's position is brought out in sharp focus.

Infrastructure and Industries

The road density of Bolangir per 100 sq. km is 80. 87 km, which is far below the average road density of Orissa, viz., 92 km. The total cultivated area in Bolangir potentially covered under irrigation projects of varying magnitude amounts to the order of 8.075 per cent in Kharif, and 2.355 per cent in Rabi, while the corresponding figures for Orissa are 32.7 per cent and 13.31 per cent respectively.

While there is one post office per 3928 people in Orissa, in Bolangir there is one Post Office per 4397 people. The concentration of commercial banks in Bolangir is low in as much as only 3.35 per cent of the total number of commercial banks in Orissa are situated in Bolangir.

Rich deposits of quartz and graphite are found in Bolangir, and the district's contributions to total production of these two minerals work out to be 10.4 per cent and 65.3 per cent respectively. However, Bolangir's contribution to Orissa's total production of minerals of all kinds is negligible, being only 0.138 per cent, which, in value terms, amounts to a paltry 0.16 per cent of state's total value of mineral produced.

Literacy Status

Only 38.6 per cent of people in Bolangir are literate, while the literacy percentage of Orissa is in excess of 49 and the national average is 60 per cent. The female literacy percentage of 21.3 per cent falls far short of the state mark of 35 per cent and the national figure of 40 per cent. Out of the thirty districts in Orissa, Bolangir ranks 21st on the literacy front. This is symptomatic of a situation, where though Bolangir accounts for 8.7 per cent of the state population, it accounts for 4.76 per cent of the total number of primary schools in the state. And its share in the total number of middle and secondary schools in the state were 3.38 and 2.99 per cent only respectively. Of all the enrolments at the primary stage in Bolangir, 15.89 per cent are drawn from the scheduled castes and 23.84 per cent from the scheduled tribes

Health Status

Bolangir is one of the highly disease-prone districts of the state. Calorific and nutritional food items like animal protein, poultry and dairy products are available to a smaller percentage of people in Bolangir as compared to the percentage of people who have access to these foods in Orissa as a whole. It has the dubious distinction of having, amongst all the districts in Orissa, the third largest prevalence rate of leprosy, which is as high as 4.47 per thousand population–almost two and a half times the prevalence rate for Orissa. Additionally, the district is also prone to diseases like malaria, tuberculosis and several other communicable diseases.

Of the total number of primary health centres in Orissa, 3.4 per cent are located in Bolangir, as against Bolangir's population in the total population of Orissa being 3.7 per cent. Only 3.25 per cent of total number of beds available in different kinds of medical institutions in Orissa are located in district.

However, the infant mortality rate (IMR) is lower in Bolangir as compared to the IMR for the state. There were 60.935 registered infant deaths per thousand registered births in Orissa for the year 1992, the corresponding figure for undivided Bolangir being 54.617. And though the corresponding death rate was 57. 81 per thousand registered births of female infants for Orissa, in Bolangir this figure was 52.319. The lower IMR and lower death rates in Bolangir vis-à-vis Orissa can be on account of the high rate of migration out of Bolangir every year. This migration has in its turn left many people in Bolangir suffering from several sexually transmitted diseases, the most widespread being Syphilis and Gonorrhea. Malnutrition is a dominant problem of the district, and apart from Protein Energy Malnutrition (PEM), Vitamin A deficiency and Anemia are widely prevalent. Majority of the pregnant women are anemic and suffer from iron and folic acid deficiency. Incidences of genetic diseases like Sickle-cell trait, HBSS and G-6-PD deficiency are found to be extremely high in Bolangir.

The Drought Factor

What makes Bolangir a nightmare for the surviving poor is the vulnerability of the district to the worst forms of disasters born out of droughts. As per the district Gazetteer, the district has a history of drought since the last one hundred years. There are records on occurrences of severe droughts during 1934-35, 1935-36 and in 1938-39 in the ex-Patna state and even after independence, Bolangir has witnessed worst forms of drought in 1954-55 and 1965.

The district suffers a five-year drought cycle, and the cost of living through one season of drought easily spills over throughout the whole cycle, making it virtually impossible for the poor to stage any form of recovery. Poverty is perpetuated through natural disaster in the form of droughts. The costs of such disasters to the poor include, but not restricted to, crop loss of an extreme kind, inevitable burden of debts, starvation deaths and consequent loss of earning members of the households (in many cases the only one), land-alienation, distress-sale of assets and irreparable damage to the forest and other common property resources.

It is interesting to note that despite the normal annual rainfall of Bolangir exceeding the state average, it still suffers from drought because of the erratic pattern of rainfall in the district. While there was 1795 mm of rainfall in 1994, it dwindled to 1548 mm in 1995 and to 608 mm in 1996.

Indeed, the rainfall in 1996 was 57.88 per cent less than the normal rainfall and 50.58 per cent less than the average rainfall of the last ten years. Unequal distribution of rainfall and short-duration intensive downpour are common phenomena in Bolangir.

A strong correlation between drought and poverty has been long established and disasters being endemic in nature in Bolangir inflict a never-ending cycle of poverty on a large segment of the population.

Table 9.2 provides a consolidated picture of the relative position of Bolangir with respect to the overall scenario in Orissa on some selected parameters having bearings on the district's poverty profile.

Table 9.2 Comparative Picture of Bolangir and Orissa

Parameters	Bolangir	Orissa
Population density per sq. km	199	203
Total literacy rate (1991)	38.6	49
Female literacy rate (1991)	21.3	35
Percentage of marginal workers (1991)	6.17	4.75
Percentage of non workers (1991)	59.25	27.37
Per capita milk available per day	44g	50g
Per capita eggs available per year	14	17
Per cent cultivated area under irrigation (Kharif, 95-96)	8.075	32.7
Per cent cultivated area under irrigation (Rabi, 95-96)	2.355	13.31
No. of people served by one PHC (1993-94)	39841	34843
Prevalence rate of leprosy per 1000 people	4.47	1.85
Road density per 100 sq. km (1981)	80.87 km	92 km
Composite economic development index (1981)	0.95254	0.99691

Bolangir produces the highest amount of rice in Orissa, yet thousands of people suffer from hunger and an equal number migrate to other parts of the state in search of food and work every year. Three villages of Bolangir, from which Food Calendar, Seasonality Diagram and Seasonality Matrix in respect of food that are available, have been examined. Details on the three villages and the Food Calendar, Seasonality Diagram and Seasonality Matrix have been obtained from PRAXIS, 1998. The villages are Jogimara, Ganta Bahali and Chikili.

II. The General Perceptions

The general perception is that poverty is closely related to short falls in household food consumption. And that food availability, accessibility and consumption are important aspects of food security at the household level in the rural areas of the district. With subsistence resource base and limited employment opportunities, families in rural areas face severe food insecurity, especially during lean employment periods. Natural calamities compound the situation to worse. For instance, the super cyclone that hit Ersama, Kendrapara, Jagatsinghpur, Paradip and other coastal areas of the state of Orissa in 1999 had left 7656 people dead, 1.73 lakh people taken ill, 9.25 lakh houses damaged and 2.97 livestock destroyed. Total crop area damaged is estimated to be over 12.52 lakh hectares. The loss of crops, ill health and loss of assets make serious inroads into the fragile food security situation of the affected people.

Box 9.1

Food in a Hunger Stricken Area

Far away, in the Mahakalpara coastal town of Kendrapara district, 72 sacks of rice are ferried to the local jetty, counted twice over by the police, army and district administration officials. They are then loaded into a ferrying country boat for a one hour long journey downstream to Khatansi, a marooned village of refugee fishermen near the mouth of the river. As the boat docks at the devastated fishing hamlet and hungry villagers welcome a third consignment of rice in a fortnight, one sack is missing. Says villager Gouranga Saha: "*Every adult here is entitled to 500 grams of rice but we often end up getting 100 gm less*".

Soutik Biswas and Swapan Nayak: "Tales of the Living Dead", *Outlook,* 22 November 1999

In the villages studied, the concept of a prosperous household is that the household has food round the year (*PRAXIS,* 1998). That is, the household is self sufficient in food throughout the year. However, in the villages studied, most of the households do not fall under this category. Landless households, households with small farms and households having marginal farms, all face hunger and food insecurity during some parts of the year or the other. They eke out a bare subsistence living. These households are on the threshold of poverty.

Poor households in these villages not only suffer from the pangs of poverty and hunger, they are also subjected to the fury of nature. Drought is a recurrent feature in these villages. Generally, their production levels are low and when they are hit by drought, the food available with these households leave nothing for consumption. This means that for these households the systemic availability of food is very low. Lack of employment opportunities make their food security even more fragile, because in the absence of gainful employment, these households are seriously handicapped in their economic access to food.

III. The Village: Chikili

Let us look at Food Calendar of Chikili first. Reference is invited to Figure 9.1. In this discussion we have used the names of the months as given by the villagers in Bolangir, which are slightly different from the Indian names we have discussed earlier.

Quantity

The Food Calendar starts from Asharh and runs up to Jaistha according to the lunar calendar months. If we look at the consumption pattern of the villagers in Chikli in terms of frequency of consumption of food, the year can be divided into two parts: from Asharh to Pousa, (corresponding roughly from mid-June to mid-January) and then from Magh to Jaistha (corresponding roughly to mid-January to mid-June). During the seven-month period starting Ashad till Pousa, the poor villagers have three meals a day and from Magh to Jaistha, they have 4 meals a day. That is, the

Figure-9.1

FOOD AVAILABILITY

CHIKILI

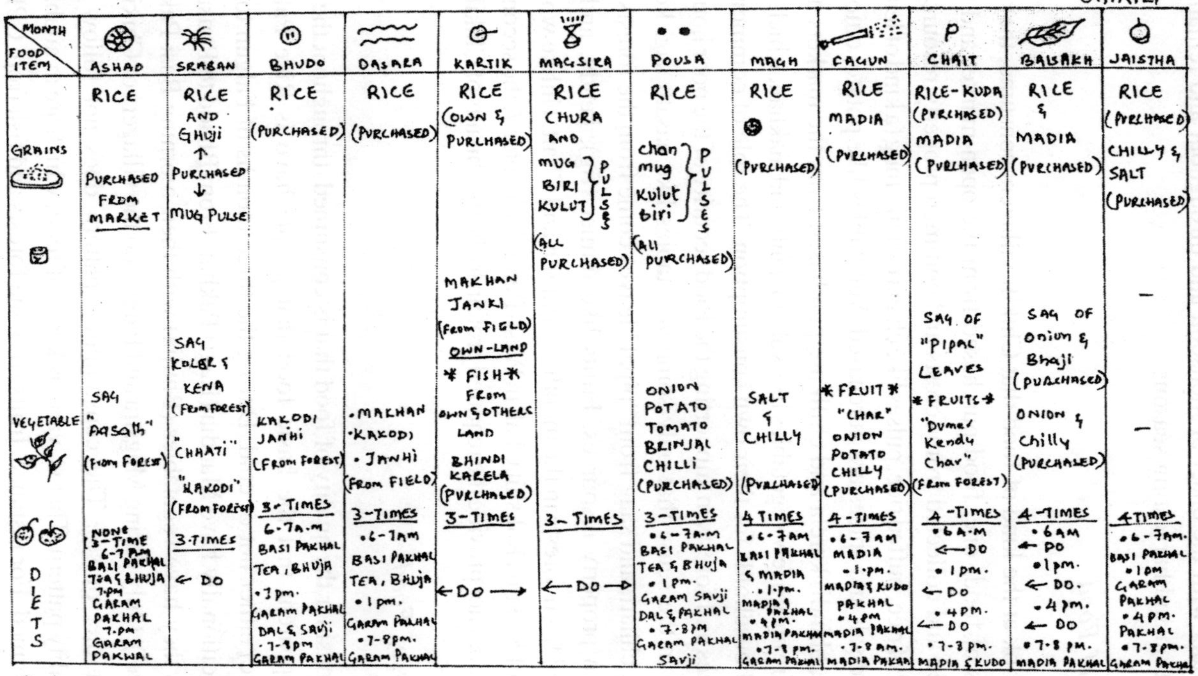

MONTH / FOOD ITEM	ASHAD	SRABAN	BHUDO	DASARA	KARTIK	MAGSIRA	POUSA	MAGH	CAGUN	CHAIT	BAISAKH	JAISTHA
GRAINS	RICE PURCHASED FROM MARKET	RICE AND GHUJI ↑ PURCHASED ↓ MUG PULSE	RICE (PURCHASED)	RICE (PURCHASED)	RICE (OWN & PURCHASED)	RICE CHURA AND MUG, BIRI, KULUT } PULSES (ALL PURCHASED)	RICE chan, mug, Kulut, biri } PULSES (ALL PURCHASED)	RICE (PURCHASED)	RICE MADIA (PURCHASED)	RICE-KUDA (PURCHASED) MADIA (PURCHASED)	RICE & MADIA (PURCHASED)	RICE (PURCHASED) CHILLY & SALT (PURCHASED)
VEGETABLE	SAG "Aasath" (From Forest)	SAG KOLBR & KENA (From FOREST) "CHHATI" "KAKODI" (FROM FOREST)	KAKODI JANHI (FROM FOREST)	• MAKHAN • KAKODI • JANHI (FROM FIELD)	MAKHAN JANKI (From FIELD) OWN-LAND * FISH * FROM OWN & OTHERS LAND BHINDI KARELA (PURCHASED)		ONION POTATO TOMATO BRINJAL CHILLI (PURCHASED)	SALT & CHILLY (PURCHASED)	* FRUIT * "CHAR" ONION POTATO CHILLY (PURCHASED)	SAG OF "PIPAL" LEAVES * FRUITS * "Dumer Kendu Char" (FROM FOREST)	SAG OF Onion & Bhaji (PURCHASED) ONION & Chilly (PURCHASED)	— —
DIETS	NONE / 3-TIME 6-7 AM BALI PAKHAL TEA & BHUJA 7 PM GARAM PAKHAL 7 PM GARAM PAKWAL	3-TIMES ← DO	3-TIMES 6-7 A.M BASI PAKHAL TEA, BHUJA • 1 pm. GARAM PAKHAL DAL & SAVJI • 7-8 pm GARAM PAKHAL	3-TIMES • 6-7 AM BASI PAKHAL TEA, BHUJA • 1 pm. GARAM PAKHAL • 7-8 pm. GARAM PAKHAL	3-TIMES ← DO →	3-TIMES ← DO →	3-TIMES • 6-7 A.M BASI PAKHAL TEA & BHUJA • 1 pm. GARAM SAVJI DAL & PAKHAL • 7-8 PM GARAM PAKHAL SAVJI	4 TIMES • 6-7 AM BASI PAKHAL & MADIA • 1 pm. MADIA & PAKHAL • 4 pm. MADIA PAKHAL • 7-8 pm. GARAM PAKHAL	4-TIMES • 6-7 AM MADIA • 1 pm. MADIA & KUDO PAKHAL • 4 PM MADIA PAKHAL • 7-8 AM. MADIA PAKHAL	4-TIMES • 6 A.M ← DO • 1 pm. ← DO • 4 PM. ← DO • 7-8 pm. MADIA & KUDO	4-TIMES • 6 AM ← DO • 1 pm. ← DO. • 4 pm. ← DO • 7-8 pm. MADIA PAKHAL	4 TIMES • 6-7 Am. BASI PAKHAL • 1 pm GARAM PAKHAL • 4 pm. PAKHAL • 7-8 pm. GARAM PAKHAL

Participants:-

Chand■ Tandi, Bhumi Kumhar

Kavsalya Bhoi, Niva Shond

frequency of eating improves after Magh and continues to be so till Jaistha and it falls with the onset of monsoon and throughout and remains low the cultivation and harvesting seasons.

Kinds of Food

If we look at the kind of food that Chikili villagers consume, they have two sources of food: one, food purchased from the open market and two, food gathered and collected from forests and common property resources.

All of rice, puffed rice, pulses like chana (gram), mug (a kind of lentil), kulut, biri, and salt and spices are purchased. Vegetables like potato, onion, brinjal, tomato, bhindi, karela and chilli are purchased from the markets and Haats. There are only a few vegetables like kakodi, janhi and makhan, which are grown by the households for their own consumption. The role of common property resources and forests in supporting the food security of the poor households is limited in the sense that only some vegetables like aasath sag, koler kena, kakodi, chhati, and saag from "pipal" leaves come from the forests and from common property resources. Fruits like dumer (fig), kendu, and char are accessed from forests in the months of Falgun and Chait. Unlike what we saw in case of Krishna Rakshit Chak in West-Bengal, Chapter 7, the secondary food system does not provide the required protein to the inhabitants of Chikili

Quality of Food

If we consider the quality of food that is consumed, throughout the year, it is quite apparent that the basic food that people have is Rice Pakhal (rice porridge) either hot or cold. During the three months of Falgun to Baisakh, they additionally have Mandia (Ragi) Pakhal. From Bhado to Pousa, for four months they have vegetables (Bhujia) with their morning Basi Pakhal (cold rice gruel). Only during Magsira and Falgun do the villagers of Chikili include in their diet pulses. The consumption pattern does not follow the food availability pattern. That is, various kinds of food, which are available, are not all consumed. For instance, fruits from the forests and fish from CPRs are not consumed but sold.

Thus both in terms of variety and palate the food consumption pattern in Chikli is dull and monotonous. The food value of their diet is low on account of the preponderance of starch and is deficient in fiber, vitamins, animal protein and fruits. Thus, from a nutritional perspective, though villagers in Chikili have food at fairly regular intervals, their nutritional value and content remains abysmally poor.

Overall Picture

The overall picture that thus emerges is that the inhabitants of Chikili face three phases of hunger: they are most hungry from Ashad to Kartik (for 5 months) surviving mostly on 3 meals of Rice Pakhal with a very small quantity of minor vegetables. For two months of Magsira and Pousa, they are hungry but less than the earlier 5 months as they add to their diet pulses and Chura (pound/flattened rice). And for five months from Magh to Jaistha their level of hunger is the least with 4 meals a day, though the quality of food consumed deteriorates.

Generally, the nutritional content of their food is very low and variety extremely limited, barring the two months of Magsira and Pousa.

IV. The Village: Ganta Bahali

The story in village Ganta Bahali is different from Chikili. Reference is invited to Figure 9.2. The months are according to Indian calendar and the year starts in Baisakh.

Quantity of Food

The general diet of a villager in Ganta Bahali consists of rice, pulses and vegetables. The Seasonality Diagram on food does not tell us about the quantity of food consumed on a cardinal basis. It does tell us, however, how much food is consumed by the villagers, in ordinal terms. Stones were placed against items of food consumed to shown the level of consumption consumption of that item of food. Larger the number of stones placed, higher was the level of food consumed. During Ashwin, Kartick, Magsira and Pousa, six stones show that the consumption of food is the highest during these months for the villagers of Ganta Bahali. In Magh to Jaith the consumption level successively falls till it reaches the lowest level in Jaith. It then rises sharply to the level of Fagun in Asharh and Sraban and then falls to a bare minimum, a situation so desperate that the villagers thought even one stone would give an exaggerated picture of food consumed. A "no stone" situation according to the villagers gives a true and fair account of their level of food consumption after Sraban.

Kinds of Food

The kinds of food that the villagers of Ganta Bahali consume are very limited. Rice is their main item of consumption. Pulses like urd, mung and kuluth are available for only three months or so. They have home grown vegetables for three months from Magh to Falgun. Vegetables are mainly tomato, brinjal, radish, pumpkin, cucumber, karela (bitter goud), onion and bhindi (lady's finger). For the villagers of Ganta Bahali, protein and fruits (bitter goud) are conspicuous by their absence from their diet.

Quality of Food

The quality of food consumed in Ganta Bahali varies from month to month. The villagers have determined their own criterion to specify the quality of food they consume. That criterion is the proportion of water content of their food. Given that they consume as their staple food Pakhal (a kind of gruel) the higher the water content the poorer the quality of the gruel. Notice the three symbols in row 2 of Figure 9.2: a plate, a glass and a vessel. The plate signifies rice. The vessel signifies pulses and the glass signifies how much watery their rice gruel is. From Ashwina to Pausa, the plate is full and the vessel is partly filled showing that they do consume pulses. There is no glass. That is, the rice they consume is proper rice. In Magh and Fagun, the vessel disappears, meaning that there is no pulse to consume content. The glass is still not there, meaning that the rice they eat have the right moisture. But the amount of rice consumed falls in Fagun. In Chait, the quantity of rice on the plate has reduced and the glass appears, signifying that the rice they eat has started becoming watery. In Baisakh, the quantity of rice has fallen further and the water in the glass has increased. That is, the rice they eat has become even more watery, and the trend intensifies in Jaith. In Asar and Sraban, the quantity of rice has increased but then in Bhadrab the plate is nearly empty and the glass almost full. The poor in Ganta Bahali survive on a near fluid diet.

There are no fruits and there is none of animal protein, not even from the common property resources. Vegetables are consumed only during Magh, Fagun and Chait. Thus, in nutritional terms, the food consumed is poor. The availability of vegetables is mostly restricted to the three months of Magh, Fagun and Chait (see sixth row of Figure 9.2). And the vegetables are seasonal vegetables.

Box 9.2
Shrinking Land and Meals of Seeds.....

By Poornima Joshi in Phulbani

"...of Badgaon's 585 inhabitants, 265 belong to the Scheduled Tribes (mainly Kandha) and 123 to the Scheduled Castes. The rest are upper caste and have built concrete houses in the nearby upcoming town of Baliguda...

There is something static about Badgaon: in the broken plough propped against the cattle-sheds, in the algae-covered pond, in the women carrying pitchers on their heads, and in the resigned, almost numb expressions of villager elder Sarveshwar Malik and his companion sitting in the afternoon sun.

Most tribals have "sold" off their land to the money lenders that can buy them provisions for a year at most. An official ban on the sale of tribal land has done little to stop this. This shrinking of cultivated land has further reduced their yield and finding two meals a day is a problem for almost half the year.

Their meals comprise water boiled with rice and, when even that is not available, they boil mango seeds with water and drink the syrup residue. "We have a tradition of eating five meals a day. We never get that much food, so eat twice a day. When that also is difficult we make do with water", says Sarveshwar.

The Hindusthan Times, New Delhi, Sunday, February 6, 2000

Figure-9.2

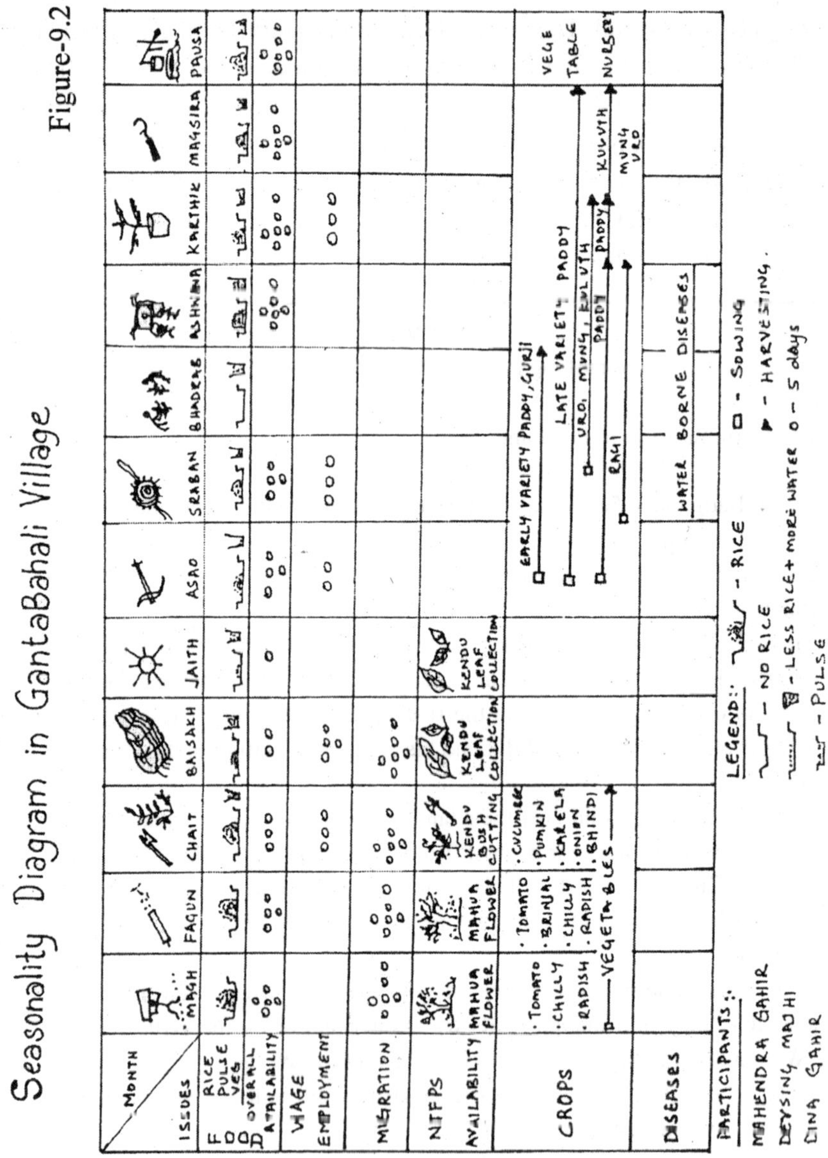
Seasonality Diagram in GantaBahali Village
MONTH
ISSUES
MAGH FAGUN CHAIT BAISAKH JAITH ASAO SRABAN BHADRAB ASHWINA KARTHIK MAGSIRA PAUSA
FOOD RICE PULSE VEG OVERALL AVAILABILITY
WAGE EMPLOYMENT
MIGRATION
NTFPS AVAILABILITY
MAHUA FLOWER
KENDU BUSH CUTTING
KENDU LEAF COLLECTION
CROPS
TOMATO CHILLY RADISH
TOMATO BRINJAL CHILLY RADISH
CUCUMBER PUMKIN KARELA ONION BHINDI
VEGETABLES
EARLY VARIETY PADDY, GURJI
LATE VARIETY PADDY
URD, MUNG, KULTH
PADDY
RAGI
KULTH MUNG URD
VEGETABLE NURSERY
DISEASES
WATER BORNE DISEASES
LEGEND:
- RICE
- NO RICE
- LESS RICE + MORE WATER
- PULSE
- SOWING
- HARVESTING
O - 5 days
PARTICIPANTS:
MAHENDRA GAHIR
DEYSING MAJHI
DINA GAHIR

The Common Property Resources

People of Ganta Bahali have access to Non-Timber Forest Produce (NTFP) for five months from Magh to Jaith. In Magh and Fagun they gather Mahua flowers, and in Baisakh and Jaith they collect kendu leaf. Though these do jack up the income of the poor households of Ganta Bahali, they are unable to make any perceptible dent on poverty or hunger. The poor households of Ganta Bahali have no holding capacity. Hence they sell the mahua at the going rate which during these months is very low because of excess supply. Kendu leaf also should fetch them handsome dividend, but the prices given by the government approved contractors and the rate of rejection of leaves, do not let them travel very far. In some cases, the payment comes with a lag and kendu leaf is purchased only during a specified period of time, when the leaves may not have even matured, whcih means the villagers earn a lower income from sale of kendu leaves.

The Overall Picture

In Ganta Bahali the intensity of hunger takes various forms. Hunger sets in Chait (mid-February to mid-March) and deepens in Jaith (mid-May to mid-June). These are the three hot summer months. With the onset of rain, employment becomes a reality from agricultural operations, people are able to buy food and improve their food availability. Hunger is at its worst in Bhadrab when neither there is any food available in the system nor is there employment in the fields. The symbols in the second row show an empty plate and a glass of watery substance.

In Ashwina, the overall availability of food in the system improves and people start harvesting the early variety of rice, called Gurji. Hunger is on the decline and gets successively reduced from then on till Magh. In Falagun food availability falls but there is enough to eat. Come Chait and real hunger sets in.

Thus the months of Chait, Baisakh, Jaith, Asad, Sraban and Bhadrab, are hunger months, with some respite in Asharh and Sraban, but then Jaith and Bhadrab are the worst hunger months. There is a five-month long hunger period, inclusive of two acutely hungry months. Significantly, the people of Ganta Bahali would have suffered even greater hunger in Chait, Baisakh, Asharh and Sraban but for the availability of employment which increases their purchasing power. This enables them to access food from the wages they earn.

And the balance seven months from Ashwin to Falgun, people do not suffer hunger. This is primarily because of two reasons. One, this is the period after the harvest which gives them paddy and pulses like urd, mung, kuluth, and two, this period also corresponds with the season for growing of vegetables, like tomato, radish, brinjal, pumpkin, karela (bitter gourd), onion and bhindi. Not only is availability of food they grow higher during these months, but part of the vegetables grown is also sold to give them some liquidity to purchase other items of consumption. Wage employment to increase access to food, which helps them tide over food shortages in Chait, Baisakh, Asharh and Sraban (the last two months in agriculture), is non-existent during this period.

V. The Village: Jogimara

Jogimara is the third village studied in Bolangir. The Seasonality Matrix drawn up by the villagers in Jogimara is not only very comprehensive, but is also the most interesting.

The row heads are names of months and the column heads are the names of the sources from which the poor villagers access food. The villagers used Sal leaves against the name of food and months, to specify the quantity of food they consumed. The larger the number of leaves placed against an item of food, the greater is the quantity they consumed. These are all relative scoring. The number of leaves against a food item does not signify consumption of that food in as many kilos or grams or whatever. They indicate how much more or less of the food item is consumed by them in a month viz-a-viz the level of consumption of the same food item in the earlier or later month(s). Reference is invited to Figure 9.3.

Kinds of Food

The kinds of food consumed by the households in Jogimara display a wide variety. Like the other eastern states, the villagers of Jogimara indicated that their principal diet consists of dal and bhat (rice and lentil). There is some combination of rice, mandia (ragi), kudo, bajra, gunji, juar (jowar), gaham and mug, harhad and biri.

They have seasonal vegetables of considerable variety ranging from Alu (potato) to brinjal, cauliflower (kobi), tomato, piaja (onion), bhindi (ladys finger), jhunga (ridge gourd) and radish (mula). Whether the households consume all these vegetables or not is another matter, to which we shall return later, but they grow some vegetable or the other in every month. If the households consume whatever vegetables they have shown in row 2 and whatever cereals they have depicted in row 1, then they would have a fairly balanced diet. But unfortunately that is not the case.

The consumption of meat and fish forms part of the diet of households in Jagimara but not on all months. And all such consumption is mostly through purchase of these items from the open market. This gives an impression that villagers in this village do not rear animal for meat. They do have animals, but they are for milk and drought power. There is no pisiculture in the village. As a result, they have to buy whatever fish they consume.

Quantity of Food

Villagers of Jogimara gave a detailed account of the levels of consumption in ordinal terms. There is a clear seasonality in the intensity of hunger faced by the households and there is inter-month variation in the intensity of food shortages that villagers confront.

During Ashwin, Kartik, Margasira, Pausa and Magh, the villagers have the highest level of consumption. These are the months when their diet has a fairly decent mix of rice, dal, mandia, juar (jowar), gaham (wheat) and bajra as also mug, harad and biri. This is shown by the three leaves, which the villagers placed against these months, to indicate their levels of consumption in row 1 of the Seasonality Matrix at Figure 9.3. These are the

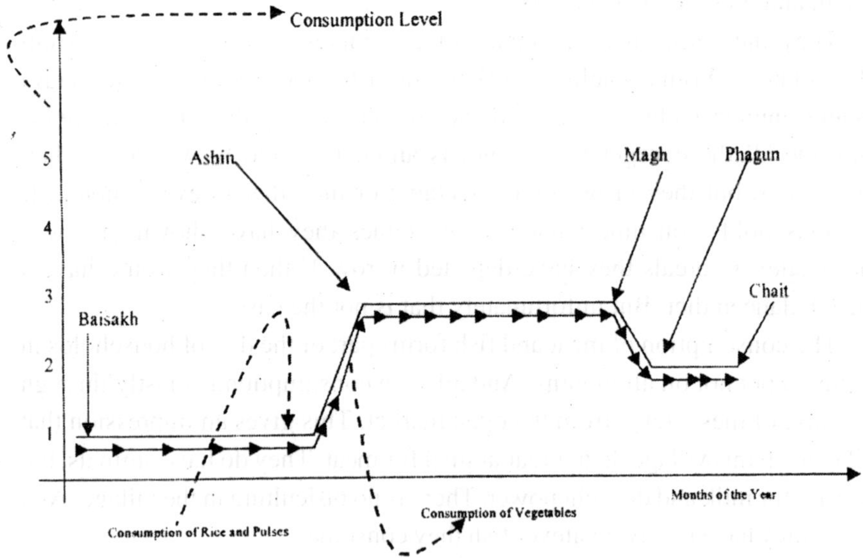

Figure-9.3 : Trends in Consumption in Village JOGIMARA

months which overlap both harvesting of crops and post-harvest season, a stretch of period when availability of food in the system is at its peak.

In Falgun and Chaitra food consumption drops to a lower level, shown by two leaves. That is, after the conclusion of the post-harvest operations, when food availability starts to decline, people start coping with the situation by curtailing consumption. Then from Baisakh to Bhado (for five months) spreading over the summer and the cultivation seasons, consumption level drops even further. During this period the lower level of consumption is shown by only one leaf. Since availability of food in the system is at its lowest during the summer months and the cultivation season, people have no alternative but further curtail their consumption. This shows that the poor households have neither economic nor physical holding power to stock foodgrains to be used during periods of shortages and hence as the systemic food availability varies, consumption is also varied.

Since the Oriya Calendar starts from Baisakh, if we look at the consumption pattern beginning from Baisakh the trend looks like the following: food consumption is at a low level in Baisakh (mid-April to mid-May) and stays at that level till Ashwin. In Ashwin, there is a sharp jump in consumption level which continues at that level till Magha. It then starts to fall, to reach the lowest level in Baisakh. Figure 9.4 shows the trend. The level of food consumed, therefore, shows significant variations during the different months in the year.

Consumption of seasonal vegetables also has a clear pattern. From Ashin to Magasira, the consumption of vegetables, like sag, mula (radish), tomato, makhan, baigan (brinjal), and piaja (onion) is at a perceptible level. Then in Pousa, Magha and Falgun a new set of vegetables enters their diet, such as, simha (beans), kobi (cauliflower), alu (potatoe) and kadu (bottle gourd). For the six months beginning Ashwin to Magha, vegetable consumption is at its highest, shown by three leaves. But in Chait as summer starts setting in, vegetable consumption falls, shown by two leaves and then from Baisakh onwards till Bhado, it is at its lowest shown by only one leaf. Thus, if we view it from the beginning of the Oriya calendar year, consumption of vegetables shows the same pattern as shown by the consumption of rice and pulses.

The villagers of Jogimara therefore, have, two clear periods: from Baisakh to Bhado, for five months, they face a hunger period. This is the

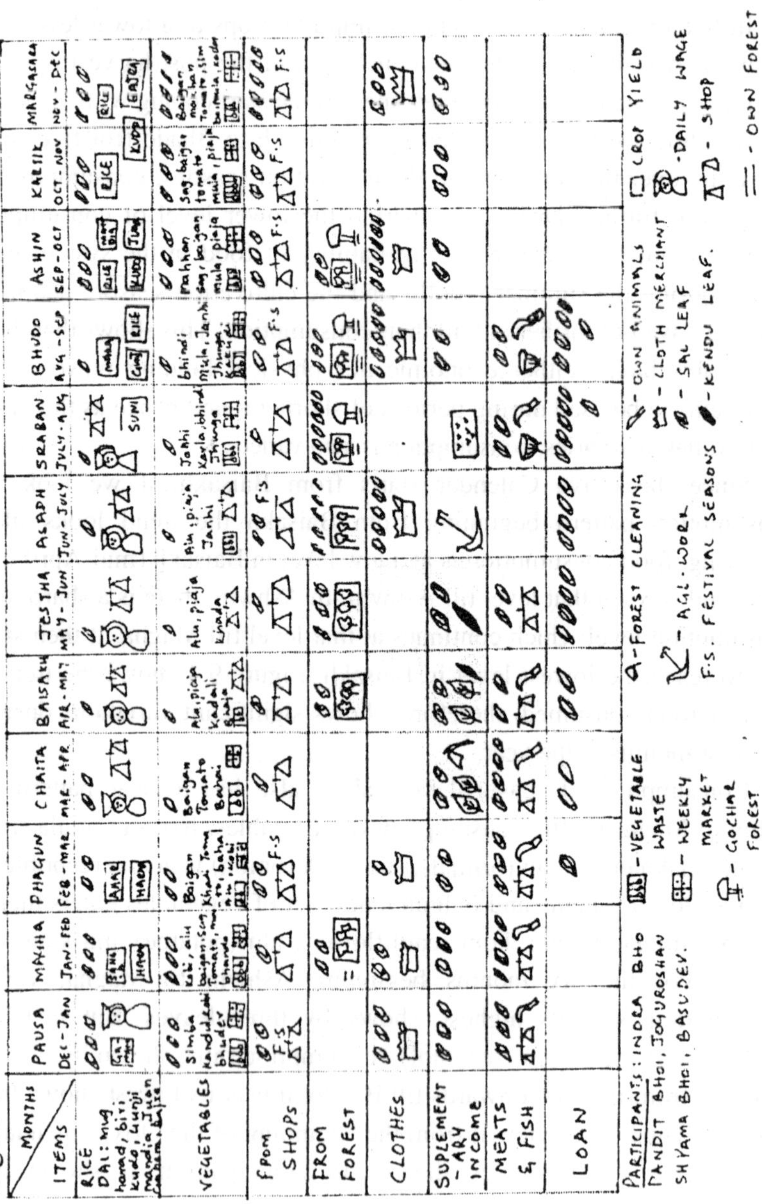

Figure-9.4 SEASONALITY MATRIX

first period. In the second period, from Ashwin to Chait, they have enough food to eat though during Chaita consumption levels start declining. During the hunger period they not only consume less of rice and pulses but also less of vegetables.

Curiously enough, the villagers have protein in the form of fish and meat in their diet on only some months. Baisakh, Jaistha, Sraban and Bhado are the four months when they consume moderate amounts of fish and meat. Then from Pousa to Chait they have a much higher level of protein consumption. The meat and fish that they consume are both home grown and bought from the market. They do not consume meat or fish in the months of Asharh, Ashin, Kartik and Margasira.

Quality of Food

On first inspection it seems that the kinds of food consumed in Jogimara clearly indicate that they do not suffer as much hunger as in some other villages. They have a fair variety and have a good mixture of rice, pulses, vegetables, meat and fish. Meat and fish are consumed either from goats and poultry raised at home or by purchase from the market. However, the villagers explained that things were a bit more difficult than what they seem at first sight.

If we see the first row of Figure 9.3, it is apparent that whatever food the poor villagers grow on their own land is enough for partially meeting their consumption needs for 7 months from Bhodo till Phagun. The sign of the "measure" indicates that they buy food from shops and the squares with the names of the food item show that they grow it at home. For the remaining five months they buy all of what they consume or collect from the CPRs, which are in the main forests of three kinds found in and around the village.

Meeting consumption needs by buying food is not an easy task for the villagers of Jogimara. To buy food for meeting their consumption needs (even if only partially) they do three things. One, they work on daily wages during the five months of Chait to Sraban (shown by the figure of a women with a basket on her head). Two, they borrow heavily from the village money lender who often is the shopkeeper himself, as shown by the last row of Figure 9.3. The borrowing starts in Falgun, as food availability from their own fields starts declining (row 1) and then reaches its peak in Sraban: from one leaf in Falgun borrowing reaches six leaves in Sraban. In Bhado, rice, maka and gund are harvested from their fields but the borrowing continues during Bhudo as well. This is to meet the expenses associated with their festival in Bhudo and Ashin (see row 3). Three, they sell off whatever good quality vegetables they grow on their own land, to have liquid cash, with which they buy other items of food consumption.

This brings us to vegetable consumption. Let us look at the second row of Figure 9.3. The sign of three leaves inside the rectangle indicates that the vegetable the villagers consume are vegetable waste. That is, vegetables that are not saleable: vegetables that are diseased, decolourised by hail storm, damaged by pests, insects and animals. The better quality vegetables are all sold off at the weekly market (shown by a rectangle with four partitions and dots in them) to have liquid cash and only the ones for the "garbage" as it were, are consumed at the household level.

Consumption of meat and fish is only during the winter and summer months starting from Pousa till Jaistha. There are moderate amounts of meat and fish consumption in Sraban and Bhado as well.

If we compare row 2 with row 7 of Figure 9.3, an interesting cultural phenomenon is projected. People consume only vegetables' that go as waste and sell of whatever good vegetables they harvest from their fields, in the market to supplement their income. But they consume meat and fish either purchased from the shop and/or procured from what they rear in home and not generally sold in the market. Thus, people substitute vegetables by meat and fish. Though the rate of substitution between vegetables, meat and fish, is not known but the fact remains that people sell the better quality vegetables they grow for supplemental income and buy meat and fish as also rear them at home. The preference for rice and fish is clearly demonstrated. Even people, who go hungry on some months of the year, do not like to change their food habits and continue to buy fish and meat milk with whatever little income they get.

Common Property Resources

Common property resources, as we have mentioned earlier, available to Jogimara villagers are restricted to forests. They have three kinds of forests, viz., Own Forests, Gochar Forests and Resource Forest. Food from all these sources is accessed for seven months in a year, the maximum being in the months of Asharh and Sraban followed by Bhado. Leafy vegetables, mushrooms and bamboo shoots are commonly gathered from the CPRs. Tubers and fruits in more modest quantities are also collected.

Overall Food Security Situation

Overall, Jogimara is a village, which has a reasonable amount of food security. Reference is invited to figure 9.4 in this regard. But people are still hungry and avoid greater starvation by accessing non-timber forest produce (NTFP), by accessing food through supplemental income earned through daily wage earning. Their diet is a mixture of cereals, pulses, vegetables and animal protein. The quality of the food eaten varies from month to month but they do consume cereals, pulses, vegetables and animal protein in varying proportions. The villagers clearly have a seasonality problem: food consumption starts declining in Chaitra and reaches the lowest level in Baisakh and stays at that level till Bhado, that is, till the new crops start flowing in. Once the new harvests of Kharif crops starts flowing into the system, consumption picks up. Thus, the people have the lowest intake during the summer and rainy seasons, the period during which people work the hardest and require the greatest amount of energy. Fortunately because availability of NTFP and employment opportunities correspond with the lean period, the suffering of the poor households is lesser than what it would have otherwise been.

VI. Discussion and Conclusions

The general picture that appears from the above is that most households are food insecure. The fact that they are poor has bearing on the households' level of consumption: the poor households are also "hungry" households. The perception in the villages is that a household is prosperous if the family is self sufficient in food all round the year.

Though the households in the villages are food insecure throughout the year, seasonal patterns of food availability for actual consumption do not exhibit any marked inter-village variations. For the marginal farmers, the food they grow on their own land is sufficient to see their households through for three to four months in normal years. They depend on wage and "other" sources for meeting their consumption needs. The conditions faced by the landless labourers are distressing. The role of food from the common property resources and forests during periods of stress is important for the food deficit households in all the villages.

If we look at the Food Calendar, Seasonality Diagram and Seasonality Matrix of the three villages, viz., Jogimara, Ganta Bahali and Chikili respectively, the cultural characteristic of a preference for rice is distinct. Rice is cooked in water and mostly consumed as Pakhal (kind of gruel). The other cereals that generally find place in the diet of the villages are ragi, gunji and kudo. Consumption of pulses is very minimal. The variety and palate in the food of households in these villagers are limited.

As is expected, food consumption is higher in the months when harvests come home. This is also the season for vegetables and pulses. This is also, therefore, the period when the availability of vegetables goes up. All this contributes towards making higher availability of aggregate food in the households and hence improves the overall level of food consumption in the poor houeholds.

Food from the forests and common property resources (food from the secondary food system) is accessed mostly during the rainy season. The kinds of food that people by and large have from the secondary food system are leafy vegetables (called Saag in local language), wild mushroom (called Chatu, perhaps a derivation from the word "*Chaata*", meaning Umbrella) and bamboo shoots (called Kardi). The villagers gave a clear impression that the variety of food available from the secondary food system had been diminishing over the years. According to their estimates, though food is no longer available from the CPRs and forests etc. in quantities and varieties as they used to be earlier, their dependence on such sources has not reduced. They have lost the variety and palate that such food added to their diet. Nevertheless, the quantity of food from the secondary food system is significant.

In most cases for the poor households, the summer months of Baisakh and Jestha and the rainy months of Asharh, Sraban and Bhado, that is, a period of five months, are *Hunger Months*. Jaistha is the nadir of the hunger period. This is very similar to what we saw in Krishna Rakshit Chak in Chapter-7. During these months, ironically, the energy needs of the people are the highest. For the households of small and marginal farmers, this is when agricultural activities peak, and for the landless labourers, these are the only months when they get employment in the villages. During the summer months of Baisakh and Jaistha, the stock of rice in the households gets exhausted and the overall availability of rice in the system at the same is very low. Hence, the going price of rice during these months is very high and the economic access of the poor people to food is so much less.

The summer months are particularly oppressive because during these months not only is the energy-need high, but availability of water the least. In consequence, people notably the women, have to work a lot harder to fetch potable water for the households. The poor quality of available water often results in intake of poor quality (read muddy) water in poor households. As a result, absorption of whatever little food is consumed is even lower and energy requirement even less met. This also has serious policy implications.

During the rainy season, particularly, in Asharh and Sraban, few households start getting what is called "Chhot Dhan" (short duration paddy) which relieves some hunger for a few of the lucky ones. The others continue to suffer. Because the going prices of food are very steep, households stop consuming anything else other than rice. The concentration of Pakhal (rice gruel) is also at its minimum and its liquidity highest. These facts are abundantly illustrated by the first row of the Seasonality Matrix of Jogimara and the first row of the Seasonality Diagram of Ganta Bahali, respectively.

Luckily during these months, in villages with relatively better forest cover, saag (leaves), tubers and wild fruits from the secondary food system are available. This is best seen if we compare the Seasonality Matrix prepared by the villagers of Jogimara, with the Seasonality Diagram prepared by the villagers of Ganta Bahali and Food Availability Chart of Chikili. Jagimara has relatively more forest cover than both Ganta Bahali and Chikili. Thus, forests provide quite a range of food to the households of Jogimara throughout the year, particularly during the hunger months. For poor households of Chikili the bounties of forest are less, but they do get mushrooms and leafy vegetables like saag, chaati, kakodi, koler and kena in Asharh and Sraban. They also get some fruits like dumer, kendu and char in Falgun and Chait. When we come to Ganta Bahali, it is apparent that food from the forest is virtually nil. But they do get non-timber forest produce like mahua flowers in Magh and Falgun; kendu and fuel from cutting bushes in Chait, and some income from collection of kendu leaf in Baisakh and Jaisth which provides valuable supplementary income. But these run out for seven months from Asharh to Magh.

The coping mechanism adopted by the villagers are different in different villages and one of the many factors that determine the coping behviour of the poor households is the availability of food from the secondary food system. In case of Jogimara migration is not an option for the hungry households: they survive on the basis of, *inter alia*, food from the secondary food system. In case of poor households of Chikili, migration is also not a preferred option and they do derive support from the secondary food system. For the households of Ganta Bahali, the picture is different. They have to migrate for at least four months from Magh to Baisakh. The migrants get back to the village at the start of the cultivation season in Jaisth and survive till Pousa, that is, till the harvesting and post-harvest operations are completed, a period during which either they work on their small pieces and parcels of land and/ or on others' land. Wage employment is also available to the people of Ganta Bahali for only three of the eight months that they stay in the village.

Forests play an important role in the food security scenario of the villages under study. Though the role of forest in providing food directly to the villagers may not be apparent in all cases, but the vegetables and fruits for consumption, income from non-timber forest produce and employment opportunities that forests offer to the villagers are significant. There is a need to relook at property rights and redefine the same to better preserve the forests and at once provide the much needed food for the hungry poor.

It has to be underscored that the villagers in these villages do not access food from the public distribution system. There is a wide spectrum of awareness about food available from the "ration shops" as they put it, but there is a virtual unanimity that they do not find the food supplied through the Public Distribution System (PDS) as being of help in meeting their food needs and mitigating hunger. On the question of why the pathetic state of physical and economic access to food through the PDS has been reached, there are different shades of reasons. For some, the ration cards, due to the fragility of poor quality paper on which these are printed, have perished under human sweat and folds. For others the cards were never there, and for some others, though physical access may be there yet the timing when food is supplied and the units in which food is made available, deny them the economic access that PDS is designed to provide. This is an area where public action is warranted and can have positive impact on food security of poor households.

The role of wage employment is critical. Since there is no scope to increase on-farm employment and the scope for off-farm employment is very limited, wage employment is the only means available for providing large sections of poor people with economic access to food. The roll back of the state does not seem to be in consonance with the stark realities of the life. There is need to re-examine the issue *de novo.* We are not advocating any particular programme and we are painfully aware of the fact that there is as much leakage from resources allocated to these programmes as from any other. But the fact remains that the state has to provide productive employment opportunities to the poor in order to provide them with economic access to food. Even in this era of LPG (liberalisation, privatisation and globalisation), it can be nobody's case that the market will take care of these hapless citizens.

10 Summary and Conclusions: The Reality Check

I. Introduction

We started writing the book at a time when the country was said to be comfortable with its food security position and the substantive debate revolved around whether to continue with cuts in food and fertiliser subsidy. Food security, hunger and indeed poverty had fallen off the national agenda. This has happened despite serious students like us having consistently argued that there is need to focus national attention on the issues of poverty and hunger. It is somewhat ironical that at the time when we are writing the last Chapter of the book, India is facing the grim prospect of an impending famine in Rajasthan, Gujarat and large parts of Andhra Pradesh, and of course, in famine's favourite hunting ground Western Orissa. An estimated 70 million people and many more animals in these states are standing face to face with the stark realities of hunger and food insecurity. In some cruel way we feel we are vindicated.

II. Entitlement and Deprivation Perspective

The conquest of hunger and food insecurity is a much more complex phenomenon than merely increasing food production and improving food distribution. Hunger and food insecurity has to be seen as the characteristic of people not having enough to eat. This is not tantamount to saying, " there isn't enough to eat". Hunger statements are about the relationship of people to food. To understand why people go hungry and face food insecurity, one has to go into the structure of ownership of food as best shown by a long series of Sen's pioneering work.

Ownership relations, according to Sen, are one kind of entitlement relationship, which as accepted in a private ownership market economy, typically include the following: (a) *Trade-based Entitlement, where an* individual is entitled to own goods and services, which the individual obtains by trading something, owned by her/him. (b) *Production-based Entitlement,* where an individual is entitled to own goods and services, he/she obtains by arranging production using resources owned by him or her. This could be done also by hiring resources. (c) *Own Labour Entitlement, where* an individual is entitled to one's own labour power. He/she is thus entitled to the trade-based and production-based entitlements related to the individual's labour power. (d) *Inheritance and Transfer Entitlement, where* an individual is entitled to own commodities, that are willingly given to the individual by another individual. These transfers could be in the nature of a gift, inheritance or bequest.

What an individual owns is called the endowment entitlement or *direct entitlement*. But individuals can also exchange the commodities they own for another commodity, or another collection of commodities. The set of all alternative bundles of commodities that an individual can acquire has been collectively called *exchange entitlement* of what the individual owns.

Hunger faced by people and their ability to avoid it depends upon both individuals' ownership of commodities and on the exchange entitlement mapping. A general decline in food supply may indeed cause an individual to be exposed to hunger but an individual can also be exposed to hunger through a rise in prices with an unfavorable impact upon the individual's exchange entitlement. Even where hunger of the person is thus caused by food shortage, the immediate reason for the individual's food insecurity will be the decline in that individual's exchange entitlement.

People (and their number runs into billions) go hungry either because there is not enough food to meet everybody's needs, or there is a decline (read failure) in entitlement. Entitlement failure or decline can be due to various factors including absence of institutional sanctions to access the available food and available food being culturally unacceptable. In many cases people may be more hungry than they otherwise would have been if there is no CPRs, micro-environment, forests, etc. which provide food, from what we have called the secondary food system. Thus, entitlement failure or decline in entitlement or absence of institutional sanction to access food etc. are the proximate causes of hunger. For instance, if an elderly person faces hunger due to entitlement failure, what are the reasons behind the entitlement failure: is it lack of income, absence of physical access to food or absence of economic access or what? The basic causes of hunger need to be looked at.

III. What Causes Hunger: The Economic Perspective?

There are seven basic reasons why people are unable to exercise their right to food and go hungry. Powerlessness and politics, violence and militarism, poverty, rapid population growth exerting strain on environment and over-consumption, racism and ethnocentrism, gender discrimination and vulnerability and age are the seven of the more important causes of entitlement failure.

The discussion on the causes of hunger logically leads to a discussion on the nutrition poverty trap.

Those, who all fail to enjoy the right to food, are usually the poor. There are fundamental issues in the economics of food deficiency involved here. Those who cannot access food are the ones who are undernourished, bearing in mind that undernutrition is not the same thing as starvation. The link between nutritional status and capacity to work imply that assetless people are simply assetless, except perhaps their potential labour power. This is also not necessarily true. Labour power is *ipso facto* not an asset because to convert their potential labour power (over a long period of time) into actual labour power, poor people need adequate food and nutrition over that period. Because the poor are undernourished they fail to convert their full potential labour power to actual labour power. Because the conversion of potential labour power into actual labour power is inadequate for the poor, their capacity to obtain food to improve their nutritional status is also low. The situation is even worse in case of early childhood undernourishment, which is damaging both for well being and for productive abilities and cognitive skills of the people involved. There is a clear link between early childhood undernourishment and poor cognitive skills. Thus over time, undernourishment and ill health can both be a cause and consequence of individuals' and households' falling in the poverty trap.

And such poverty can be inter-generational: once a household falls into a poverty trap, successive generations tend to remain trapped in poverty. For a family in poverty, its descendents fail to get out of it even if the economy in the aggregate sense was experiencing growth in output. The vicious cycle of undernourishment traps the households continuously. It is also well-known that early childhood undernourishment cause long-term damage to individuals and this is perpetuated from one generation to another. Thus, hunger and undernourishment in one generation sets a chain reaction that penetrates deep into the subsequent ones, especially in societies where there is inequity in intra-familial distribution of power and hence where inequity in access to food and education is loaded against women.

In this nutrition-poverty trap, maintenance requirements of individuals take a severe beating. It has been long established that 60-75 per cent of the energy intake of someone in nutritional balance is expended towards maintenance and the much smaller 40-25 per cent is expended on "discretionary activities" such as work and play. Thus, those who are undernourished cannot provide nutrition for the maintenance function of their bodies. They are able to work less and burn out early. Large maintenance requirements are a reason why in poor societies one can expect the emergence of inequality among people who may have been similar to begin with. Thus, poor people who subsist on diets of low calorific value are effectively excluded from the workforce. Thus when we see a beggar, as Das Gupta (*Das Gupta,* 1997) beautifully puts it, it gives a picture which "contains both physiological and behavioral adaptation with vengeance. It tells us that emaciated beggars are not lazy: they have to husband their precarious hold on energy".

IV. How to Overcome Hunger?

While increased food production is very important there is much more that needs to be done, if we are to get rid of poverty trap, hunger and food insecurity. A programme to conquer hunger must include among other things, measures for enhancement of general economic growth, expansion of employment, decent rewards for work, diversification of production, enhancement of medical and health care, arrangement of special access to food on the part of poor people (including deprived mothers, aged, disabled and small children), spread of basic education and literacy, strengthening democracy and the news media and reduction in gender-based inequalities. As Sen puts it in his 1997 Dr. Rajendra Prasad Memorial Lecture, "*These different requirements call for an adequately broad analysis alive of the diversity of causal antecedents that lie behind the many-sided nature of hunger in the contemporary world*".

In order to achieve this broad-based approach towards ensuring a hunger free and food secure society, it is essential to recognise and manage several interdependencies. These interdependencies include: interdependence between consumption and income, between distinct sectors, between different countries, between food and macroeconomic stability, between intra-familial distributional equity and sharing of food, between women's standing and fertility decline, between political incentives and public policies, between wars, military expenditure and economic deprivation, between early undernourishment and cognitive skills and finally between public activism and social policies.

V. Can Hunger be a Social Problem?

Hunger can be seen as a societal problem as well. The development of society is determined by both the technical and material conditions, as also the social conditions of production. Ideology, politics, culture, religion, customs, usage, social norms and practices, legal system, customary rights, system of justice, etc., all having a bearing on development, are called the "*super-structure*".

The *technical* and *material* conditions of production reflect the relationship between people on one hand, the means of production and nature on the other, where the means of production are identical with the existing tools, technology, ecology, environment, bio-diversity, etc. They are the *objective* elements in the conditions of production process.

But there are also *subjective* elements in production process like vision, mission in life, values, attitudes, behaviour and inherent qualities of human beings. These include, but are not restricted to, technical knowhow, professionalism, imagination and ideas, skills, entrepreneurial spirit, risk aversion, spirit of adventure, will power and cultural traits, religious beliefs, customs, practices, pride and prejudice, and even altruism. The subjective elements as a basket of resources in the production process have been called "*potential resources*".

The *social conditions* of production, which reflect the interrelationship between people and the means of production, determine what is produced, where the existing property relations, the division of labour, the societal power-status structure, institutional arrangements, etc. are the critical elements. These have been called the "*economic structure*" of society.

There is a relationship between the *potential resources* and the *economic structure* of society, of continuous interaction resulting in a certain mode of production, which is called the "*economy*". But the basic interaction between the *potential resources* and the *economic structure* of a society also influences people's perceptions, their culture, their religion, their beliefs and their ideology. When contradictions are overcome or solved by changes in the *economic structure* of the society, then the *superstructure* (ideology, culture, etc.) will slowly change. Such a change will in turn affect the basic interaction between *potential resources* and the *economic structure.* In summary, the economy and the political and ideological superstructure interact in every society.

A perspective of hunger and society has been developed through this dialectical model of society. And that is, we are told, the way forward because "mono-disciplinary" and political perspectives, or reductionistic approaches, used to analyse hunger and formulate policy prescriptions emanating from these analyses, produce unsatisfactory results and yield partial remedies to a complex problem. Hunger and food insecurity at the household, community and national levels are systemic problems and complex phenomena. Granted that, the problem of hunger deserves a characteristically multi-faceted remedy.

It is possible to distinguish four general levels of depth of analysis, viz., symptoms or signs, immediate/proximate causes, underlying causes and basic causes. Basic causes themselves can take many forms and are of different kinds. Generally, the immediate causes and the symptoms and signs attract far more public and media attention than the underlying or basic causes. However, to tackle hunger on a comprehensive scale, it is important to deal with all of these causes in an original manner.

Symptoms are the direct observable manifestations of hunger in a society.

The *proximate causes* of hunger include inadequate intake of food, calories and nutrition, and sudden onset of diseases like cholera, malaria and dengue fever.

The *underlying causes* of inadequate intake of food and nutrition and affliction of diseases are many and complex. But most of the factors are a result of unequal and inadequate access that the hungry people have to, for example, goods, services and other resources. The production, distribution and consumption of all these goods and services are determined by the socio-economic structure of the society, including its political and ideological superstructure.

There are several contradictions and the interrelationships in society that have bearing on hunger through development of a society. The contradictions and interrelationships within the economy *inter se* and between the economy, and between the economy and the political and ideology superstructure are the ultimate determinants of the development of a society. The *basic causes* explain how the potential resources of a given society are mobilized for production of goods and services and how these are distributed.

There is the need to have a categorization of the basic causes of hunger into different types of basic causes. These basic causes could be historical, ecological, technological, economic, ideological, cultural and political.

There are at least five levels at which hunger and food insecurity may exist. These are: (i) at the *international* level, (ii) at the *national* level, (iii) at the *area* level (iv) at the *village* level and (v) finally at the *household* level. However, the incidence of hunger is always on the individuals, where the symptoms manifest themselves. We see emanciated men, we see anemic pregnant women, we notice men struggling to get out of the drought affected areas. We do not see an emanciated country or an emanciated state, village or area. But the causes of hunger can be located at different levels.

Causes that lead to hunger, whether underlying or basic, may work at any or all of the five levels, either severally or jointly. Elimination of symptoms of hunger, that manifest in individuals and many of which are visually perceivable, requires elimination of hunger itself. This warrants interventions at those levels where the causes are situated. This is what makes a strong case for a, for want of a better word we say, integrated approach. Such an integrated approach will be, by definition, complex but a complex problem of hunger does not have a simple solution.

Hunger, thus, manifests itself at the individual or household level as inability to have physical and economic access to food, undernourishment, malnourishment, nutrient deficiency, metabolic disorders, loss of weight, apathy, entitlement failure, etc. and even loss of dignity as in the case of a beggar. Hunger thus is a symptom of a complex economic and social disorder, where the causes are to be traced via immediate and underlying causes to the basic causes. The basic causes of hunger can only be understood in relation to the specific historical, ecological, economic, cultural and political contexts in which the hungry people and their contemporary economy and society are situated. The basic causes have to be contextualised and categorized within this framework to arrive at an appropriate response to deal with the problem of hunger comprehensively.

VI. Any Commonality Between Economic and Social Perspectives?

A comparison of the perspectives of hunger reveals several important common elements. In both the economic perspective and social perspective of hunger, its complexity is well recognised. In consequence whether one is approaching hunger from the social perspective or the economic perspective, an integrated, as opposed to a "mono-directional" approach, is commended. The problem of hunger is too complex to be treated on one single plane. The need to look at hunger at different levels is brought forth and, therefore, a differentiated approach is warranted to eradicate hunger from different levels, starting from the individual to the national level or even the international level. This foreshadows the fact that if hunger is to be attacked and food security ensured at different levels, starting from the individual (especially the women and girl children), then people have to play a crucial role.

VII. Community Perspectives of Non-Tribal Communities

Having discussed the theoretical and conceptual basis of hunger, we have got the perspectives of the economists, the political scientists, gender activists and the sociologists. This in sum is the "experts" perspective on hunger. We now turn to see the perspectives of those who suffer hunger. The people. The community.

Communities' perspective on hunger and food insecurity was learnt through a process of cumulative learning. Hence, we began with an understanding of their livelihoods and the agro-ecosystems within which they operate and move on to deeper discussions. The discussion in this book follows the same route as was followed with the communities. We take a discussion of their livelihood and agro-ecosystem as our point of departure.

Livelihood and Agroecosystems

The livelihood option exercised by a majority of the villagers, within the hierarchy of agroecosystems, is biased in favour of the farming system. The livelihood of a minority, may be a significant minority, of the people fall under off-farm employment and trading. There is none of gathering/hunting and handicraft/manufacture systems. Within the farming system, the dependence is more on the cropping system than on the livestock system. And within the livestock system, they are confined to the paddock system only (there being no herdsmen). Thus, in operational terms most of our village folks are either into growing crops or into raising herds of milch animals and selling milk to meet their food security needs. Nearly everywhere, agriculture is critical as a means of livelihood, even in cases where farmers have a secondary source of income, and in cases where agriculture partakes the nature of a secondary source of income. Agriculture is carried out on land handed down from one generation to another as bequest.

With the flux of time, the dismantling of the joint family system and growth in population, the villagers pointed out, the land-man ratio has turned adverse in the villages. The pressure on inherited land, which they cultivate, is on the rise, resulting in a steady decrease in size of landholdings and increasingly smaller size of farming plots.

Fragmentation of land coupled with the high cost of cultivation for different reasons, including high external input and irrational application of inputs in the absence of extension, have made farming a losing proposition. These have disillusioned the farmers with farming in most of the villages, as manifested in the seeming decline in interest that agriculturists have in pursuing agriculture as a means of livelihood. The community clearly perceives significant variations in climatic conditions, which have increased the risks in agriculture, which, as it is, forms the riskiest end of the farming system. And the growing list of constraints, man-made and nature-bestowed like shortage of power, lack of credit, falling water table, increased pests, insect and weed attack, taken one with the other, have added several folds to the burden on the farmers.

The data of the last six decades, for our study on livelihood systems currently in vogue as provided by the villagers, tell us a story of difficulty. Whereas in the 1940s and the 1950s, most of the villagers were into farming, significant changes set in the 1960s and by 1980s, as villagers started diversifying their livelihood systems. The trend got further entrenched in the 1990s. Selling milk, serving the government and private industry, self-employment, petty trade, working in the transport sector and working as pure labourer made their way into the pattern of livelihood systems in the villages. Two forces were working on the rural economy, viz., One, agriculture losing its position as a lucrative calling, and two, state sponsored employment opportunities out side of agriculture, including self employment opportunities through credit from the formal system, were increasing. The villagers saw the importance of state sponsored employment since in the villages, like the ones in Chandpur and Tikri in Uttar Pradesh, they perceived that agriculture could no longer absorb all the people who were available for employment. Not only had natural growth in labour force outstripped growth in demand for labour in farming, but also because people were being slowly displaced from agriculture due to its mechanisation (at least partially). Alternative means of employment had to be sought and both state sponsored employment opportunities and job created in the nearby towns provided the outlet, though partially.

Thus for the farmers the "mantra" of "diversify or perish", that pervades farming at end of the 1990s, started catching as early as in the sixties. The findings in these villages are abundantly corroborated by events overtaking agriculture elsewhere as well. Even medium and large farmers have launched a spectrum of parallel non-agricultural ventures to beef up their dipping incomes, in Punjab and other parts of Haryana.

Intra-village diversification of livelihood patterns shows considerable inter-state variations. In U.P, the diversification of livelihood was *mostly in and around* the villages. For instance, in Chandpur, the diversification led to farmers scouting around for options within the village, like setting up powerloom and handloom weaving, stitching, earning daily wages, farm and agricultural work, working in transport sector or in self-employment like running auto rickshaws, vegetable hawking, setting up of petty shops and electric repairing outlets and so on. In Tikri, the diversification led to "Agriculture +": agriculture along with another source of income. For instance, agriculture and selling milk, agriculture and working as labourers, agriculture and working in the service sector like shops etc. Some villagers even migrated out of the village in search of work retaining their land and property in the village, to return only during cultivation and harvesting.

In Haryana, the diversification was *outside* the village. For example, in Uncha Gaon, working in the Police and Defense Forces, working for the Government Departments, serving in the industrial complexes, and selling milk in the industrial townships of Ballabgarh and Faridabad were the options. In Uncha Gaon, agriculture in growing cash crops, backed up by selling milk, provide bulk of the employment. These variations are a reflection of both the mindset of the people as also the opportunities available. In case of Haryana villages, the prospects of agricultural lands being acquired by the government has also set the farmers thinking on exploring alternatives to agriculture. Returns from agriculture for the community in these villages seem to be a major consideration in continuing or otherwise with farming and in judging the importance of agriculture.

The villagers see land not only as the biological basis for growing food and a means of livelihood, but also as the source of power and social standing. For the villagers land forms the basis for accessing other inputs like credit, and it acts as a hedge against inflation. Land is to them an excellent avenue to increase their net worth, because land prices are on the rise, particularly in the Haryana villages. This does not imply that the villagers in any way discount the facts that agriculture provides food (as one farmers called it "nutritious and good food"), and that it provides a certain amount of money to access "other" food that they do not themselves grow. They are appreciative of the fact that agriculture provides the much-needed fodder for feeding and maintaining their milch animals at a tolerable cost, which helps them in their food security. The critical place that agriculture has in providing employment to the villagers, which increases their economic access to food, particularly for women, is invariably highlighted.

Farming Practices

In 1940s and 1950s, agriculture was wholly rainfed. Farming was carried out with all traditional practices. Seeds, water-harvesting structures, soil nutrients and implements were all of the traditional variety and accessed from local resources. It was basically a household affair. The farmers and the community were in total control of the inputs, barring rains where they were fully dependent upon nature's bounties. There was virtually none of inputs required to be imported from outside the village.

Two decades later mechanization and electrification of agriculture took roots: deployment of electrified tubewells and tractors, with different degrees of intensity in the villages, more in Haryana and less so in Uttar Pradesh, was a common sight. In 1970s we see evidence of agriculture in all the villages exposed fully to "new technology", though adoption of the new technology was more pronounced in Haryana villages than in the U. P. villages. The induction of hybrid or HYV seeds replacing traditional varieties; chemical fertilisers crowding out organic manure; emergence of insecticides and pesticides in place of pest-resistant and insect-resistant plants became the in-thing in farming. This mirrored the sad fact that more than 300 plant species that have been traditionally used for pest control in India and a large storehouse of knowledge verified by continuous practice, which is available, fell into disuse. Tractors substituting the bullocks and the wooden plough, and electricity driven irrigation facilities in place of traditional irrigating methods, have become distinctly noticeable in almost all the villages, more in Haryana and less in Uttar Pradesh.

Cultivators apply fertilisers to their plots of land according to their gut feeling. They generally have no training and there is no extension service. The agriculture department is unhelpful in disseminating information to the farmers on use of fertiliser, pesticide and insecticide and even on HYV seeds. Consequently, the farmers in case of a new pest/disease attack use whatever they think would stop the disease or pest. If it works, others follow suit, with the full knowledge that there is no guarantee that a "medicine" which has worked in one plot of land will do wonders elsewhere as well. For instance a farmer in Uncha Gaon found out the hard way that DDT mixed with Urea in the chilli fields to tackle *moriya* (a pest) did not work though it has worked for another farmer. Farmers went by the advice they receive from the pesticide dealers, which has been reduced, for all practical purposes, into a single line advice: "spray as long as the pests/ insects persists". The experimentation based on pure gut feeling of others and the advice of shopkeepers, fail more often than succeed. This entails considerable waste of resources and time and increases the cost of farming.

Villagers were unequivocal that they are more dependent now upon seed companies and government seed farms, pesticide and insecticide companies, the respective State Electricity Boards, tractor companies and the fertilisers companies than they were ever before. The farmers also wasted resources in dealing with the dysfunctionality associated with bureaucracy that go with agencies and companies. The control of the farmers and the community on inputs vital for their survival, as a consequence, has gone out of their hands. With the process of globalisation proceeding at the current pace and the WTO Agreements implemented, the control of inputs to agriculture will further shift away from the farmers to a larger domain, may be even a global domain.

What the community pointed out means that farming is now a High External Input Agriculture (HEIA) from Zero External Input Agriculture (ZEIA)/Low External Input Agriculture (LEIA). That is agriculture is in the process of abandoning Chambers' *"unimproved" agriculture* as we travel through time from 1940s to 1990s. In the 1940s and 1950s, agriculture was based on what the farmer and the community had: seeds, labour, bullocks, plough and the wooden hoe, manure, moats and rains. In the 1980s and 1990s, agriculture has come to be based on inputs more from outside the households and the community: HYV seeds, pesticides, insecticides, chemical fertilisers, electricity, tractor power, tubewells and pump sets. This is a copy-book case confirming the framework of "internal resources vs. external resources" provided by Francis and King (1988). We have compared the sourcing of resources in the 40s and 50s vis-a-vis 80s and 90s and the picture is that except for receiving energy from sun for plant photosynthesis and a portion of family labour, the farmers are buying a whole lot of inputs from outside.

In the process, since farming in the 1980s and 1990s has become more dependent on sourcing inputs from outside the villages, farming has come to use resources that are not always renewable. Internal resources are "inherently renewable". The external inputs in the 1990s are in most cases not renewable. Since agriculture in the villages has become more or less dependent on external resources, much of it is *not* provided as a "free good". This implies that the farming households must buy most of the inputs and hence must generate a surplus of production, cash or whatever else of value, to exchange for external resources.

The transition from ZEIA to LEIA and eventually to HEIA, has made agriculture a high *open* cost operation because, as we stated in the previous paragraph, the farmers in the villages have to buy most of the inputs. There is little of the resources required which is free of charge, as virtually nothing is a free good. Thus, the cost of farming operation has gone up so much so that it has put sustainability of peasant agriculture in jeopardy. The high cost of external inputs is pinching the farmers since the last 4-5 years.

The transition from ZEIA to HEIA has also made a noticeable impact on the *hidden* cost of operation. The increase in fossil fuel used to keep outputs high also means more energy consumption. Shift from ZEIA to HEIA has led to substitution of manual labour and animal power by tractors, threshers and pump sets, which implies that external energy sources have substituted sources of energy found in the household and the community. All of these along with use of fertilisers, which is mostly NKP, have caused agriculture to become highly energy intensive activity now. For India as a whole it is estimated that 10-20 per cent increase in yields following mechanisation costs an additional 43-260 per cent more in energy consumption. Thus, it seems from the community perspective, as farming moved from traditional methods of low external input cultivation to mechanised or partially mechanised high external input agriculture, yield increased, but at once, energy consumption also increased, which for an energy-deficient economy is not good news. The differentials in yield increase and extra energy requirement depends on local conditions and micro-level environments.

High external input agriculture entails a lot more increases in *real costs*. Even where there is no direct monetary outgoing to acquire a resource, there are steep hikes in real cost incurred by the farming household. The most obvious examples are the time and energy spent in procuring seeds and other inputs from local distributors, time expended in fetching diesel for pump sets (in case the pump sets are not electricity operated), chasing the State Electricity Board employees for power, etc. Add to this the loss in terms of crops lost or land left fallow, owing to non-availability or untimely availability of any of the inputs. The waste of time, energy and paper required to obtain credit from formal purveyors of credit is oppressive. And the control over prices and supply of inputs does not rest with the farmers and their community.

This system of costs and prices and markets is also encouraging part-time farming as is apparent from the communities' perspectives. Either farmers are also in employment, trade, business in and around the village, or are emigrants serving in the Military, Police and other employers in Private/ Public sector. In the former case, the farmers treat agriculture as their primary means of livelihood and the "other" employment as their secondary source of income. In the latter case, they impose the burden of farming on their families or they return to the farms during cultivation and harvesting, considering agriculture as their secondary source of income.

The different kinds of chemical fertilisers and to a lesser degree the insecticides/ pesticides applied directly to the fields and insecticides applied to store HYV seeds, means that agricultural inputs have come to include a whole range of chemicals. Since much of it is applied without the necessary technical details being available with the farmers, they disturb the chemical balance of the soil. Their combined impact on the health of soil may be far more severe than what is perceived, because the farmers everywhere complained that the dealers short change them by supplying spurious "medicines". Indeed, the farmers often approach the dealers with the name of the pest or disease and request them for a remedy. There being no extension, they feel obliged to take to their fields whatever the dealers "prescribe" as the remedy. Experts believe that what is worrying is the number of sprayings of pesticides and insecticides that are done to the crops.

Diversity: Whither Poly-Culture?

The cropping pattern and crop diversity have also seen a sea change. In 1950s, a large number of crops were cultivated, though the villagers did not specify on what percentage of arable land each crop was grown. The crops were a mixture of staple, coarse cereals, lentils, pulses, beans of different kinds and condiments and sugarcane (for Jaggery). The main crops were coarse grains and cereals: barley, jowar, bajra, grams, maize and so on. There were wheat and paddy of different varieties. By growing this diverse mosaic of crops, the farmers not only diffused their risk of failure, on account of pests, insects, drought, flood, disease or whatever, but also ensured that their households consumed a basket of food which contained fibre, nutrition and protein: carbohydrates, cereals and pulses.

In 1960s, winds of change had begun to hit the villages. Some of the crops started being looked at with less of interest. In the 1990s, farmers in the villages are left with wheat and mustard, and some vegetables like cauliflower and radish, as principal Rabi crops. During Kharif, paddy constitutes the main crops, with bits of bajra, moong, arhar, dhencha and sesame. Jowar is grown for fodder. In the 1980s, some attempt at promoting "Yellow Revolution" to grow more mustard, was made but the revolution died in its infancy.

A large menu of factors determines the crops chosen for cultivation. Water requirements and water availability, size of the landholdings, experience the farmers have gathered in growing the crop, time required to grow the crop, its labour intensity, cost of cultivation and return and finally the risks involved, all enter the decision making process of the farmers. The principal trade-off is between cost and return on the one hand and risks involved on the other. In case of wheat, the additional factor has been the response of the farmers to price incentives in the form of minimum support price and the procurement price declared by the Government of India. It has to be underscored that the community clearly indicated that considerable amount of the changes in the cropping pattern had been on account of the farmers' response to technological changes, observable principally from mid 1960s onwards.

In one of the villages studied, Uncha Gaon, vegetables grown are grown primarily for sale in the market where there is a demand for vegetable. Vegetable cultivation is a highly water intensive activity and with erratic and insufficient rainfall, much of this agriculture depends on irrigation by drawing ground water. In the absence of any water market and extension service, this has resulted in drawing ground water beyond sustainable limits set by parameters of the agro-climatic zone in which the village is situated. The community indicated that water table has predictably fallen below 85 feet. Food is, therefore, being produced in Uncha Gaon, according to the information provided by the community's perspective, by using natural resources beyond sustainable limits in response to demands of, not the villagers, but those who can pay for it.

What about variety and diversity? In terms of variety and diversity, there is a marked reduction in almost all the villages, to which extent, the capacity of the farmers to diffuse risk is pruned. This fall in diversity of crops signals a movement away from poly-culture towards bi-culture. It signals reduction in palate and nutritional value of the food for the villagers in all the villages. It also indicates that there is a movement from growing crops to meet food requirements of households and of the community, to growing crops for the market's consumption and for money.

This is a copy-book case of destroying diversity for higher productivity. Unfortunately, it was not realised that diverse native varieties are very often high yielding or yield higher crop production than industrially bred varieties. More importantly, killing diversity in farming system is tantamount to killing higher output (as distinct from higher productivity) by moving toward monocultures. Let us take the comparison of yields from native varieties and the high yielding varieties as shown in Tables 10.1 and 10.2. "Green Revolution varieties (meaning HYV) are not higher yielding under conditions of low capital availability and fragile ecosystems. Farmers varieties are not intrinsically low yielding and Green Revolution varieties or industrial varieties are not intrinsically high yielding" (*Shiva, 1998*). If we compare the outputs of the two systems of agriculture, output from the traditional system is much higher. Hark these words:

Table 10.1 Yield in Indigenous Varieties in Garhwal Himalaya

Indigenous Rice Variety	Yield 1992 Grains	Straw	Total	Yield 1993 Grains	Straw	Total
Thapachini	66	94	160	66	92	158
Hansraj	50	80	130	48	75	123
Rikhva	56	64	12	50	66	116
Jhumka	72	104	176	66	90	156
Rekhalya	48	80	128	58	90	168
Ghiyasu	48	80	128	58	90	168
Basmati	50	80	130	42	75	117
Ramjawan	52	64	116	40	50	90

Source: "*Sustaining Diversity: Renewing diversity and balance through conservation*" (New-Delhi: Research Foundation for Science Technology and Ecology) 1994.

Table 10.2 Yield in High Yielding Paddy Varieties in Garhwal Himalaya

Green Revolution Rice Variety	Yield 1992 Grains	Straw	Total	Yield 1993 Grains	Straw	Total
Kasturi	40	56	96	40	54	94
Pant 6	52	40	92	50	40	90
Saket 4	48	36	84	68	64	132
Saket 4	–	–	48	36	84	–
Dwarf	33	36	68	48	40	88

Source: *Sustaining Diversity: Renewing diversity and balance through conservation.* (New-Delhi: Research Foundation for Science Technology and Ecology) 1994.

"A study comparing traditional polycultures with monocultures shows that a polyculture system can produce 100 units of food from 5 units of inputs whereas an industrial system requires 300 units of input to produce the same 100 units. The 295 units of wasted inputs could have provided 5900 units of additional food. Thus, the industrial system leads to a decline of

5900 units of food. This is a recipe for starving people, not feeding them" (*Francesa,* 1994, as quoted in *Shiva,* 1998). Though there is higher productivity from HYV, the output is more in traditional varieties.

In terms of Boserup's classification of agriculture, the villages under study are moving further away from multiple cropping to annual cropping. We have to add here that it is no one's position that a mixture of crops is invariably better than mono/bi-cropping. Much depends upon the local conditions and the characteristics of the crops themselves. However, there is evidence that pest infestation frequently gets reduced in inter-cropping, because of various factors. Host plants for these pests and insects are more widely spread and so the pests and insects find it so much more harder to locate them. One plant species may trap a pest or one specie may repel a pest. There may be plants to which predators may be attracted. Weeds are more likely to be suppressed by mixture of plants/crops

Changes in Agriculture and Food Security.

Households in the villages produced their own food directly and also brought food from the open market. In 1998 and 1999, the period of this study, harvests were normal and yields were not dispersed. There was, therefore, food security ensured mostly by direct entitlements and partially through exchange entitlement. Though earnings out of wages were low in almost all the villages, the villagers complained, not of fluctuations, but irregularity, in that those who offered their services did not always find employment even on a daily wage basis.

The basic diet of the villagers is chappatis and rice eaten with dal. Chilly chutney (paste) was found the more frequent accompaniment of chappatis for the poorer farmers. Vegetables and milk were rarer occupants of their plates and mostly during seasons when they were harvested. The villagers as a part of their daily intake of food did not mention animal protein. In some villages they had meat (goat meat) once a month or so. Poultry and fish were conspicuous by their absence from the villagers' menu of what they eat. Families frequently ate a mixture of water and leafy vegetables (spinach, Sarson da Saag, cabbage, tender pumpkin-creepers and tender bottle-gourd creepers, fenugreek plants, etc.) with chilies and salt. The high fibre diet and malabsorption, as evidenced especially from bouts of diarrhoea that all villagers complained of, probably results in low digestibility, which may be further reduced in summer and rainy season. Assessed against local standards, many families in the villages were eating a diet, which indicated household poverty.

The constraints to agriculture pointed out by the villagers have a large number of insects and pests like caterpillar, locust, termites and other predators. These ravage crops frequently and though the losses in all cases are not large, in value and volume terms, yet these losses had perceptible impact on the diet, which the villagers ate. For instance, pulses when attacked by any of these predators not only robs the villagers of a source of income, it also means that the villagers would consume so much less of pulses (Daal) and hence so much less of protein.

The changes in cropping pattern could have also led to changes in consumption pattern. Since in the days of the ZEIA most of what was produced was for sustenance and subsistence, it is not hard to imagine that the consumption basket had a variety of food stuff. With reduction in the number and kinds of crops grown, there is no way that the same variety and palate would be maintained. The quality of the villagers' staple diet, wheat, had lost some of the good tastes it had in the days of the yore. The villagers were categorical that taste of wheat was still deteriorating.

In all the villages, there is food insecurity. The intensity and duration of hunger varies. Food insecurity is more in Uttar Pradesh than in Haryana. The intensity of food insecurity is higher in Uttar Pradesh, the poorer of the two States. This lends some credence to the widely held theory that the overall growth of the economy is an important component of the composite mechanism for eliminating poverty and hunger.

In some villages in Uttar Pradesh people suffer hunger for long months. For example in Chandpur, villagers silently bear hunger for five months from Baisakh till Bhado. They generally have one meal of chapatis with chilli paste and occasionally some cheap vegetables. It is only (in Kartick) after the first flush of harvests comes, that people's food intake improves. In Tikri people suffer hunger for five months from Jeth to Kuar, when they have a single meal of chappatis and chilli paste. This is particularly damaging because these are the months when people, particularly women, hardest as it is the main cultivation season for Uttar Pradesh. And this is the season when employment outside their farms are hardest to get.

Even in villages where the thrust of agriculture is commercial agriculture and despite these villages being in peri-urban areas, people suffer food insecurity all round the year. And they suffer hunger during the months of Sawan, Bhado and Kuar. In other months their diet lacks nutrition, is deficient in calorie intake and there is no variety.

Since many of these villagers have no secondary source of food, like food from common property resources, micro-environment and forests, any option of reducing their hunger from "hunger foods" is closed. In at least one case, there is direct evidence that contamination of a pond and destruction of mango and guava orchards have robbed the poor of a natural source of nutrition and diet. The pollution of Ganges has added to the misery of Malhas in Tikri, as marine life has been damaged by pollutants in the river, robbing them of a vital source of food and income to access food.

Men in most of the villages studied control the income and expenditure of the household. Because men in the villages control the income generated by the household and expenditure in a "single household accounting system", individuals within the households do not keep and dispose off some or all of the product of their labour. Because women have little access to resources or markets, they have no alternative but to seek and keep the protection of their men through the adoption of attitudes of submissiveness, propriety and self sacrifice.

In the villages women carried out most of the domestic tasks and their activities affected food production—especially marketable milk from the buffaloes and/or cows they keep at home. Milk production and care of livestock are closely bound to the home. Women and girl children made fuel from dung, collected fuelwood and engaged in deweeding fields, processed, prepared and cooked food at home. As a general rule, men do buying and selling at markets, being in a privileged position vis-à-vis women when deciding what and how much to buy, including not infrequently liquor. Men thus exercise basic control over the supply of food to the family through deciding on the crops for cultivation on household land (direct entitlements) and market transactions (exchange entitlements).

The gender division of labour in food production, distribution and processing, influence the nutritional needs of the households. Women in the villages have a long and arduous routine of domestic and household farm work.

From the employment picture painted by the villagers, it is apparent that the opportunities for employment for women are severely constrained. Women's hours of leisure and sleep are so much less. Different activity levels of men and women and compulsions to provision the household with commodities or to reproduce the family, loaded against women do result in lower output capacity and risk of ill health in women.

VIII. Community Perspectives from Tribal Villages

Hunger persists in all the tribal villages.

The nature and intensity of hunger varies from month to month. The situation is worst in the summer and monsoon months. Villagers face a long hunger period from Chaitra to almost Kartick. As in case of the non-tribal villages, in the tribal villages the consumption of food is the lowest in the months when the energy needs are highest due to work-load on account of employment and harsh climate. Food consumed by the villagers lack in nutritional content and are mostly starch. The women face additional work-load of maintaining supply of fuel during the period under reference, when particularly the latter part of the hunger period, fuel availability from "conventional sources" get reduced.

The poor households try to deal with their lives as if they are circumscribed by only the village or villages they visit. There is attempt at migration in some cases but the proclivity to migrate is higher in villages where the secondary food system is weak. This is true of both the villages of West Bengal and Orissa. There is no attempt (or may be better still, "failed attempt") to access food from the public distribution system. There is no attempt to seek any outside help to mitigate their sufferings.

The role of the secondary food system (common property resources, micro-environments and forests etc.) is critical in reducing hunger of the poor, all through the year but more so during the hunger period. Access to CPRs, micro-environments and forests plays critical roles in enabling the hungry villagers to obtain food, diversify income sources and increase the stability of the family livelihood systems. CPRs serve as a source of various kinds of food, the only source of animal protein, fodder, fuel, etc. for household consumption and for sale to supplement income. Thus, the villagers depend heavily on the CPRs for sustaining them.

There are two aspects of the dependency that warrants a few comments. First, the dependence on the CPRs and forests is not constant. It varies from season to season. It gets intensified during the slack season. Two, the availability of food and other resources from the CPRs and forests also varies but the slack season, as it were, for the output from the secondary sources is not co-terminus with the slack season for food availability from the primary food system. This helps the poor villagers to cope with reduction in food supply from the primary food system.

In the food systems of the village, the role of the women remains what they are traditionally required to do. They bear the burden of providing food to the households. They have a more detailed knowledge of food from the primary and the secondary food systems than men. More generally, the women in the tribal community are the principal gatherers, collectors and gleaners of food from the secondary food system.

Collecting food from the secondary food system is time consuming and entails very hard work. Since there is a disparity in the intra-familial distribution of power, the task of collecting produce from the secondary food system falls on the younger women and girl children. Because they spend considerable part of their school-going time in collecting and foraging food from the secondary food system, they miss their schools.

The concept of CPR as an element of the secondary food system itself has been distinctly different for the tribal people of West-Bengal and Orissa. The women of the West Bengal village consider negotiated rights, or their customary right, to collect and glean foodgrains and vegetables from the rich farmers' land, even in neighbouring villages, as part of their CPR. In case of the villages of Orissa, the concept of CPR is the orthodox concept of what is owned communally and more specifically forests of different kinds.

Though the secondary food system robs the young women and the girl children of valuable opportunities to study in the village schools, yet its influence in providing women, girl children and even the aged with a independent source of subsistence cannot be over emphasized. It eliminates the need for a mediated dependency relationship on the able bodied (read younger) male adults. Thus, food from the secondary food system is not merely helping in reducing hunger but also helping in empowering the women and the vulnerable groups in society.

IX. The Force Field Analysis

Looking at the Force Field Analyses of the four villages there are a few implications that are clear. The number of negative forces operating on food security situation, in the villages under reference, exceed the number of the positive forces and that too by a wide margin.

The negative forces affecting food security are unleashed by both men and nature, where natural forces are dominant. The villagers take little cognizance of the role of the state programmes in ensuring food security in their villagers. Neither the Public Distribution System (PDS) for supply of food nor the employment generation programmes to increase the accessibility of food find any mention in the food security mapping.

The nature of the negative and positive forces acting on food security in the villages of Varanasi and Faridabad also varies because the major crops in Faridabad villages studied are vegetables and wheat, whereas the major crops grown by the villages in Varanasi are wheat and some vegetables. And then the major cropping season in Varanasi is Kharif whereas the major cropping season in Faridabad is Rabi.

Of the positive forces that have helped the villagers in all the villages to maintain their fragile food security, employment in the nearby industrial estates and township and sale of milk have played important roles. With the Agreement, which came into force on December 28, 1999, between Government of India and the U.S., that quantitative restrictions on imports from 1429 items will be lifted, these sources of food security will probably vanish. The small and medium enterprises (SMEs) in the Industrial Estates near Tikri and Chandpur will also probably nearly vanish. This will mean a large number of people from Tikri, Chandpur, Uncha Gaon who get employment in the Industrial Areas of Varanasi and Faridabad will be rendered unemployed.

Secondly, the removal of restrictions from imports of milk, cheese, butter, ghee, condensed milk and malted milk, amongst the hundreds of others, will mean that the sale of milk in Faridabad will nose dive. There is no way that the milk produced by the women of Uncha Gaon and Sagarpur will compete with imported milk, which is heavily subsidised. Much of the demand for milk and milk products like ghee and cottage cheese will also go down. Thus, the supplementary income to support food security will be lost in the not too distant future.

Villages like Uncha Goan, which survive on sale of vegetables and villages like Chandpur which partially survive from income from sale of vegetables, will be doubly hit. They will not only not have the same market in nearby industrial townships, if the SMEs close down as we discussed above but they will have to scout around for fresh pastures. Secondly, with quantitative restrictions out from vegetables including on imports of ginger, edible roots and tubers (includes onion), cabbage, cucumber, sweet potato, cauliflower, etc., these small farmers may be called upon to compete with global players in selling their home grown vegetables in India itself.

X. Findings And Conclusions

The fact that we produced an estimated over 200 million tons (or thereabout) of food in 1999/2000 and that the government holds buffer stocks in excess of the warranted level at 32 million tons, may give the illusion of food security at the national level, but many areas of hunger persist. Despite huge strides made in increasing agricultural productivity, despite establishment and successful functioning of the Panchayati Raj system in at least some states, despite a PDS system honed and refined several times, that we are told "works" and despite significant measures taken to provide land to the landless and asset to the assetless, there are large sections of people who suffer hunger in rural and peri-urban areas. That is, ensuring that the country achieves a massive food output, a more than adequate food stocks as buffer, rapid rise in food output at the state levels and at the national level, a functioning democracy at the local level and a PDS are not enough for elimination of hunger. Ravages of food insecurity and pangs of hunger linger in substantial measure at the houschold levels despite there being a mirage of food security at the national and sub-national levels. We have to look for ways and means to achieve sustainable food security at all levels, remembering all the time that food security is best ensured at the household level and that is the best way to secure a hungerless society.

We had seen that for food security and freedom from hunger, several measures are warranted. If we mean business and if we are serious about relieving our people of the pain and indignity of hunger, we have to enhance the general economic growth of the economy, expand employment opportunities for the people and ensure decent rewards for work, diversify our production base, enhance access to medical and health care facilities, arrange for special access to food on the part of vulnerable people (including deprived mothers and small children), spread basic education and literacy, strengthen democracy and the news media and reduce gender based inequalities. If we realistically assess how far have we progressed on these fronts then we will have an idea of how near are we to the goal of a hunger-free India. We take the case of general economic growth first.

General Economic Growth and Expansion

A redeeming feature of the nineties is that the GDP has increased at the rate of 5.8 per cent as opposed to a slightly lower figure of 5.46 per cent in the eighties. But given the stubbornness of the percentage of people below the poverty line, there seems to have been nothing for the poor to cheer about. Consider the following:

After 1993-94, the percentage of people living below the poverty line has remained unchanged as against a sharp decline in poverty with the percentage of people living below the poverty line coming down to a little over 36 per cent in 1993-94, from 56.44 per cent in 1973-74 (*Guruswamy,* 2000). "In India the poverty ratio (i.e., the percentage of people below the poverty line) between 1983 and 1990-91 fell by –3.0 per cent per annum and slowed down to -0.2 per cent per in the 1990s, i.e., almost stagnant between 1990-91 and 1997" (*Gupta,* 1999). This means that the number of poor people has increased during the period 1993-1999 and around 46 million people have joined the ranks of the poor.

Add to this the fact that incidence of poverty has been increasing in the poverty heartland of central and eastern states, notably Assam, Bihar, Orissa and Uttar Pradesh, even during the period when overall percentage of people below the poverty line for the country as a whole was declining. For instance, percentage of people living below the poverty line in Bihar grew from 53.6 per cent to 58.2 per cent between 1987-88 and 1993-94 and the percentage of people living below the poverty line in Assam grew from 39.35 per cent to 45.01 per cent during the same period. The states of Bihar, Madhya Pradesh, Rajasthan and Uttar Pradesh account for 51 per cent of the country's poor (*Press Trust of India,* 2000). And these are the states where hunger is reported as a matter of routine every year and from where migration in thousands, if not in lakhs, take place every year in search of work, food and hope.

During the high growth period of the nineties upto 1997, the employment growth rate was just around 0.6 per cent, in the process lowering the employment elasticity to 0.1 per cent. Employment growth was estimated as negative in 1998 (*Gupta,* 1999). The annual average growth rate of wages of unskilled agricultural male workers in the last decade was a paltry 2.5 per cent in the nineties. When we pitch this against the increase of the Whole Sale Price Index (WPI), the picture becomes murkier. In the period 1991-2000, the WPI rose by about 8.8 per cent annually. Slow growth in wage rates, near stagnant employment opportunities and the relatively sharper rise in prices have all contributed to cutting off economic access of the poor to food. If we see the future projection of population, labour force and availability of employment, it is a trifle more distressing. The Ninth Five Year Plan Document for India projects that labour force between 1997 and 2002 will increase per annum and nearly 2.4 per cent per annum over the next fifteen years. When this is pitched against the employment growth and employment elasticity to GDP growth that we have experienced during the last decade, the decline in economic access to food for the poor will be sharper.

What has happened to literacy?[1]

The literacy rate for rural India as a whole is 54 per cent–66 per cent for males and 40 per cent for females with a gender disparity (F/M ratio) of about 40 per cent (*NCAER,* 1999). The 1991 Census data however revealed a literacy rate of 45 per cent for rural India. This difference is entirely plausible and could be due to the increase in mass education during the first half of the last decade. The gender disparity is also higher in the 1991 Census data and lower in NCAER data, which is also because the gender disparity has come down since the 1991 Census was carried out, though the winning post is still quite far way off.

Of the States under our consideration the picture is like the one shown in Table 10.3.

Table 10.3 Literacy Rates in the States and All India for 7 Years and Above

States	1991* Total	F/M* 1991	Total	Male	Female	F/M
Haryana	49.9	0.50	59.9	69.4	38.1	0.55
Uttar Pradesh	36.76	0.36	46.7	62.0	28.3	0.46
Orissa	45.5	0.52	54.5	67.8	40.7	0.60
West Bengal	50.5	0.61	58.5	66.3	49.9	0.75
Kerala	88.9	0.93	89.6	93.0	86.5	0.93
All India	**44.7**	**0.53**	**53.5**	**65.6**	**40.1**	**0.61**

Source: NCAER, 1999.
* These figures relate to 1991 Census.

Table 10.3 is almost self-explanatory. In case of Uttar Pradesh, all the variables are well below the all India average, indicating that the problems of development generally and of education in particular are very severe. In case of the other states, though most of the variables look somewhat better than the all India figures, yet they are still well below the level of achievement in Kerala. And the levels of achievement of these states on these counts are certainly below the ideal figure of total literacy, which is the national goal, reiterated and repeated without exception in all major and minor policy documents of the government. It is interesting that the states, which have a higher relative per capita State Domestic Product (SDP), are the states, which have a higher literacy levels. The per capita SDP is highest in Haryana, followed by West Bengal, Orissa and Uttar Pradesh. Their literacy levels are also in the same descending order: 54. 9 per cent for Haryana, 58.5 per cent for West Bengal, 54.5 for Orissa followed by 46.7 for Uttar Pradesh.

It has also been found that apart from this general picture, landless wage earners, scheduled tribes and other marginalised groups have very low levels of school enrolment. Enrolment rates are high among the salaried and professionals, and low among wage earners in almost all the states. Thus, since in most of the villages we studied in Uttar Pradesh, West Bengal and Orissa, the villagers are not salaried and professionals, and are landless wage earners, predictably enough their enrolment rates are lower.

If we look at the ever enrolment, discontinuation and non-attendance rates for children (aged 6-14 years) by states, the picture is similar. Reference is invited to Tables 10.4 to 10.6.

Table 10.4 Ever Enrolment Rate

States	Enrolment Rate		Ever Enrolment Rate			
	Total	F/M	Total	Male	Female	F/M
Haryana	75.2	0.73	78.1	83.8	72.3	0.86
Uttar Pradesh	48.5	0.48	64.2	73.2	53.4	0.73
Orissa	47.2	0.72	70.9	78.5	63.4	0.81
West Bengal	54.2	0.77	66.1	87.0	65.1	0.97
Kerala	97.4	0.99	98.6	99.2	98.0	0.99
All India	**57.8**	**0.69**	**71.4**	**77.1**	**64.8**	**0.84**

Source: NCAER 1999

Table 10.5 Discontinuation Rate

States	Enrollment Rate		Discontinuation Rate			
	Total	F/M	Total	Male	Female	F/M
Haryana	75.2	0.73	4.2	3.8	4.6	1.2
Uttar Pradesh	48.5	0.48	4.2	3.3	5.6	1.7
Orissa	47.2	0.72	7.6	6.2	9.3	1.5
West Bengal	54.2	0.77	6.2	5.9	6.5	1.1
Kerala	97.4	0.99	1.7	1.5	2.0	1.32
All India	**57.8**	**0.69**	**6.0**	**4.8**	**7.6**	**1.56**

Source: NCAER 1999

Table 10.6 Non-Attendance Rates

States	Enrolment Rate		Non-Attendance Rates			
	Total	F/M	Total	Male	Female	F/M
Haryana	75.2	0.73	2.3	2.4	2.2	0.88
Uttar Pradesh	48.5	0.48	6.8	6.9	6.6	0.96
Orissa	47.2	0.72	11.7	12.1	11.1	0.91
West Bengal	54.2	0.77	8.9	9.4	8.3	0.88
Kerala	97.4	0.99	3.7	3.9	3.5	0.91
All India	**57.8**	**0.69**	**7.0**	**7.0**	**7.0**	**1.00**

Source: NCAER 1999

If the ever enrolment rates, discontinuation rates and the non-attendance rates are compared, the picture is about the same or similar. The non-attendance rates (total as well as for men and women separately) are higher in West Bengal than in the other three states we have considered. The gender disparity comes out in bold relief by looking at ever enrolment rates and the discontinuation rates. On the whole, this explains why, at least one study has shown that a women have 60 per cent chance of being illiterate (*UNDP,* 1999) and in some parts of the country, as high as 90 per cent of the women are illiterate (*Institute of Social Sciences,* 1994).

Let us now see the micro-picture. We begin with village Tikri in Varanasi (*Mukherjee,* 1999). The village has four Primary Schools and two Middle Schools. It has a branch of a Bank and a Kisan Sewa Kendra is also located in the village. There is also a Post Office. In terms of social overheads, therefore, Tikri is relatively well endowed (See *Shariff,* 1999 for a comparative picture). This does not, however, seem to have any impact on the village: the literacy rate is only 40 per cent though the state average is 47 per cent, 62 per cent for men and 28 per cent for women. And most of the literate people are in the non-poor households, viz., households who are generally not at risk of facing hunger and food insecurity.

Take the case of Chandpur (*Mukherjee,* 1999). The literacy rate in Chandpur, another village in Uttar Pradesh, is 60 per cent for males and 30 per cent for the females. That is, of the total population of 4700, about 55.5 per cent are literate, which is slightly below the national average, though the state average is 47 per cent. The disaggregated litercay rate for the state is 62 per cent for men and 28 per cent for women. This is somewhat surprising given that the village has a primary school, a co-educational school and two Junior High Schools, one for Girls and the other for Boys.

The picture is not any better in Haryana villages. Consider the case of Sagarpur (*Mukherjee,* 1999). It has one high school, one recreation park (under construction), Gram Samiti in each ward to provide loans, a pond for pisciculture and 60 per cent metalled roads, all of which indicate that Sagarpur is well endowed in terms of infrastructure.

The villagers, nevertheless, face a number of problems which were listed and ranked by the women of Baghail hamlet. In this list the problem of alcoholism among men ranks highest, scoring 10 points, followed by female illiteracy and shortage of money, both scoring 8 points. The ranking is reproduced in Table 10.7.

Table 10.7 Problem Ranking by Women of Baghail Hamlet, Sagarpur

Problems	Ranking by Women of Baghail Scoring	Rank
Drinking habit of men	********** 10	1
Illiteracy of women	******** 8	2
Shortage of money	******** 8	2
No hospital in village	****** 6	3
Small landholding	***** 5	4
Insufficient electric supply	**** 4	5

Source: Mukherjee, 1999.
Village Analysts from Hawelliwalle: Rajmati,Bhagwati, Prem and Pyari.
Village Analysts from Baghail: Prem, Shanti, Saroj, Phulwati.
Facilitator: Meera Jaiswal.
Date: 5. 4. 99.

Kadhaoli is a nearby village (*Mukherjee,* 1999). In Kadhaoli, the total population is 3000, with 1550 male and 1450 females, thus giving it a sex ratio of 935 females per 1000 males, which is not very encouraging. The literacy rate is around 40 per cent, which is disappointing, given that the national average is slightly above 53.6 per cent and Haryana's literacy rate is 55 per cent. There is no separate school for girls. In the traditional community of Muslims in Kadhaoli, non-existence of a school for girl children is ranked at par with poverty as a problem by the villagers. While a male child may travel outside the village, a girl child may not do so: her schooling has to be within the perimeter of the village. As a result, the villagers explained, whereas the overall literacy rate was a low 40 per cent for the village, the literacy level was much lower among the girls (*Mukherjee,* 1999).

What is the situation in West-Bengal. We look at the social map of Krishna Rakshi Chak as at Figure 10.1. It is a literacy map of Krishna Rakshit Chak (*Mukherjee,* 1995). Taking adult literacy as an indicator of the spread of basic education, we looked at female literacy. Only 44 per cent of the households have literate females, or if the percentage is calculated on the total female population, out of a total of 59 female adults, only 22 are literate, that is, literacy rate for women is 37 per cent. Of the adult males only 3 are illiterate out of a total of 78 adult males, that is, the literacy rate among men is 96 per cent. The total literacy rate is about 67 per cent. Against the backdrop of total literacy rate of 60 per cent in the country, this *prima facie* looks satisfactory. Such satisfaction, however, has to be sobered by the fact that Midnapore (in which Krishna Rakshit Chak is located) was covered under the Total Literacy Campaign (TLC), where the district is claimed to be 100 per cent literate. A literacy level of 67 per cent in a village of a district declared to be 100 per cent literate and after 45 years of continuous efforts at providing elementary education to all, looks rather disappointing.

If we factor in the cultural factor, that in Bengal, education is highly regarded and sought after things are a little more murky. In Satyajit Ray's famous movie, *Pather Panchali*, when the wife of the poor teacher complains to him that their neighbours have all the creature comforts while their children suffer from hunger and deprivation, the teacher replies, which is symptomatic of a typically Bengali ethos, "after all I am a teacher", meaning that even if "we suffer, I am in an exalted vocation, teaching and not trading". And if we further factor in the political elements of the state, that its citizens are politically conscious which places a high premium on demands for good education, the disappointment is all the more. What is precisely more disturbing is the huge gap between female literacy rate of 37 per cent, which is well below the national literacy rate for women, and the male literacy rate of

96 per cent, which is way above the average literacy rate for men nationally.

It is significant that the female literacy is only 22 out of 57 women in the village, while male literacy is 75 out of 78 men in the village. This mirrors some form of gender bias in imparting and accepting basic education. This is further reinforced by the intra-familial distribution of power. We mentioned in Chapter 7 earlier that the arduous task of accessing food from the secondary food system falls on the younger women and girls in the family, which prevents them from attending schools. This is more so during the hunger months when they work harder as accessing food flowing from the secondary food system becomes dearer and difficult. Because accessing food from the secondary food system is the responsibility of the women and the girls, they have either no time to attend school or have such low energy levels that reading is not possible.

Thus, one of the essential elements, viz., access to primary education, for making the country free from hunger remains a pipe dream. Even if we compare the 1991 Census figures of literacy and enrolment (columns 2 and 3 of Tables 10.3 and 10.4) with the NCAER figures in columns 4, 5 and 6 of the same tables, there is little cause for cheer. Because though there have been some improvements due to the emphasis that education has received from the Government in the form of the Total Literacy Mission, from the Non-governmental Organisations and from other development actors during the nineties, there is much that needs to be done.

What is the Health Situation?

This brings us to the health situation.

Short duration morbidity prevalence measured by diarrhoea, cough and cold and fever, for all India works out to be 122 per thousand population and females have a slightly higher morbidity and gender disparity at the all India level is 1.08. Like in case of literacy, clearly the health of the people in these states viz., Haryana, Uttar Pradesh, Orissa and West-Bengal, is far worse than the standard set by Kerala and is below the international standards.

Table 10.8 Short Duration Morbidity Prevalence Rates (SDMPR)

States		SDMPR per thousand Population			
		Diarrhoea	Cold/ Cough	Fever	Total
Haryana	Persons	29	48	84	153
	Gender Disparity				1.20
Uttar Pradesh	Persons	51	26	97	132
	Gender Disparity				1.02
Orissa	Persons	54	85	22	143
	Gender Disparity				0.93
West Bengal	Persons	45	114	11	164
	Gender Disparity				1.08
Kerala	Persons	6	75	8	89
	Gender Disparity				0.99
All India	**Persons**	**31**	**72**	**25**	**122**
	Gender Disparity	**0.92**	**1.08**	**1.17**	**1.08**

Source: NCAER 1999.

Table 10.9 Major Morbidity Rates

States	Major Morbidity per Lakh of Population							
	Epi-lepsy	Hyper-ten-sion	Di-abe-tes	Heart Dis-ease	Mental Dis-ease	TB	Lep-rosy	Major Mor-bidity
Haryana	103	372	100	230	143	322	—	6697
Uttar Pradesh	120	221	158	231	120	370	27	3523
Orissa	369	863	116	245	99	206	31	5011
West Bengal	133	1049	207	795	151	636	22	6168
Kerala	81	1433	980	914	283	504	—	7319
All India Total	**120**	**589**	**221**	**385**	**132**	**423**	**57**	**4578**
All India Gender Disparity	**0.71**	**1.31**	**0.65**	**0.86**	**0.75**	**0.59**	**1.64**	**1.00**

Source: NCAER 1999.

The major morbidity rates shown in Table 10.8 may not be any indication of the access to health care facilities but what they do signify is that the morbidity of these people could be traced to early childhood undernourishment and/or undernourishment of their mothers during pregnancy. Thus except for Uttar Pradesh all these states have a health chart which is worse than the all India picture. The case of Kerala, which we use as a bench mark, does not work in this case because of the high degree of hyper tension and mental disease that distorts the picture. The higher degrees of hyper-tension and greater prevalence of mental diseases may be seen as manifesting themselves in the high rates of suicides that marks the psychological map of the state.

The demographic parameters and reproductive health care in general in these states do not inspire much confidence either. For rural India as a whole the crude birth rate (CBR) is 32 live births per thousand population, which is high particularly when judged against the backdrop of the extremely high base of nearly 1000 million people over which this occurs. Though the CBR varies considerably among states, yet failure to contain a high fertility rate is too glaring not to be any cause for discomfort. Though the CBR is easy to calculate yet it has its drawback in that it cannot depict the fertility patterns associated with the age of women. A better measure is the total fertility rates (TFRs). The TFR for the country as a whole was 4.3 but again as in case of CBR, there are inter-state variations in TFRs. Table 10.10 will give a partial picture of fertility rates in the states under reference.

Table 10.10 Fertility Rates by States

States	Crude Birth Rates			Total Fertility Rates		
	HDI (1994)	NFHS* (90-91)	SRS** (91-92)	HDI (1994)	NFHS* (90-92)	EMW 40-9 All
Haryana	30	35	33	4.2	4.3	4.7
Uttar Pradesh	38	38	36	5.9	5.2	5.1
Orissa	29	27	29	3.7	3.0	4.2
West Bengal	34	28	27	4.3	3.3	5.5
Kerala	21	20	18	2.2	2.1	3.8
All India	**32**	**30**	**30**	**4.3**	**3.7**	**4.6**

Notes: * National Family Survey, *India Report 1992-93*, IIPS, Bombay.1995.
** Registrar General, Sample Registration System, 1991-92.
EMW is Ever Married Women.

Source: NCAER 1999

When one uses the different measurements to judge the high fertility problem, the fertility rates differ both between the measures and between the States of Haryana, Uttar Pradesh, Orissa and West-Bengal. The different stages in demographic transition through which these states are passing become apparent. What is relevant, however, for the purposes of our discussion is that the fertility rates are still very high and for the states we are concerned with, viz., Haryana, Uttar Pradesh, Orissa and West Bengal the fertility rates, whichever measure one chooses, are way above what is desirable and certainly achievable as demonstrated by the figures of Kerala. Though we do not foresee any reason to press the panic button warranted by a Malthusian type crisis (*Sen,* 1994), yet a high growth rate in population does not auger well for the country. The fertility figures indicate that the use of and access to family planning facilities are limited. This fits in well with the earlier data that literacy levels are low in these states, particularly for women, because it has been established convincingly by a long list of experts that where female literacy is low, access to family planning measures is low and fertility rates high.

That family planning facilities are either not accessed or that the eligible groups are not aware of these facilities are demonstrated by the fact that the contraceptive prevalence rates (percentage) for ever married women in all the states under reference show that only 36 per cent of eligible women reported having some methods of contraception. This when coupled with the fact that about 10 per cent of those reported to be pregnant had received ante natal care (ANC) on an all India basis does not give us cause for cheers either. True, there are inter-state variations but the scenario is nowhere comfortable barring Kerala. Even in West Bengal the percentage of those reported to be pregnant having received ante-natal care (ANC) does not go beyond 18 per cent. The link between receiving ANC and literacy is as established as the positive correlation between accessing family planning services and female literacy. This has been again reconfirmed by the NCAER survey where adult literacy groups and more specifically the female literacy groups and groups where both partners were literate, had more expectant mothers who had received ANC than mothers from other groups had.

Significantly enough for rural India, only 40 per cent of total births are attended by trained dais/birth-attendants. These percentages vary again across States. For instance in Orissa, only 20 per cent of total deliveries are attended

Table 10.11 Health Calendar of Patel Basti, Chandpur

Diseases	Less than 10 years old	10-25 years old	Above 25 years	Mon-ths	Since When	Treatment: What and where?	Notes and causes
Cough	60 per cent	20 per cent	15 per cent	Sept to Dec	Since more than 10 years	Private doctor out of the village	Due to change in climate and from smoke/smog from G.T. Road
T.B.	—	—	2 persons	—	10-12 years	Outside the village	Negligence and alcoholism
Eye problem, weak eyesight and watery eyes	8 persons	—	5	—	5-6 years	Private doctor in the village	Smoke and from malnutrition
Swelling of stomach	75 per cent	—	—	—	12 years	No treatment	Eating of soil
Diarrhoea and vomiting	50 per cent	5 per cent	2-3 per cent	Summer	8-9 years	Private doctor in the village	Heat and unhygenic food

Stomach Ache	—	—	50 per cent men and 80 per cent women	Through-out the year but more during summer	5-6 years	Private doctor in the Village	Unhygenic food
Appendicitis	—	—	4 persons	—	2-3 years	Private doctor at Varanasi	Negligence in food habits
Skin Disease	1	1	1	—	5-6 years	Private doctor in the village	Hereditary and traditional medicines
Malaria	50 per cent	25 per cent	25 per cent	July to Sept	8-10 years	Private doctor in the village	Cause by garbage and mosquito breeding in the village
Pneumonia	75 per cent of children below 5 years age	10 per cent	—	Sept to Feb	15-20 years	Private doctor in the village	During winter and during change of season

Source: Mukherjee, 1999.
Village Analysts: Reeta Devi, Rampati Devi, Sabitri and Gulabi.
Facilitator: Ms. Meera Jayaswal.
Date: 17.11.98.

to by trained dais/birth-attendants. In West Bengal and Uttar Pradesh only one fifth of total deliveries are attended to by trained dais/birth-attendants. Maternal health care is nothing to write home about in these states. This is at least one reason why on the whole it is estimated that 570 deaths occur per 1000 live births among Indian mothers *(UNDP,* 1999).

Let us now compare this with the micro-situation obtaining in some of the villages (*Mukherjee,* 1999). We take village Chandpur in Uttar Pradesh. In Chandpur, increase in the incidence of malaria is a notable development in its health status (50 persons affected during 1998 June/July) due to breeding of mosquitoes in stagnant water without proper drainage facilities. For the women group said that pneumonia had become endemic for the last 7 to 8 years and at least 100 children were affected last year, of which 10 children died. Health problems of villagers caused by jaundice, gastritis (on the rise over the last 7 to 10 years supposedly due to contaminated food), frequent body ache and mild fever in elderly people, cough, cold, asthma (25 per cent of adult and almost every old men and women suffer in silence for they think that the disease is incurable and medicines provide temporary relief), have been clearly articulated. Amongst the diseases affecting children (taking 20-25 days for recovery and an expenditure of Rs. 6000 to Rs. 7000), increase in incidence of pimples all over body caused by mosquito bites (50 per cent of children were suffering at the time of field research), ear disease with pimple in the ear and pus flowing, and nagging cold and cough, have been widely reported.

The state of health of the villagers can be best assessed through the Health Calendar prepared by the villagers as at Table 10.11.

There are differences in perceptions of men and women about diseases. Diseases, which prevent men from working outside their homes, have been rated as causing the greatest distress, by Men's group. Diseases which render children sick are rated as most distressing by women, because they are the ones who look after the children, whether ill or healthy, at home.

This Health Calendar of Chandpur, Patel Basti, is striking in two respects. *One*, majority of the diseases afflict children and this was explained by the villagers as being caused by pollution owing to the major highway in the form of Grand Trunk Road, along which the village and its school are situated. *Second*, the villagers suffer from a larger number of diseases now than say 5 years ago or so. For example, asthma, skin diseases, stomach-ache, ear and eye problems have afflicted the community since last 5-6 years. The community associated some of these diseases, particularly those afflicting the children as being caused by pollution created by heavy vehicular traffic on the Grand Trunk Road.

In dealing with their health problems villagers seek the help of private practitioners both in the village and outside the village, including in Varanasi. There is no effort on the part of the community to avail of the services of government healthcare facilities. The infrastructure available in the village does include a government healthcare outlet but the community apparently does not access the available health facility as it does not inspire confidence. This also explains that the villagers spend about 15 per cent of their income on health, which is equal to 50 per cent of what they spend on their food, which for a poor community is an exceptionally high percentage of expenditure. There is no mention of any preventive and promotive health care being accessed. Thus, the coping mechanism of the villagers with their problems of health is dependent upon their own resources and efforts and lies in the realm of curative health only.

Let us now turn to compare the state of health of Chandpur to that of a Haryana village. Let Sagarpur be the chosen village (*Mukherjee,* 1999). The village has several parts. We begin with looking at the portion of the village which is most exposed to health hazard, viz., the Ita Bhatta Colony. The women of Ita Bhatta drew up a graded scoring of different health problems faced by the inhabitants of their colony. Refer to Table 10.12.The ranking of health problems in other parts of the village are in Tables 10.13 and 10.14.

Table 10.12 Graded Scoring of Health Problems in Ita Bhatta Colony, Village Sagarpur (by Women's Group)

Health Problems	Scoring	Rank
Cough	**** 4	3
Fever and headache	****** 6	2
Weakness	** 2	5
White discharge	**** 4	3
Breathing problem	******** 8	1
Tuberculosis	*** 3	4

Source: *Mukherjee*, 1999.
Village Analysts: Prem, Saroj, Shanti, Pappi, Nirmala, Sunita, Sita and Rewati.
Facilitator: Ms. Meera Jaiswal.

The range of diseases suffer varies from serious to common ailments. But the women rank breathing problem as the most serious problem. Fever and headache are ranked second, followed by cough. The women take great pains to explain that they come to live in the colony for 9 months, from October to July, that is, from the end of the rainy season till the beginning of the next rainy season, which is when their health problems get aggravated.

The health problems in the other parts of the village are similar but more extensive. The health analysis and ranking of health problems in Tables 10.13 and 10.14 give quick review of health status in Sagarpur.

TB, appendicitis and heart palpitation are at the bottom of the scale. cholera and diarrhoea are ranked last but one in this ranking, whereas "cough, cold and najla" are the top scorers. The villagers explain that they rank those health problems as being gravest, which have visible external symptoms, which spare none and which interfere with the agricultural operations most; not their killing potential. Thus cough, cold and najla rank high. Malaria also does not discriminate between men or women or children, and hits them right in the midst of the cultivating season. TB, asthma and cholera are less restrictive in their impact on the immediate capability of the farmers to carry out their duties in the fields and hence are placed at the lower end of the ranking.

Table 10.13 Ranking of Diseases by Villagers, Hawelliwalle Muhalla, Sagarpur

Problems/Diseases	No. of Rajma Placed	Rank
Cough, cold and najla	**********	1
Malaria	******	2
Gastritis	***	3
Cholera, diarrhoea, vomiting	***	3
Asthma	***	3
Gallstone	***	3
Heart Palpitation	**	4
Appendicitis	**	4
Tuberculosis	**	4

Source: *Mukherjee*, 1999.
Village Analysts: Prandei, Bhagawati, Mukesh, Prem.
Facilitator: Ms. Meera Jaiswal

Table 10.14 Health Analysis, Hawelliwalle Muhalla, Sagarpur

Health Problem	Annual Incidence	Trend	Expenses Incurred in Treatment	Perceived Causes	Treatment
Malaria	Men and children	Increasing	Minimum Rs. 100	Mosquito bites	Treatment in Balabhgarh
appendicitis	Men and women	Not known	Rs. 15000	Not known	Surgery in Faridabad
cough, cold and najla	women and children and men	Increasing 10 years ago few were affected	Minimum Rs. 100 per occasion	Excessive heat and cold	Medical help sought if condition is acute
Gallstone	Women	Increasing	Rs. 5000	Over use of spinach, tea etc.	Surgery in Ballabgarh
Heart palpitation	Women	Increasing. 20 years ago there was no incidence	—	Tension	—
Gastritis	More men and some women	Increasing	At least Rs. 3000	By birth control measures for women	Private doctor
Tuberculosis	More men than in women	Same as before	At least Rs. 3000	Cough	Private doctor
Cholera, vomiting and diarrhoea	Children and women	Increasing since last ten years	Minimum Rs. 2000	—	Treatment in extreme cases only
asthma	More men and few women	Increasing	Minimum Rs. 1000		Treatment with private doctor

Source: *Mukherjee*, 1999.
Village Analysts: Pruned, Bhagawati, Mukesh, Prem.
Facilitator: Ms. Meera Jaiswal

Fourth column read with sixth column of Table 10.14 is most revealing. The poor villagers in almost all cases seek medical advice and treatment from private practitioners. They do not avail of the medical facilities provided by the Government. And the incidence of these diseases is on the rise, suggesting that the preventive and promotive health care system in the village is either weak or non-existent.

Health is a matter of concern in Uncha Gaon also like in Sagarpur. These issues were explored at the participatory sessions. The Women's Group of Ahir Muhalla catalogued 9 health problems of the village and ranked them as well. The scoring and ranking is shown in Table 10.15.

Table 10.15 Graded Scoring of Health Problems in Ahir Muhalla (by Women's Group), Uncha Gaon

Health Problems	Scoring	Rank	Treatment	Expenditure (in Rs.)
Malaria	******** 8	1	Only in severe cases	400-500
Gastritis	********8	1	No	—
Headache	********8	1	No	—
Diarrhoea	********8	1	Only in severe cases	400-500
Najla	******6	2	Only in severe cases	200-300
Dengu	******6	2	Yes	400-500
Bai	*****5	3	No	—
Stomachache	****4	4	No	—
White discharge	****4	4	No	—

Source: *Mukherjee*, 1999.
Village Analysts: Kela, Vidya, Bhagwati.
Facilitator: Ms. Meera Jayaswal.
Date: 10.4.99.

Malaria, gastritis, headache and diarrhoea are ranked 1 and are perceived as causing the severest problems. Najla and dengu are placed at number two, followed by *Bai*. The least problematic are stomachache and white discharge. It is also apparent that the villagers seek the advice of private practitioners, which is why their outgoing on treatment of ailments is so high. They do not apparently use the health service outlets provided by the state in terms of the Public Health Centre (PHC), Maternity and Child Health Centre (MCH) and Referral Hospitals.

The state of health in West Bengal as seen in Krishna Rakshit Chak is equally distressing. The Health Map of Krishna Rakshit Chak in Figure 10.2 (*Mukherjee,* 1995, reprinted 1997), identifies diseases like polio, tuberculosis, leprosy, asthma and piles as the preponderant ones. Details in matters of family planning with households actually practising/adopted family planning, number of pregnant women in the community, lactating mothers and households with cases of miscarriage are clearly marked. Old age as an aspect of health, often neglected in general health descriptions, has been noted and households with aged people are explicitly mentioned.

Family planning is practised in 22 households, which is 44 per cent of the total households living in the village. If one were to look at the social structure, it is obvious that a little less than 50 per cent of those identified as 'poorest of the poor' are left out of the family planning net.

The leprosy cases affect almost 25 per cent of the 'poorest of the poor'. This seems to be in line with the all-India picture where the incidence of leprosy is 200 per cent higher in less developed villages than in the developed ones (*Philipose,* 1999). The incidence of tuberculosis, asthma and old-age all afflict the 'poorest of the poor' households.There is a recent study which shows that the incidence of tuberculosis is 32 per cent higher in poorer villages than in the better-off ones (*NCAER,* 1999). This in not surprising, given that the 'poorest of the poor' for one have lower capacity to buy health care services, and for the other, they are more under-nourished than the rest of the community, making them more vulnerable to diseases.

The Well Being Map at Figure 10.3 of Krishna Rakshit Chak (*Mukherjee,* 1995, reprinted, 1997), to no one's surprise indicates the existence of temples, drinking water wells, primary school and even school hostel for the tribal children, but makes no mention of any health facility, not even a Maternity and Child Health Sub-Centre. [The Health infrastructure is organised in several tiers. The District has a referral hospital. A Block, a development unit at the sub-district level with a population of approximately

1,00,000 to 1,50,000, has a Public Health Centre (PHC) and in some cases a second unit called Additional PHC. MCH sub centres at the sub-block level is to serve a population of 5000 people].

Apart from the problems of carrying the sick and the old over long distances, the social stigma and ostracisation that follows on detection of diseases like leprosy and tuberculosis makes it even more difficult for them to access basic health care facilities, even if distance is not a constraining factor. If we add to the general standard of health, the element of malnutrition, reflected by the food calendars disscused in Chapter-7, the status of health in Krishna Rakshit Chak has no reason to be happy.

What is the State of Gender Disparity?

While we would discuss separately the issue of gender discrimination, the discussion on education and health gives us enough hint that we have a long way to go in removing gender disparity. The disparity in literacy levels and limited access to and knowledge of ANC and other reproductive health care facilities, do indicate that gender disparity may be decreasing in form but in substance it is seemingly frozen in time. Small wonder, women are hesitant to receive medical advice during pregnancy, contributing to risks of death at childbirth. It is estimated that 437 women die at childbirth for every 1,00,000 births (*HDC,* 1999). The discrimination against women starts almost since her conception in her mother's womb evidenced by 5 million women seeking abortions each year to avoid giving birth to a girl child.

Women generally consume about 1000 calories less of food than the men in the household do, which is embodied in the very process by which cooked and uncooked food are distributed in the family: *the women eat last, least and leftovers*. As a result, the women from the rural households seldom reach their full growth potential and they generally stand the chance of being anemic in 50-70 per cent of the cases while an estimated 80 per cent of pregnant women are anemic.

In terms of work, everywhere the wages paid to women are lower than the wages paid to their male counterparts. Most of the work that women are required to do in the agricultural sector is during that time of the day when it is harshest and most of the tasks entrusted to their care are based on human energy without the use of implements. These are also the reason why women's work is considered unskilled and less productive (*Venkateshwaran,* 1995) and hence paid less.

Women, in addition to their work in the fields, maintain kitchen gardens and poultry, dehusk and grind foodgrains, collect water, fuel and fodder, cook food (more often than not in Biomass Ovens which is a health hazard) and tends animals at home. Cleaning and caring for the children are also her responsibility.

The cases of spousal battery are not uncommon and dowry deaths are known to have reached the staggering figure of 6000 per annum. In some villages women face a 75 per cent chance of being assaulted by their husbands (*United Nations,* 1995). There are progressive legislation for women but patriarchal traditions persist and many women do not know their rights. They continue to be subservient to their husbands, parents and sons. This is abundantly demonstrated, not only by the distribution of work, but also by the processes established for the appropriation of wealth, created by the households. In almost all the villages in Haryana and Uttar Pradesh studied, while the crops and vegetables grown and milk produced are through the conjoint efforts of all members of the households, the responsibility of taking the producce to the Mandis, Markets or Hats, for sale, rests with the male adults in the households. Thus, control over sale proceeds rests primarily with the adult males. In some cases the adult males also utilise the sale proceeds of the produce of the household, in a way strongly disapproved by other members, especially the women of the households. The case of expending household income on alcoholism is a case in point.

The foregoing is backed by the micro-evidence. We begin by Krishna Rakshit Chak. Let us consider the gender issue from three objective criteria. One, access to health; two, the state of elementary education, and three, discrimination in access to food.

Last thing first: discrimination in accessing food. We have mentioned that there is asymmetry in access to food. While men and the male children are better fed, the women and the girls eat less and poorer food. It is sad that in the history of Bengal this phenomenon has persisted for decades. Despite all the empowerment and politicization of local level governance, including reservation of seats in local level elected institutions (Panchayats), things have not changed dramatically for the better. Even those parts of Bengal which have gone through several "rounds of fire", show significantly same behaviour.

The discrimination in terms of education is brought forth both by the lower female literacy rates and the time that the women spend to access food by re-appropriating their time for school to collect and gather food from the common property resources and micro-environments and indeed process such food as well, both of which we have discussed earlier. There are other causal factors, including the social belief that girls would be married off to other households and that they do not require education for, after all they will be, in the last analysis, only managing the kitchen and the children at home.

With regard to health, there is nothing apparent in the health map of Krishna Rakshit Chak indicating discrimination in accessing health facilities. But that the women additionally suffer from mental diseases, places them on a worse health plane than their men counterparts. There is enormous pressure on the women who cannot get married for want of dowry. The paying capacity of the poor households, who cannot afford two square meals a day and the much needed primary health care, is unable to sustain the demands of paying handsome dowry to buy the eligible girls their husbands. The result is that those who remain spinster and those households, which have spinsters, are subjected to social and familial pressures, bordering on torture. Until the middle of the last century, it was not uncommon to find married women living with their parents to be occassionally visited by their husbands. It also is a matter of public history that a social norm prevailed in some parts of rural Bengal that enjoined on a family, which failed to have its girl(s) married off to men, to have the girl children married to even a Banyan Tree. Women have to be married. This demonstrates a very strong bias against unmarried women and may have been one of the sociological reasons for which very young girl, often minors, were earlier married off to old men (not infrequently with several wives).

This limited utilisation of family planning methods can have serious implication. As we noted earlier, "if the general impact of the higher population growth is curtailment of the well being and freedom of women and men in society, then there are real problems to consider,"*(Sen,* 1994) particularly in relation to hunger.

What Happened to Our Measures to Provide Special Access to Food to Vulnerable People?

The Government is aware that for food security, measures to provide special access to food for vulnerable people must be provided. The Government has made two interventions in this regard: One, the Public Distribution System (PDS) and two, the system of price incentives to farmers to grow more food and sell them for feeding into the PDS.

The PDS was started in early 1960s and entails supplying to the vulnerable sections of society essential commodities at subsidized prices. The PDS in India has a network of over 4,00,000 fair price shops (PFS) serving about 160 million families and is probably the largest such distribution system in the world. Many commentators, including Sen, maintain that India could avoid large scale famines and save millions of lives because of the PDS, something that other countries, which did not have such a system, failed to prevent *(Sen,* 1998).

In the macro-micro terminology, the PDS in India is intended to translate the so–called macro level self-sufficiency in foodgrains to micro level food security by ensuring access to food and other essential commodities to poor families. The PDS is also a way of transferring resources to the poor and providing the economically weaker sections of society with a minimum level of consumption to avoid a decline in the impairment of human capital.

The PDS was refined in 1992, called the Revamped Public Distribution System (RPDS). The RPDS was started that year in areas where the poor are concentrated, covering 1775 blocks falling under the ITDP, DPAP, DHA and DDP areas. For the RPDS, food grains were released at a price lower than the price at which food grains are released by the Government of India to the State Governments for the normal PDS. The price differential is Re. 1 per kilogram of food grains released. The RPDS was targeted at all people in the poor areas irrespective of economic status.

The issue of further streamlining the PDS was put on the agendas of both the Conference of Chief Ministers in July 1996 and of State Food Ministers in August 1996. On the basis of these discussions, the target of the PDS was changed to "poor in all areas" from "all in poor areas". The new target of the PDS was reworked at the population below the poverty line in all areas. This Targeted Public Distribution System (TPDS) was implemented in all practically all the states (baring Punjab) and Union Territories (barring Delhi, Goa and Lakshadweep).

In the Union Budget for 2000-2001, there has been substantial modifications in the scheme in terms of both the amount of food that will be available and the price at which they will be available. The amount of food available from the PDS has been increased from 10 kg to 20 kg for below poverty-line households. And the price which will be charged for the same has been increased from Rs. 2.50 to Rs. 4.20 per kg of wheat, from Rs. 3.50 to Rs. 5.85 per kg of rice and from Rs. 12 to Rs.13 per kg for sugar. The Budget also determined the amount of food that will be made available to above poverty-line households. And the prices at which such food will be made available have been fixed at Rs. 8.40 per kg for wheat, up from Rs. 6.82 kg Rs. 11.70 per kg for rice, up from Rs. 9.05. The price to be charged from people, above the poverty line, was fixed at the economic costs of food which the Government bears.

To back the PDS etc. the Government procures foodgrains, notably rice and wheat, and has built up a large stock of food grains. This procurement of rice and wheat is backed by the price policy of a procurement price and a minimum support price about which references were made in Chapters 4, 5 and 6, earlier. The prices are designed to promote farming and encourage surplus farmers to continue to grow more food in response to price incentives. For good or bad the minimum support price declared by the Government for 2000 has pitched the domestic price of foodgrains (wheat and rice) above the rate at which such foodgrains are available in the international market.

The PDS has, however, been widely criticised for its failure to reach the poor effectively, for its urban bias and lack of transparency and accountability. Although the PDS is a centrally sponsored programme, its implementation is dependent on the state governments. In states with appropriate political and administrative will and infrastructural facilities, the public distribution system has worked; in most it has floundered. Due to poor targeting the system is being used (misused) by all irrespective of the standard of living. Excepting for sugar and standard cloth, there is virtually no variation in the utilisation of items supplied according to levels of living. The objective of resources transfer has not been achieved.

The leakage from the system and other wastes associated with PDS is proverbial. The inefficiency of the entire bureaucracy of food is questioned, and very responsible and influential government functionaries were seriously debating the utility of the PDS on the plea that the state spends Rs. 5, in order to transfer Re. 1 to the poor, through the PDS. A not insignificant number of observers believe that the PDS has served the interest of the big farmers only procuring solely wheat and rice. Consequently, no attempt has been made to extend the coverage to PDS to other crops and coarse cereals like jowar and bajra and the required back up R&D has not come about in these crops except at the margin.

The Finance Minister of India was busy defending Central Government's decision to cut food subsidy bill (*Kumar,* 2000) by Rs. 1000 crore and therefore, raising the price of food distributed through the Public Distribution System by significant amounts:

The PDS is a supply side measure. Even its function as a welfare measure seems to be in doubt. Consider the following.

In Table 10.16 we have rankings of some Indian States with respect to per capita distribution of food grains through the PDS and proportion of people living below the poverty line. The Table includes all the States other than the seven States of the North East for want of comparable data. The data pertains to 1986-87 and 1987-88 as estimated by Sikha Jha and Planning Commission respectively, and quoted in Mooji (1999). It will be seen that the poorer the State, lower is the off-take from PDS. A Spearman Rank Correlation Coefficient was computed and found to be 0.04 when all the 14 states mentioned in the Table are taken into account (*Balkrishna,*

Box 10.1

Poverty Programmes Bypassing the Poor

The Public Distribution System (PDS) in India, which provided essential food supplies at below market prices to Indian consumers, has problems reaching the poorest Indians. 0-60 per cent of the beneficiaries of PDS have been estimated to be non-poor. PDS network remains limited to poorer states. Poor states like Bihar, Madhya Pradesh and Uttar Pradesh have received far less food supplies than less poorer states like Kerala and Andhra Pradesh.

Only about 40 per cent of the total wheat supply reaches the poorest 40 per cent of the Indian people. The lower monthly purchases from PDS came from the very poor in India. Thus, the actual income benefits of these subsidies remain limited for the poor: less than 22 paisa for every rupee.

In rural areas, PDS serves to raise individual incomes only modestly, amounting to 2.7 per cent of their per capita expenditure. In North and Central India, where poverty is massive, PDS provides subsidies equal to an income of only Rs. 2.5 per person per month. Thus, with a few exceptions, the coverage of PDS remains uneven—with a large number of poor being left out.

Human Development in South Asia 1999, Oxford University Press and HDC, Islamabad, 1999.

1999a). But the near perfect positive rank correlation in cases of Punjab and Haryana between rank in PDS off-take and rank in proportion of people below the poverty line, could have introduced some bias in the calculation. Hence to account for the bias, these two states were excluded from the sample and Rank Correlation was recomputed for the remaining 12 states. The rank correlation coefficient now turned out to be -0.52. This is significant. The negative correlation coefficient shows that the PDS is more than halfway towards being away from where it is most needed. The poor and the vulnerable groups do not get the benefit of the PDS run at a huge cost to the exchequer, which in 2000-2001 will be at staggering Rs. 7457 crore, despite the increase in the prices to be charged from the consumers.

Table 10.16 Statewise Ranking of PDS and Poverty

State	Rank in PDS off-take	Rank in proportion of people below poverty line
Andhra Pradesh	5	12
Bihar	11	2
Gujarat	4	10
Haryana	12	13
Karnataka	7	8
Kerala	1	11
Madhya Pradesh	9	5
Maharastra	6	7
Orissa	10	1
Punjab	13	14
Rajasthan	8	9
Tamilnadu	3	3
Uttar Pradesh	14	6
West Bengal	2	4

Source: *Balkrishna*, 1999.

This also brings home the point that not only should food be available but that food so available should be economically and physically accessible to the people. We mentioned at the beginning of this chapter that the number of people below the poverty line has increased in the states of Bihar, Uttar Pradesh, Rajasthan, Orissa and Madhya Pradesh. As poverty has increased and people have become poorer, they have been economically cut off from accessing food from the PDS. And hence they are not buying food from the PDS.

XI. Divergence in Farmers Perspectives and Policy Conclusions

In sum then many of the essential elements of a scheme that makes a nation free from hunger and ensures food security at the household levels are missing. There have been giant strides made in each of these areas and spectacular achievements seen in matters of food production. But the lurking danger of hunger visiting us is always there and the apparent complacency displayed by the powers in tackling the latent danger has forced the nation to pay very dearly. The false sense of comfort that we are self sufficient in foodgrains has complicated an already difficult situation.

If we look at the perspective of the villagers, then for them the factors that have contributed to persistent hunger are different, though some of the strands of policy emanating from the views of the "outsiders" are significantly visible. For instance, the problem of accessing health care facilities, reflected in the ultimate analysis, in higher population growth and sufferance from a catalogue of diseases, has been adequately registered by the community. So have they brought forth the importance of providing basic education be it for making a representation to the powers that be for redressal of their grievances, or for reading what all is written on the labels of "medicines" supplied by the dealers to deal with pests, insects and weeds.

But they have a longer and a more complex story to tell. Its understanding requires deep empathy and a capacity and patience to listen to their muted voices.

In the non-tribal areas the absence of extension services, spurious pesticides and fertilisers have been negative factors operating on their state of hunger and food security. In their perception in the absence of any extension service, they have to rely on their own gut feeling or on their per chance experimentation results or on hearsay about the efficacy of agricultural practices from other farmers who have been through similar experience. They make choices but they are not informed choices. They, most of the time, whistle in the dark. When they realise that they are unable to cope withi the situation on the strength of their gut feeling or limited experience, they seek the assistance of apparently the most knowledgeable person around, the pesticide dealer. This leads them down the garden path of irrational application of pesticides, often repeatedly, not only leading to huge increases in cultivation costs but also to damage to crops and health of the soil.

Uncertainty of rains has been a constant refrain from the farmers in all the villages studied: droughts, excess rains, uneven distribution of rain and untimely (unseasonal seasonal would have been a better word) rain damage their food production and hence food availability. The remedy given to them has been, in one sense, worse than the cure. They were all lured into lift irrigation through electric pump sets. For one, the uncertainty and shortage of power supply, (nothwithstanding that it is free of charge) from the respective State Electricity Board, often disables them from irrigating their land when they are needed most. For the other, the sinking of the pump sets has resulted in withdrawal of ground water far beyond the sustainable limits, evidenced by falling water table and salination of land due to excess of water discharge. The current generation of farmers is, in effect, living on the resources that rightfully belongs to the future generations. The cumulative effect is that in the long run these households will run into even greater food insecurity and hunger.

A singular lack of the entire gamut of agrarian reforms, impinging upon the current state of hunger and food security in the villages, is perceived as having a strong negative impact on food security. Fragmentation of land and the consequent uneconomic holding have been isolated as contributory factors towards the deterioration in food security of the villages. The fact that the tenant-farmers perceive the landlord's contribution as positive is expressive of the failure of public policy to redistribute land and abolish tenancy *de facto*, or at least record the tenants so that they do not face eviction at will. The contribution of landlords has to be perceived as positive by the tenant farmers because the alternative to this scenario is starvation and even more deprivation. When we add to this landscape the element that the PDS designed to increase economic access to food for the poor, which attracts so much public attention, is nowhere to be seen in the hunger picture drawn by the villagers, it reconfirms that public policy has played a minimalist role in assisting the poor farmers and poor households to conquer hunger. The incremental variation in economic access to food that employment can provide is also mostly, though not wholly, brought about through increased employment in the informal sector and SME enterprises in the private sector. The employment opportunities in government programmes for poverty alleviation appears to be operating only at the margin. Taking one with the other, these factors indicate that there is certainly an urgent need to look at the entire gamut of public policy for ensuring food security for all.

Amongst the negative factors that require corrective action relate to pests, weeds, insects and animals. Much more attention has been paid towards tackling the problems of pests but not much seems to have been done to deal with animals, weeds and insects. The answers to these problems have been sought mostly in chemical pesticides, and of late some murmur is heard about use of pest-resistant seeds. While the former has led to an enormous increase in cost of farming taking the small peasant-farmer to the edge of migrating out of the agricultural sector, the latter tried in cash crops like cotton has resulted in such a surge in cost of production and hence weight of debt on the already indebted farmers that the only course open to them was to commit suicide. [2]. The large scale suicides by the cotton farmers of Andhra Pradesh, Karnataka, Maharastra and even Punjab speak volumes on the issue. The need is not to jack up chemicalisation of agriculture even more but to return to integrated pest management successfully tried in many parts of the country and abroad. We have seen that the so-called scientific solutions have only worsened the conditions of the peasants and the need is to return to our age-old tested and tried methods (*Phongphit and Bennoun,* 1988).

While the negative factors need to be circumvented, the positive factors need to be strengthened. Amongst the role of off-farm income, selling milk deserves special mention. As the farmers pointed out, selling maintaining bovine wealth and selling milk were possible without additional financial burden on the communities. They could feed the animals from the bye-product of the farms and from the common property resources, yet they could reap sizeable income from sale of milk, without any value addition. In any scheme of ensuring food security and eliminating hunger, on-farm activities should be added to off-farm livelihood systems, depending on the traditional knowledge and skill of the community, not only as supplementary source of income to cause increase in physical and economic access to food but also to tide over difficulties in stressful years. We are not for once saying that farmers should be encouraged to rear milch animals and consume milk products because there are much more efficient and cheaper sources of protein and energy available, such as peanuts and grams. Indeed the villagers of all the villages do not consume all the milk they produce. They rather sell their milk output to have economic access to other items in their consumption basket and satisfy other consumption needs. All we are trying to drive at is, that there is need to join on-farm and off-farm livelihood systems in our villages to kill hunger.

The strength of community support and self-help warrants a few comments. Much of what the communities do to have food has been possible through these two forces. It is important that organising the community receives a high priority. This is more so in case of civil society actors. They can render singular service by being the catalyst in this process. It seems to us clear that the impact of civil society actors in poverty eradication would be increased several times over if they laid greater emphasis on strengthening community support and self-help, for these would be the bed rock on which the communities could be galvanised to seek and assert their rights. Asserting their rights is the only way by which communities can be empowered and developed through a self propelling mechanism (*Mukherjee,* 1999a). The signal service that the Panchayats can also render in this regard can hardly be over-emphasised.

There is the need to rework a new system of agriculture, the brief outline of which is presented below:

One: In the current age when agriculture has become like any other business, maximising profits through agricultural production is seemingly catching on as the main goal of farming. This is reflected in the preference of members of farming households to seek employment elsewhere. There has to be conscious effort at changing this mindset. Meeting human needs has to be restored at the centre stage as the goal of agriculture, where livelihood security has a very high priority.

Two: The current thinking that decisions should be made by experts and only experts can question each other is fallacious. The need for the common people to have access to information that enables and empowers them to question the decisions of the experts, participate in the planning process by making informed choices and undertake evaluation of development interventions and even paradigm, must be put in place. And the passage of the Bill by the Rajasthan Assembly on the Right to Information is a significant achievement in this regard, that has not come a day too early and without ceaseless struggle by dedicated activists like

Aruna Roy and others. Thus, a majority of the natural resources management decisions pertaining to agriculture must be made at the field level by primary users of resources. The technology development priorities and decision process must be through interactive participatory process. Passive participation is insufficient.

Three: The current philosophy in the LPG era, where self-centredness and competitiveness are great virtues, and profit the only basis of our progress, need a thorough re-examination. We need to seriously ponder whether the Keynesian edict (discovered and reinvented several times over in different incarnations) that the more we consume, the more we contribute to development by generating effective demand has to be subjected to searching scrutiny. There is no alternative to sharing, caring and collaboration and the degree of co-operation and harmony that exists in our socio-economic environment are true barometers of the quality of life. Unbriddled consumption is self destructive, so eloquently borne out by the precipice of environmental calamity to which the consumption of the rich has brought the world.

Four: The technical parameters of sustainable agriculture have also to be changed. The three parameters can be best summarised in three words: "Poly-culture, integration and reduction". *Poly-culture,* multi-storey farming and diversification of the agricultural production system to improve the stability of food output all through the year and over the years, must replace the current trend towards mono-culture. *Integration* of seasonal, annual and perennial crops, trees and shrubs, birds and animals, aquatic plant and animals, insects, reptiles and micro-organism, etc. for ensuring energy efficiency and low external input, is essential for move away from HEIA. And then, all agro-chemicals and agricultural practices that cause injury to the life of the soil must be *reduced* and eventually *eliminated* to free agriculture from high fossil fuel intensity, together with adoption of biological and physical techniques and methods of soil and water conservation, to restore lost health of soil.

Five: The design parameters of sustainable agriculture have to be rewritten. It has to be recognised that every element in the agricultural process is multi-purpose. For instance, a fence to ward off predatory animals can also be a source of fuelwood and green leaf for manuring, food, shelter for birds and animal, and also be a windbreaker and help soil erosion. In the design parameters, all problems are also to be viewed as potential as well. While termites and white ants, that create, havoc in villages like Uncha Gaon that we saw in Chapter 6 and Kadhaoli and Sagarpur (*Mukherjee,* 1999), are also a rich source of poultry feed. Gullies created by erosion are ideal sites for afforestation and horticulture, to provide fuel, fodder and food for the people. Farm design must change its orientation from *use* and *exploitation* to *conservation*. Soil, water, energy and genetic resources conservation has to be in-built into the farm design. Finally, the design parameters must build the farming system on the foundation of indigenous plants and animals, local knowledge and traditional farming system. The focus of the farming system should be to improve the entire system, rather than gearing to improve only yield or income by changing a single element.

Six: The choice of agricultural techniques must be set in the Indian context. In so doing the following elements have to be factored in while choosing agricultural techniques:

(a) Much of India has fairly high rainfall, but it is very unevenly distributed. And droughts and floods are regular features, often one following the other, such as the case in Orissa.[3].
(b) Torrential seasonal rains cause massive soil erosion and approximately no more than 20 per cent of annual rainfall infiltrates into the soil to recharge water aquifers.
(c) Generally, ground water withdrawal throughout India has far exceeded the rate at which it is recharged leading to water table falling. This is exemplified by what the villagers said about their search for irrigation water in Ucha Gaon. The dry water bodies, wells, ponds and canals leading to severe water shortage and drought, under which as many as eleven states, particularly Rajasthan, Gujarat, large parts of Madhya Pradesh, Orissa and Andhra Pradesh, are reeling, are mute witnesses to the tragic phenomenon (*Agarwal,* 2000). Such withdrawal of ground water also increases salinity in coastal areas.

Box 10.2
Rich Farmers and Water Exploitation

The whole Nimar and Malwa region comprising Dewas, Dhar, Jhabua, Mandsaur and Ratlam districts in Madhya Pradesh are under a dry spell. Jhabua, which borders Gujarat and has similar climatic conditions, is the worst hit. Rajesh Rajora District Collector, Dhar remarked: "Rich farmers or patidars have bored deep into their plots of land and use them to grow, at least, three crops a year. This has led to lowering of water table." The same has been the case in Rajasthan. Rich farmers, aware of the political clout they enjoy, they have dug up a deep as they can to get the maximum number of crops possible in a year. This has led to over utilisation of soil and water. Governments, faces with the effect of past sins, are offering more of the same.

(d) Major dams have so far created as many new problems as they have solved the old ones for agriculture and forestry, and canal based irrigation has also led to water logging and salinity as is apparent in several parts of Punjab, Haryana and Rajasthan, notably Bikaner, along the Indira Gandhi Canal. In Lunkaransar in Bikaner district one can see white sheets of salt covering vast stretches of yellow sands of the Thar along even the state highways.

(e) Common property resources, forests, woodlots, common grazing lands, river beds, rivulets, water bodies such as small ponds etc. are dwindling fast leading to severe shortage of biomass in rural areas and making severe inroads into the secondary food systems of the poor households.

(f) Despite all the progress made, 70 per cent of the Indians still live in the rural areas, a majority of whom are landless or are small and marginal farmers, who rely on the production of milk, eggs, meat, etc. through birds and small animals.

(g) Biological activity is very high in most of the States and therefore trees grow at a fast pace. This is because most parts of the country have a warm climate.

(h) There is a wide variation in inter-state and intra-State soil and climatic conditions, highlighting the need for any model of agricultural development to be adapted to local conditions.

(i) There exists a wide variety of natural vegetation and fauna, though the knowledge about their use, location, reproduction techniques, origin, etc. are inadequately documented.

From the forgoing it is manifest that a wide range of solutions are needed. Thus, for instance, separate farming systems are required for the irrigated areas, for arid and semi-arid areas, for low land in humid areas and for uplands in humid areas. "One jacket fits all" system, that we were pursuing under the aegis of Green Revolution, is unlikely to yield results.

Endnotes

1. There are various sources of data relevant for the discussion on the social sectors. For our purposes we will use the data provided by NCAER. Consequently all data on literacy and health are from NCAER 1999.

2. The cotton variety tried was BT Cotton.

3. The situation in Orissa, which a few months ago was battling water, now cannot find it anywhere. In the Erasama block, which was the worst hit by the cyclone, sweet water is not available at a depth of 1,500 feet. Chief Minister Navin Patnaik has requested for special trains to be run to carry water into the remote districts of the state. Patnaik additionally needs more central assistance for "sinking more tubewells and organising tankers for water supply."

Figure-10.1 **LITERACY MAP, KRISHNA RAKSHIT CHAK**

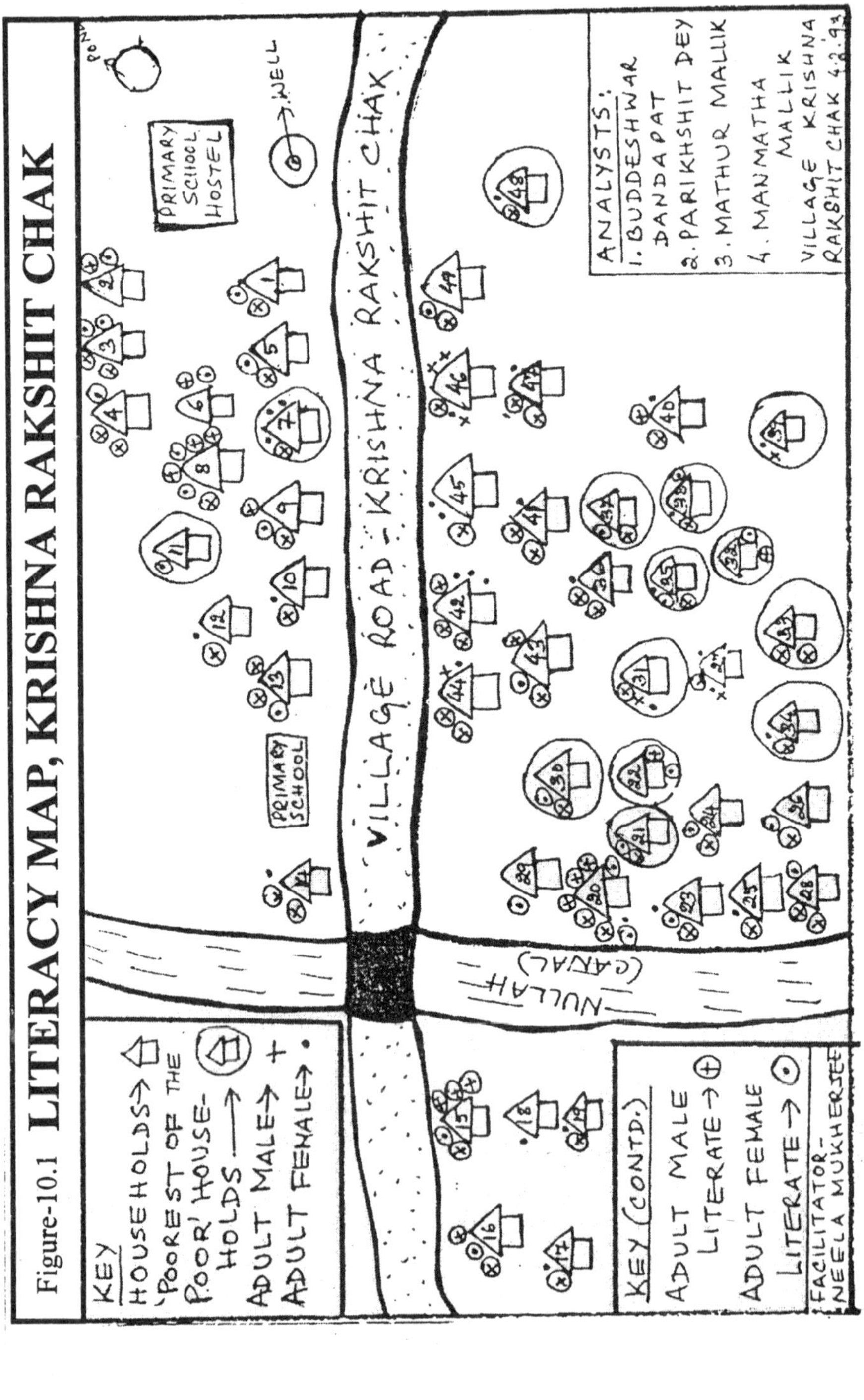

Figure-10.2

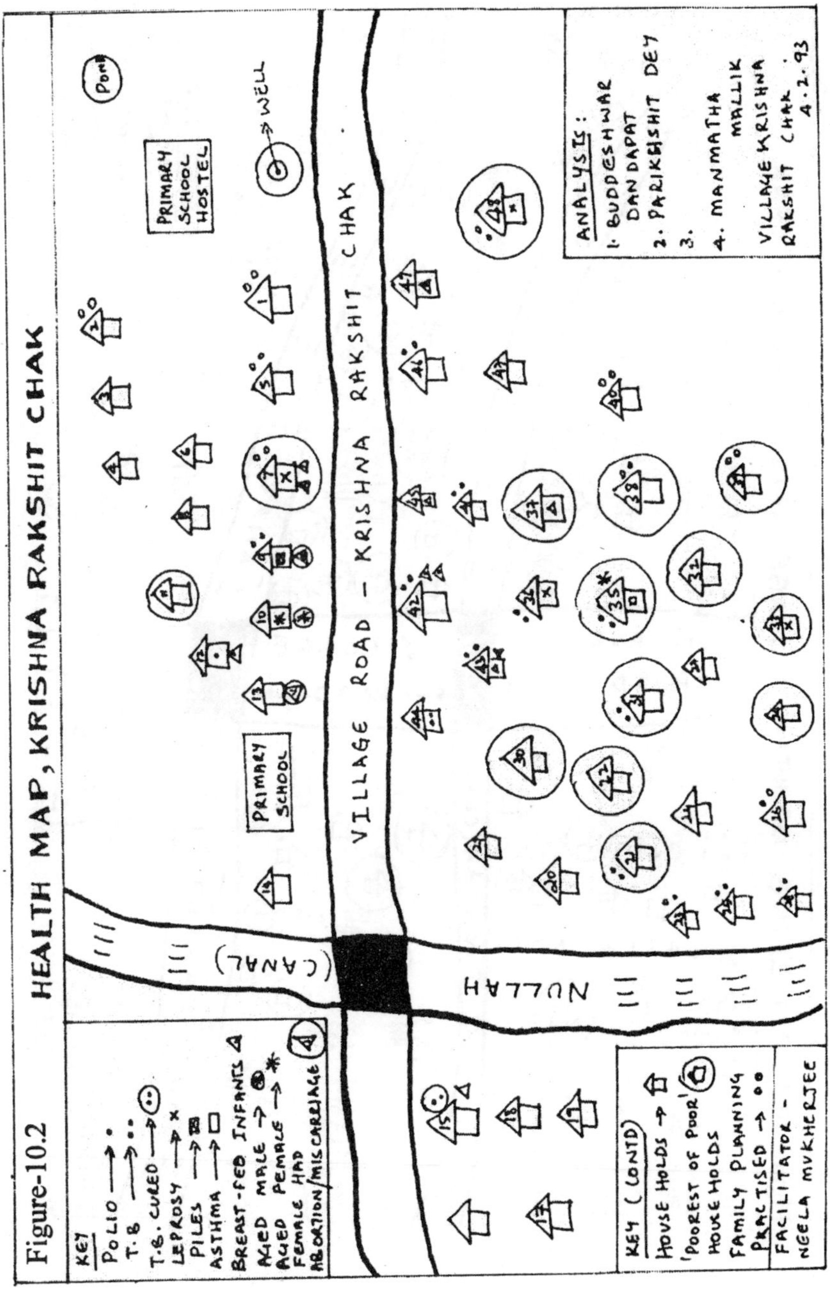
HEALTH MAP, KRISHNA RAKSHIT CHAK
KEY
POLIO
T.B
T.B. CURED
LEPROSY
PILES
ASTHMA
BREAST-FED INFANTS
AGED MALE
AGED FEMALE
FEMALE HAD ABORTION/MISCARRIAGE
KEY (CONTD)
HOUSE HOLDS
'POOREST OF POOR' HOUSE HOLDS
FAMILY PLANNING PRACTISED
FACILITATOR - NEELA MUKHERJEE
CANAL
NULLAH
VILLAGE ROAD - KRISHNA RAKSHIT CHAK
PRIMARY SCHOOL
PRIMARY SCHOOL HOSTEL
WELL
POND
ANALYSTS:
1. BUDDESHWAR DANDAPAT
2. PARIKSHIT DEY
3.
4. MANMATHA MALLIK
VILLAGE KRISHNA RAKSHIT CHAK
4.2.93

Figure-10.3 WELL-BEING GROUPING, VILLAGE KRISHNA RAKSHITCHAK

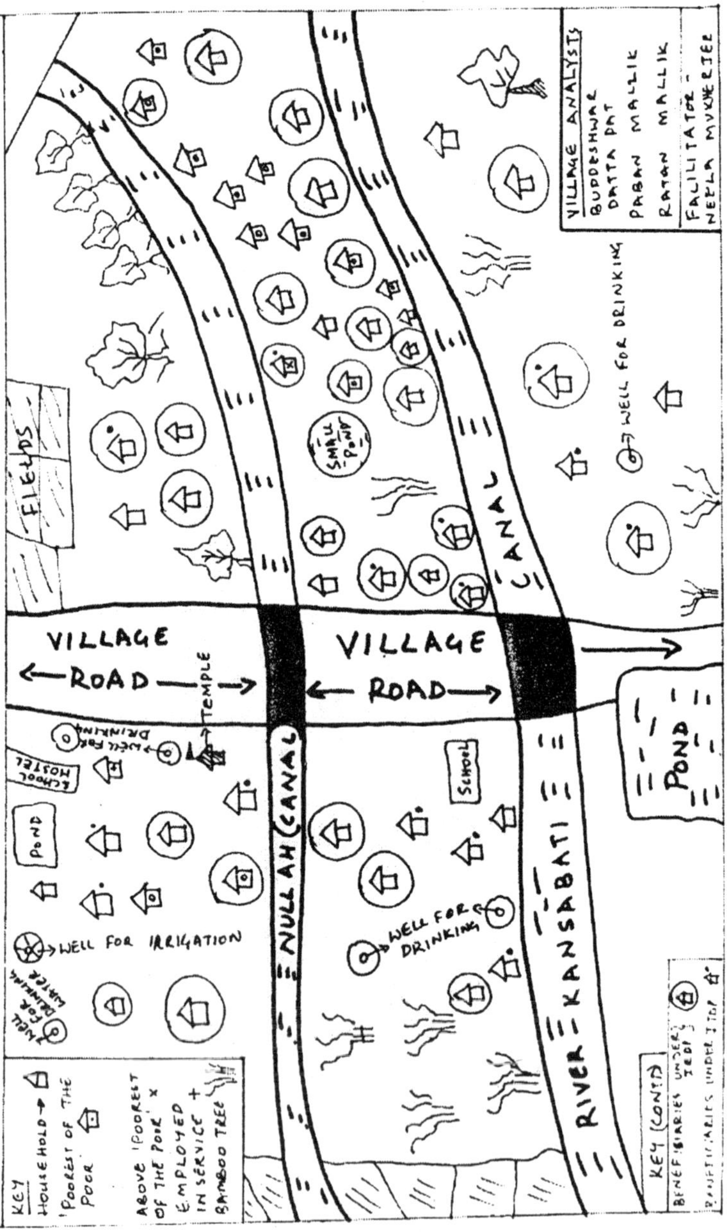

References and Select Bibliography

ACC/SN (1990): "Some Options for Improving Nutrition in the 90s", *SCN News* No.7, ACC/SCN, Geneva.

Acharya, S (1991): "Labour Use in Indian Agriculture Analysis at Macro Level for the Eighties", *Working Paper Series, No.105*, Institute of Social Studies, The Hague.

Acharya, S.S. (1994): *Discussant's Comments,* in G.S. Bhalla (ed.): *Economic Liberalization and Indian Agriculture*, Institute for Studies in Industrial Development, New Delhi.

Addition, T. and Demery, L. (1987): "Rural Poverty Alleviation under Adjustment: What Room for Manoeuvre?" Paper read in September 1987 at the *Overseas Development Institute Conference on the Design and Impact of Adjustment Programme on Agriculture and Agricultural Institutions*, London.

Adedeji, A. (1989): "Interaction between Structuralism, Structural Adjustment and Food Security Policies in Development Policy Management", *ECDPM Occasional Paper*, Maastricht.

Advisory Council on Development Cooperation (1995): *Food Security in Africa, Report and Recommendations*, December, Republic of Ireland, Ireland.

Africa Leadership Forum (1989): *The Challenges of Agricultural Production and Food Security in Africa, Report of a Conference,* 27-30 July 1989, Ota, Nigeria.

Agarwal, A. (1986): *The Wood Fuel Crisis in the Third World* (New-Delhi: Allied Publishers).

Agarwal, A., Chopra, R. and Kalpana, S. (1987 rev. edn of 1982): *The State of India's Environment 1985. The Second Citizen's Report* (New-Delhi: Centre for Science and Environment).

Agarwal, Anil: *Indian Express,* May, 2000.

Agarwal, Bina (1986): "Women, Poverty and Agricultural Growth in India", *Journal of Peasant Studies*, Vol. 13, No. 4, 165-220.

Agarwal, Bina (1988): "Who sows? Who reaps? Women and land rights in India", *Journal of Peasant Studies*, Vol. 15, No. 4, 531-81.

Agarwal, Bina (1989): "Rural Women, Poverty and Natural Resources: Subsistence, Sustainability and Struggle for Change", *Economic and Political Weekly*, WS 46-65.

Agarwal, Bina (1994): *A Field of One's Own: Gender and Land Rights in South Asia* (Cambridge: Cambridge University Press).

Agarwal, Bina (1995): "Gender, environment and poverty interlinks in rural India: regional variations and temporal shifts, 1971-1991", *Discussion Paper Number 62*, United Nations Research Institute for Social Development, Geneva.

Agarwal, Bina (1999): "Social Security and the Family: Coping with Seasonality and Calamity in Rural India", in Ehtisham Ahmed, Jean Dreze, John Hills and Amartya Sen (eds.): *Social Security in Developing Countries* (New-Delhi: Oxford University Press) Oxford India Paperbacks.

Agarwal, P. K. and D. P. Garrity (1987): *Intercroping of Legumes to Contribute Nitrogen in Low-input Upland Rice-based Cropping System,* paper read at the International Symposium on Nutrient Management for Food Crops in Tropical Farming System, Malang, Indonesia, 1987.

Aggarwal, R. (1983): "Price Distortions and Growth in Developing Countries", *Staff Working Paper, No.575*, World Bank.

Ahluwalia, Deepak (1993): "Public distribution of food in India: Coverage, Targeting and Leakages", *Food Policy*, Vol.18, No.1, 33-54.

Ahmed, Farzand (1992) "The Mushara: The Rat-eaters of Bihar", *India Today*, October 15th, 1992, p.21.

Ahmed, Iftikar (1994): "Technology and Feminisation of Work", *Economic and Political Weekly*, Vol. XXIX, No. 18, April, 30th, 1994.

Alagh Y.K.: *Towards a Policy System for Food Security* (Mimeo).

Alagh, Y. K.: "Listen to the Views of the Poor, Grain of Truth", *Indian Express*, New-Delhi, 28th September, 1999.

Althusser L. (1965): *Lire le Capital*, Paris.

Amsden, Alice (1988): "Taiwan's Economic History. A Case of Etatisme and a Challenge to Dependency Theory", in Bates, Robert H. (ed.), *Towards a Political Economy of Development—A Rational Choice Perspective* (Berkeley: University of California Press).

Anand, S. and C. Harris (1990): "Food and Standard of Living: An Analysis Based on Sri Lankan Data", in J. Dreze and A. Sen (eds.): *The Political Economy of Hunger*, Vol. 1 (Oxford: Clarendon Press).

Anand, S. and S. M. Ravi Kanbur (1991): "Public Policy and Basic Needs Provision: Intervention and Achievement in Sri Lanka", in J. Dreze and A. Sen (eds.): *The Political Economy of Hunger*, Vol. 3 (Oxford: Clarendon Press).

Anandan, Sujatha (2000): "Farmers Might Have to Sell Their Milch Cows", *Outlook*, 21st February 2000, p. 26-27.

Arnold, David (1988): *Famines, Social Crisis and Historical Change* (Oxford: Basil Blackwell).

Arnold, J.E.M. (1991) *Three Products in Agroecosystems: Economic and Political Issues* (London: International Institute for Environment and Development)

Atkin, Michael (1993): *Snouts in the Trough: European Farmers, the Common Agricultural Policy and the Public Purse* (Cambridge: Woodhead Publishing Ltd.).

Atkin, Michael, (1995): *The International Grain Trade*, 2nd edition (Cambridge: Woodhead Publishing Ltd.).

Baden, Sally and Kirsty, Milward (1995): *Gender and Poverty, Briefings on Development and Gender Report Number 30,* Institute of Development Studies, Brighton, U.K.

Badiana, O. (1988): *National Food Security and Regional Integration in West Africa* (Kiel: Wissenschaftsverlag Vauk).

Balakrishnan, P. (1991): *Pricing and Inflation in India* (Delhi: Oxford University Press).

Balakrishnan, P. (1999): *Land reforms and the question of food in Kerala,* the Eighth Daniel Thorner Memorial Lecture delivered at the Centre for Development Studies on 25 February 1999, reprinted in the *Economic and Political Weekly*, pp. 1272-1280.

Balakrishnan, P. (1999a): "Agricultural Growth and Economic Welfare Since 1991", paper read at the Foundation Day Seminar on Rural Prosperity and Agricultural Strategies held at Hyderabad, November, 4-5, 1999.

Balakrishnan, P. and B. Ramaswami (1999): "Analysing government intervention in foodgrain markets", in N. Krishnaji (ed.): *Public support for Food Security* (New Delhi: Sage) 2000.

Balakrishnan, P. and Ramaswami, B. (2000):. "On Targeting Food Subsidies", in K. Seeta Prabhu (ed.): *Reforming India's Social Sectors: Strategies and Prospects* (New-Delhi: Sage Publications) forthcoming.

Ballam, D. N. (1986): "Self Sufficiency in Japanese Agriculture: Telescoping and Reconciling the Food Security-Efficiency Dilemma", in Browne, W. P. and Hadwiger, D. F. (eds.): *World Food Policies: Toward Agricultural Interdependence* (Boulder: Layne Rienner Publishers).

Bambawale, O. M.: "Evidence of Ozone injury to a crop plant in India", in *Atmospheric Environment,* Vol. 20, 1986.

Bandopadhyay, J. and Shiva, V. (1987): "Chipko: Rekindling India's Forest Culture", *The Ecologist*, Vol. 17, No.1, pp.26-34.

Bansil, P. C. (1985): *Feed, seed and wastage rates: A regional study* (New Delhi: Techno Economic Research Institute).

Bansil, P.C. (1997): "India's Demand for Foodgrains in 2000 AD Simple Incremental Demand Model", *Indian Farming,* February, 1997.

Bapna, S. L. (1990): "Food Security through the PDS: the Indian Experience", in Tyagi, D. S. and Vyas V S (eds.): *Increasing Access to Food: The Asian Experience* (New-Delhi and London: Sage Publications).

Barbier, E. B. (1988): "Sustainable Agriculture and the Resource Poor: Policy Issues and Options", *London Environment Economics Centre Paper*, pp.88-92, International Institute for Environment and Development, London; University College, Environment Economics Centre, London and Land Environment Economics Centre, London.

Bardhan, P. K. (1973): "A Model of Growth of Capitalism in a Dual Agrarian Economy", in Bhagwati, J. N. and Eckaus, R. (eds.): *Development and Planning: Essays in Honour of Paul Rosentein Rodan* (Cambridge, Massachussets: MIT Press).

Bardhan, Pranab K (1974): "On life and death questions", *Economic and Political Weekly*, 9 (32-34): 1293-1304.

Bardhan, P. K. (1984): "Work Patterns and Social Differentiation: Rural Women of West Bengal", in Binswanger, H. et. al. (eds): *Contractual Arrangements, Employment and Wages in Rural Labour Markets in Asia* (Connecticut: Yale University Press).

Bardhan, Pranab (1998): *The Political Economy of Development in India* (expanded edition with an epilogue on the political economy of reform in India) (New-Delhi: Oxford University Press).

Barmark J., and G. Wallen (1975): *Knowledge Production in Interdisciplinary Groups* being Report No.37 of the Department of the Theory of Science, University of Gothenburg, Gothenburg, Sweden.

Barraclough, S. and Utting, P. (1987): *Food Security Trends and Prospects in Latin America, Working Paper, No.99*, Helen Kellog Institute for International Studies, University of Notre Dame, USA.

Barraclough, Solon (1996): *The End of Hunger: The Social Origin of Food Strategies* (London: Zed Books)

Barratt, Brown, Michael and Tiffen, Pauline, (1994): *Short Changed: Africa and World Trade* (London and Boulder: Pluto Press, with Transnational Institute).

Basu, Alalka Malwade (1996): *Women's Economic Roles and Child Health: An Overview in Population and Women* (New York: Population Division, United Nations).

Beck, Tony (1994): *The Experience of Poverty* (London: Intermediate Technology Press).

Begum, A. (1985): *Women and Technology in Rice Processing in Bangladesh, in Women in Rice Farming* (Gower: International Rice Research Institute).

Behera Bhagirath and V. Ratna Reddy (2000): *Killing Fields: Lifesavers and Externalities (A Study of the Impact of Industrial Pollution on Rural Communities)* (Hyderabad: Centre for Economic and Social Studies).

Behrman, Jere R. and Anil B. Deolalikar (1987): "Will Developing Country Nutrition Improve with Income? A case study for Rural South India", *Journal of Political Economy*, Vol. 95, No.3.

Behrman, Jere R. and Anil B. Deolalikar (1989): "Is Variety the Spice of Life?· Implications for Calorie Intake", *The Review of Economics and Statistics*, Vol. LXXI, No.4, pp. 666-672.

Behrman, Jere R., Anil B. Deolalikar and Barbara L. Wolfe (1988): "Nutrients: Impacts and Determinants", *The World Bank Economic Review*, Vol. 2, No.3, pp. 299-320.

Beneria, Lourdes and Savitha Bisnath (1996): *Gender And Poverty, An Analysis for Action* (New-York: United Nations Development Programme) Gender and Development Monograph Series No. 2, February 1996.

Benson, C., Clay, E. J. and Green, R. H. (1986): *Food Security in Sub-Saharan Africa,* Paper presented at the Other Economic Summit, IDS University of Sussex, Brighton.

Berg, A. (1973): *The Nutrition Factor* (Washington DC: The Brookings Institute).

Berg, A. and Austin (1984): "Nutrition Policies and Programmes", *Food Policy*, Vol. 9, No.4, November.

Berg, A., N. Scrimshaw, and D. L. Call (eds.) (1973): *Nutrition, National Development and Planning* (Cambridge, Mass., USA: MIT Press).

Berry, S. (1984): "Households, Decision-Making and Rural Development: Do We Need to Know More?" *Discussion Paper, No.167*, (Cambridge, Massachusetts: Harvard Institute for International Development).

Besley, T. (1997): *Political Economy of Alleviating Poverty: Theory and Institutions,* paper presented at the Annual World Bank Conference on Development Economics, 1996, IBRD.

Besley, T. and Ravi Kanbur (1987): "Food Subsidies and Poverty Alleviation", *Discussion Paper, No.75*, October 1987 (Coventry: University of Warwick, Department of Economics).

Bhalla, G. S. et. al. (2000): *Prospects of India's Cereal Supply and Demand to 2000,* paper read at the National Seminar on Food Security held at the Centre for Economic and Social Studies, Hyderabad, from 25th to 27th 2000.

Bhalla, G. S. (ed.) (1994): *Economic Liberalization and Indian Agriculture* (New Delhi: Institute for Studies in Industrial Development), 1994.

Bhalla, G. S. and G. Singh, (1997): *Draft Report-1 on Recent Developments in Indian Agriculture: A State Level Analysis*, submitted to the Planning Commission, Government of India for Planning Commission project on "Agricultural Growth in India during 1980-83 to 1990-93 – a District Level Study" (New Delhi: Centre for Study of Regional Development, Jawarhalal Nehru University).

Bhalla, G. S. and Singh, Gurmail, (1997): "Recent Development in Indian Agriculture: A State Level Analysis", *Economic and Political Weekly*, Vol. 32, No. 13.

Bhalla, G.S and Peter Hazell (1997): "Food Grains Demand in India to 2020–A Preliminary Exercise", *Economic and Political Weekly*, December 27.

Bhalla, G. S., P. Hazell and J. Kerr (1999): "Prospects for India's Cereal Supply and Demand till 2020", *Food, Agriculture and the Environment Discussion Paper 29*, International Food Policy Research Institute (IFPRI), Washington, DC.

Bhalla, G. S. and Tyagi, D. S. (1989): *Patterns of India's Agricultural Development: A District Level Study* (New Delhi: Institute of Economic Growth).

Bhalla, G. S. and Vashistha, P. S. (1988): "Income Distribution in India: A Re-Examination", in Srinivasan, T. N. and Bardhan, P. (eds.): *Rural Poverty in South Asia* (New York: Columbia University Press).

Bharati, P. and Basu, A. (1988): "Uncertainties in food supply, and nutritional deficiencies in relation to economic conditions in a village population in Southern West Bengal, India", in De Graine, I. And G. A. Harrison (eds.): *Coping with Uncertainty in Food Supply* (Oxford: Oxford Science Publications).

Bhatia, B. M. (1988): *Indian Agricultural: A Policy Perspective* (New-Delhi: Sage Publications, New Delhi).

Bhowmick, P. (1963): *Lodhas of West Bengal: A Socio-Economic Study* (Calcutta: Punthi Pustak).

Bigman, D. (1982): *Coping with Hunger: Toward a System of Food Security and Price Stabilization* (Cambridge, Massachusetts: Ballinger Publishing Co.).

Bigman, D. and P. V. Srinivasan, (2000): *Geographical Targeting of Agricultural R&D for Poverty Alleviation: Possibilities and Prospects for India,* mimeo, (Bombay: IGIDR).

Binswanger, H., S. R. Khandkerm and M. Rescnzweig (1993): "How infrastructure and financial institutions affect agricultural output and investment in India", *Journal of Development Economics*, Vol. 41, No. 2, 337-366.

Bliss, C. J. and Stern, N. H. (1986): *Palanpur: The Economy of an Indian Village* (Oxford: Clarendon Press).

Borosag, R. (1984): *Foreword* to Susan George, *Ill Fares the Land: Essays on Food, Hunger and Power* (Washington: Institute of Policy Studies).

Borton, J. and Shoham, J. (1991): *Mapping, Vulnerability to Food Insecurity: Tentative Guidelines for WFP Office,* mimeo, Study Commissioned by the World Food Programme (London: Relief and Development Institute).

Boserup, Ester (1970): *Women's Role in Economic Development* (London: George Allen and Unwin).

Boserup, Ester (1993): *The Conditions of Agricultural Growth, The Economics of Agrarian Change under Population Pressure* (London: Earthscan).

Boulding, E. (1976): *The Underside of History: A View of Women Through Time* (Boulder: Westview Press).

Bowbrick, Peter (1986): *The Causes of Famine: A Refutation of Professor Sen's Theory,* in *Food Policy*, May 1986, p. 105-124.

Brandt Commission (Independent Commission on International Development Issues) (1980): *North–South: A Programme for Survival* (Cambridge, Mass., USA: MIT Press).

Brandt, H. (1990): "Food Security Aspects in Price and Market Policies for Grain-Based Food Systems of sub-Saharan Africa", in Chole, E. (ed.): *Food Crisis in Africa: Policy and Management Issues* (New Delhi: Vikas Publishing House Pvt. Ltd.).

Brara, R. (1989): *Shifting Sands: A Case Study of Rights in Common Pastures* (Jaipur: Institute of Development Studies).

Bray, Francesca (1994): "Agriculture for Developing Nations", *Scientific America,* July, 1994, pp. 33-35.

Bread for the World Institute (BFWI) (1994): *Causes of Hunger*, Fourth Annual Report on the State of World Hunger (Silver Spring: Bread for the World Institute).

Bread For the World Institute (BFWI) (1995): *Hunger 1995*, Fifth Annual Report on the State of World Hunger (Silver Spring, MD, USA: Bread For the World Insitute).

Bread For the World Institute (BFWI) (1999): *Changing Politics of Hunger,* (Silver Spring: Bread for the World Institute).

Bread For the World Institute (BFWI) (2000): *A Program to End Hunger,* (Silver Spring: Bread for the World Institute).

Brown, J. L. (1997): "Release of National Food Security Measurement Study Results by USDA", Tufts University School of Nutrition, Science and Policy, 16th September, 1997.

Brown, L. (1992): *State of the World 1992* (London: Earthscan Publications Ltd.).

Brundtland, Gro Harlem, (1993): *Population, Environment and Development* (New-York: UNFPA, New York).

Buchanan-Smith, M. and Young, H. (1990): "Food security planning in the wake of an emergency: Relief operation: The case of Darfur, Western Sudan", *IDS Discussion Paper, No.278*, Institute of Development Studies, University of Sussex, Brighton, U.K.

Burki, S. J. (1986): "The African Food Crisis: Looking Beyond the Emergency", *Journal of Social Development in Africa*, Vol. 1, pp.5-22.

Cadwell, J. et. al. (1986): "Periodic High Risk as a Cause of Fertility Decline in Rural Environment: Survival Strategies in the 1980-83 South India Drought", *Economic Development and Cultural Change*, Vol. 34, No. 4.

Cain, M. (1977): "The Economic Activities of Children in a Village in Bangladesh", *Population and Development Review*, Vol. 7, No. 3.

Call, D. L., and F. J. Levison. (1973): "A Systematic Approach to Nutrition Intervention Programmes", in Berg, A., Scrimshaw, N. and Call, D. L. (eds.): *Nutrition, National Development and Planning* (Cambridge, Mass., USA: MIT Press).

Calon, M. L. H. (1990): *Population Farming Systems and Food Security, Paper No. 7(E)* International Course for Development Oriented Research in Agriculture: Farming Systems Analysis.

Campbell, D. J. (1982): "Community Based Strategies for Coping with Food Scarcity: A Role in African Famine Early Warning System", *Geo Journal*, Vol. 20, No. 3, pp.231-41.

Campbell, D. J. (1990): "Strategies for Coping with Severe Food Deficits in Rural Africa: A Review of the Literature", *Food and Foodways*, Vol. 4, No. 2, pp.143-62.

Campbell, D. J. and Trechter, D. D. (1982): "Strategies for Coping with Food Consumption Shortage in the Madara Mountains Region of North Cameroon", *Social Science and Medicine*, Vol. 16, pp. 2217-27.

CARE (1988): *Project Food Aid: A Classification of its Uses as a Development Resource* May, (New-York: CARE).

Carr, M. (ed.) (1991): *Women and Food Scarcity: The Experience of the SADCC Countries* (London: Intermediate Technology Press).

Cathie, J. and Dick, H. (1987): *Food Security and Macro Economic Stabilisation: A Case Study of Botswana 1965-84*, Institute for Weltswirtschaft an der University Keil, Tubingen, Boulder (Colarado: Westview Press).

Cecelski, E. (1987): "Energy and Rural Women's Work: Crisis Response and Policy Alternatives", *International Labour Review*, Vol. 1216, No.1, pp. 41-44.

Centre for Food Security (1991): *Background Paper on Food Security: Draft Final*, Centre for Food Security (Ontario: University of Guelph).

Centre for Science and Environment (1985): *The State of India's Environment, 1984-85, The Second Citizens' Report* (New-Delhi: Centre for Science and Environment).

Centre for Science and Environment (1987): *The State of India's Environment 1987* (New-Delhi: Centre for Science and Environment).

Cernea, M. M.: *Putting People First* (Oxford: Oxford University Press) 1991.

Cernea, M. M (1993): "Culture and Organisation, The Social Responsbility of Induced Development", *Sustainable Development*, Vol. 1, No. 2, 1993, pp.18-29.

Chakravaty, Aunindyo (2000): "The Nation State, The Self-enclosed Worlds of Village India", *Times of India*, 18th April.

Chambers, Roberts: *Rural Development, Putting the Last First* (London: Longman) 1983.

Chambers, R, (1988): "Sustainable Rural Livelihoods: A Key Strategy for People, Environment and Development", in C. Conroy and M. Litvinoff (eds.): *The Greening of Aid, Sustainable Livelihoods in Practice* (London: Earthscan and International Institute for Environment and Development).

Chambers, R. (1989): "Editorial Introduction: Vulnerability, Coping and Policy", *IDS Bulletin*, Vol.2, No.2, pp.1-7.

Chambers, Roberts: *Micro-Environment Unobserved*, GateKeeper Series (London: Institute of Environment and Development) 1992.

Chambers, Robert: *Foreward* in Scoones, Ian and John Thompson (eds.): *Beyond Farmer First* (London: Intermediate Technology) 1994.

Chambers, Robert, N. C. Saxena and Tushar Shah (1989): *To The Hands of the Poor: Water and Trees* (New Delhi: Oxford and IBH and London: Intermediate Technology).

Chambers, R., Pacey, A. and Thrupp, L. A. (1989): *Farmer First: Farmer Innovation and Agricultural Research* (London: Intermediate Technology Press).

Chand, Ramesh and Birthal, Pratap S. (1997): "Pesticide use in Indian Agriculture in Relation to Growth in Area and Production and Technological Change", *Indian Journal of Agricultural Economics*, Vol. 52, No. 3, July-September.

Chand, Ramesh and Haque, T. (1997): "Sustainability of Rice-Wheat Crop System in Indo-Gangetic Region", *Economic and Political Weekly*, Vol. 32, No.18.

Chandra, Parul (2000): "For Nalia, the village well is just a mirage", *Times of India*, New Delhi, 21st April 2000.

Chandrasekhar, C. P. and J. Ghosh, (1997): "Targeted Public Distribution System; Is it getting more Food to the Poor?" *Business Line*, July 22.

Chattopadhyay, B. (1991): *Food Insecurity and the Social Environment, Food Systems and the Human Environment in Eastern India*, Vol. 1 (Calcutta and New Delhi: K. P. Bagchi and Co.).

Chen, Lincoln C., Huq, Emdadul, and Stan D'Souza (1981): "Sex bias in the family allocation of food and health care in rural Bangladesh", *Population and Development Review*, Vol. 7, No.1, pp. 55-70.

Chen, Martha Alter (1999): *Widows in India* (New-Delhi: Sage Publications).

Chen, R. S . (1990): "The State of Hunger in 1990" in *The Hunger Report: 1990*, Allan Shawn Feinstein World Hunger Program (Providence: Brown University).

Chengappa, Raj (1997): "The Haldi Battle", *India Today*, September 8, 1997, p. 56.

Chisholm, A. H. and Tyers, R. (eds.) (1992): *Introduction and Overview, Food Security: Theory, Policy and Perspectives from Asia and the Pacific Rim* (Massachusetts: Lexington Books).

Chopra, Kanchan (1996): "The Management of Degraded Land: Issues and an Analysis of Technological and Institutional Solutions", *Indian Journal of Agricultural Economics*, Vol. 51, Nos. 1 and 2, January-June.

Chopra, Kanchan, Gopal K. Kadekoedi and M. N. Murthy (1990): *Participatory Development: People and Common Property Resources* (New Delhi: Sage Publications).

Christensen, G. (1991): "Towards Food Security in the Horn of Africa", *Working Paper No.4* (Oxford: Food Studies Group).

Christian Science Monitor (1994): "Developing World will Claim Huge Share of Population Growth", *Christian Science Monitor*, April 29th, 1994.

Clay, E. (1981): *Food Policy Issues in Low Income Countries: An Overview* in *Food Policy Issues in Low Income Countries*, World Bank Staff Working Paper No. 473, August (Washington DC: World Bank).

Cohen, Bernard (1994): "A View from the Academy" in *Taken by the Storm: The Media, Public Opinion and US Foreign Policy in the Gulf War* (Chicago: University of Chicago Press) 1994.

Collins J. J. and D. Harris (1983): "Air Pollution Assessment at the International Crops Research Institute for the Semi-arid Tropics, India", *Environmental Technological Letters*, Vol.8, 1983, pp.10785-10787.

Commission of the European Communities (1989): "Food Security Policy: Examination of Recent Experience in Sub-Saharan Africa", *Commission Staff Paper*, Brussels, 28 July.

Conelly, W. T. and Chaiken, M. S. (1987): *Land, Labour and Livestock: The Impact of Intense Population Pressure on Food Security in Western Kenya*, paper presented at the 1987 Meeting of the American Anthropoligical Association, November 18-22, Chicago, Illinois, USA.

Conway, G. R. and Jules, Pretty (1991): *Unwelcome Harvest* (London: Earthscan Publications).

Conway, G. and Barbier, E. G. (1990): *After the Green Revolution: Sustainable Agriculture for Development* (Earthscan: London).

Conway, Gordon R. (1987): "The Properties of Agroecosystems", *Agricultural Systems*, Vol. 24, No. 2, 1987.

Coon, Carleton S. (1984): *A Reader in General Anthropology* (New-York, Chicago and San Francisco: Hold, Rinehart and Winston).

Corbett, J. E. M. (1988): "Famine and Household Coping Strategies", *World Development*, Vol. 16, No. 9, pp.1099-1112.

Cornia, G.A. and F. Stewart, (1993): "Two Errors of Targeting", *Journal of International Development*, Vol. 5, No. 5, pp. 459-490.

Correa, Carlos (1999a): "Developing Countries and the TRIPS Agreement", *Third World Economics*, Issue No. 217, 16th – 30th September, 1999.

Correa, Carlos (1999b): *Intellectual Property Rights, the WTO and the Developing Countries: The Trips Agreement and Policy Options* (Penang: Third World Network) 1999.

Cravioto, J. (1970): "Complexity of Factors Involved in Protein-Calorie Malnutrition in Malnutrition is a Problem of Ecology", *Bilbliotheca Nutrition et Dieta*, No.14.

Crossette, Barbara (1998): "Where the Hunger Season is Part of Life", *New York Times*, 16th August 1998.

Crow, B. (1984): "Warning of Famines in Bangladesh", *Economic and Political Weekly*, pp.1 754-1758.

Cummings, R. W. and Ray, S. K. (1969): "1968-69 Foodgrains Production, Relative Contribution of Weather and New Technology", *Economic and Political Weekly*, No. 4, September 27, 1969, pp. A163-A174.

Currey, B. (1981): *The Famine Syndrome: Its Definition for Relief and Rehabilitation,* in J. Robson (ed.): *Famine, Its Causes, Effect and Management* (London: Gordon and Breach).

Curtis, D., Hubbard, M. and Modaran, A. (1991): "Tragedy of the Commons and Comedy of Common Property Resources", *Economic Political Weekly*, 21 September 1991, pp. 2213-15.

Dandekar, V. M., and N. Rath (1971): "Poverty in India", *Economic and Political Weekly*, 2 January 1971, pp. 25-42, and 9 January 1971, pp. 106-46. A seminal work.

Dantwala, M. L. (1996): "My Academic Dialogues: Agricultural Price Policy and the Green Revolution", *Indian Journal of Agricultural Economics*, Vol. 51, Nos.1 and 2, January-June.

Dantwala, M. L. (1967): "Incentives and Disincentives in Agriculture", in *Indian Journal of Agricultural Economics,* April-June, 1967.

Dantwala, M. L. (1976): "Agricultural Policy Since Independence", in *Indian Journal of Agricultural Economics*, October-December, 1976.

Das, Veena (2000): "Ways of Dying", in *A Future Past the Present*, (New Delhi: Hindusthan Times Special Issue), 1st January 2000

Dasgupta, Biplab, (1997): "The New Political Economy: A Critical Analysis", in *Economic and Political Weekly*, January.

Dasgupta, Biplab, (1997a): "Indian Agriculture in the Global Context and Under Structural Adjustment", in Chaddha, G. K and Sharma, Aloke N. (eds.), *Growth, Employment and Poverty in Rural India: Change and Continuity*, (Delhi: Allied Publishers).

Dasgupta, Biplab (1999): *Structural Adjustment, Global Trade and the New Political Economy of Development* (Zed and Sage-Vistaar, London and Delhi), 1998.

Dasgupta, Partha and Debraj Ray (1990): "Adopting to Undernourishment", in Jean Dreze and Amartya Sen (ed.): *The Political Economy of Hunger*, Vol. 1 (Oxford: Clarendron Press).

Dasgupta, Partha (1993): *An Inquiry into Well Being and Destitution* (Oxford: Oxford University Press).

Dasgupta, Partha (1995): "The Population Problem: Theory and Evidence", *Journal of Economic Literature*, Vol. 33, No. 4, pp. 1879-1902.

Dasgupta, Partha (1997): *The Economics of Food* (London: STICERD, London School of Economics, London).

Dasgupta, S. (1985) "Adivasi Politics in Midnapur, c. 1760-1924" in Guha, Ranajit (ed.) (1985): *Subaltern Studies* IV (New Delhi: Oxford University Press).

Davies, O. and Writer, M. (1986): *Issues in Food Security in Jamaica,* National Food and Nutrition Coordinating Committee of Jamaica, Kingston.

Davies, S. (1989): *Micro Level Food Monitoring in the Sahel,* The Food Information Project in Mali, mimeo, Institute of Development Studies, University of Sussex, Brighton.

Davies, S. (1991): *What Can Markets Tell Us About Food Entitlements?* mimeo, Institute of Development Studies, University of Sussex, Brighton.

Davies, S. and Buchanan-Smith, M. (1990): *Can Local Communities in the Sahel Use Seasonal Rainfall Forecasts*? mimeo, Report for the Climatic Research Unit, University of East Anglia dnd Institute of Development Studies, University of Susses, Brighton, UK.

Davies S, Buchanan-Smith, M. and Lambert, R. (1991): *Early Warning in the Sahel and Horn of Africa: The State of the Art, A Review of the Literature,* IDS Research Report, No. RR220, Vol.1 of a 3 part series, IDS, University of Sussex, Brighton.

Davies S, Leach, M. and David, R. (1991): "Food Security and the Environment: Conflict or Complementarity?" *IDS Discussion Paper, No. 285*, IDS, University of Sussex, Brighton.

Davies, S. and Lipton, M. (1985): *A New Start: Preconditions for a Food Strategy in Zaire,* Report of 18 March 1985, Food Strategy Team's Mission to Zaire.

Davis, M. (1983): *Rank and Rivalry: The Politics of Inequality in Rural West Bengal* (Cambridge: Cambridge University Press).

De Waal, A. (1988): "Famine Early Warning Systems and the Use of Socio-Economic Data", *Disasters,* Vol.12, No.1, pp.81-91.

De Waal, A. (1991): "Emergency Food Security in Western Sudan: What is it for?" in S. Maxwell (ed.): *To Cure All Hunger: Food Policy and Food Security in Sudan* (Intermediate Technology, London).

De Waal, A. (1989): *Famine that Kills:* Darfur, Sudan, 1984-85 (Clarendon Press: Oxford, U.K.).

Dev, S. Mahendra (1987): "Growth and Instability in Foodgrains Production: An Inter-State Analysis", *Economic and Political Weekly*, Review of Agriculture, Vol. XXII, No.39, pp. A-82-A-92.

Dev, S. Mahendra (1995): "India's (Maharashtra) Employment Guarantee Scheme: Lessons from Long Experience", in von Bruan, Joachim (ed.): *Employment for Poverty Reduction and Food Security* (Washington: International Food Policy Research Institute, Washington, D.C.) pp.108-143

Dev, Mahendra, S. (1996): "Food Security: PDA Vs EGS, A Tale of Two States"; *Economic and Political Weekly*, Vol. 31, No.27..

Devereux, S. (1988): "Entitlements, Availability and Famine: A Revisionist View of Wollo 1972-74", *Food Policy*, Vol. 3, No.3, pp.270-82.

Devidayal, Sucheta (2000): "Is this the 21st century budget?" *Times of India*, 5th March, 2000, p.16.

Dey, J. (1984): *Women in Food Protection and Food Security in Africa* (Rome: Food and Agriculture Organisation, Rome).

Dinham, B. (1993): *The Pesticide Hazard* (London: Zed Books).

Diouf, Jacques: "Food for All, The World Food Summit", *Our Planet*, Vol.8, No.4, 1996.

Dirks, R. (1980): "Social Responses during Severe Food Shortages and Famine", *Current Anthropology,* Vol. 21, No.1.

Dixon, Ruth (1978): *Rural Women at Work: Strategies for Development in South Asia* (Baltimore, Johns Hopkins University Press).

Dommen, A. (1983): *Mali's National Food Strategy,* Paper prepared for the Food and Agriculture Organisation Political Panel, Annual Meeting of the African Studies Association, Boston.

Donovan, D. J. (1981): "Real Responses Associated with Exchange Rate Action in Selected Upper Credit Tranche Stabilisation Programmes", in *International Monetary Fund Staff Papers*, December, Vol.28, pp.681-727.

Dornbush, R. (1985): "Policy and Performance Links between LDS Debtors and Industrialised Nations", *Economic Activity No.2*, Brookings Institution, New York.

Dougill, Andrew and Jonathan Cox (eds.): "Land Degradation and Grazing in The Kalhari: New Analysis and Alternative Perspectives", *Pastoral Development Network Series 38*.

Dowler, E. A. and Seo, Y. O., Thompson, A. M. and Wheeler, F. F. (1982): "Nutritional Status Indicators: Interpretation and Policy Making Role", *Food Policy,* Vol. 7, No. 2, pp. 99-112.

Downing, T. E. (1990): *Assessing Socio-Economic Vulnerability to Famine: Frameworks, Concepts and Applications,* FEWS Working Paper, Vol. 2, No.1, USAID Famine Early Warning System Project, Washington DC.

Downing, T. C. E., Giru, K. W. and Crispin, M. K. (eds) (1989): *Coping with Drought in Kenya* (Boulder and London: Lynne Rienner Publishers).

Dreze, Jean (1988): *Famine Prevention in India,* paper presented at the World Institute for Development Economic Research, Helsinki.

Dreze, Jean (1990): "Famine Prevention in India", in Dreze, Jean and Amartya Sen (eds.): *The Political Economy of Hunger* (Oxford: The Oxford University Press.).

Dreze, Jean and Sen, Amartya (1989): *Hunger and Public Action* (Oxford: The Claredon Press).

Dreze, Jean and Amartya (eds.) (1990): *The Political Economy of Hunger* Vol. 1 Entitlement and Well-Being (Oxford: Clarendon Press).

Dreze, Jean and Amartya Sen (1995): *India: Economic Development and Social Opportunity* (New Delhi: Oxford University Press).

Dreze, J. and Amartya Sen (eds.) (1999): *Indian Development, Selected Regional Perspectives* (Oxford: Oxford University Press).

Dutta, H. S. (1988): *Irrigation Investment vis-à-vis Price Incentives for Continuous Self-Sufficiency of Food Grains in India,* mimeo, Punjab Agricultural University, Ludhiana.

Dyson, Tim (1996): *Population and Food: Global Trends and Future Prospects* (London: Routledge).

Economic and Political Weekly (1999): "Women and Work", *Economic and Political Weekly*, October 9, 1999, p. 2893.

Edwards, C. A., M. K. Wali, D. J. Horn and F. Miller (1993): *Agriculture and the Environment* (London: Elsevier Science Publishers).

Ehrlich, Paul R., Ehrlich, Anne H., and Gretchen C. Daily (1993): "Food Security, Population, and Environment", *Population and Development Review*, Vol. 19, No. 1, p. 132.

Eide A., Oshaug, A. and Eide, W. B. (1991): "Food Security and the Right to Food", *International Law and Development, Transnational Law and Contemporary Problems*, Vol. 1, No.2, pp.415-67.

Eide, A. (1989): *Right to Adequate Food as a Human Right* (Geneva: Centre for Human Rights).

Eide, W, B., Holmboe-Ottesen G, Oshaug, A., Pereta, D., Tilakaratna, S. and Wandel, M. (1986): *Introducing Nutritional Considerations into Rural Development Programmes with Focus on Agriculture: Towards Practice,* Development of Methodology for the Evaluation of Nutritional Impact of Development Programmes, Institute for Nutrition, *Research Report No. 2,* March, University of Oslo.

Eide, W. B. (1990): *Household Food Security: A Nutritional Safety Net, Discussion Paper*, International Fund for Agricultural Development, October.

Ellis, F. (1988): *Peasant Economics* (Cambridge: Cambridge University Press).

Elwin, V. (1964): *The Tribal World of Verrier Elwin: An Autobiography* (Oxford: Oxford University Press).

Evans, A. (1991): "Gender Issues in Rural Household Economics", *IDS Bulletin*, Vol. 22, No.1, pp.51-59.

Express News Service (2000): "Going deep into woes of urban water supply", *The Indian Express*, February 9, 2000, p. 10.

Falconer, J. (1989): *Forestry and Nutrition: A Reference Manual* (Rome: Food and Agriculture Organization of the United Nations.).

Falconer, J and Arnold, J. E. M. (1989): *Household Food Security and Forestry: An Analysis of Socio-Economic Issues* (Rome: Food and Agriculture Organization of the United Nations).

FAO (1993): *The State of Food And Agriculture* (Rome: FAO).

FAO (1996): *The World Food Summit Plan of Action* (Rome: Food and Agricultural Organisation).

Fernandes, Walter and G. Menon (1987): *Tribal Women and Forest Economy: Deforestation, Exploitation and Status Change* (New Delhi: Indian Social Institute).

Fernandez, Aloysius (1999): "The impact of technology adaptation on productivity and sustainability: MYRADA's experiences in Southern India", in F. Hinchcliffe, J. Thompson, J. Pretty, I. Guijt and P. Shah (editors): *Fertile Ground: The Impacts of Participatory Watershed Management* (London: Intermediate Technology Publications).

Fieldhouse, Paul (1995): *Food and Nutrition* (London, Glasgow etc: Chapman Hall).

Fogel, R. W. (1994): "Economic Growth, Population Theory and Physiology: The Bearing of Long Term Processes on the Making of Economic Policy", *American Economic Review*, Vol. 84, pp. 369-395.

Folbre, N. (1986): "Cleaning House: New Perspectives in Households and Economic Development", *Journal of Development Economics*, Vol. 22, No.1, pp. 5-40.

Fones-Sundell M and Brasch D (1989): "World Food Crisis: Myth and Reality", *Issue Paper No. 11*, Swedish University of Agricultural Sciences, Uppsala.

Food and Agriculture Organization (1974): *Annual Report* (Rome: FAO).

Food and Agriculture Organization (1976): *Indicative World Plan for Agricultural Development.* (Rome: FAO, Rome).

Food and Agriculture Organisation (1979): *The Struggle for Food Security*, (Rome: Food and Agriculture Organisation, Rome).

Food and Agriculture Organisation (1981): *Forest Resources of Tropical Asia* (Rome: Food and Agriculture Organisation, Rome).

Food and Agriculture Organisation (1981): *Agriculture Towards 2000* (Rome: Food and Agriculture Organisation, Rome).

Food and Agriculture Organization (1982): *Fruit Bearing Forest Trees* (Rome: Food and Agriculture Organization of the United Stations) Forestry Paper No. 34.

Food and Agriculture Organisation (1983): *World Food Security: A Reappraisal of the Concepts and Approaches, Director-General's Report* (Rome: Food and Agriculture Organisation).

Food and Agriculture Organisation (1983a): "Approaches to World Food Security", *Food and Agriculture Organisation Economic and Social Development Paper, No.32* (Rome: Food and Agriculture Organisation Commodities and Trade Division, Rome).

Food and Agricultural Organisation (1983b): *Fruit Bearing Forest Species 1: Examples from Eastern Africa* (Rome: Food and Agriculture Organisation of the United Nations) Forestry Paper No. 44/1.

Food and Agriculture Organisation (1984a): *Public Expenditure on Agriculture in Developing Countries, 1978-82,* Policy Analysis Division, Food and Agriculture Organisation, Rome.

Food and Agriculture Organisation (1984b): *Food and Fruit Bearing Forest Species 2: Examples from South Eastern Asia,* Forestry Paper No. 44/2 (Rome: Food and Agriculture Organisation, Rome).

Food and Agriculture Organisation (1986a): *Food and Fruit Bearing Forest Species 3: Examples from Latin America,* Forestry Paper No. FO:MISC/88/7 (Rome: Food and Agriculture Organisation, Rome).

Food and Agriculture Organisation (1988): "Agricultural Policies, Protectionism and Trade: Selected Working Papers, 1985-87", *Food and Agriculture Organisation Economic and Social Development Paper, No.75*, (Rome: Food and Agriculture Organisation, Rome).

Food and Agriculture Organisation (1988): *Methodology for Preparing Comprehensive National Food Strategies* (Rome: Food and Agriculture Organisation, Rome).

Food and Agriculture Organisation (1988a): *An Interim Report on the State of Forest Resources in the Developing Countries*, No. FO: MISC/88/7 (Rome: Food and Agriculture Organisation).

Food and Agriculture Organisation (1988b): *Structural Adjustment, Food Production and Rural Poverty,* Food and Agriculture Organisation paper presented at the International Conference on Human Dimension of Africa's Economic Recovery and Development, held on March 1988 at Khartoum, Sudan.

Food and Agriculture Organisation (1989): *Food Security Assistance Programme: Methodology for Preparing Comprehensive National Food Security Programmes,* Paper presented at the Symposium on Food Security in Africa, Dakar.

Food and Agriculture Organisation (1989a): *Preparation of Comprehensive National Food Security Programmes: Overall Approach and Issues,* Second Ad hoc Consultation on 27 October, with FSAS Donors, Rome.

Food and Agriculture Organisation (1989c): "Effects of Stabilisation and Structural Adjustment Programmes on Food Security", *Economic and Social Development Paper, No.89* (Commodities and Trade Division, Food and Agriculture Organisation, Rome).

Food and Agriculture Organisation (1989c) *Household Food Security and Forestry, An Analysis of Socio-Economic Issues* (Rome: Food and Agriculture Organisation of the United Nations) Forestry paper No. 44/3.

Food and Agriculture Organisation (1990): Annex 10, *Incorporating Nutrition and Socio-Economic Information into Early Warning and Food Information Systems in Strengthening National Early Warning and Food Information Systems in Africa,* Food and Agriculture Organization of the United Nations Workshop, 23-26 October 1989, Accra, Ghana.

Food and Agriculture Organisation (1990a): Annex 4, *National Early Warning and Food Information Systems—Their Purpose, Method and Use,* Food and Agriculture Organisation of the United Nations Workshop, 23-26 October 1989, Accra, Ghana.

Food and Agriculture Organisation (1990b): Annex 9, *Use of Food Balance Sheets for the Estimation of Deficits and Surpluses in Strengthening National Early Warning and Food Information Systems in Africa,* Food and Agriculture Organization of the United Nations Workshop, 23-26 October 1989, Accra, Ghana.

Food and Agriculture Organisation (1991): *Analysis of National Policies to be Pursued and the External Assistance Needed to Attain Food Security,* Paper presented to the Symposium on Food Security in Africa, Dakar.

Food and Agriculture Organisation (1993): *Harvesting Nature's Diversity* (Rome: FAO).

Food and Agriculture Organisation (1998): *Poverty Alleviation and Food Security in Asia: Lessons and Challenges* (Bangkok: Food and Agricultural Organization of the United Nations Regional Office for Asia and the Pacific, December 1998).

Fowler, C. and P. Mooney: *The Threatened Gene: Food, Policies and the Loss of Genetic Diversity* (Cambridge: The Lutterworth Press) 1990.

Francis, C. and Harwood, R. (1985): *Enough Food: Achieving Food Security Through Regenerative Agriculture* (Pennsylvania, USA: Rodale Press).

Francis, C. A. and J. A. King (1988): "Cropping Systems Based on Farm Derived Renewable Resources", *Agricultural Systems,* Vol. 27, pp. 67-75, 1988.

Francis, David G.: *Family Agriculture, Tradition and Transformation* (London: Earthscan Publications Ltd.) 1994.

Franke, R and Chasin, B. H. (1980): *Seeds of Famine: Ecological Destruction and the European Development* (Mont Clair: Allanheld and Asmun, Mont Clair).

Frankenberger, T. R. (1990): *Production Consumption Linkages and Coping Strategies at the Household Level,* Paper presented at the Agriculture-Nutrition Linkage Workshop, February 1990, Bureau of Science and Technology, USAID, Washington DC.

Frankenberger, T. R. and D. M. Goldstein (1990): "Food Security, Coping Strategies and Environment Degradation", *Arid Lands Newsletter,* Vol.30, Office of Arid Lands Studies, University of Arizona, pp.21-27.

Frankenberger, T. R. and D. M. Goldstein (1991): *The Long and Short of It: Household Food Security, Coping Strategies and Environment Degradation in Africa,* mimeo, Office of Arid Land Studies, The University of Arizona.

Frankenberger, T. R. and D. M. Goldstein (1991): "Linking Household Food Security with Environmental Sustainability Through an Analysis of Coping Strategies", in K Smith (ed.), *Growing Our Future* (New-York: Kumarian Press).

Friedman, Harriet (1991): "Changes in the International Division of Labor: Agri-food Complexes and Export Agriculture", being Chapter 3, in Friedland, William H. Busch, Laerence, B., Frederick, H. and Rudy Alan, P. (eds.): *Towards a New Political Economy of Agriculture* (Boulder: Westview Press).

Friedman, Harriet (1995): "Food Politic: New Dangers, New Possibilities", in McMichael, Philip (ed): *Food and Agrarian Orders in the World Economy* (London: Praeger).

Gadgil, Madhav and Guha, Rmamchandra (1992): "State Forestry and Social Conflict in British India", in Hardiman, David (ed.): *Peasant Resistence in India 1858-1914* (New Delhi: Oxford University Press)

Galbraith, J. K. (1991): "Economics in the Century Ahead", *Economic Journal*, Vol. 101, No.404.

Galtung, Johan (1978): *Goal, Processes and Indicators of Development: A Project Description* (Tokyo: UN University, Tokyo).

Galtung, Johan (1994): *Human Rights in Another Key* (Cambridge: Polity Press).

Galvin, K. (1988): "Nutritional Status as an Indicator of Impending Food Stress", *Disasters*, Vol. 12, No. 2, pp.147-56.

Gandhi, V., G. Desai, S. K. Raheja, and Prem Narain (1994): "Fertilizer response function environment and future growth of fertilizer use on wheat and rice in India", in G. Desai and A.Vaidyanathan (eds.): *Strategic Issues in Future Growth of Fertilizer Use in India* (New Delhi: Macmillan India).

Gandhi, Vasant, P. and Patel, N. T. (1997): "Pesticides and Environment: A Comparative Study of Farmer Awareness and Behaviour in Andhra Pradesh", *Indian Journal of Agricultural Economics*, Vol. 52, No. 3, July-September.

Garine, I. and G. A. Harrison (eds): *Coping with Uncertainty in Food Supply* (Oxford: Oxford Science Publication, Clarendon).

Gavan, J. and Indrani, C. (1979): *The Impact of Public Food Grain Distribution and Food Consumption and Welfare in Sri Lanka, Research Report, No. 13*, International Food Policy, Washington.

Gelbach, J. B. and L. H. Pritchett, (1996): *Does More for the Poor Mean Less for the Poor? The Politics of Tagging*, Washington D.C, The World Bank, *Policy Research Working Paper 1523*.

George, P. S. (1979): *Public Distribution of Food Grains in Kerala – Income Distribution Implications and Effectiveness, Research Report 7*, International Food Policy Research Institute, Washington.

George, P. S. and Mukherjee, C. (1986): "Rice economy of Kerala: A disaggregated analysis of performance", *Indian Journal of Agricultural Economics*, Vol. 41, No.1.

George, Susan (1977): *How the Other Half Dies: The Real Reason for World Hunger* (Montclaire: Allanheld and Osmun Publishers).

George, Susan (1978): *Feeding the Few: Corporate Control of Food* (Washington: Institute of Food Policy Studies, Washington).

George, Susan (1985): *Ill Fares the Land: Essays on Food Hunger and Power* (London: Writers and Readers, London).

George, Susan (1989): *A Fate Worse than Debt* (London: Penguin).

George, Susan and Nigel, P. (1982): *Food for Beginners* (San Fransisco: Institute for Food and Development Policy, San Fransisco).

Ghosh, Buddhadeb (1999): "Land Reforms: Lessons from West Bengal", in Sinha, B.K. and Pushpendra (eds.): *Land Reforms in India* (New Delhi: Sage).

Gillespie, S. and Mason, J. (1991): "Nutrition Relevant Actions: Some Experience from the Eighties and Lessons for the Nineties", *Nutrition Policy Discussion Paper, No.10, ACC/SCN*, Geneva.

Gittinger, J. P., Chernick, S, Horenstein, N. R and Saiter, K. (1990): "Household Food Security and the Role of Women", *World Bank Discussion Paper, No.96*, The World Bank, Washington DC.

Glower Jonathan (1995): "The research programme of development ethics", in Nussbaum, Martha and Jonathan Glower (eds.): *Women, Culture and Development: A Study of Human Capabilities* (Oxford: Clarendon Press).

Goonesekere, Savitri (1998): *Children, Law and Justice, A South Asian Perspective* (New-Delhi: Sage Publications).

Gopalan, C. (1987): *Nutrient Value of Indian Food* (Hyderabad: National Institute of Nutrition, Hyderabad).

Gordon, J.E. (1976): "Synergism of Malnutrition and Infectious Disease", *Nutrition in Preventive Medicine*, WHO Series, No. 62. WHO, Geneva.

Government of Haryana (1998): *Statistical Abstract of Haryana, 1985-86 to 1996-97* (Chandigarh: Government of Haryana).

Government of Haryana: *Statistical Data Base (1997)*, Sub-Divisional Agricultural Office, Ballabgarh, Faridabad, 1997.

Government of India (1945) *Famine Enquiry Commission Report*, Report on Bengal (New Delhi: Government of India).

Government of India (1976): *Report of the National Commission on Agriculture*, Part III: Demand and Supply (New Delhi: Ministry of Agriculture and Irrigation, New Delhi).

Government of India (1976): *Report of the National Commission on Agriculture*, Part V (New Delhi: Ministry of Agriculture).

Government of India (1990): *Agriculture in Brief* (New Delhi: Controller of Publications, Government of India).

Government of India (1992): *Economic Survey* (New Delhi: Ministry of Finance, Government of India).

Government of India (1992): *Economic Survey 1991-92*, Part II *Sectoral Developments* (New-Delhi: Department of Economic Affairs, Economic Division, Government of India).

Government of India (1993): *National Nutrition Policy* (New Delhi: Ministry of Human Resource Development, Department of Women and Child Development).

Government of India (1997): *Focus on the Poor,* Guidelines for the implementation of the Targeted Public Distribution System (New-Delhi: Ministry of Civil Supplies, Consumer Affairs and Public Distribution, Government of India).

Government of India, Planning Commission (1993): *Report of the expert group on estimation of the proportion and number of the poor* (New Delhi: Planning Commission).

Government of India (1997): *Economic Survey*, 1995-96 (New-Delhi: Ministry of Finance) 1997.

Greely, M. (1987): *Post Harvest Losses, Technology and Employment: The Case of Rice in Bangladesh* (Colorado: Westview Press).

Greely, M. and A. K. Huq (1980): *Rice in Bangladesh: An Empirical Analysis of Farm Level Food Losses in Five Post-Production Operations* (Dhaka: Bangladesh Institute of Development Studies) mimeographed.

Greenough, P. (1982): *Prosperity and Misery in Modern Bengal: The Famine of 1943-1944* (New York: Oxford University Press).

Grierson (1926): *Bihar Peasants Life Being a Discursive Catalogue of the Surrounds of the People of that State* (London).

Guhan, S. (1981): *Social Security: Lessons and Possibilities from Tamil Nadu Experience,* (Madras: Madras Institute of Development Studies) *Bulletin No.11*.

Gulati, A., and C. H. Hanumantha Rao (1994): "Indian agriculture: Emerging Perspectives and Policy Issues", *Economic and Political Weekly*, December 31, A158-A169.

Gulati, Ashok and A. N. Sharma (1992): "Subsidising Agriculture: A Cross Country View", *Economic and Political Weekly*, Vol. XXVII, No.39, September 26.

Gulati, Ashok, and Anil Sharma (1997): "Freeing Trade in Agriculture: Implications for Resource Use Efficiency and Cropping Pattern Changes", *Economic and Political Weekly*, Vol. 32, No. 52, pp. A154-A164.

Gupta, S.P. (1999): *Globalisation, Economic Reforms and the Role of Labour,* Society for Economic and Social Transition, New Delhi.

Gupta, S. P. (2000): "Trickle down theory revisited: The role of employment and poverty", *Indian Journal of Labour Economics*, Jan-March.

Guruswamy, Mohan (2000): "The Sad Face of Liberalisation", *Indian Express*, 10th April, 2000.

Haddad, L., Sullivan, J. and Kennedy, E. (1991): *Identification and Evaluation of Alternative Indicators of Food and Nutrition Security: Some Conceptual Issues and an Analysis of Extant Data* (Washington DC: International Food Policy Research Institute).

Haddad, Lawrence and Howarth E. Bouis (1991): "The Impact of Nutritional Status on Agricultural Productivity: Wage Evidence from the Philippines", *Oxford Bulletin of Economics and Statistics*, Vol. 53, No.1, pp.45-68.

Halbwachs, G (1984): "Organisational responses of higher plants to atmospheric pollutants: sulphur dioxide and fluoride", in M. Treshow (ed.): *Air Pollution and Plant Life* (Chichester: John Wiley and Sons) 1984.

Hanumantha Rao, C. H. (1989): *Technological Change in Indian Agriculture, Emerging Trends and Perspectives, Presidential Address* to The Golden Jubilee Conference of The Indian Society of Agricultural Economics, Bombay, December 1989.

Hanumantha Rao, C. H. (2000): "Declining Demand for Foodgrains in Rural India: Causes and Implications", *Economic and Political Weekly*, Vol. 35, No. 4, pp.201-206.

Hanumantha Rao, C. H. and Radhakrishna, R. (1998): *National Food Security: A Policy Perspective for India* (Mimeo).

Harle, V. (ed.) (1976): *Political Economy of Food: Proceeding of an International Seminar Tampere Peace Research Institute*, Research Report No. 12, Tampere.

Harrington, Michael (1962): *The Other America: Poverty in the United States* (New-York: Macmillan).

Harriss, Barbara (1990): "The intra-family distribution of hunger in South Asia", in Deze, Jean and Amartya Sen (eds.): *The Political Economy of Hunger*, Volume 1 (Oxford: Clarendon Press).

Hartmann, B. and J. Boyce (1983): *A Quite Violence: View from a Bangladesh Village* (London: Zed Books).

Heald, C. and Lipton, M. (1984): *African Food Strategies and the EEC's Role: An Interim Review, Commissioned Study, No.6*, Institute of Development Studies, Brighton.

Heiser, C. B. Jr. (1981): *Seeds to Civilization: The Story of Food* (2nd edition) (San Francisco: W H Freeman & Co).

Helleniner, G. K. (1990): "Free Strategy in Medium-Term Adjustment", in *World Development*, Vol. 18, No. 16, pp. 879-97.

Hindle, R. (1990): "The World Bank Approach to Food Security Analysis", *IDS Bulletin*, Vol. 21, No. 3, pp.62-66.

Hines, C. and Dinham, B (1984): "Can Agri Business Feed Africa", *The Ecologist*, Vol. 14, No. 2.

Hobbelnik (eds.) (1992): *Growing Diversity: Genetic Resources and Local Food Security* (London: IT Publications).

Hobbs, P., and M. Morris (1996): *Meeting South Asia's Future Food Requirements from Rice-Wheat Cropping Systems: Priority Issues Facing Researchers in the Post-Green Revolution Era*, Natural Resources Group (Mexico City: International Maize and Wheat Improvement Center).

Hobsbawm, Eric (2000): *The New Century* (London: The New Press).

Hoehn, Richard A. (1999): *Introduction, The Changing Politics of Hunger* (Maryland: Bread For the World Institute).

Holmes, Joan (2000): *Women and Ending Hunger—the Global Perspective*, lecture at the Institute of Social Sciences, New-Delhi, 2nd March 2000.

Hopkins, R. F. (1986): "Food Security Policy Options and the Evolution of State Responsibility", in Tullis, F. L. and Hollist, W. L. (eds.): *Food, the State and International Political Economy: Dilemmas of Developing Countries* (Lincoln and London: University of Nebraska Press).

Hopper, G. R. (1999): "Changing Food Production and Quality of Diet in India", *Population and Development Review*, Vol. 25, No. 3, September.

Howes, M. (1985): *Whose Water? An Investigation of the Consequences of Alternative Approaches to the Small Scale Irrigation in Bangladesh* (Dhaka: Bangladesh Institute of Development Studies).

Huang, J., and H. Bouis (1996): "Structural changes in the demand for food in Asia; Food, Agriculture, and the Environment", *Discussion Paper 11*, Washington, DC: International Food Policy Research Institute.

Hubbard, M. (1995): *Improving Food Security: Guide for Rural Development Managers* (London: Intermediate Technology Press).

Huddleston, B. (1990): "Food and Agriculture Organisation's Overall Approach and Methodology for Formulating National Food Security Programmes in Developing Countries", *IDS Bulletin*, Vol. 21, No. 3, pp.72-80.

Human Development Centre (1999): *Human Development Report for South Asia, 1999* (New York: Oxford University Press).

Hutchinson, B. and Frankenberger, T. (1992): *A Selected Annonated Bibliography on Indicators with Application to Household Food Security (draft)*, Office of Arid Lands Studies, University of Arizona.

IFDA (1987): *Annual Report 1987*, (Rome: International Fund for Agricultural Development).

IFDA (1991): *Food Security in Africa,* Paper presented at the Symposium of Food Security in Africa, pp. 3-4, Dakar.

IFPRI (1984): *Assessment of Food Demand-Supply Prospects and Related Strategies for Developing Member Countries of the Asian Development Bank* (Washington, D.C.: International Food Policy Research Institute). Mimeo.

IGADD (1990): *Food Security Strategy Study*, Vol. 1, Final Report, October (Dijibouti: IGADD, Dijibouti).

Ikerd, J., S. Monson and D.V. Dyne (1992): *Potential Impacts of Sustainable Agriculture* (Missouri: University of Missouri, Department of Agricultural Economics).

Ikerd, J., S. Monson and D. V. Dyne (1992): *Potential Impacts of Sustainable Agriculture* (Missouri: University of Missouri, Department of Agricultural Economics).

Indian Express (1999): "No Rains Means More Pesticides in Your Subzi", *Express Newsline*. New-Delhi, 25th September 1999.

Indrakant, S. (1995): *Food Security and Public Distribution System in Andhra Pradesh,* Workshop on Food Security and Public Distribution System in India, Planning Commission, New Delhi, April.

International Fund for Agricultural Development (1992): *The State of the World Rural Poverty, A Profile of Asia* (Rome: IFAD).

Institute of Social Studies (1994): *Status of Panchayati Raj in the States of India,* (New Delhi: Institute of Social Studies), mimeograph.

International Institute for Environment and Development: *RRA Notes, No.15* (London: IIED) 1992.

J. M. (1992): "Waiting for the Rains", *Economic and Political Weekly,* 1992.

J. M. (1994): "Food Exports and Food Requirement", *Economic and Political Weekly,* Vol. XXIX, No. 35, pp. 2261.

Jain, Anrudh K. (1985): "Determinants of regional variation in infant mortality in Rural India", *Population Studies*, Vol. 39, No. 3, pp. 407-24.

Jain, L.R. and B.S. Minhas (1991): "Rural and urban consumer price indices by commodity groups (States and all India: 1970-71 to 1983)", *Sarvekshana*, Vol. XV, No. 1, pp.1-21.

Jain, Onu (1999): "No Rains means more pesticides in your subzi", *Indian Express*, New-Delhi, 25th September 1999.

Jaiswal, Meera (1999): *Second Round of the Study on Impact of Air Pollution on Agriculture in Urban and Peri-Urban Areas of Faridabad* (Ranchi: Ranchi University) 1999, mimeograph.

Jaizairy, Idriss, Mohiuddin Alamgir and Theresa Panuccio (1992): *The State of World Rural Poverty* (Rome: International Fund for Agricultural Development).

Jeffery, Patricia, Roger Jeffrey and Andrew Lyon (1989): *Labour Pains and Labour Power* (london: Zed Books and New-Delhi: Manohar).

Jefrey, Patricia and Jefrey, Roger (1996): *Don't Marry Me to a Plowman* (New Delhi: Sage).

Jha, D., P. Kumar, Mruthyunjaya S. Pal, S. Selvarajan and A. Singh (1995): "Research Priorities in Indian Agriculture", *NCAP Policy Paper* 3, New Delhi.

Jha, Shikha and P. V. Srinivasan (1999): "Grain price stabilization in India: Evaluation of policy alternatives", *Agricultural Economics*, Vol. 21, pp. 93-108.

Jharwal, S. M. (1998): *Public Distribution System in India Reassessed* (New-Delhi: Manak Publications).

Jodha, N.S. (1975): "Famine and Famine Policies: Some Empirical Evidence", *Economic and Political Weekly*, October 11, 1975, pp. 1605-23.

Jodha, N. S. (1978): "Effectiveness of Farmers' Adjustment to Risk", *Economic and Political Weekly*, pp. A28-38..

Jodha, N. S. (1978a): "Population Growth and Decline in Common Property Resources in Rajasthan", *Population and Development Review*, Vol. 11.

Jodha, N.S. (1986): "Common Property Resources and Rural Poor in Dry Regions of India", *Economic and Political Weekly*, Vol. 21, No. 27.

Jodha, N. S. (1989): *Management of Common Property Resources in Selected Areas in India,* a paper read at the Seminar on Approaches to Participatory Development and Management of Common Property Resources, held on 10th March, 1989, at the Institute of Economic Growth, New Delhi.

Jodha, N.S. (1990): "Rural Common Property Resources: Contribution and Crisis", *Economic and Political Weekly*, pp. A65-A78. A slightly modified version is his *Rural Common Property Resources: A Growing Crisis* (London: International Institute for Environment and Development), Gatekeeper Series (1990).

Jodha, N. S. (1991): *Rural Common Property Resources: A Growing Crisis* (London: International Institute for Environment and Development), Gatekeeper Series No. 24.

Jodha, N.S. (2000): "Waste Lands Management in India: Myths, Motives and Mechanisms", *Economic and Political Weekly*, Vol. 35, No. 6, February 5-11.

Jonsson, U. and Toole, D. (1991): *Household Food Security and Nutrition: A Conceptudl Analysis,* mimeo (New York: UNICEF).

Jonsson, U. (1984): "The Socio-Economic Causes of Hunger", in Asbjorn Eide, Winche Barth Eide, Susantha Goonatilake, Joan Gussow and Omawale (ed.): *Food As a Human Right* (Tokyo: United Nations University).

Jonsson, U. and Toole, D. (1991a): *Conceptual Analysis of Resources and Resource Control in Relation to Malnutrition, Disease and Mortality,* mimeo, UNICEF, New York.

Jonsson, U., and Thierry Brun (1978): *The Politics of Food and Nutrition Planning* in L. Joy, (ed.) *Nutrition Planning: The State of the Art* (London: IPC Technology Press).

Joshi, Hema and Sunita Bisht (1999): *Report on Impact of Air Pollution on Agriculture in Urban and Peri-Urban Areas* (New-Delhi: National Institute of Urban Affairs).

Joshi, P. K, S. P. Wani, V. K. Chopde and J. Foster (1996): "Farmers Perception of Land Degradation: A Case Study", *Economic and Political Weekly*, Vol. 31, June 29.

Joshi, P. K. (1997): "Farmer's investments and government intervention in salt-affected and waterlogged soils", in J. M. Kerr, D. K. Marothia, K. Singh, C. Ramasamy, and W. R. Bently, (eds.) *Natural Resources Economics: Concepts and Applications to India* (New Delhi: Oxford and IBH).

Joshi, P. K. and D. Jha (1992): "An Economic Inquiry into the Impact of Soil Alkalinity and Water Logging", *Indian Journal of Agricultural Economics*, Vol. 47, No. 2, April-June.

Joshi, Sharmila (1999): *The Girl Child, Free and Compulsory Education is Imperative,* in *The Unseen Workers, On the Trail of the Girl Child*, writings by Fellows of the National Foundation for India (Bangalore: Books for Change) 1999.

Joy, L. (1973): "Food and Nutrition Planning", *Journal of Agricultural Economics*, Vol. 24, No. 1, pp. 165-197.

Judd, M. A., J. K. Boyce and R. E. Evenson (1983): *Investing in Agricultural Supply* (Connecticut: Economic Growth Center, Yale University) Mimeo.

Kabeer, Naila (1991): "Gender, Production and Well Being: Rethinking the Household Economy", *IDS Discussion Paper No. 288*, (Brighton: IDS, University of Sussex).

Kabeer, Naila (1990): "Women, Household, Food Security and Coping Strategies", *ACC/SCN Symposium Report, Nutrition Policy Paper 6*, ACC/SCN, Geneva.

Kabeer, Naila (1991): "Monitoring Poverty as if Gender Mattered: A Methodology for Rural Bangaldesh", University of Sussex, Institute of Development Studies *Discussion Paper No. 255* 1989, and *Journal of Peasant Studies*, 1991.

Kakwani, N. C. and K. Subha Rao (1990): "Rural Poverty and its Alleviation in India", *Economic and Political Weekly*, Vol. XV, No. 13.

Kannan, K. P. and K. Pushpangadan (1990): "Dissecting agricultural stagnation in Kerala: An analysis across Crops, Seasons and Regions", *Economic and Political Weekly*, Vol. XXV, Nos. 35 and 36, pp. 1991-2004.

Kannan, K.P. (1999): *State Assisted Social Security in Kerala,* paper presented at the National Seminar on Social Security in India, India International Centre, New Delhi during April 1999 and organized by the Institute of Human Development, New Delhi.

Kannan, K. P. (2000): *Food Security in a Regional Perspective: A View from Food Deficit Kerala,* paper read at national seminar on food security at Hyderabad, March 25-27, 2000.

Kanwar, J. S. (1982): Presidential Address to the XII International Congress of Soil Science, organized at New Delhi, held in February 1982 under the auspices of the Indian Society for Soil Science, Division of Soil Science and Agricultural Chemistry, Indian Agricultural Research Institute, New Delhi.

Kashyap, S. P. and Niti Mathur (1999): "Ongoing changes in Policy Environment and Farm Sector: Role of Agro-Climatic Regional Planning Approach", *Economic and Political Weekly*, Vol. XXXIV, No. 26, June 26-July 2 (Review of Agriculture).

Kates, R, and V. Haarmann (1992): "Where The Poor Live: Are The Assumptions Correct?" *Environment*, Vol. 34, No. 4, pp. 5-11, 25-28.

Keatinge, G. F. (1993): "Agricultural Progress in Western India", *Poona Agricultural College Magazine*, July, 1913.

Kelly, M. R. (1982): *The Economics of Land Reform and Farm Size in India* (New Delhi: Macmillan).

Kelly, T. G. and P. Parthasarthy Rao (1994): "Chickpea Competetiveness in India", *Economic and Political Weekly*, Vol. 29, No. 26, March 25.

Kenmore, P. (1991): *How Rice Farmers Clean Up the Environment, Conserve Biodiversity, Raise More Food, Make Higher Profits* (Manila: Food and Agriculture Organisation).

Kennedy, E, and Cogill, B. (1988): "The Commercialization of Agriculture and Household Level Food Security: The Case of South-Western Kenya", *World Development*, Vol. 16, No. 9, pp. 1075-1081.

Kennes, W. (1990): "The European Community and Food Security", *IDS Bulletin*, Vol. 21, No.3, pp 67-71, Institute of Development Studies, Brighton.

Kenya, Republic of (1982): *The Concept of Food Security and How it Relates to Kenya,* Proceedings of the Workshop on Food Policy Research Priorities, held on 14-17 June 1982.

Keonig, D. (1988): "National Organizations and Famine Early Warning: The Case of Mali", *Disasters*, Vol. 12, No. 2, pp. 157-68.

Kerr, John M.; Dinesh K. Marothia, Kartar Singh, C. Ramaswamy and William R. Bentley (eds.): *Natural Resources Economics* (New-Delhi and Calcutta: Oxford and IBH Publishing Co.) 1997, Chapter 3.

Khadka, N. (1990): "Regional Cooperation for Food Security in South Asia", *Food Policy*, Vol. 15, No. 6, December 1990, pp. 492-504.

Khadka, N. (1991): "Regional Food Security Through Regional Food Reserve in South Asia: The Prospect", *Quarterly Journal of International Agriculture*, Vol.30, No.3, July-September, pp.264-83.

Khare, Arvind et. al. (2000): *Joint Forestry Management: Policy, Practice and Prospects* (London: International Institute for Environment and Development and New-Delhi: WWF).

Khoshoo, T.N. (1984), *Environmental Concerns and Strategies* (New-Delhi: India Environmental Society).

Kielman, A. and McCord, C. (1978): "Weight for Age as an Index of Risk of Death in Children", *The Lancet* 1, p.1247.

Kielman, A. A., et. al. (1977): *The Narangwal Nutrition Study: A Summary Review*, Department of International Health, mimeo, School of Hygiene and Public Health, John Hopkins University, Baltimore.

Koester, U. (1986): *Regional Cooperation to Improve Food Security in Southern and Eastern African Countries* (Washington: International Food Policy Research Institute).

Koshy, A., A. A. Gopalakrishnan, V.Vijayachandran and N. K. Jayakumar (1989): *Report of the Study on Evaluation of the Public Distribution System in Kerala*, Centre for Management Development, Trivandrum.

Krachut, U. (1981): "Food Security for People in the 1980s", Paper prepared for discussion at the North-South Food Roundable Meeting, Washington.

Kriesel, S. and S. Zaidi, (1999): *The Targeted Public Distribution System in Uttar Pradesh, India—A Evaluation,* Draft Paper, The World Bank, Washington, August.

Krishnaswamy, P. B. (1977): *Micro-Macro Links in Planning*, Monograph No.9, (Canbera: The Australian National University, Development Studies, Canberra).

Kuchli, C. (1997): *Forests of Hope: Stories of Regeneration* (London: Earthscan, London).

Kuhn, B. A., P. A. Dunn, D. Smallwood, K. Hanson, J. Blaylock and S.Vogel (1996): "The Food Stamp Program and Welfare Reform", *Journal of Economic Perspectives*, Vol. 10, No. 2, Spring, pp. 189-198.

Kuliraj, B. F. (1982): "Impact of Cash Crop Economy of the Tribes of Wyanad", *Journal of Indian Anthropological Society*, Vol. 17, No. 1, 1982.

Kumar, Davinder (2000): "Hunger's Warning Call", *Indian Express* dated 2nd March 2000.

Kumar, K. (1989): *Indicators for Measuring Changes in Income, Food Availability and Consumption, and the Natural Resource Base,* Program Design and Evaluation Methodology, No.12, USAID, Washington DC.

Kumar, Navika (2000): "Ration Wheat, Rice Prices to go up", *The Indian Express,* New Delhi, 29th February, 2000, p.11.

Kumar, P. (1998): *Food demand and supply projections for India, Agricultural Economics Policy Paper 98-01* (New Delhi: Indian Agricultural Research Institute).

Kumar, Praduman, (1996): "Agricultural Productivity and Food Security in India: Implication for Policy Analysis", *Agricultural Economic Research Review,* Vol. 9 No. 2, pp. 128-141.

Kumar, Praduman and Joshi, P. K. (1998): "Sustainability of Rice-Wheat Based Cropping Systems in India: Socio-Economic and Policy Issues", *Economic and Political Weekly,* Vol. 33, No. 39.

Kumar, Praduman and Mathur, V.C. (1996): "Measurement and Analysis of total Factor Productivity and Sources of Growth for Rice in India", *Economic and Political Weekly,*

Kumar, Praduman and Mathur, V.C. (1997): "Agriculture in Future Demand—Supply Perspective", in Bhupat M. Desai (eds.): *Agricultural Development Paradigm for the Ninth Plan under New Economic Environment* (New-Delhi: Oxford & IBH Publishing Co. Pvt. Ltd.).

Kumar, Praduman and M. W. Rosegrant (1994): "Productivity and Sources of Growth for Rice in India", *Economic and Political Weekly,* A183-88.

Kumar, Praduman and M. W. Rosegrant (1997): "Dynamic Supply Response of Cereals and Supply Projections: A 2020 Vision", *Agricultural Economic Research Review,* Vol. 10, No. 1, 1-24.

Kumar, Praduman, Mark W. Rosergrant and Howarth E. Bouis (1996): *Demand for Foodgrains and Other Food in India, Indian Agricultural Research Institute,* New Delhi and International Food Policy Research Institute, Washington, D.C., Mimeo.

Kumar, S. K. (1988): "Effects of Seasonal Food Shortage on Agricultural Productions in Zambia", *World Development,* Vol. 16, No. 9, pp. 051-63.

Kumar, Somesh (1999): "Application of Force Field Analysis in PRA", *Exchanges,* Bangalore, Issue Nos. 25 and 26, June and September 1999.

Kyle, R (1987): "Rodents Under the Carving Knife", *New Scientists,* June 1987, pp.58-61.

Kynch, Jocelyn and Amartya Sen (1983): "Indian Women: Well-being and Survival", *Cambridge Journal of Economics,* Vol. 7, Nos. 3-4, pp. 363-80.

Kynch, Jocelyn and Mike Maguire (1994): *Food and Human Growth in Palanpur* (London: STICERD, London School of Economics).

Kynch, Jocelyn and Mike Maguire (1989): "Wasted Cultivators and Stunted Little Girls: Variations in Nutritional Status in a North Indian Village", *Discussion Paper 69*, (Oxford: University of Oxford, Institute of Economics and Statistics).

L.B.S. National Academy of Administration (1991): *Report of Tenancy Situation in Bihar.* Paper presented in Workshop on Land Reforms in Bihar, Februrary 8-11.

Lappe, F. M. and Collins, J. (1986): *World Hunger: Twelve Myths* (New-York:Grove Press Inc.).

Leach, M. and Mearns, R. (1991): *Poverty and Environment in Developing Countries: An Overview Study,* Global Environmental Change Initiative Programme Final Report to Economic and Social Research Council, Society and Politics Group and ODA, IDS University of Sussex, December.

Leslie, K. and Rankine, L. B. (eds.) (1987): *Papers and Recommendations on Food and Nutrition Security in Jamaica in the 1980s and Beyond,* National Food and Nutrition Coordinating Committee of Jamaica, Kingston.

Levinson, F. J. (1974): *Morinda: An Economic Analysis of Malnutrition Among Young Children in Rural India, International Nutrition Policy Series* (Mass: Cornell–MIT, Massachusetts).

Lewin, Kurt (1951): *Field Theory in Social Sciences* (New-York: Harper Row).

Lewis, J. (1992): "Brundtland Commission Urges New Global Partnership", *Perspective, No. 8*, Spring, 1992.

Lipton, M. (1983): "Poverty, Under-Nutrition and Hunger", *World Bank Staff Working Paper, No. 597,* The World Bank, 1983.

Lipton, M. (1984): "Urban Bias Revisited", *Journal of Development Studies*, Vol. 20.

Lipton, M. (1985): "Land Assets and Rural Poverty", *World Bank Staff Working Paper, No.774*, World Bank, Washington DC.

Lipton, M. (1985): *Modern Varieties: International Agricultural Research and the Poor, Study Paper, No .2*, Consultative Group on International Agriculture, Washington.

Lipton, Micheal and R. Longhurst (1989): *New Seeds and Poor People* (London: Unwin Hyman).

Ljungqvist, B., O. Mgaza and U. Jonsson (1980): *The Role of Nutrition Surveys in Solving Nutrition Problems,* Nutrition in Europe: Proceedings of the Third European Nutrition Conference, Uppsala, Sweden, 19-21 June 1979.

Lobao, Londa M. (1990): *Locality and Inequality: Farm and Industry Structure and Socio-Economic Conditions* (Albany: State University of New-York Press) 1990.

Longhurst, R. (1986): "Famines: Issues and Opportunities for Policy and Research", *Food and Nutrition*, Vol. 9, No.1.

Longhurst, R. (1986): "Household Food Strategies in Response to Seasonality and Famine", *IDS Bulletin,* Vol. 17, pp.27-35.

Longhurst, R. (1987): "Rapid Rural Appraisal: An Improved Means of Information Gathering for Rural Development and Nutrition Projects", *Food Nutrition*, Vol.13, No.1, pp.44-47.

Longman, K. A. and Jenik, J. (1990): *Tropical Forest Ecology* (Cambridge: Cambridge University Press).

Maganda, B. F. (1989): "Surveys and Activities of the Central Bureau of Statistics Related to Food Monitoring", in Downing, T. E., Gitu, K. W. and Crispin M. K. (eds.): *Coping with Drought in Kenya* (Boulder and London: Lynne Rienner).

Mahendra, Dev S. (1996): "Food Security PDS Vs EGS", *Economic and Political Weekly*, July 6.

Mahendra, Dev S. (1998): "Public Distribution System: Impact on Poor and Options for Reform", *Economic and Political Weekly*, August 29.

Majumdar, N.A (1999): "Investment in Agriculture and the Globalization Syndrome", *Economic and Political Weekly*, Vol. 34, No. 14, April 3.

Malambo, L. (1988): *Rural Food Security in Zambia,* Studies Related to Integrated Rural Development, No. 29, (Hamburg: Justus-Liebing Giessen University).

Malhotra, K.C. and Gadgil, M. (1988): "Coping with uncertainty in food supply: Case studies among the pastoral and non-pastoral nomads of western India", in Garine, I. and G. A. Harrison (eds): *Coping with Uncertainty in Food Supply* (Oxford: Oxford Science Publication, Clarendon).

Malhotra, K. C. et. al. (1992): *Role of Non-Timber Forest Produce in Village Economy* (Calcutta: IBRAD).

Mallik, R. M. (1997): *Forest Dweller Economy and Non-Timber Forest Produce in Orissa: An Empirical Exercise on Seclected Items* (Dehradun: Centre for Minor Forest Produce).

Manuliak, Kristy (1999): "Women and Children Last?" in Bread for the World Institute*: The Changing Politics of Hunger* (Maryland: Bread for the World Institute).

Margolius, R. and Mukhier, M. O. (1989): *Community Based Information Systems for Food Security Monitoring: The Role of the Sudanese Red Crescent Drought Monitoring Programme in Northern Darfun,* mimeo, Sudan.

Markhan, Adams (1994): *A Brief History of Pollution* (London: Earthscan Publications Ltd.).

Marothia, Dinesh (1997): "Agricultural Technology and Environmental Quality: An Institutional Perspective", *Indian Journal of Agricultural Economics*, Vol. 52, No. 2. July-September.

Marshall, Fiona; Mike Ashmore and Fiona Hinchcliffe (1997): *A Hidden threat to food production: air pollution and agriculture in the developing world* (London: International Institute for Environment and Development) Gatekeeper Series No. 73, 1997.

Mason, J., et. al. (1985): "Identifying Nutritional Consideration in Planning and Rural Development Project in Haiti", *Food Nutrition*, No. 18, pp.1-17.

Mason, J., Habicht, J. P., Tabetan H and Valverde, V. (1984): *Nutritional Surveillance* (Geneva: WHO).

Maxwell, S., Swift, J. and Buchanan-Smith, M. (1990): "Is Food Security Targeting Possible in Sub-Saharan Africa? Evidence from North Sudan", *IDS Bulletin*, Vol. 21, No. 3, pp. 52-61.

Maxwell, S. (1988): *National Food Security Planning: First Thoughts from Sudan*, Paper presented at Workshop on Food Security in the Sudan, *Discussion Paper, No.262*, IDS, Sussex, 3-5 October 1988.

Maxwell, S. (1989): "Food Insecurity in North Sudan", *Discussion Paper, No.262*, IDS, University of Sussex, Brighton.

Maxwell, S. (1989): "Rapid Food Security Assessment: A Pilot Exercise in Sudan", *RRA Notes*, No.5, International for Environment and Development, London.

Maxwell, S. (1990): "Food Security in Developing Countries: Issues and Options for the 1990s", *IDS Bulletin*, Vol.21, No.3, Institute of Development Studies, University of Development Studies, University of Sussex, Brighton.

Maxwell, S. (ed.) (1991): *To Cure All Hunger: Food Policy and Food Security in Sudan* (London: Intermediate Technology Publications).

Maxwell, S. and Fernando, A. (1989): "Cash Crops in Developing Countries: The Issues, the Facts, the Policies", *World Development*, Vol. 17, No. 11.

Maxwell, S. and Smith, M. et. al. (1992): *Household Food Security: A Conceptual Review*, mimeo, March, Institute of Development Studies, Univesity of Sussex, Brighton.

McCracken J., Pretty, J. and Conway, G. (1988): *An Introduction to Rapid Rural Appraisal for Agricultural Development*, mimeo, International Institute for Environment and Development, London.

Mchemet, O. (1983): "Market Imperfections and Equity Efficiency Conflicts in Project Evaluation Export Agriculture Versus Local Food", *South East Asian Economic Review*, December, Vol.4, No.3.

McInerney, J. (1983): "A Synoptic View of Policy Making for the Food Sector", in Burns, J. McInerney, J. and Swinbank, A. (eds.): *The Food Industry* (London: Heineman).

McIntire, J. (1981): "Food Security in the Sahel: Variable Import Levy, Grain Reserves and Foreign Exchange Assistance", *IFPRI Research Report*, No.26, IFPRI, Washington.

Mehta, Jaya (1997): "Employment and Unemployment in Indian Economy", in *Alternative Economic Survey 1996-1997* (New- Delhi: Delhi Science Forum).

Mellor, J. (1988): "Global Food Balances and Food Security", *World Development*, Vol. 16, No. 9, pp.997-1011.

Mellor, J. (1990): "Global Food Balances and Food Security", in Carl, K. Eicher and John, M. Staatz (eds.): *Agricultural Development in the Third World* (Baltimore: John Hopkins University Press).

Mellor, J. W. (1976): "Food Aid for Security and Development", in Clay, E. and Shaw, J. (eds.): *Poverty, Development and Food*, (London: Macmillan).

Mellor, J. W. (1988): "Towards an Ethical Redistribution of Food and Agricultural Science", in LeMary B. W. J. (eds.): *Science, Ethics and Food* (Washington DC: Smithsonian Institution).

Mellor, J. W. and Raisuddin Ahmed (eds.) (1988): *Agricultural Prone Policies for Developing Countries* (Baltimore: John Hopkins Press).

Merrick, Laura (1990): "Crop Diversity and its Conservation in Traditional Agroecosystems", in M. E. Altieri and S. B. Hecht (eds.): *Agroecology and Small Farm Development* (Bosca Raton: CRC Press).

Messer, E. (1989): "Seasonality in Food Systems: An Anthropological Perspective on Household Food Security", in David, E. S. (ed.): *Seasonal Viability in Third World Agriculture* (Baltimore: John Hopkins University Press for the International Food Policy Research Institute).

Messer, E. (1990): "Food Wars: Hunger as a Weapon of War", in *The Hunger Report: 1990*, The Alan Shawn Feinstein World Hunger Problem (Providence RI: Brown University).

Minear, Larry, Colin Scott and Thomas Weiss (1996): *The News Media, Civil War and Humanitarian Action* (Boulder: Lynne Rienner).

Minhas, B. S. (1976): "Presidential Address—Towards National Food Security", *Indian Journal of Agricultural Economics*, Vol. 31, No. 4, October-December 1976, pp.8-19.

Minhas, B. S. (1991): "On Estimating the Inadequacy of Energy Intake: Revealed Food Consumption Behaviour Versus Nutritional Norm (Nutritional Status of Indian People in 1983)", *The Journal of Development Studies*, Vol.28, No.1, pp.1-38.

Mlambo, L. (1988): *Rural Food Security in Zambia,* Studies related to Integrated Rural Development, N-29 (Hamburg: Justus-Liebing Giesen University).

Mlbogoh, S. G. (1982): *A Review of Kenya's National Food Policy,* Proceedings of the Workshop on Food Policy Research Priorities, 14-17 June 1982, Nairobi.

Moghe, K., (1997): "Redefining the Poor", *Frontline,* 14-21, Oct. 31.

Mooij, J. (1999): *Food Policy and the Indian State* (Delhi: Oxford University Press).

Mooij, Jos (1999b): "Food Policy in India: The importance of electoral politics in policy implementation", *Journal of International Development,* Vol.11, pp. 625-636.

Morgan, D. (1985): "Merchants of Grain", in Beradi, G. M. (ed.): *World Food, Population and Development* (Totowa, New Jersey: Rowman and Allanheld).

Morgan, D. H. (1982): *Coping with Uncertainty in Food Supply* (Oxford: Clarendon, Oxford Science Publication).

Morgan, D. H. (1982): "The Place of Harvesters in Nineteenth-Century Village Life", in Samuel, R. (ed.): *Village Life and Labour* (London: Routeledge and Kegan Paul).

Morris, B. (1982): *Forest Traders, A Socio Economic Study of the Hill Pandaram* (New-Jersy: Athlone Press)

Moris, J. R. (1989): "Indigenous Versus Introduced Solutions to Food Stress", in David, E. Sahn (ed.): *Seasonal Variability in Third World Agriculture: The Consequences for Food Security* (Maryland, USA: International Food Policy Research Institute, John Hopkins University Press).

Muhammed, A. (1987): *Present Situation and Future Outlook for Food Security in the Muslim World,* in *Food Security in the Muslim World,* Proceedings of the Seminar on Food Security in the Muslim World, 5-7, December, organized by the Islamic Academy of Sciences, Amman, Jordan.

Mukherjee, Amitava (1993): *Structural Adjustment Programme, Putting the First Things, Poverty and Environment Last* (New Delhi: Segment Books).

Mukherjee, Amitava (1994): *Structural Adjustment Programme and Food Security: Hunger and Poverty in India* (Avebury: Aldershot, Brookfield, Honkong, Singapore and Sydney).

Mukherjee, Amitava (1997): "Institutional Sanction, Choice and the Secondary Food System: Incompleteness of Sen's Entitlement and Depreciation Thesis as an Explanation of Hunger", in George K. K. et. al. (eds.): *Economic Development and the Quest for Alternatives* (NewDelhi: Concept) and *Indian Economic Journal,* Vol. 43, No. 4, April-June, 1995-1996.

Mukherjee, Amitava and Mukherjee Neela (1994): "Rural Women and Food Insecurity: What a Food Calendar Reveals", *Economic and Political Weekly,* No.11, March 12.

Mukherjee, N. and Mukherjee, A. (1997): "Rural Women's Participation: Food Gathering, Food Insecurity and Hunger Periods: Some Policy Implications from Village Krishna Rakshit Chak", in Agarwal, Anil (ed.): *The Challenge of the Balance Environmental Economics in India* (New Delhi: Centre for Science and Environment).

Mukherjee, Neela and Mukherjee, Amitava (1997): "Food Calendar Once Again", *PRA, M&E Information Pack,* IDS, University of Sussex, Brighton.

Mukherjee, Amitava (1999): *Voices of the Silent Majority: Community Perspectives on Air Pollution, Crop Yields and Food Security, Report on the Project on Impact of Air Pollution and Crop Yield* of the T. H. Huxley School at the Imperial College of Science, Technology and Medicines, University of London, London and The International Institute for Environment and Development, London.

Mukherjee, Amitava (1999a): *What Johan Galtung Did Not Say,* paper read at the Foundation Day Seminar of the National Institute of Rural Development, Hyderabad, 22nd November, 1999, reprinted in Choudhury, R.C. and R.P. Singh (2000): *Rural Prosperity and Agriculture Policies and Strategies* (Hyderabad: National Institute of Rural Development).

Mukherjee, Amitava and Mukherjee, Neela (2000): "Rural Women and Food Insecurity: a Longitudinal Study", in Mukherjee Neela et. al., (eds.): *Learning to Share* (New-Delhi: Concept Publishing Company).

Mukherjee, Neela (1995, 1997 reprint): *Participatory Rural Appraisal* (New-Delhi: Concept Publishing Company).

Mukherjee, Neela (1997): *Participatory Rural Appraisal and Questionnaire Survey (Comparative Field Experience and Methodological Innovations)* (New-Delhi: Concept Publishing Company).

Mukherjee, Neela: "Villagers Perceptions of Rural Poverty Through the Mapping Method of PRA", *RRA Notes, No. 15*, IIED, London.

Mukul (1999): "The untouchable present. Everyday life of Musahars in North Bihar", *Economic and Political Weekly*, Vol. 34, No. 47. pp. 3465-3470.

Murakami, Shimpei (1991): *Lessons from Nature: A Guide to Ecological Agriculture in the Topics* (Manikganj, Bangladesh: Proshika) 1991.

Murthi, Mamta, Anne-Catherine Guio and Jean Dreze (1995): "Mortality, Fertility and Gender Bias in India: A District Level Analysis", *Population and Development Review*, Vol. 21, December 1995.

Mydral, Gunnar (1968): *Asian Drama: An Inquiry into the Poverty of Nation* (New-York: Pantheon).

NCAER (1999): *India Human Development Report* (New Delhi: Oxford University Press).

NABARD (1994): *Tractorisation in Hrayana-An Ex-Post Evaluation Study*, NABARD, 1994.

Nadkarni, M.V. (1989): "Use and Management of Common Lands: Towards an Environmentally Sound Strategy", in Cecil Saldhana (ed.): *Karnataka: State of the Environment* Report IV, Bangalore.

Nadkarni, M.V. (1993): *Agricultural Policy in India: Context, Issue and Instruments*, Development Research Group Study No. 5, Reserve Bank of India, Bombay.

Nair, Kusum (1979): *Blossom in the Dust: The Human Face in Indian Development* (Chicago and London: Chicago University Press). Midway Reprint.

Narain, D. (1977): "Growth of Productivity in Indian Agriculture", *Indian Journal of Agricultural Economics*, Vol. 32, pp.1-44, January-March.

Narayan, Deepa, Robert Chambers, Meera Shah and P Petesch (1999): *Global Synthesis: Consultation with the Poor* (Washington D.C.: The World Bank), September 1999.

Natarajan, I. (1995): "Trends in Firewood Consumption in Rural India", *Margin*, October-December.

Natarajan, Shriram and Utsa Patnaik (1999): *Post Reform Trends in Crop Area, Output and Employment in China and India,* Paper presented at the International Seminar on Economic Reforms in India and China, Department of Economics, University of Hyderabad, Hyderabad, March 10-12.

Nath, Lalit M. (2000): "Curing will not Cure", in *A Future Past the Present, New Delhi: Hidusthan Times Special Issue,* 1st January 2000.

National Council of Applied Economic Research (NCAER) (1999): *The India Human Development Report* (New Delhi: Oxford University Press).

National Nutrition Monitoring Bureau (1996): *Nutritional Status of Rural Population*, Report of NNMB Surveys, Hyderabad.

National Sample Survey Organization (NSSO) (1983): "Survey Results: Per capita per diem intake of nutrients, NSS 27th round, October 1972-September 1973", *Sarvekshana*, Vol. VI, Nos. 3-4, Issue No.18, pp.S1-S88.

National Sample Survey Organization (NSSO) (1986): "Results on the Third Quinquennial Survey on Consumer Expenditure: NSS 38th Round", *Sarvekshana*, Vol. IX, No. 4, pp.S1-S102.

National Sample Survey Organization (NSSO) (1989): "Results on Per Capita Consumtion of Cereals for Various Sections of Population: NSS 27th Round (1983)", *Sarvekshana*, Vol. XIII, No. 2, pp.S1-S176.

National Sample Survey Organization (NSSO) (1990): *Report on the fourth quinquennial survey on consumer expenditure: Patterns of consumption of cereals, pulses, tobacco and some other selected items*, NSSO 43rd Round (July 1987-June 1988), *Report No.374,* New Delhi: Department of Statistics, Government of India.

National Sample Survey Organization (NSSO) (1996): *Consumption of some important commodities in India, NSSO 50th Round 1993-94,* Department of Statistics, Government of India, *Draft Report No.404*, New Delhi, India.

National Sample Survey Organization (NSSO) (1996): *Level and Pattern of Consumer Expenditure, 5th Quinquennial Survey 1993-94,* Report No.402, Department of Statistics, Government of India, New Delhi.

National Sample Survey Organization (NSSO) (1997a): "Survey Results on Nutrititional Intake in India-NSS 50th Round (July 1993-June 1994)", *Sarvekshana*, Vol. XXI, No.2, pp.S-1-S-214.

National Sample Survey Organization (NSSO) (1997b): "Operational Land Holdings in India, 1991-92, Salient Features", Department of Statistics, Ministry of Planning and Programme Implementation, New Delhi.

Nelson, G. O. (1983): "Food and Agricultural Production in Bangladesh", *IDS Bulletin*, Vol. 14, No. 12, April.

Nesmith, C.A. (1990): *People and Trees: Gender Relations and Participation in Social Forestry in West Bengal, India,* unpublished Ph.D Thesis, University of Cambridge, Cambridge, UK.

Newhouse, P. (1987): "Monitoring Food Supplied", *UNDRO NEWS,* Jan/Feb., Geneva.

Ninan, Sevanti (2000): "The Cost of War", *The Hindu Magazine*, June 25, 2000.

Nolan, Peter and Sender, John (1992): "Death Rates, Life Expectancy and China's Economic Reforms: A Critique of A. K. Sen", *World Development*, Vol. 20, No.9, pp.1279-1303.

Norton, A. (1992): *Analysis and Action in Local Institutional Development,* paper read at the GAPP Conference on Participatory Development, 9th-10th July, London).

NSSO: *Sarvekshana*, Vol. XVI, July-September, 1992.

NSSO: *Sarvekshana*, Vol. XX, No. 3, 70th Issue, January-March 1977

O'Brien, Place P. and Frankenberger, T. R. (1988): *Food Availability and Consumption Indicators: Nutrition in Agriculture Cooperative Agreement, Report No.3*, Office of Arid Land Studies, University of Arizona, Tucson, Arizona, USA.

O'Malley, L. S. S. (1914): *Bengal District Gazetteers: 24 Parganas* (Calcutta: Bengal Secretariate Book Depot).

Obbo, C. (1985): "Food Sharing During Food Crisis: Case Studies from Uganda and Ciskei", in Pottier, J. (ed.): *Food Systems in Central and Southern Africa* (London: School of Oriental and African Studies, University of London).

Observer Research Foundation (1999): *Demand for Foodgrains by 2020* (New Delhi: Observer Research Foundation).

OECD (1997): *Environmental Benefits from Agriculture: Issues and Policies, The Helsinki Seminar* (New-Delhi: Oxford & IBH Publishing Co. Pvt. Ltd.).

Ogle, B. (1991): "Learning More about Dependency on Forest and Tree Foods for Food Security", *Forest, Trees and People Newsletter*, June, IRDC/Food and Agriculture Organisation.

Oomen, I. A. (1988): *Food Security: Experiences and Prospects,* in *From Beyond Adjustment*, SDA, Africa Seminar, Maastricht.

Oshaug, A. (1985): "The Composite Concept of Food Security", in Eide W. B. et. al. (ed.) (1985): *Introducing Nutritional Consideration into Rural Development Programmes with Focus on Agriculture: A Theoretical Contribution, Development of Methodology for the Evaluation of Nutritional Impact of Development Programmes, Report No.1*, June (Oslo: Institute for Nutrition Research, University of Oslo).

Osmani, S. R. (1991): "The Food Problem of Bangladesh", in Dreze, J. and Sen A. K. (eds.): *The Political Economy of Hunger* (Oxford: Clarendon Press, Oxford).

Osmani, Siddiq (1993): *Nutrition and Poverty* (Oxford: Oxford University Press).

Oxford Forestry Institute (1991): *Common Property Resource Management in India, Tropical Forestry Paper 24* (Oxford: Oxford Forestry Institute).

Panikar, P. G. K. (1980): "Inter-regional Variation in Calorie Intake", *Economic and Political Weekly*, Vol. XV, Nos. 41,42 and 43.

Pankhurst, R. (1986): *The Economic History of Ethiopia* (Addis Ababa: Artistic Press).

Panneerselvan, A. S. (2000): "Import of Food, or of Unemployment", *Outlook,* 21st February, 2000, p. 27.

Parikh, Kirit S. (1994): "Who Gets How Much from PDS: How Effectively Does it Reach the Poor", *Sarvekshana*, Vol.XVII, No.3.

Parikh, Kirit S., N. S. S. Narayana, Manoj Panda, A. Ganesh Kumar (1995): "Strategies for Agricultural Liberalization—Consequences for Growth, Welfare and Distribution", *Economic and Political Weekly*, Vol. XXIX, No. 39, September 30.

Paroda, R. S. and Praduman Kumar (1999): *Food Production and Demand Situations in South Asia,* Paper presented in the Study Week on Food Needs of the Developing World in the Early Twenty-First Century, January 27-30, Pontifical Academy of Sciences, Vatican City.

Payne, P. (1990): "Measuring Malnutrition", *IDS Bulletin*, Vol. 21, No. 3, pp.14-30.

Payne, P. and Lipton, M. with Longhurst, R., North, J. and Treagust, S. (1990): *How Third World Rural Households Adapt to Dietary Energy Stress: Statement of Issues and Surveying the Literature,* mimeo, January, International Food Policy Research Institute, Washington.

Pender, J., and J. Kerr (1996): *Determinants of farmers indigenous soil and water conservation investments in India's semi-arid tropics, EPTD Discussion Paper No.17*, Washington, DC: International Food Policy Research Institute.

Pereira, Winin and Seabrook, Jeremy (1990): *Asking The Earth, Farms, Forestry and Survival In India* (London: Earthscan).

Perspective Planning Division (1993): *Report of the Expert Group on Estimation of Proportion and Number of Poor*, (New Delhi: Government of India).

Philipose, Pamela, (1999): "Rhythm of the Countryside", *The Express Magazine*, New Delhi, 8th November, 1999.

Philipose, Pamela (2000): "UN panel grills India on unkept promises of equality for women", *The Indian Express*, January 27, 2000, p.7.

Phillips, T. and Taylor, D. (1990a): *Food Security: An Analysis of the SEARCA/ Guelph Survey*, Centre for Food Security WPO11, University of Guelph, Ontario, July.

Phillips, T. and Taylor, D. (1990b): "Optional Control of Food Insecurity: A Conceptual Framework", *American Journal of Agricultural Economics*, Vol. 72, No. 5, December pp.1304-10.

Phillips, T. et. al. (1991): *Background Paper on Food Security: Penultimate Report*, University of Guelph, Ontario, September.

Phongphit, Seri and Robert Bennoun (1988): *Turning Point of Thai Farmers* (Bangkok: Thai Institute for Rural Development).

Pillai, Ajith (2000): "The Trade Locusts", *Outlook*, 21st February, 2000, pp. 26-27.

Pillai, Ajith (2000a): "Trade, A Nation of Shopkeepers", *Outlook*, 7th Februray, 2000.

Pillai, Ajith (2000b): "WTO, The Trade Locusts", *Outlook*, 21th February, 2000.

Pimbert, M. (1993): *The Making of Agricultural Biodiversity in Europe*, in V. Rajan (ed.): *Rebuilding Communities, Experiences and Experiments in Europe* (London: Resurgence Books).

Pinstrup-Anderson P. (1987): *Impact of Economic Adjustment on People's Food Security and Nutritional Levels in Developing Countries*, in WFC, May 1987.

Pinstrup-Anderson P. (ed.) (1988): *Food Subsidies in Developing Countries: Costs, Benefits and Policy Options* (Baltimore and London: John Hopkins University Press).

Pinstrup-Anderson, P. (1986): "An Analysis Framework for Assessing Nutrition Effects of Policies and Programmes", in Charles K. Mann and Barbara Huddleston (eds.): *Food Policy: Frameworks for Analysis and Action* (Bloomington, USA: Indiana University Press).

Planning Commission (1993): *Report of The Expert Group On Estimation of the Proportion And Number of Poor* (New-Delhi: Perspective Planning Division, Planning Commission, Government of India).

Ployani, Karl (1957): "The Economy as Instituted Process", in Karl Polyani, C. W. Arensberg and H. W. Pearson (eds.): *Trade and Market in Early Empires* (New-York: Free Press).

Popkin, S.L. (1979): *The Rational Peasant: The Political Economy of Rural Society in Vietnam* (Berkeley and Los Angeles: University of California Press).

PRAXIS (1998): *Participatory Poverty Profile Study: Bolangir District, Orissa* (New-Delhi: U.K. Department of International Development) mimeo.

PRAXIS (1999): *Consultations with the Poor, A Study to Inform WDR 2000-01, Site 1 Synthesis Report* (Patna: PRAXIS) 1999 mimeograph.

PRAXIS (1999a): *Consultations with the Poor, A Study to Inform WDR 2000-01, Site 6 Synthesis Report* (Patna: PRAXIS) 1999, mimeograph.

PRAXIS (1999b): *Country Synthesis Report, Consultations with the Poor, India,*(Patna: PRAXIS) 1999, mimeograph.

Press Trust of India (2000): "Poverty declines in India, but still nags BIMARU States", *The Indian Express*, New-Delhi, February 13, 2000, p.10.

Pretty, J., Gujit I., Scoones, I. and Thompson, J. (1992): "Regenerating Agriculture: The Agroecology of Low External Input and Community Based Development", in Holmberg, J., et. al. (ed.): *Policies for a Small Planet* (London: Earthscan Publications, London).

Pretty, J. (1991): "Farmers Extension Practice and Technology Adaptation: Agricultural Revolution in XVII-XIX Century Britain", *Agriculture and Human Values*, Vol. 8, No.1-2.

Pretty, J. N. (1996): *Regenerating Agriculture* (London: Earthscan and New Delhi: Vikas Publishing Co.).

Pretty, J. N.and R. Howes (1993): *Sustainable Agriculture in Britain: Recent Achievements and New Policy Challenges*, International Institute for Environment and Development Research Series (London: IIED) Vol. 2, 1993.

Pretty, Jules; Thompson, John and Hinchcliffe, Fiona (1996): *Sustainable Agriculture: Impact on Food Production and Challenges for Food Security*, IIED Gatekeeper Series No.60, International Institute for Environment and Development, London.

PROBE (1998): *Report on the State of Elementary Education in India* (New Delhi: Oxford University Press).

Public Interest Research Group (1992): *Structural Adjustment Who Really Pays?* (New Delhi: Public Interest Research Group, March).

Pursell, Gary and Gulati, Ashok (1995): "Liberalizing Indian Agriculture: An Agenda for Reform", in Cassen, Robert and Joshi, Vijay (eds.): *India—the Future of Economic Reform* (Bombay: Oxford University Press).

Radhakrishna, R. (1991): "Food and Nutrition: Challenge for Policy", *Journal of the Indian Society of Agricultural Statistics*, Vol. XLIII, No.3, pp. 211-227.

Radhakrishna, R. (1996): "Food Trends, Public Distribution and Food Security Concerns", *Indian Journal of Agricultural Economics*, Vol. 51, Nos. 1 and 2.

Radhakrishna, R. (1999): "Food Security and the Poor", in Chelliah, R. J. and Sudarshan, R. (eds.): *Income Poverty and Beyond: Human Development in India* (New-Delhi: Social Science Press).

Radhakrishna, R. and C. Ravi (1992): *Effects of Growth, Relative Prices and References on Food and Nutrition* (Hyderabad: Centre for Economic and Social Change, Hyderabad).

Radhakrishna, R. and C. Ravi (1994): *Food Demand Projections for India: Emerging Trends and Perspectives,* Mimeo. Center for Economic and Social Studies, Hyderabad.

Radhakrishna R., Subbarao K., Indrakant S., and Ravi, K. (1997): "Public Distribution: A National and International Perspective", *World Bank Discussion Paper No. 380* (Washington DC: The World Bank).

Rahman, M. (1981): "The Causes and Effects of Famine in Rural Population", in J. Robson (ed.): *Famine, Its Causes, Effect and Management* (London: Gordon and Breach).

Rai, K., N. Srinivas and R. K. Grover (1987): "Economic Analysis of Renting Agricultural Land in Haryana", *Indian Journal of Agricultural Economics*, Vol. XLII, No.3, pp.355-56.

Raj Krishna and G. S. Raychaudhuri (1979): "Some aspects of wheat price policy in India", *The Indian Economic Review'*, Vol. 14 pp. 101-25.

Rajan, S. I., U. S. Misra and P. S. Sarma (1999): *India's Elderly, Burden or Challenge* (New-Delhi: Sage).

Ramakrishna, G. (1993): "Growth and Fluctuations in Indian Agriculture", *Asian Economic Review*, The Journal of the Indian Institute of Economics, Vol. 35 (April), pp. 47-60.

Ranade, Ajit and S. Mahendra Dev (1997): "Agriculture and Rural Development", in Kirit S. Parikh (ed.): *India Development Report* (New-Delhi: Oxford University Press) 1997.

Rao, C. H. Hanumantha (1994): *Agricultural Growth, Rural Poverty and Environmental Degradation in India* (New-Delhi: Oxford University Press).

Rao, C. H. Hanumantha (1999): *Sustainable Development of Agriculture,* paper presented at the First Biennial Conference of the Indian Society of Ecological Economics, ISEC, Bangalore, December 20-22.

Rao, C. H. Hanumantha (2000): "Declining Demand for Foodgrains in Rural India: Causes and Implications", *Economic and Political Weekly*, Vol. 35, No. 4.

Rao, C. H. Hanumantha and Ashok Gulati (1994): "Indian Agriculture: Emerging Perspectives and Policy Issues", *Economic and Political Weekly*, Vol. XXIX, No. 53, December 31.

Rao, V.M (1990): "Village Studies From The Economic Perspective: Some Priority Issues And Themes", *The Administrator*, Vol. XXXVI, No.3.

Rao, V. M.; Alakh N. Sharma and Ravi Srivastava (1999): *Voices of the Poor, Poverty in People's Perceptions in India*, (New-Delhi: Institute for Human Development) mimeograph.

Ravallion, M. (1987): *Markets and Famines* (Oxford: Clarendon Press, Oxford).

Ravallion, M. (1990): "Market Responses to Anti-Hunger Policies: Effects on Wages, Prices and Employment", in Dreze, Jean and Amartya Sen (eds.): *The Political Economy of Hunger*, Vol. 2, Famine Prevention (Oxford: Clarendon Press).

Ravindran, Sundari T. K. (1995): "Women's health in a rural poor population in Tamil Nadu", in Das Gupta, Monica; Chen, Lincoln C., and T. N. Krishnan (eds.): *Women's Health in India: Risk and Vulnerability* (Bombay: Oxford University Press).

Ray S. K. (1998): *Sources of Change in Crop Output* (New Delhi: Institute of Economic Growth, Delhi).

Ray, Sudipta (1999): *Participatory Field Research Report: Impact of Air Pollution on Agriculture in the Urban and Peri-Urban Areas of Varanasi* (New-Delhi) 1999. Mimeograph.

Ray, Sudipta (1999): *Impact of Air Pollution on Agriculture in Urban and Peri-Urban Areas of Faridabad, Field Report-Round II* (New-Delhi) 1999. Mimeograph.

Rayan, J. G., P. D. Bidinger, N. P. Raw and P. Pushmpamma (1984): "The Determinants of Individual Diets and Nutritional Status in Six Villages of Southern India", *ICRISAT, Hyderabad, Bulletin No.7*.

Reardon T and Matlon P (1989): "Seasonal Food Insecurity and Vulnerability in Drought-Affected Regions of Burkina Faso", in D. E. Sahn (ed.): *Seasonal Vulnerability in Third World Agriculture: The Consequences for Food Security* (Baltimore and London: John Hopkins University Press).

Reardon T, Matlon P and Delgado C (1988): "Coping with Household Level Food Insecurity in Drought Affected Areas of Burkina Faso", *World Development*, Vol. 16, No. 1065-74.

Reddy V. Ratna (1993): "New Technology in Agriculture and Changing Size-Productivity Relationships: A Study of Andhra Pradesh", *Indian Journal of Agricultural Economics*, Vol. 48, No. 4, October-December.

Reddy V. Ratna (1998): "Institutional Imperatives and Co-production Strategies for Large Irrigation Systems in India", *Indian Journal of Agricultural Economics*, Vol. 53, No. 3, July-September.

Reddy, V. Ratna and R. S. Deshpande (1992): "Input Subsidies: Whither the Direction of Policy Changes", *Indian Journal of Agricultural Economics*, Vol. XLVII, No. 3, July-September.

Reddy, V. Ratna (1995): *Willingness and Ability to Pay for Water: A Study of Rajasthan*, Project Report, Institute of Development Studies, Jaipur.

Reijntjes, Coen; Haverkort, Bertus, and Bayer-Waters, Ann (1992): *Farming for the Future: An Introduction to Low External Input and Sustainable Agriculture*, (London: Macmillan).

Repetto, R. (1994): *The "second India" revisited: population, poverty and environmental stress over two decades* (Washington, DC: World Resources Institute).

Reutlinger, S. (1977): "Food Security: Magnitude and Remedies", *Staff Working Paper, No.267*, World Bank, Washington DC.

Reutlinger, S. (1982): "Policies for Food Security in Food Importing Developing Countries", in Chisholm A. H. and Tyers, R. (eds.): *Food Security: Theory, Policy and Perspectives from Asia and the Pacific Rim* (Massachusetts: Lexington Books).

Reutlinger, S. (1985a): "Policy Options for Food Security", *Discussion Paper, Report No. ARU 44,* Agriculture and Rural Development Department Research Unit, World Bank, Washington DC.

Reutlinger, S. (1985a): "Food Security and Poverty in LDCs", *Finance and Development*, Vol. 22, No .4, pp.7-11.

Reutlinger, S. and Knapp, K. (1980): "Food Security in Food Deficit Countries", *World Bank Staff Working Paper, No. 393,* (Washington DC: The World Bank).

Reutlinger, S. and Selowsky, M. (1976): "Malnutrition and Poverty: Magnitude and Policy Options", *World Bank Staff Occassional Paper, No.23*, (Washington DC: World Bank).

Ridge, Milan (1999): "Poverty an Unhealthy Start to Ageing", in *The Sunday Nation*, Singapore, July 4, 1999, pp. A5.

Rizvi, N. (1986): "Food Categories in Bangladesh and Its Relationship to Food Beliefs and Practices of Vulnerable Groups", in R. S. Khare and M. S. A. Raw (eds.): *Food, Society and Culture: Aspects of South Asian Food Systems* (Durham: Caroline Academic Press).

Roberts, T. M. (1984): "Long Term Effects of Sulphur Dioxide on Crops: An Analysis of Dose-Response Relations", *Phil. Trans. Royal Society London, No.305,* 1984.

Roche, C. (1991): "An NGO Perspective on Food Security and the Environment: ACORD in the Sahel and Horn of Africa", *IDS Bulletin,* Vol. 22, No. 3, July, Institute of Development Studies, University of Sussex, Brighton.

Rodhe, H. and R. Harrera (1988): *Acidification in Tropical Countries* (Chister: John Wiley and Sons).

Rogaly, B., Barbara Hariss-White and Sugata Bose (1999): *Sonar Bangla?* (New Delhi: Sage).

Roger, Lois and Lilian Nduta (2000): "Obesity rates soar among the world's poor", *The Sunday Times*, as quoted in *The Times of India*, New-Delhi, January 27, 2000.

Rosegrant, M. R., M. Agcaoili and N. Perez (1995): "Global food projections to 2020: Implications for Investment, Food, Agriculture and the Environment", *Discussion Paper No. 5,* Washington, DC: World Resources Institute.

Rosenzweig, Mark and T. Paul Schultz (1982): "Market Opportunities, Genetic Endowments and Intrafamily Resource Distribution: Child Survival in Rural India", *American Economic Review*, Vol. 72, No. 4, pp. 803-15.

Roumasset, J. (1982): "Rural Food Security", in Chisholm, A. H. and Tyers, R. (eds.): *Food Security: Theory, Policy and Perspectives from Asia and the Pacific Rim* (Massachusetts: Lexington Books).

Rukuni, M. and R. H. Bernsten (1988): "Major Issues in Designing a Research Programme on Household Food Insecurity", in M. Rukuni and R. H. Bernsten (eds.): *Southern Africa: Food Security Policy Options*, Proceedings of the third annual conference on Food Security in Southern Africa, 1-5 November 1987, University of Zimbabwe, Michigan State University Research Project, and Department of Agricultural Economics and Extension, Harare.

Rukuni, M. and R. H. Bernsten (1988): "The Food Security Equation", in C. Bryant (ed.): *Poverty, Policy and Food Security in Southern Africa* (London: Mansell Publishing Ltd., England).

Runeckles, V. C. (1984): "Impact of Air Pollutant Combinations on Plants", in M. Treshow (ed.): *Air Pollution and Plant Life* (Chichester: John Wiley and Sons) 1984.

S. Karger, D. Basel, K. Freebairn (eds.): *Food, Population and Employment* (New-York: Praeger).

Sahn, D. E. (1989): "A Conceptual Framework for Examining the Seasonal Aspects of Household Food Security" in D. E. Sahn (eds.):. *Seasonal Variability in Third World Agriculture: The Consequences for Food Security* (Baltimore and London: John Hopkins University Press).

Sahn, D. E. (ed.) (1989): *Seasonal Variability in Third World Agriculture: The Consequences for Food Security,* (Baltimore and London: John Hopkins University Press, Baltimore, Maryland, USA).

Sahni, B. (1998): *Tamas* (London: Penguin) and the film based on it by Govind Nihalini.

Sanderson, F. H. and Shyamal Ray (1979): *Food Trends and Prospects in India* (Washington: Brookings Institution, Washington).

Sandhu P. S. and Grewal, S. S. (1987): "The Changing Land Holdings Structure in Punjab", *Indian Journal of Agricultural Economics*, Vol. XLII, No. 3, pp. 294-300.

Sann, A. L. (1998): *A Livelihood from Fishing—Globalization and Sustainable Fisheries Policies* (London: Intermediate Technology).

Sanyal, Manoj K., Pradip K. Biswas and Samaresh Bardhan (1998): "Institutional Change and Output Growth in West Bengal Agriculture", *Economic and Political Weekly*, November 21-28, 1998.

Sargent, C. and Bass, S. (1992): "The Future Shape of Forests", in Holmberg, Johan (eds.): *Policies for a Small Planet* (London: Earthscan Publications).

Sarma, J. S. and Vasant, P. G. (1990): *Production and Consumption of Foodgrains in India: Implications of Accelerated Economic Growth and Poverty Alleviation*, Research Report, No. 81 (Washington: International Food Policy Research Institute).

Sarma, J. S. and Shyamal, R. (1979): "Foodgrain Production and Consumer Behaviour in India—1960-77", in Sarma, J. S. and Shyamal, R. (1979): *Two Analysis of Indian Foodgrain Production and Consumption Data*, Research Report, No. 81, 1990 (Washington DC: International Food Policy Research Institute).

Sarris, A. H. (1985): *Domestic Price Policies and International Distortions: The Case of Wheat and Rice,* Paper prepared for Food and Agriculture Organisation, Rome.

Sarris, A. H. (1988): "Agricultural Stabilization and Structural Adjustment Policies in Developing Countries", *Economics and Social Paper*, Food and Agriculture Organisation, Rome.

Sarris, A. H. (1989): "Food Security and International Security", *Discussion Paper, No. 301*, (London, Ma.: Centre for Economic Policy Research).

Scherr, S. J. and P. Hazell (1994): "Sustainable Agricultural Development Strategies in Fragile Lands", *EPTD Discussion Paper No. 1* (Washington, DC: World Resources Institute).

Scheveningen Report (!980): "Towards a New International Development Strategy: The Scheveningen Report", *Development Dialogue, No.1,* pp.56-67.

Schumaker, J. and Holt, J. (1980): "Markets and Famines in the Third World", *Disasters*, Vol. 4, No. 3, pp.283-97.

SCN (1991): "Some Options for Improving Nutrition in the 1990s", *SCN News, No. 7* in Supplement, UN, Geneva.

Scoones, I. and Thompson, J. (1994): *Beyond Farmer First* (London: Intermediate Technology Press, London).

Scott, J. (1976): *The Moral Economy of Peasants* (New Haven: Yale University Press).

Scrimshaw, Nevin (1997): "The Lasting Damage of Early Nutrition", *World Food Programme,* May31, 1997.

Segal, Sondra and Roberta Sklar (1987): *Women's Body and Other Natural Resources*, 1987.

Sehgal, J. and I. P. Abrol (1994): *Soil Degradation in India: Status and Impact*, (New-Delhi: Oxford & IBH Publishing Co. Pvt. Ltd).

Sen, A. K. (1981): *Poverty and Famines: An Essay on Entitlement and Deprivation* (Oxford: The Clarendon Press).

Sen, A., (1992): *Poverty Alleviation: Targeting Versus Universalisation,* Convocation Address at Management Development Institute, Gurgaon, India, July 3.

Sen, A., (1995): *The Political Economy of Targeting,* in van de Walle, D. and Nead, K. (eds.): Op. Cit., pp. 11-24.

Sen, Abhijit and Utsa Patnaik: "A Country Study on Poverty in India", *DSA Working Paper*, Centre for Economic Studies and Planning, Jawaharlal Nehru University, New- Delhi, December 1997.

Sen, Abhijit: "Economic Reforms, Employment and Poverty: Trends and Options", *Economic and Political Weekly*, Special Number, Vol. 31, Nos. 35-37, August, 1996.

Sen, Amartya (1986): "The Causes of Famine, A Reply", in *Food Policy*, May, 1986, p 125-131.

Sen, Amartya (1990): "Gender and Co-operative Conflict", in Tinker, Irine (ed.): *Persistent Inequalities: Women and World Development* (New York: Oxford University Press).

Sen, Amartya (1992): "Life and Death in China: A Reply", *World Development*, Vol. 20, No.9. p.p. 1305 – 1312.

Sen, Amartya (1994): "Population and Reasoned Agency: Population Growth and Food Security", *Development,* No. 3, 1994.

Sen, Amartya (1997): *Hunger in the Contemporary World* (London: STICERD, London School of Economics, London) November, 1997.

Sen, Amartya (1998): "Famines: The Man-Made Disaster", *The New-York Times*, July 26, 1998, pp. 14.

Sen, Amartya (1999): *Freedom as Development* (Oxford: Oxford University Press).

Sen, Amartya (1999a): "Alternative Approaches to Development", *The Statesman Festival 99*, Calcutta.

Sen, Amartya and Sunil Sengupta (1983): "Malnutrition of Rural Children and the Sex Bias", *Economic and Political Weekly*, Annual Number, May.

Sengupta, S. and M. G. Ghosh (1978): *State Intervention in the Vulnerable Food Economy of India and the Problem of the Rural Poor,* paper presented at the Workshop on Problems of Public Distribution of Foodgrain in Eastern India, mimeographed.

Shah, Tushar (1987): *Gains from Social Forestry: Lessons from West Bengal,* paper read at the workshop on Commons, Wastelands, Trees and the Poor: Finding the Right Fit, at IDS, University of Sussex, Brighton.

Shah, Tushar (1993): *Ground Water Markets and Irrigation Development: Political Economy and Practical Policy* (New-Delhi: Oxford University Press).

Shah, Amita (1994): "Moisture-yield Interaction and Farmers' Perceptions: Lessons from Watershed Projects in Gujarat", *Economic and Political Weekly*, Vol. 34, No. 4, December.

Shah, Amita (1997): "Food Security and Access to National Resources: A Review of Recent Trends", *Economic and Political Weekly*, Vol. 32, No. 26.

Shah, Amita (1999): *Environment and Ecology* (unpublished) paper presented for the NGO-Academics Paper on Poverty in India, Centre for Development Alternatives, Ahmedabad.

Shah, Mihir, et.al., (1998): *India's Drylands* (New-Delhi: Oxford University Press).

Shamala, M. (1982): *Food Security and Storage Policies,* Proceedings of the Workshop on Food Policy Research Priorities, Field in Nairobi, 14-17 June 1982.

Shanker, Kripa (1999): *The Question of Tenancy Reforms,* paper read at the National Workshop on Tenancy Reform, Lal Bahadur Shastri National Academy of Administration, Mussoorie, September 24-25th 1999.

Shariff, Abusaleh (1999): *India Human Development Report* (New-Delhi: Oxford University Press and NCAER, 1999).

Sharma, Devinder (2000): "Indian Farmers not Benefitting from WTO Agreements", in *National Herald,* 1st November, 2000, p. 8.

Sharma, M. L. and Punia, R. K. (1989): *Land Reforms in India* (New-Delhi: Ajanta Publications).

Sharma, V. K. and Haque, T. (1987): *Impact of Fertilizer Subsidy on Agricultural Growth and Equity,* IASRI Souvenir, Indian Agricultural Statistics Research Institute, New Delhi.

Shears, P. (1991): "Epidemiology and Infection in Famine and Disasters", *Epidemiol Infect,* No.107, pp.241-51.

Shetty, P. S. and W. P. T. James (1994): "Body Mass Index, A Measure of Chronic Energy Deficiency in Adults", Food and Agriculture Organisation, *Food and Nutrition Paper, No. 6* (Rome: Food and Agriculture Organisation).

Shiva, M. P. (1998a): *Inventory of Forest Resources for Sustainable Management and Bio-Diversity Conservation* (Dehradun: Centre for Minor Forest Produce).

Shiva, M. P. and Mathur, R. B. (1997): *Management of Minor Forest Produce for Sustainability* (New-Delhi: Oxford and IBH).

Shiva, Vandana (1988): *Staying Alive: Women, Ecology and Survival in India* (Delhi: Kali for Women).

Shiva, Vandana (1991): *The Violence of the Green Revolution* (Penang, Malaysia: Third World Network).

Shiva, Vandana (1991): *Staying Alive: Women, Ecology and Development*, (London: Zed Books).

Shiva Vandana (1998): *Betting on Bio-Diversity: Why Genetic Engineering will not Feed the Hungry,* (New Delhi: Research Foundation for Science, Technology and Ecology).

Shiva Vandana (2000): Talk at the "International Conference on Community Initiatives for Food Security and Nutrition", held by CARE-India and Ministry of Human Resources Development, Government of India, at Vigyan Bhawan, New Delhi on 6th March, 2000.

Shivshankar, Rahul (2000): "The Problem now is Aid Addiction", *The Sunday Times of India*, April, 23, 2000.

Shoham, J. and Clay, E. (1989): "The Role of Socio-Economic Data in Food Needs Assessment and Monitoring", *Disasters*, Vol. 13, No. 1, pp.41-60.

Shuttleworth, G., Bull, R. and Hodgkinson, P. (1988): "Food Security Through Seasonal Destabilization: The Case of Madagascar", *Food Policy*, Vol. 13, No. 2, May, pp. 150-53.

Siamwalla, A. and A. Valdes (1980): "Food Insecurity in Developing Countries", *Food Policy*, Vol. 5, No., November, pp.258-72.

Siamwalla, A. and A. Valdes (1984): "Food Security in Developing Countries: International Issues", in Eider, C. and Staaz, M. (eds.): *Agricultural Development in the Third World* (Baltimore: John Hopkins University Press).

Siddiqui, K. (1982): *The Political Economy of Rural Poverty in Bangladesh* (Dhaka: National Institute of Local Government).

Sidhu, R. S. and Dhillon, M. S. (1996): "Land and Water Resources in Punjab: Their Degradation and Technologies for Sustainable Use", *Indian Journal of Agricultural Economics*, Vol. 52, No. 3, July-September.

Simmons, I. G. (1993): *Interpreting Nature, Cultural Constructions of the Environment* (London: Routledge).

Sindhu, D. S. and D. Byerlee (1992): "Technical Change and Wheat Productivity in the Indian Punjab in Post-Green Revolution Period", *Working Paper 92-02*, Economics, CIMMYT, Mexico.

Singer, H.W. (1991): "Terms of Trade: New Wine and New Bottle", *Developing Policy Review*, Vol. 9, No. 4, December.

Singh, B. P. (1989): *The Hindu: Survey of Agriculture* (New Delhi: The Hindu).

Singh, J. and S. S. Miglani (1976): "An Economic Analysis of Energy Requirements in Punjab Agriculture", *Indian Journal Of Agricultural Economics*, No. 3, July- September 1976.

Singh, J. P. and Alok Dash (1998): "Agriculture", in *Alternative Survey Group: Alternative Economic Survey, 1991-1998, Seven Years of Structural Reforms* (New-Delhi: Rainbow Publishers Ltd., Lokyayan and Azadi Bachao Andolan).

Singh, J. S., K. P. Singh and M. Agarwal (1990): *Environmental Degradation of Obra-Renukoot-Singhrauli Areas and its Impact on Natural and Derived Ecosystems*, Project Report submitted to the Ministry of Environment and Forests, Government of India, 4/167/84/MAB/EN-2RE, 1990.

Singh, L. R. and B. Singh (1976): "Level and Pattern of Energy Consumption in an Agriculturally Advanced Area of Uttar Pradesh", *Indian Journal of Agricultural Economics*, No. 3, July-September, 1976.

Singh, M. (1995): *Inaugural Address,* delivered to the Fifty Fourth Annual Conference of the Indian Society of Agricultural Economics held at Kolhapur on 26th November 1994, reprinted in the *Indian Journal of Agricultural Economics,* Vol. 50.

Singh, R. P., and M. L. Morris (1997): "Adoption, management and impact of hybrid maize seed in India", *Economics Working Paper 97-06.* (Mexico City: International Maize and Wheat Improvement Center).

Singh, R. P., N. S. Jodha and H. P. Binswanger (1985): "ICRISAT Village Studies Management System", *Economics Group Paper No. 237* (Pancheru: ICRISAT).

Singh, Ram D. (1996): "Female Agricultural Workers' Wages, Male-Female Wage Differentials, and Agricultural Growth in a Developing Country, India", *Economic Development and Cultural Change*, Vol. 45, No. 1.

Sinha, Poonam (2000): "Too Many People in Too Little Space Can Only Amount to a Scarcity of Natural Resources", *Hindusthan Times,* 13th May 2000, p. 15.

Sinha, Rajesh (2000): "The Men are Leaving and Cattle are Dying", *The Indian Express*, New-Delhi, 22nd April 2000, pp.1.

Siston, J. S (1915): *Final Report of the Survey and Settlement Operation of the District of Hararibag 1908—1915* (Hazaribag: Settlement Officer Chotanagpur) August 1915.

Smith, M. et. al. (1992): *Household Food Security, Concepts and Definitions: An Annotated Bibliography,* mimeo, IDS, Brighton.

Sobhan, Rehman (1990): "The Politics of Hunger and Entitlement", in Dreze, Jean and Amartya Sen (eds.): *The Political Economy of Hunger,* Volume 1 (Oxford: Clarendon Press).

Srinivas, Ravi, K. (1996): "Sustainable Agriculture Biotechnology and Emerging Global Trade Regime", *Economic and Political Weekly*, Vol. 31, No. 29.

Srinivas. M. N. (ed.): *India's Villages* (Bombay: Asia Publishing House) 1955. This is an all time classic in the field.

Srinivasan, T. N. (1983): "Hunger: Defining it, Estimating its Global Incidence and Alleviating it", in Johnson, D. Gale and Schuh, G. E. (eds.): *The Role of Markets in the World Food Economy* (Boulder: Westview Press Inc.).

Staatz, J. (1990): *Food Security and Agricultural Policy: Summary,* Proceedings of the Agriculture Nutrition Linkage Workshop, Vol.1, February 12-13, Virginia.

Stewart, Frances (1993): "War and Development", *Developing Studies Working Papers No. 56,* International Development Centre, Oxford.

Streeten, P. (1987): *What Price Food?* (London: Macmillan).

Stryker, J. D. (1978): *Food Security, Self Sufficiency and Economic Growth in the Sahelian Countries of West Africa,* prepared for USAID from Food Research Institute, Stanford University.

Sudan, Republic of (1988): *Proceedings of the National Food Security Workshop,* Khartoum, 4-5 June.

Sukhatme, P. V. (1965): *Feeding India's Growing Millions* (Bombay: Asia Publishing House).

Suryanarayana, M. H. (1995): "PDS: Beyond Implicit Subsidy and Urban Bias – The Indian Experience", *Food Policy*, Vol. 20, No .4.

Suryanarayana, M. H. (1996): "Food Security and Calorie Adequacy Across States: Implication for Reform", *Journal of Indian School of Political Economy*, Vol. VII, No. 2.

Suryanarayana, M. H. (1997a): "Food Policies: Need for an Integrated Perspective", *Productivity,* Vol. 38, No. 2.

Suryanarayana, M. H. (1999): "Poverty, Food Security and Levels of Living: Maharashtra", *Journal of Indian School of Political Economy*, Vol. XI, No.1.

Suryanarayana, M. H. (2000): "Backdoor Closure of PDS?" in *The Hindu*, March.

Swaminathan, M. S. (1989): "Why are Rural People Vulnerable to Famine?" *IDS Bulletin*, Vol. 20, No. 2, Institute of Development Studies, University of Sussex, Brighton.

Swaminathan, M. (2000a): *Weakening Welfare, The Public Distribution of Food in India* (New Delhi: Left World Books).

Swaminathan, M. (1997): "Dangers of Narrow Targeting", *Frontline,* October 31,12-16.

Swaminathan, M. (2000b): *Targeting Welfare: Theory and Lessons from Policies of Food Distribution in India* unpublished paper, Mumbai.

Swaminathan, M. S. (1999): *A Century of Hope* (New-Delhi: East West Books) 1999.

Swaminathan, Madhura (1999): "Understanding the Costs of the Food Corporation of India", *Economic and Political Weekly*, Vol. 34, No. 52, December 25.

Swaminathan, Madhura and V. K. Ramachandran (1999): "New Data on Calorie Intakes", *Frontline*, 12 March 1999.

Swift, J. J. (1989): "Why are Rural People Vulnerable to Famine?" *IDS Bulletin*, Vol. 20, No.2, pp.8-15.

Syarief, H. (1990): "Combating Malnutrition Through Improvements in Food and Nutrition Systems", in Tyagi, D. S. and Vyas, V. S. (eds.): *Increasing Access to Food: the Asian Experience* (New Delhi and London: Sage Publications).

Taal, H. (1989): "How Farmers Cope with Risk and Stress in Rural Gambia", *IDS Bulletin*, No. 20, pp.16-22.

Tapsoba, E. K. (1990): "Food Security Policy Issues in West Africa: Past Lesson and Future Prospects", *Economic and Social Development Paper*, No. 93, Food and Agriculture Organisation, Rome.

Tata Energy Research Institute (1990): *Energy Survey and the Preparation of Project Document in the Selected Block Gopikander of Dumka District* (New Delhi: TERI).

Taylor, L. (1982): "Food Price Inflation, Terms of Trade and Growth", in Gersovitz, M. et. al. (eds.): *The Theory and Experience of Economic Development* (New-York: George Allen and Unwin) New York.

Tekolla. Y. (1990): "The African Food Crisis", in E. Chole (ed.): *Food Crisis in Africa: Policy and Management Issues* (New-Delhi: Vikas Publishing House).

TERI (1998): *Green India 2047: Looking Back to Think Ahead* (Bombay: Tata Energy Resource Institute, Bombay).

Thamarajakshi, S. (1999): "Agriculture and Economic Reforms", *Economic and Political Weekly, pp. 2293-5.*

The Economist (1992): "Freeing India's Economy: The Elephant Awakes", *The Economist*, 23 May 1992.

The Economist (2000): "Hopeless Continent", *The Economist,* May 13th – 19th 2000, p. 15.

The Economist (2000a): "Marxism Today, Looking Back", *The Economist*, May 13th – 19th 2000, p. 8.

The Indian Express (2000): "Desert Sands of Habit: Public Apathy Plus Bad Governance Equals a Drought", Lead Editorial, *The India Express*, New-Delhi, 22nd April, 2000.

The World Bank (1985): *The Bank's World*, Vol. 4, No. 12.

The World Bank (1986): *Poverty and Hunger: Issues and Options for Food Security in Developing Countries* (Washington D.C.: The World Bank).

The World Bank (1989): *Gender and Poverty in India* (Washington D.C.: The World Bank).

Third World Network: *Third World Resurgence*, Issue No. 108-109, August/ September 1999.

Thomas, D. (1991): *Gender Differences in Household Resource Allocation, Population and Human Resources Department Living Standard Measurement Study*, Working Paper No. 79 (Washington D. C.: World Bank).

Thomas, R. B., Paine, S. H. B. H. and Brenton, B. P. (1989): "Perspectives on Socio-Economic Causes of and Responses to Food Deprivation", *Food Nutrition Bulletin*, Vol. 11, pp. 41-54.

Thompson, A. (1986): "The Social Goals of Agriculture", *Agriculture and Human Values*, Vol. 3, No.4, 1986, pp. 32-42.

Thompson, E. P. (1986): *The Making of the English Working Class* (London: Penguin).

Thompson, R. L. (1983): "The Role of Trade in Food Security and Agricultural Development", in Dale G. Johnson and G. E. Schuh (eds.): *The Role of Markets in the World Food Economy* (Boulder: Westview Press Inc.).

Tidewell, Billy J. (1993): *The State of Black America 1993* (New-York: National Urban League).

Tiffen, Mary, et. al. (1994): *More People Less Erosion* (Chictester: John Wiley).

Tilakafgna, S. (1986): "Household Food Security Within a Framework of Basic Human Needs", in Eide, W. et. al.: *Introducing Nutritional Considerations into Rural Development Programmes with Focus on Agriculture: Towards Practice*, Report 2, Development of Methodology for the Evaluation of Nutritional Impact of Development Programmes, March, Institute for Nutrition Research, University of Oslo.

Timberlake, Lloyd (1991): *Africa in Crisis* (London: Earthscan).

Times of India (2000): "Famines as Photo-ops", Lead Editorial, *Times of India*, New Delhi, 21st April, 2000.

Times of India (2000a): "Protest Against Women", p. 3.

Tomasevski, K. (1984): "Human Rights Indicators: The Right to Food as a Test Case", in P. Alston and K. Tomasevski (eds.): *The Right to Food* (The Netherlands: Martinus Nijhoff).

Tomkins, A. and Watson, F. (1989): *Malnutrition and Infection: A Review, ACC/ SCN State of the Art Series Nutrition Policy*, Discussion Paper, No.5.

Toole, M. and Waldman, R. (1990): "Prevention of Excess Mortality in Refugee and Displaced Populations in Developing Countries", *Journal of the American Medical Association*, Vol. 263, No. 24, June.

Tullis, F. L. and Hollist, W. L. (eds.) (1986): *Food, the State and International Political Economy: Dilemmas of Developing Countries,* (Lincoln and London: University of Nebraska Press).

Turnbill, C. (1984): *The Mountain People* (London: Triad and Paladin Books).

Twose, M. (1984): *Cultivating Hunger: An Oxfam Study of Food Power and Poverty* (Oxford: Oxfam, Oxford).

Tyagi, D. S. (1984): *Farmers Response to Agricultural Prices in India* (NewDelhi: Heritage Publishers).

Tyagi, D. S. (1990): "Increasing Access to Food Through Interaction of Price and Technology Policies: The Indian Experience", in D. S. Tyagi and V. S. Vyas (eds.): *Increasing Access to Food: The Asian Experience* (New-Delhi: Sage Publications).

Tyagi, D. S. (1993): "Pricing of Fertilizers: Some Reflections on Subsidy Question", in Vidya Sagar (ed.): *Fertilizer, Pricing Issues Related to Subsidies* (Jaipur: Classic Publishing House).

Tyagi, D.S. (1990): *Managing India's Food Economy: Problems and Alternatives* (New-Delhi: Sage Publications).

UN (1974): *Universal Declaration on the Eradication of Hunger and Malnutrition,* endorsed by the General Assembly Resolution 3348 (XXIX) of 17 December 1974.

UN (1975): *Report of the World Food Conference,* Rome, 5-16 November 1974, New York.

UN (1988): *Towards Sustainable Food Security: Critical Issues,* Report by the Secretariat, World Food Council, Fourteenth Ministerial Session, Nicosia, Cyprus, 23-26 May.

UN (1989): *Right to Adequate Food as a Human Right* (New York: United Nations, New York).

UN (1990): *Nutrition-Relevant Actions in the Eighties: Some Experiences and Lessons from Developing Countries,* Background Paper for the ACC/SCN Ad Hoc group Meeting on Policies to Alleviate Under-Consumption and Malnutrition in Deprived Areas, 12-14 November, London.

UN (1996): *International Covenant on Economic, Social and Cultural Rights,* Adopted and opened for signature, ratifications and accession by the General Assembly Resolution 2200 A (XXI) of 16 December 1996.

UN Department of Economics and Social Affairs (1971): *Strategy Statement on Action to Avert the Protein Crisis in Developing Countries* (New-York: United Nations).

UNDP (1990): *Human Development Report, 1990* (New York: UNDP).

UNDP (1992): *Human Development Report,* 1992 (New Delhi: Oxford University Press).

UNDP (1997): *Human Development Report 1997* (New-Delhi: Oxford University Press).

UNDP (1998): *Human Development Report 1998* (New-Delhi: Oxford University Press).

UNDP (1998): *Human Development Report for South Asia 1998* (New-Delhi: Oxford University Press).

UNDP (1999): *Human Development Report 1999* (New-Delhi: Oxford University Press).

UNDP (1996): *Report on Human Development in Bangladesh*, A Pro-Poor Agenda, Volume 3, (Dhaka: United Nations Development Programme, Dhaka).

UNICEF (1990): *Poverty Reduction from Below: A Household Food Security Approach,* mimeo, UNICEF, Lilongwe, Malawi.

UNICEF (1990): *Strategy for Improved Nutrition of Children and Women in Developing Countries,* a UNICEF Policy Review, (New York: UNICEF).

UNICEF (1991): *A Situation Analysis of Children and Women in Namibia,* mimeo, Windhoek, Namibia.

UNICEF (1991): *Nutrition Surveillance Workshop,* UNICEF, New York, 27-28 September 1991, Report by the Nutrition Cluster, UNICEF (New York: UNICEF).

UNICEF (1994): "A Year to Renew the Family", in *First Call for Children*, January-March, 1994.

UNICEF (1995): *The Progress of Indian States* (New-Delhi: UNICEF).

UNICEF: "Malnutrition", in *The State of the World's Children 1998* (New-York: Oxford University Press) 1998.

United Nations (1995): *Declaration and Programme of Action*, from the World Summit for Social Development, Copenhagen, March, 1995.

United Nations (1995): *The World's Women 1995, Trends and Statistics* (New York: United Nations).

University of Guelph, Centre for Food Security (1991): *Background Paper on Food Security: Draft Final,* University of Guelph, Ontario, Canada.

UNSTD (1986). *Report of the Ad hoc Panel of Specialists on Science, Technology and Food Security*, 7-13 January, United Nations Advisory Committee on Science and Technology for Development, Harare.

Uphoff, Norman (1992): *Approaches and methods for monitoring and evaluation of popular participation in World Bank-assisted projects,* Paper for World Bank Workshop on Popular Participation, 26th to 27th February 1992 (Washington D.C.: The World Bank).

Uphoff, Norman (1992): *Learning from Gal Oya: Possibilities for Participatory Development and Post Newtonian Science* (Ithaca: Cornell University Press).

US Agency for International Development (1992): *Definition of Food,* Policy Determination, No.19, Document PN-AAV-468, USAID, Washington, April.

US Dept. of Agriculture, Office of the Secretary (1977): *The Relationship Between Trade and World Food Security,* Speech by Dale Hathaway, Assistant Secretary for International Affairs and Commodity Programmes before the International Food Conference at the Pan American Health Organizations, April 29, Washington DC.

Vaidyanathan, A. R. (1999): *Agricultural Development: Imperatives of Institutional Reforms,* Lead Paper read at the NIRD Foundation Day Seminar on Rural Prosperity and Agriculture: Strategies and Policies for the Next Millenium, November 4th to 5th, 2000 at Hyderabad.

Valdes, A. and Ammar, S. (1981): "Introduction", in Alberto Valdes (eds.): *Food Security for Developing Countries* (Boulder: Westview Press).

Valdes, A. and Panos Konandreas (1981): "Accessing Food Insecurity Based on National Aggregates in Developing Countries", in Alberto Valdes (ed.): *Food Security for Developing Countries* (Boulder: Westview Press).

Van Ayl, J. and Coetzee, G. K. (1990): "Food Security and Structural Adjustment: Empirical Evidence on the Food Price Dilemma in Southern Africa", *Development Southern Africa*, Vol.7, no.1, pp.105-16.

Van de Walle, D. and K. Nead (eds.) (1995): *Public Spending and the Poor, Theory and Evidence, A World Bank Book* (Baltimore: John Hopkins University Press).

Van Hoof, G. J. H. (1984): "The Legal Nature of Economic, Social and Cultural Rights: A Rebuttal of Some Traditional Views", P. Alston and K. Tomasevski (eds.): *The Right to Food* (The Netherlands: Martins Nijhoff).

Van Schendel, W. (1989): "Self Rescue and Survival: The Rural Poor in Bangladesh", in Lieten, G. et al. (eds.): *Women, Migrants and Tribals, Survival Strategies in Asia* (Delhi: Manohar).

Varshney, B. K.; M. Agarwal, K Ahmed, P. S. Dubey and S. H. Raza (1997): *Effect of Air Pollution on India Crop Plants,* Project report Submitted to Imperial College Centre for Environmental Technology, London, 1997.

Venegas, M. (1986): "Meeting World Food Objectives: Towards an Improved Trade Environment in Agriculture", *Food Policy*, Vol. 11, No. 3, August.

Venkateshwaran, Sandhya (1995): *Croplands, Environment, Development and Gender Gap* (New Delhi: Sage).

Vidyasagar (1991): "Fertilizer Pricing: Are Substitutes Essential", *Economic and Political Weekly*, 14 December 1991, pp. 2861-64.

Von Braun, J. (1988): "Effects of Technological Change in Agriculture on Food Consumption and Nutrition: Rice in a West African Setting", *World Development*, Vol. 16, No. 9.

Von Braun, J. (1991): *A Policy Agenda for Famine Prevention in Africa,* Food Policy Report, International Food Policy Research Institute, Washington DC.

Von Braun, J., et. al. (1992): *Improving Food Security of the Poor: Concept, Policy and Programmes,* International Food Policy Research Institute, Washington DC.

Von Braun, J., Bovis, H., Kuman S. and Pandya-Lorch, R. (1991): *Improving Household Food Security,* A theme Paper in Preparation for the Food and Agriculture Organisation/WHO International Conference on Nutrition, International Food Policy Research Institute, Washington D.C.

Von Braun, J., Hotchkiss, D. and Immink, M. (1989): *Non-Traditional Export Crops in Guatemala: Effects on Production, Income and Nutrition,* (Washington DC.: Research Institute, Washington DC).

Vyas, V. S. (1996): "Diversification of Agriculture: Concept, Rationale and Approaches", *Indian Journal of Agricultural Economics*, Vol. 51, No. 4, October-December.

Wahid, A.; R. Maggs, S. R. A. Shamsi, J. N. B. Bell and M. R. Ashmore (1995): "Air pollution and its impacts on wheat yield in Pakistan Punjab", *Environmental Pollution*, Vol. 88, 1995.

Walker, P. (1989): *Famine Early Warning Systems - Victims and Destitution* (London: Earthscan Publications Ltd.).

Wallerstein, M. B. (1980): "Inter-disciplinary Dialogue on World Hunger: A Summary of the Workshop on Goals, Processes and Indicators of Food Nutrition Policy", *Food and Nutrition Bulletin*, Vol. 2, No. 3, pp. 16-23.

Warley, T. K. (1983): "Discussion", in Johnson, D. G. and Schuh, G. E. (eds.): *The Role of Markets in the World Food Economy* (Boulder: Westview Press Inc.).

Watts, M. (1983): *Silent Violence: Food, Famine and Peasantry in Northern Nigeria* (Berkeley. University of California Press, Berkeley).

Watts, M. (1987): *Drought, Environment and Food Security: Some Reflections on Peasants, Pastoralists and Commoditizations in Dryland West Africa,* in M. Glantz (ed.): *Drought and Hunger in Africa: Denying Famine a Future* (Cambridge: Cambridge University Press).

Watts, M. (1988): "Coping with the Market: Uncertainty and Food Security among Hausa Peasants", in I. De Garine and G. A. Harrison (eds.): *Coping with Uncertainty in Food Supply* (Oxford: Clalrendon Press).

Weber, M. T. and Jayne, T. S. (1991): "Food Security and its Relationship to Technology, Institutions, Policies and Human Capital", in G. Johnson et. al. (eds.): *Social Science Agricultural Agendas and Strategies* (East Lansing: Michigan State University Press).

Weber, M. T., Staatz, J. M., Holtzman, J. S., Crawford, E. W. and Bernsten, R. H. (1988): "Informing Food Security Decisions in Africa: Empirical Analysis and Policy Dialogue", *American Journal of Agricultural Economics*, Vol. 70, No. 5, December, pp. 1044-52.

Westerveen G. (1984): "Towards a System for Supervising States: Compliance with the Right to Food", in P. Alston and K. Tomasevski (eds.): *The Right to Food* (Netherlands: Martinus Nijhoff).

Whiteford, M. B. and Ferguson, A. E. (1991): "Social Dimensions of Food Security and Hunger: An Overview", in Whiteford, M. B. and Ferguson, A. E. (eds.): *Harvest of Want: Hunger and Food Security in Central America and Mexico* (Boulder, Coloradao: Westview Press).

Whitehead, A. (1990): "Rural Women and Food Production in Sub-Saharan Africa", in Sen, A. K. and Dreze, J. (eds.): *The Political Economy of Hunger*, Volume 1 (Oxford: Clalrendon Press).

Whyte, R.O. (1974): *Rural Nutrition in China* (London: Oxford University Press).

Wijewardene, R. and P. Waidyantha (1994): *Systems Techniques and Tools for Small Farmers in Humid Topics* (Colombo: Department of Agriculture, Government of Sri Lanka and CCGAAP) 1994.

Wisner, B., O'Kneefe, P. and Westgate, K. (1977): "Global Systems and Local Disasters: The Untapped Power of Peoples' Science", *Disasters*, Vol.1, No.1, pp. 47-57.

Witcombe, J. R. et. al., (ed.) (1998): *Seeds of Choice: Making the Most of New Varieties for Small Farmers* (New-Delhi: Oxford & IBH Publishing Co. Pvt. Ltd.).

Wolfe, E. C. (1986): *Beyond the Green Revolution: New Approaches for Third World Agriculture* (Washington DC: Worldwatch Institute).

World Bank (1980): "Food Security in Food Deficit Countries", *World Bank Staff Working Paper*, No. 393, June (Washington DC: The World Bank).

World Bank (1981): *World Development Report 1981*, (The World Bank, Washington D. C.).

World Bank (1983): *World Development Report 1983*, New-York: Oxford University Press).

World Bank (1986): *Poverty and Hunger: Issues and Options for Food Security in Developing Countries*, World Bank, Policy Study (Washington D. C.: The World Bank).

World Bank (1986): *World Development Report 1986* (Washington D. C.: The World Bank).

World Bank (1988): *Food Security in Africa, Task Force Report* (Washington D. C.: The World Bank).

World Bank (1988): *The Challenge of Hunger in Africa* (Washington D. C.: The World Bank).

World Bank (1989): *Analysis Plan: Food Security and Nutrition* (Draft) (Washington D. C.: The World Bank).

World Bank (1989a): *Mozambique Food Security Study,* (Draft) (Washington D. C.: The World Bank).

World Bank (1989b): *Gender and Poverty in India* (Washington D. C.: The World Bank).

World Bank (1990): *Symposium on Household Food Security and the Role of Women* Harare, January 21-24, 1990.

World Bank (1992): *World Development Report (1992)* (Washington D. C.: The World Bank).

World Bank (1993): *World Development Report 1993: Investing in Health* (Oxford: Oxford University Press).

World Bank (1996): "India's Public Distribution System: A National and International Perspective", Poverty and Social Policy Department (Washington D. C.: The World Bank), *World Bank Discussion Paper, No.380,* 1999.

World Bank (1997): *The Indian Oilseed Complex: Capturing Market Opportunities*, Vol.1 and II, Report No.15677-IN, July 31 (Washington D. C.: The World Bank).

World Bank (1999): *Towards rural development and poverty reduction,* Paper presented at the NCAER-IEG-World Bank conference on "Reforms in the Agricultural Sector for Growth, Efficiency, Equity and Sustainability", April 15-16, New Delhi, India.

World Bank (1999): "India Foodgrain Marketing Policies: Reforming to Meet Security Needs", Rural Development Unit, South Asia Region, *Working Paper, Report No. 18329*, May 27 (Washington DC: The World Bank).

World Bank (1999): *World Development Report, 1998-99* (Washington D. C.: The World Bank).

World Bank (2000): *World Development Report 2000* (Washington D. C.: The World Bank)

World Bank and World Food Programme (1991): *Food Aid in Africa: An Agenda for the 1990s,* (Washington D. C.: The World Bank).

World Commission on Environment and Development (1987): *Our Common Future* (Oxford: Oxford University Press).

World Food Conference (1974): *Declaration on the Eradication of Hunger and Malnutrition* (FAO: Rome).

World Food Council (1988): *Towards Sustainable Food Security: Critical Issues,* Report by the World Food Council Secretariate, Fourteenth Ministerial Session, 23-26 May WFC, 1988, Nicosia, Cyprus.

World Food Council (1989): *Ending Hunger: The Cyprus Initiative,* Fifteenth Ministerial Session of the World Food Council, Cairo.

World Resource Institute and HRD (1989): *World Resources 1988/89,* Report by the World Resource Institute, UNEP and UNDP (New-York: Oxford University Press).

World Resources Institute (1994): *World Resources 1994-1995* (New-York: Oxford University Press).

World Resources Institute (1998-99): *World Resources, A Guide to the Global Environment* (New-York: Oxford University Press), 1998.

Wright, Nancy, A. Cecilia Snyder and Don Reeves (1994): "Population, Consumption and Environment" in Bread for the World Institute: *Causes of Hunger, Fifth Annual Report on the State of World Hunger* (Silver Spring: Bread for the World Institute) 1994.

Wright, Nancy, A. Cecilia Snyder and Don Reeves (1996): "Secure Access to Land by the Poor", *Development*, December 1996, pp. 22-27.

Young, H. and Jaspars, S. (1991): *Nutrition Surveillance for Rural People—Action and Impact in Darfur, Sudan, 1984-91,* mimeo, University of Sussex, Institute for Development Studies, Brighton.

Young, H. and Jaspars, S. (1992): *Nutrition Surveillance: Help or Hindrance in Times of Famine?* Paper presented at IDS Workshop, 8 May 1992.

Yugandhar, B. N. and P. S. Datta (eds.) (1995): *Land Reforms in India, Rajasthan—Feudalism and Change* (New Delhi: Sage).

Zaki, E., von Braun, A. A. J. and Teklu, T. (1991): "Drought and Famine Prevention in Sudan: Famine and Food Policy", *Discussion Paper, No. 5,* Food Consumption and Nutrition Division, International Food Policy, Washington D. C.

Zalla, T. (1979): *Incorporating Nutrition and Consumption in Farming Systems Research and Rural Development Projects,* Bureau for Science and Technology, Office of Rural Development, USAID, Washington D. C.

Zinyama, L. M., Campbell, D. J. and Matiza, T. (1987): "Traditional Household Strategies to Cope with Food Insecurity in the SADCC Region", in Rukuni, M. and Bernsten, R. H. (eds.): *Southern Africa: Food Security Policy Options* (University of Zimbabwe UZ and East Lancing Michigan: MSU).

Zipperer, S. (1987): *Food Security and Agricultural Policy and Hunger* (Harare: Zimbabwe Foundation for Education with Production).

INDEX